The Ethics of
Deuteronomy

Rabbi Dr. Abba Engelberg

Kodesh Press

The Ethics of Deuteronomy
© Abba Engelberg 2021

Hardcover ISBN: 978-1-947857-61-2
Paperback ISBN: 978-1-947857-62-9

All rights reserved. Except for brief quotations in printed reviews, no part of this publication may be reproduced, stored in a retrieval system, or transmitted in any form or by any means (printed, written, photocopied, visual electronic, audio, or otherwise) without the prior permissions of the publisher.

The Publisher extends its gratitude to
Michele Scheer for her editing work.

Published & Distributed by

Kodesh Press L.L.C.
New York, NY
www.KodeshPress.com
kodeshpress@gmail.com

TABLE OF CONTENTS

FOREWORD 9
INTRODUCTION TO DEUTERONOMY 11

DEVARIM 17
   JUDGING THE NATION 18
   COMPARISON TO THE U.S. CONSTITUTION 30
   SUMMARY 32
VA'ETCHANAN 33
   SABBATH OBSERVANCE 37
   IS THERE A COMMAND TO WORK? 43
   SUMMARY 46
EKEV 47
   MANNA: A MEANS OF AFFLICTION 47
   MANNA: A STIMULUS TO REPENT 52
   MANNA: THE FREQUENCY OF ITS DESCENT 55
   SUMMARY 60
RE'EH 61
   THE DIETARY LAWS 61

    Answering the First Question:
        Why Observe the Dietary Laws? 63
    Answering the Second Question:
        What Is the Meaning of Holiness? 90
    Summary 91
SHOFTIM 92
    The Ends Do Not Justify the Means 96
    The Ends Justify the Means 114
    Summary 122
KI TEITZEI 124
    Tza'ar Ba'alei Chaim 125
    Modern Questions 140
    Summary 147
KI TAVO 148
    The Ceremony on Mt. Gerizim and Mt. Ebal 149
    The Blessings and the Curses 155
    Four Questions about Later Tragedies 158
    Summary 176
NITZAVIM 177
    Messianic Times 182
    The Messiah 187
    Summary 206
VAYEILECH 207
    The *Hakhel* Ceremony 207
    Women's Learning 219
    Summary 225
HA'AZINU 226
    The World to Come (*Olam ha-Ba*) 231
    Rambam's Description of *Olam ha-Ba* 233
    Saadiah Gaon's Description of *Olam ha-Ba* 242
    Summary 249
VEZOT HABRACHAH 250
    The Blessings of the Tribes 254

THE ORDER OF THE BLESSINGS	256
THE CONTENT OF THE BLESSINGS	265
SUMMARY	285

APPENDIX I: JEWISH DIETARY HISTORY 286
   FROM ADAM TO NOAH 286
   FROM NOAH TO THE EXODUS 289
   FROM THE EXODUS TO THE GIVING OF THE TORAH 294
   FROM THE GIVING OF THE TORAH
      UNTIL ENTERING THE LAND OF ISRAEL 300
   UPON ENTERING THE LAND OF ISRAEL 305
APPENDIX II: VEGETARIANISM 307
APPENDIX III: THE SANCTITY OF MARRIAGE 321
APPENDIX IV: THE VALUE ATTACHED TO LIFE 325
APPENDIX V: THE LATER YEARS OF THE SECOND TEMPLE . 334
   HEROD IN THE TALMUD 345
APPENDIX VI: THE WAR OF GOG AND MAGOG 349
APPENDIX VII: MASHIACH B. YOSEF 355
   WHY ARE TWO MESSIAHS NEEDED? 362
APPENDIX VIII: BIRTH PANGS OF THE MESSIAH 371
APPENDIX IX: ENTITLEMENT TO THE WORLD TO COME . 375
APPENDIX X: THE HALACHIC
   DECISION REGARDING *TZA'AR BA'ALEI CHAIM* 377

SOURCE MATERIAL 385
COMMENTATORS 393

Foreword

This is the fifth in a series of books which analyze the ethical behavior and values which may be gleaned from close examination of the five books of Moses. In *The Ethics of Genesis*, the ethical, and sometimes unethical, behavior of the patriarchs and their progeny was discussed. In *The Ethics of Exodus*, the seeds of anti-semitism were presented, followed by a description of the crystallization of the twelve tribes into a nation, guided by a divinely-inspired leader and lawgiver, who taught the people its constitution, the Torah, and prepared a sanctuary for prayer and thanksgiving to its Redeemer. That service was enlarged upon in *The Ethics of Leviticus*, but more emphasis was placed on the moral, ethical, and sexual laws which were investigated in detail. *The Ethics of Numbers* described the experiences and comportment of the Israelites in the desert, which consisted of frequent backsliding on both the communal level, as exemplified by the sin of the spies, and the idol worship and prostitution at Baal Peor; as well as on the individual level, as demonstrated by the rebellious Korah and even the uncharacteristic misbehavior of the brother and sister of Moses our teacher. Heroes appeared on the scene as well, such as Phineas, the daughters of Zelophehad, and of course Moses himself (supplemented by his virtuous wife, Zipporah), whose outstanding leadership enabled the nation to navigate through the obstacle-infested wilderness.

In *The Ethics of Deuteronomy*, the short history of Israel is reviewed, with emphasis on the nation's shortcomings for edificatory reasons, since "those who do not learn from history are doomed

The Ethics of Deuteronomy

to repeat it" (Winston Churchill), and adequate warnings are pronounced with respect to the pitfalls which lay ahead until the final redemption. In the meantime, the laws, especially those with moral and ethical content, must be adhered to, which can only happen if there exist adequate systems of judgment and enforcement, integrated into a supportive cultural environment consisting of Sabbath, holidays, and uniform dietary prescription.

In preparing this material, I have utilized the Talmud and Midrash, as well as the many commentaries which have been written from the Middle Ages until the present. I have availed myself of the Soncino translation of the Talmud, as well as Chabad's translation of the Bible with Rashi and of the *Yad ha-Chazakah* of Rambam, all freely available on the Internet. To give the reader an idea of the scope of the material upon which the book is based, I have included a glossary of sources, followed by a glossary of the authorities quoted. Most of the information which appears in these lists has been culled from the Internet, especially from Wikipedia. Since the title Rabbi appears frequently, I have abbreviated it using the letter "R." I have also used "b." to denote *ben*, meaning "son of."

I would like to take this opportunity to thank my loving wife Ruthie, who made many helpful suggestions, and in addition did a very thorough job of commenting on and proof-reading the entire book. I also drew much inspiration from my wonderful sons, whose behavior in both joyous and sometimes trying circumstances helped me develop my moral compass, which I have tried to illuminate in this commentary. I fervently hope that this book will be of benefit to those who read it.

Abba Engelberg
Jerusalem 2021

Introduction to Deuteronomy

The Hebrew name for the fifth book of Moses is *Devarim,* meaning "words," based on the first phrase in the book: "These are the words." The original name is *Mishneh Torah,* meaning "repetition of the Torah," based on the verse in Deut. 17:18, in which future kings are ordered to write a *mishneh ha-Torah,* literally, "a copy of the entire Torah." They are actually required to write two Torah scrolls, one to be kept with their valuables and one to carry with them (BT *Sanhedrin* 21b). However, since they are assumed to already have one, just as every Jew must, the verse only speaks of one additional Torah. Tosafot interpret the Talmudic text in a different manner, holding that the second Torah was not complete, but rather just contained the Ten Commandments, which (according to Tosafot) are composed of 613 letters, symbolizing the 613 commands in the Torah, thus justifying its being referred to as a Torah (*Da'at Zekenim,* Deut. 17:20).

Even though the Biblical usage of *Mishneh Torah* refers to a copy of the entire Torah according to most authorities, since the fifth book essentially reviews the most important aspects of the Pentateuch, it alone became known as *Mishneh Torah* in rabbinic literature. When used in the Bible, the Midrash interprets the appellation as referring to the entire Torah, because the need for a king to have it is rationalized as being "to keep all the words of this Torah and these statutes, to perform them" (*Sifrei,* Deut. 160). Otherwise, the term would have referred only to the fifth book. *Mishneh Torah* is the source for the

The Ethics of Deuteronomy

English name Deuteronomy, which is based on the Greek name *Deuteronomion*, meaning "Second Law."[1]

Rediscovery of the Torah

During the reign of the righteous King Josiah (637-607 BCE), while rummaging through the Temple grounds, Hilkiah the priest found an old Torah scroll, as described in the Bible: "And Hilkiah the high priest said to Shaphan the scribe, 'I have found the Scroll of the Law in the House of the Lord'" (2 Kings 22:8). The discovery is detailed in the book of Chronicles, where the find is described as "the Scroll of the Law of the Lord, by the hand of Moses" (2 Chron. 34:14), implying that it was the entire Pentateuch, and the scroll discovered was indeed said by Josephus to contain "the holy books of Moses" (*Antiquities* 10:57, 58, 63). Rashi, in 2 Kings (as expanded by *Metzudat David*), explains that the wicked King Ahaz had burned Torah scrolls and the Rabbis of that generation feared that he might do the same to the original copy in Moses' handwriting, which had been placed on a shelf adjoining the Ark, so they hid it under a layer of stones. After the death of Ahaz, the new generation of priests were unable to locate it, and it was only when Hilkiah was searching for valuables that he inadvertently discovered it. Radak points out that the king who followed Ahaz was his son, Hezekiah the righteous, who would have certainly made a thorough search and uncovered it. He accordingly prefers to ascribe the Torah-burning to King Hezekiah's son, the wicked King Manasseh, an appropriate choice in that the Talmud (BT *Sanhedrin* 103b) portrays him as a mass murderer who installed an idol in the Temple. The Talmud itself (ibid.) ascribes sealing the Torah (closing the houses of study) to Ahaz, but burning the Torah to Amon, the son of Manasseh and father of Josiah, who also installed Manasseh's idol in the Holy of Holies. Perhaps the similarity of the names of Ahaz and Amon was the source of the confusion.

Both Radak and Malbim, in 2 Kings, accept the view that the

---

1. J.H. Hertz, *The Pentateuch* (1938), p. 735.

scroll being referred to here is the one that Moses wrote, as indicated by its description in Chronicles as "the Scroll of the Law of the Lord, by the hand of Moses," which was kept adjacent to the Ark until it was hidden. Malbim points out that this is emphasized by Hilkiah using the definite article when he referred to it as "*the* Scroll of the Law"— the one that dated back to the time of Moses and was heretofore missing—and that this is "the Scroll of the Covenant" from which King Josiah read before the congregation (2 Kings 23:2).

There are, however, other views as to what was found by Hilkiah. Rashi says that it was not the entire Torah, but rather *Mishneh Torah* (2 Chron. 34:14).[2] Although it is termed "the Scroll of the Law," Joshua as well was told to be totally immersed in "the Scroll of the Law" (Josh. 1:8), yet the Midrash states that the latter reference is to Deuteronomy (*Gen. Rabbah* 6:9). Furthermore, the narrative continues with the king reading before the elders "all the words of the Scroll of the Covenant" (2 Kings 23:2). If the entire Pentateuch is being referred to, certainly this would be far too much verbiage to present orally to even the most disciplined gathering. On the other hand, there exists a precedent for public readings by the king from the book of Deuteronomy at the ceremony of *hakhel* (Deut. 31:10-13; *Sotah* 7:8). Finally, the language used in the covenant enacted between God and the congregation (2 Kings 23:2) is highly reminiscent of that found in various locations in Deuteronomy (4:45, 6:5, 6:20, 11:13, 13:5, 29:9, 30:2).

Sforno (Deut. 31:26) limits Hilkiah's scroll even further, specifically to the portion of the Torah which had been given by Moses to the Ark-bearers (Deut. 31:9) and which discusses the duties of a king (Deut. 17:14-20). At a later stage, Joshua added the covenant that he

---

2. Biblical criticism of course takes this idea much further and says that Hilkiah actually authored Deuteronomy (Eugene Merrill, "Deuteronomy and de Wette: A Fresh Look at a Fallacious Premise," *Journal for the Evangelical Study of the Old Testament* (2012), pp. 25–42.) Rashi clearly meant no such thing. Louis Ginsberg, in *The Legends of the Jews*, Vol. 6, "The Later Kings of Judah," note 116 (1928), found other Jewish sources for assuming that it was Deuteronomy which was discovered.

made with the nation in exchange for the Israelites' commitment to worship God in "sincerity and truth" (Josh. 24:14). The covenant embodied in this scroll was certainly of a length which could feasibly be read to the assembly.

CONTENTS OF DEUTERONOMY

Deuteronomy is intrinsically different from the four preceding books, which present God's message to Israel through the medium of Moses. God's direct communication may thus be considered to have been completed at the end of the book of Numbers. In Deuteronomy, Moses embarks on a series of monologues—introduced by the phrase: "These are the words which Moses spoke to all Israel" (Deut. 1:1)—tracing the history of Israel from the time of its emergence as a nation until his death, which takes place as the congregation is about to cross the Jordan and enter the main land of its future home. Moses reviews the past narrative and also adds details and even previously unmentioned commands (which Moses had received at Sinai but not yet promulgated) to those which had already appeared. A new element, stressed in this book for the first time, is the emotional tone accompanying alternating words of reproof (*musar*) and encouragement. Moses draws mainly on material included in the books of Exodus and Numbers. Genesis precedes the existence of Israel as a nation, and much of Leviticus specializes in sacrificial details and the priestly code of conduct. Deuteronomy is directed at the congregation as a whole, although it does include prescribed interactions between commoners and the clerical (Levitical and priestly) classes.

The Vilna Gaon (*Aderet Eliyahu*, Deut. 1:1) divides Deuteronomy into three discourses, each of which parallels one of the three previous books of the Torah. Exodus starts with the Hebrew words *ve-eleh shemot* (Exod. 1:1), which is paralleled *by eleh ha-devarim* (Deut. 1:1). This first discourse reviews the journey of the nation from Sinai to Kadesh. Leviticus starts with *va-yikra* (Lev. 1:1), which is paralleled by *va-yikra* in Deut. 5:1. This second discourse deals with the religious foundations of the covenant, including the Ten Commandments, and the laws and statutes which compose it. Numbers starts with *va-yedabber* (Num. 1:1), which is paralleled by *va-yedabber* in Deut. 27:9. This third discourse deals with the immediate and long-term future of the nation as it enters the Promised Land. Similarly, the three halachic Midrashim have the same subdivision, *Mechilta* covering Exodus, *Sifra* covering Leviticus, and *Sifrei* covering Numbers (and Deuteronomy).

R. Elia Shmuel Hartom (1887-1965), in his introduction to Deuteronomy, on the other hand, divides it into three sections based on subject matter. He defines the first part as stretching from the first through the eleventh chapters (comprising the portions of *Devarim*, *Va'etchanan*, and *Ekev*). It retells the simultaneously wondrous, but sordid, saga of the nation, interweaving historical narrative with reprimands and exhortations. The second part, legal in nature, consists of chapters 12 through 26 (comprising the portions of *Re'eh*, *Shoftim*, and *Ki Teitzei*), and reviews and expands upon previously recorded laws.[3] Finally, the third section, from chapter 27 until the end of the book (*Ki Tavo*, *Nitzavim*, *Vayeilech*, *Ha'azinu*, *Vezot Habrachah*) includes Moses' blessing of the tribes (ch. 33), but mostly concentrates on inculcating the concept of reward and punishment.

Even the historic references are *musar*-oriented. For example, Egypt (*Mitzrayim*) is mentioned over 20 times in the following contexts:

1. Israel's lack of gratitude (Deut. 1:27, 8:14, 9:7) and threatened punishment (Deut. 28:27, 60, 68).
2. Encouraging Israel to remember and be grateful for their redemption from slavery (Deut. 4:20; 5:14; 6:12; 7:18; 11:3, 4;

---

3. These three portions contain the largest concentration of *mitzvot* in the entire Torah and, according to Hertz (*The Pentateuch*, 1938, p. 737), 70 of the 100 laws recorded therein are new.

29:1, 15; 34:11) and to empathize with the unfortunate (Deut. 10:19; 15:15; 24:22).
3. Relating to attributes of God, Israel's liberator (Deut. 5:6; 13:6, 11; 20:1), Who loves Israel (Deut. 7:8), and will prevent further suffering (Deut. 7:15).

The three discourses presented in Deuteronomy took place in a very concentrated manner. They started on the first of the eleventh Hebrew month, Shevat (Deut. 1:3), and ended upon the death of Moses, just two months later on the seventh of Adar II (BT *Kiddushin* 38a; Prof. Eli Merzbach, *Daf Shavu'i* 433, Bar Ilan University). This certainly gives credence to the Biblical claim that upon his death at the age of 120, "his eye had not dimmed, nor had he lost his [natural] freshness" (Deut. 34:7).

Devarim

Moses' first discourse in the book of Deuteronomy starts in the first portion, *Devarim*, with the phrase "Moses commenced [and] explained this Law, saying…" (Deut. 1:5), and continues well into the second portion, *Va'etchanan*. The discourse is divided into two sections. In the first, Moses reviews the most important events which occurred from the time the people were commanded to depart from Mt. Sinai (Deut. 1:6) until they arrived at the fields of Moab, which is apparently where the soliloquy took place (Deut. 3:29). Moses recalls the spying incident, which turned the journey into a forty-year trek and led to the demise of all of the adult males (including Moses himself) other than the virtuous spies—Joshua and Caleb—in the desert (Deut. 1:19-46).[4] Moses then focuses on the route of the journey, which skirted the land of the Edomites, Moabites, and Ammonites, all of whom the nation was commanded not to attack, even though it would have been possible to save a lot of mileage by passing through some of those lands (Deut. 2:1-23). With regard to

---

4. Based on the phrase "when all the men of war finished dying from among the people" (Deut. 2:16), the Talmud (BT *Bava Batra* 121b) assumes that the men who died were between the ages of twenty and sixty, i.e., men who were capable of waging war, which *Chizkuni* (Num. 14:29) explains to be commensurate punishment for those who should have participated in the conquest of the Land of Israel. See Rashbam, BT *Bava Batra* 121a, s.v. *she-kalu*, and Tosafot, BT *Ta'anit* 30b, s.v. *yom*. Whether this incident was the cause of Moses not entering the land is in dispute between Ramban and *Or ha-Chaim* (Deut. 1:37).

the Amorites, however, the story was different. After Israel's peace offer was rejected, the nation proceeded to march through the land, and was intercepted by the Amorite King Sichon and his army, whom they readily defeated. The situation developed similarly with regard to King Og of the Bashan (Deut. 2:24-3:11; Num. 21:21-35). Moses then recalls the emotion-laden negotiations with the tribes of Reuben, Gad, and Manasseh, who wished to settle in the lands of the Amorites to the east of the Jordan.

Judging the Nation

One of the events that occurred at the beginning of the journey of the Israelites in the desert was the appointment of assistants to help Moses lead and maintain order. The Jewish nation was never easy to lead. On the verse "How can I bear your trouble, your burden, and your strife all by myself?" (Deut. 1:12), Rashi (based on *Sifrei*, Deut. 12) explains each of the direct objects mentioned by Moses:

- **your trouble**: This teaches that the Israelites were troublesome [people]. If one saw his opponent in a lawsuit about to win, he would say: "I have [other] witnesses to bring, [more] evidence to introduce, I [will exercise my right to] add judges to you [in your tribunal]."
- **and your burden**: This teaches that they were cynical. If Moses left early, they said: "Why does the son of Amram leave? Perhaps he is not at ease inside his house." If he left late, they said, "Why did the son of Amram not leave? What do you think? He is sitting and devising evil schemes against you, and is thinking evil thoughts about you."
- **and your strife:** This teaches that they were contentious.

In short, according to Rashi, Moses complained that the people were troublesome, cynical, and contentious. Ramban, on the other hand,

Devarim

maintains that Moses was referring to the difficulties (trouble) of teaching the congregation the basic laws and statutes, the prayers (called burdens) which he supplicated for them, and the judgments (to assuage strife) which he made on their behalf. Sforno relates trouble, burden, and strife to interpersonal arguments, communal administration, and lawsuits (of a financial nature or otherwise), respectively. As most of their years in the desert were spent in a relatively calm and peaceful atmosphere, Sforno is quite surprised by the rampant contentiousness.

The exhausting nature of Moses' office was even noticed by a relative outsider, his father-in-law Jethro, who shortly after his arrival, upon seeing Moses in action, had said "You will certainly get worn out, together with your nation, for the task is too heavy for you, you cannot perform it alone" (Exod. 18:18).

COMPARING THE DESCRIPTIONS IN EXODUS AND DEUTERONOMY

Both Exod. 18:13-27 and Deut.1:9-18 portray attempts by Moses to ease his onerous load. The outline of the events described is parallel to the extent that, at first blush, one might consider the Deuteronomic version to be a rehashing of the previous story, such as occurs with many of the commandments which appear for a second time in Deuteronomy, and is implied by its byname, *Mishneh Torah*—Replication of the Torah. Before discussing this question in depth, it will be instructive to cite the respective verses in each description.

Jethro's analysis of Moses' dilemma is described in Exod. 18:

> **18** You will surely wear yourself out, both you and the nation that is with you, for the matter is too heavy for you; (A) you cannot do it alone. **19** Now listen to my voice, I will advise you, and may the Lord be with you. [You] represent the people before God, and you will bring the [difficult] matters to God. **20** And you should admonish them concerning the

statutes and the teachings and make known to them the path that they should trod and the deed[s] that they should perform.

The leaders whom Moses was to choose are described by Jethro as follows:

> **21** And you should choose from the entire nation able [alternatively, morally worthy, see Ruth 3:11] men, God-fearers, men of truth, who hate unjust gain, and you should appoint [those chosen] over them [as] (B) rulers of thousands, rulers of hundreds, rulers of fifties, and rulers of tens. **22** And they will judge the people at all times, and behold, any major matter they will bring to you, and every minor matter they themselves will judge, thus making it easier for you, and they will bear [the burden] with you. **23** If you do this thing, and the Lord commands you [indicating His approval, then] you will be able to survive, and also, all this people will come upon their place in peace.

Moses' acquiescence to Jethro's advice is described as follows:

> **24** Moses listened to the voice of his father-in-law, and he did all that he said. **25** And Moses chose able men from all of Israel and appointed them as heads of the people, rulers of thousands, rulers of hundreds, rulers of fifties, and rulers of tens. **26** And they judged the people at all times; (C) the difficult cases they would bring to Moses, but any minor case they themselves would judge.

The parallel verses from the book of Deuteronomy (ch. 1) are:

> **9** And I spoke to you at that time, saying, (A) "I cannot

carry you alone. **10** The Lord, your God, has multiplied you, and behold, you are today as the stars of the heavens in abundance. **11** May the Lord, God of your forefathers, add to you a thousand-fold as many as you are, and may He bless you, as He spoke concerning you. **12** How can I bear your trouble, your burden, and your strife all by myself? **13** Get for yourselves men who are wise and understanding, known among your tribes, and I will make them heads over you." **14** And you answered me and said, "The thing you have spoken is good for us to do."

After suggesting the means for improving the judicial system, Moses implemented the aforementioned policy:

15 And I took the heads of your tribes, men wise and well known, and I made them heads over you, (B) rulers of thousands, rulers of hundreds, rulers of fifties, and rulers of tens, and officers, over your tribes. **16** And I commanded your judges at that time, saying, "Hear [disputes] between your brothers and judge justly between a man and his brother and his litigant. **17** You may not favor persons in judgment; [rather] you must hear the small just as the great; you should fear no man, for judgment is by the Lord [and man is only His representative], (C) and the case that is too difficult for you, bring to me, and I will hear it."

The similarities and differences between the two narratives will now be examined. The following similarities, indicated in the respective texts by the letters A, B, and C, can be identified:

(A) Adding judges, based on the realization that Moses cannot possibly judge the interpersonal disputes of an entire nation by himself.

(B) The ruling hierarchy will group the nation by thousands, hundreds, fifties, and tens.

(C) Moses will only handle the most difficult cases, which require greater expertise.

Despite these similarities, an even greater number of differences between the two texts is listed below:

1. Jethro's Name Is Not Mentioned in Deuteronomy
In Exodus, discovery and analysis of the problem, as well as the proposed solution, is attributed to Moses' father-in-law, Jethro (Exod. 18:17, 24), while in Deuteronomy there is no mention of his name. Ramban (Deut. 1:18), who believes that the texts provide alternate descriptions of the same event, suggests three reasons for the failure to mention Jethro's name:

a. It was due to Moses' innate modesty. Exactly what Ramban means is questionable. R. Aryeh Leib Steinhardt (*Kur Zahav*) says that Jethro's brilliance would ultimately reflect on Moses himself, since this generation was unacquainted with Jethro, and Moses looked upon mentioning that Jethro was his father-in-law as a form of name-dropping. R. Avraham Lieblein (*Kesef Mezukak*) says that by revealing the evolution of the system, it would become apparent that Moses could have managed on his own if not for Jethro's proposal, which would reflect even more directly on Moses' supernatural capabilities.

b. Moses did not wish to embarrass the nation by noting that it had to rely on outside counsel to organize its legislative system (*Tur*'s version of Ramban, as cited in R. Charles B. Chavel's edition of Ramban).

c. Although Jethro made the initial suggestion, and he was given full credit in the portion of *Yitro*, which is even named for him (together with only two other portions named after non-Jews,

Devarim

Noach and *Balak*), the decision to actually adopt Jethro's proposal only followed God's final approval. Ramban bases himself on the *Mechilta* on the verse: "Moses listened to the voice of his father-in-law, and he did all that he said" (Exod. 18:24). The simple explanation of the last phrase is that Moses did all that Jethro said, but R. Elazar ha-Moda'i interprets it to mean that Moses did all that God said, i.e., "all that He said."

2. Who Made the Suggestion to Appoint Judges?

In the portion of *Yitro*, Jethro suggests to Moses that he appoint the judges ("And you should choose from the entire nation," Exod. 18:21), while in *Devarim* it is Moses who offers that option to the community ("Get for yourselves men who are wise and understanding," Deut. 1:13).

3. What Type of Qualities Are Required?

The qualifications outlined by Jethro were of a moralistic nature, namely moral worthiness, piety, truthfulness, and beneficence (Exod. 18:21), while those enumerated by Moses were more external and measurable, namely wisdom, cleverness, and public recognition (Deut. 1:13).

Rashi, based on *Sifrei* (in Malbim, Deut. 1:15) and *Midrash Rabbah* (*Deut. Rabbah* 1:10), combines the qualifications mentioned in both portions to obtain the seven traits which characterize a good judge. It has been suggested that Moses in the present portion mentioned only the external traits, since only those could be known to the members of the community, who would be making the initial selection, while the spiritual qualities would be taken into account by God, Who would be giving His final approval. It is thus clear how Rashi and Ramban would account for this difference between the narratives as described above.

There is a difference of opinion between the two previously mentioned Midrashim as to the exact identification of the seven traits. Rashi, based on *Sifrei*, derives four of them from the phrase "men who are wise and understanding, known among your tribes" (Deut. 1:13), as follows:

a. Men (*anashim*): *Sifrei* (Malbim, Deut. 1:13) questions the necessity of this word. "Could we ever imagine [that judges could be] women [in accordance with the culture of the times]? It tells us that the judges must be silver-haired (*kesufim*), men of seniority (*vatikim*)." According to Rabbeinu Hillel on *Sifrei*, *vatikim* implies expertise in Torah, while *kesufim* (from the root *kesef*—money) designates skillfulness in accounting, although others have interpreted *kesufim* to mean versatile and many-faceted, based on Greek etymology (M. Rosenbaum and A.M. Silbermann, Deut. 1:13, note 1), or bashful and ashamed of doing anything wrong (R. Akiva Eiger on *Sifrei*).
b. Wise (*chachamim*)
c. Understanding (*nevonim*): *Sifrei* (Malbim, ibid.) explains:

> This is what Arius asked R. Yosi: "What is the difference between wise men and understanding men?" [R. Yosi said:] "A wise man is like an [unambitious] money changer: When people bring him dinars to examine, he examines them. When they do not bring [money] to him, he sits doing nothing. An understanding man, however, is like a [creative] money changer: When they bring him money to examine, he examines it, and when they do not bring it to him, he [goes out and] brings his own [money—i.e., he does not wait for people to come to him—he goes to them].

The meaning is that the wise man (*chacham*) grasps what he is told, but cannot derive knowledge on his own, nor does he take initiative. The understanding man (*navon*), on the other hand, is an original thinker who can decipher a matter and is thus not dependent on others to teach him. The Hebrew description of such a person is *meivin davar mi-toch davar* (one who understands a matter by comparing it with another matter).

Some compare the *chacham* to a rich man who does not have to think out of the box, others to a poor man who is indigent specifically because he cannot think out of the box. The *navon* (understanding man) is consequently either a poor man who is forced to improvise, or a rich man who is wealthy specifically because he is able to do so. Taking the latter approach, the Vilna Gaon emended the *Sifrei* to read: "An understanding man, however, is like a rich money changer."

d. Known among your tribes (*yedu'im le-shivteichem*): *Sifrei* (Malbim, ibid.) explains:

[Men] whom you recognize. If one were to come before me [Moses] wrapped in his robe, I would not know [from where he comes and of what tribe he is], and what are his actions [whether he is suitable]. But you know him, for you have raised him. Therefore, it says, "well-known among your tribes."

If the initial four requirements were defined as "men who are wise and understanding, known among your tribes" (Deut. 1:13), *Sifrei* notes that when it came to implementation, Moses found men with only three of the traits, as described by the phrase "men wise and well-known" (Deut. 1:15), having been unable to locate *nevonim* (men of understanding).

The remaining three traits mentioned in Exod. 18:21 are:
    e. God-fearers
    f. Men of truth
    g. Haters of unjust gain.

The Ethics of Deuteronomy

Deut. Rabbah (1:10) tallies the seven traits slightly differently, speaking of only three traits in Deuteronomy and adding *anshei chayil* (morally worthy men) from Exod. 18:21. The Midrash goes on to say:

> Why were the seven traits not written in one place [but rather split between Exodus and Deuteronomy]? [To tell us that] if they did not find [judges] with four [of the traits], three would suffice, and if they did not find [judges] with three [of the traits], one would suffice, as it says: "A woman of valor [*eishet chayil*] who can find" (Prov. 31:10).

The verse from Proverbs is cited to show that even men with just the one general trait of *anshei chayil* is not especially easy to find, but sometimes such judges must suffice, as stressed in the following Talmudic extract (BT *Rosh Hashanah* 25b):

> Jeruba'al [Gideon] in his generation is like Moses in his generation, Bedan [Samson] in his generation is like Aaron in his generation, Jephthah in his generation is like Samuel in his generation. The most worthless [person], once he has been appointed a leader of the community, is to be accounted like the mightiest of the mighty. Scripture says also: "And you will come to the priests, the Levites, and to the judge who will be in those days" (Deut. 17:9). Can we then imagine that a man should go to a judge who is not in his days? This shows that you must be content to go to the judge who is in your days. It also says: "Do not say: 'How was it that the former days were better than these'" (Ecc. 7:10).

The three judges mentioned—Gideon, Samson, and Jephthah—are all considered to be lightweights. Of Gideon, the Zohar (*Noach* 67b) says that he was neither righteous, nor the son of a righteous man.

Devarim

Samson was said to be overly familiar with women (*Gen. Rabbah* 98:14). Jephthah was the son of a harlot (Judg. 11:1) and was said to have made an improper request of the Lord, which led to the lifetime incarceration of his daughter (*Gen. Rabbah* 60:3). The point of the extract is to stress that even if a generation is not blessed with people of caliber who possess all of the seven desirable traits, the appointed leaders must be accepted and respected.

4. Proper Judgment Is Only Defined in Deuteronomy

As previously noted, both the portion of *Yitro* and that of *Devarim* list desirable traits for judges, with the former emphasizing the spiritual and the latter stressing the external, measurable qualities. However, only in the portion of *Devarim* is proper judgment characterized by the strictures stating that judges must "judge justly between a man and his brother and his litigant" (Deut. 1:16), and that "you may not favor persons in judgment; [rather,] you must hear the small just as the great; you should fear no man" (Deut. 1:17).

5. Are These Leaders or Judges?

Jethro referred exclusively to the judicial system: "And they will judge the people at all times" (Exod. 18:22), while Moses added the aspect of leadership: "And I took the heads of your tribes… and I made them heads over you… and officers over your tribes. And I commanded your judges at that time" (Deut. 1:15-16).

At this point, the original question will once more be broached: Do the texts in Exodus and Deuteronomy relate to the same or different events? In enumerating the similarities and differences, it has already been pointed out that both Rashi and Ramban take the former approach, so there is certainly no need to justify the similarities. Five differences were noted, namely (1) who made the initial suggestion, (2) who did the appointing, (3) what were the qualifications, (4) what instructions were given to those chosen, and (5) were judges or leaders being appointed? Differences (1) and (3) were already reconciled according to Rashi and Ramban. It is extremely important for judges to be impartial, so that difference (4) is certainly relevant to the judges whom Jethro advocated. As far as the other differences, since the same event is being described, it will have to be assumed that Moses broadened Jethro's suggestion somewhat and looked upon the judges as leaders as well, and this would answer question (5). In fact, Moses' extension of Jethro's original plan was so significant that this might provide another reason why his name is not mentioned in the present portion, since the metamorphosis from the original scheme was so great. As far as question (2) is concerned, although in *Yitro* it says that Moses made the appointments (Exod. 18:25), and in *Devarim* it implies that the people themselves chose ("Get for yourselves men," Deut. 1:13), note that two verses later it says: "And I took the heads of your tribes." It may thus be proposed that perhaps the people presented their initial choices, which were afterwards filtered by Moses, so that in the end, as mentioned previously, Moses was only able to find men having the one trait of being *anshei chayil* (Exod. 18:24).

R. Amnon Bazak (*Parshat Devarim: Eichah Esah Levadi*, VBM) has taken the latter approach, which claims that *Yitro* and *Devarim* represent separate events. Jethro confined his suggestion to the appointment of judges, who had their traits outlined in Exodus and were appointed by Moses, while in *Devarim* the tribal leaders— who would serve as the managers of all tribal functions, including the judicial system for the settlement of internecine disputes—were chosen by popular vote.

According to this approach, judges and leaders fill different roles and command different talents and abilities, so it is quite understandable that they would be chosen by different mechanisms and would possess different traits.

R. Bazak also calls attention to a third location where Moses bemoans his limited ability to deal with the congregation. After hearing their complaints concerning the difficulty of their journey and the inferiority of manna compared to their Egyptian diet, he had said to the Lord: "Why did I not find favor in Your eyes that You put the burden of this entire people on me?" (Num. 11:11), and he soon declared his inability to handle the situation on his own when he said: "I cannot carry this entire people alone, for it is too dificult for me" (Num. 11:14). In this case, God answered Moses by saying: "Assemble for Me seventy men of the elders of Israel, whom you know to be the people's elders and officers… and I will take of the spirit that is upon you and bestow it upon them. Then they will bear the burden of the people with you, so that you need not bear it alone" (Num. 11:16-17) [Rashi: in answer to Moses' complaint that: "You put the burden of this entire people on me" (Num. 11:11)]. These seventy elders, together with Moses, were sufficient to compose a Great Sanhedrin (BT *Sanhedrin* 3b), which would be able to help Moses deal with complicated issues and laws. However, it would seem that one of the main tasks of this group would be to inspire, influence, and edify the Israelites so that they would be more considerate of each other and more grateful for the Lord's beneficence. After all, these elders were initially mobilized in response to the murmurings of the nation (Num. 11:1).

The basis for the last claim is the specific background of those chosen. Rashi, based on *Sifrei*, points out that the officers chosen here were:

> the self-same officers who were appointed over them in Egypt [to oversee] the rigorous labor, and they had mercy on them, and were beaten on their account, as it says, "the officers of the Children of Israel were beaten" (Exod. 5:14). Now they will be chosen in their greatness, just as they had suffered in their [Israel's] distress (Rashi, Num. 11:16).

Such people would be respected and listened to by the nation, which recalled their self-sacrifice in order to protect them. Furthermore, the meaning of "bestowing the spirit on them" is spelled out in the description of what actually took place:

> The Lord descended in a cloud and spoke to him [Moses], and took of the spirit that was on him and bestowed it on the seventy elders [Rashi, based on *Tanchuma Beha'alotcha* 12: What did Moses resemble at that time? A candle placed upon a candelabrum; everyone lights from it, yet its brightness is not diminished]. And when the spirit rested upon them, they prophesied, and they did not cease [translation of Onkelos] (Num. 11:25).

As prophets, the seventy assistants would be looked up to and would naturally serve as mentors to the untutored masses. Such highly respected people would be able not only to adjudicate, but to legislate new laws as well.

Comparison to the U.S. Constitution

In 1787 the leaders of the thirteen existing states on the American mainland gathered to write the Constitution—a set of principles that outlined how the new nation would be governed.

The leaders of the states wanted a strong and fair national government, but they also wanted to protect individual freedoms and prevent the government from abusing its power. They believed they could do this by having three separate branches of government—executive, legislative, and judicial. This separation is described in the first three articles of the Constitution of the United States of America.

These principles would certainly have been vital to the Jewish nation as well. It may be suggested that the three Biblical texts referred to previously correlate with the three branches of the U.S. government: the judicial branch with Exod. 18:13-27, the legislative branch with Num. 11:11-17, and the executive branch with Deut. 1:12-18.

Devarim

THE JUDICIAL BRANCH

Jethro, on a short visit, certainly was not in a position to analyze the overall workings of the Jewish system of government. However, he couldn't help but notice the long queues in front of the tent of Moses, and so he made an operational suggestion to improve efficiency. Instead of Moses serving as a lone judge, he would serve only as the adjudicator of last resort. Below him would be various levels of courts, similar to the city, state, and supreme courts in the U.S. Just as Supreme Court justices are chosen by the president of the U.S., so in the Bible, the judges were chosen by Moses. And it is certainly understandable why it was suggested that Moses choose only people of unblemished integrity.

THE LEGISLATIVE BRANCH

The function of the legislative branch is to legislate laws. In the U.S., laws are instituted in response to popular request, as transmitted by the congressmen and senators. At the inception of the Jewish nation, by contrast, the God-given laws of the Torah were presented to the Israelites. The seventy elders appointed by Moses in the book of Numbers would serve the Children of Israel as spiritual guides who would enable them to comprehend and assimilate the laws of the Torah.

THE EXECUTIVE BRANCH

The president of the U.S., elected by the electoral college, ensures that the laws of the country are implemented. Additionally, he is responsible for the smooth functioning of all arms of the government, including the armed forces and international relations. The function of the leaders referred to in Deuteronomy was to help Moses develop an efficiently administered government. It is clear, then, why Moses had directed the nation to choose people who were sufficiently intelligent to execute his ambitious program. And, of course, they would have to be well-liked in order to be democratically chosen.

The Ethics of Deuteronomy

To what extent the framers of the U.S. Constitution were influenced by their knowledge of the Bible is hard to know, but we can certainly utilize the clear delineation of the U.S. Constitution to appreciate the inherent logic in the Biblical system of government.

Summary

The topic of appointing assistants to help Moses govern the nation was examined. The subject was raised in three distinct locations in the Pentateuch: in Exodus by Jethro, and in Numbers and Deuteronomy by Moses himself. The question dealt with was whether the three texts all refer to the same event or whether three different tribunals are being described. Since the functions of the seventy elders described in Numbers are quite different, it seems to be accepted that that event exists independently and describes a group of senior scholars who would make an intellectual contribution to Moses' legislative, judicial, and educational efforts. Regarding the remaining two, Rashi and Ramban are of the opinion that they refer to the same event, and the descriptive terms which appear in the first text coalesce with those listed in the latter one, while R. Amnon Bazak has substantiated the hypothesis that these are really two different groups having distinctly different functions. Extending the analysis of R. Bazak, it was noted that the three branches of government established by the U.S. Constitution roughly parallel the three sets of helpers designated for Moses, as described in the Pentateuch.

Va'etchanan

In the opening paragraph of this portion, Moses' historical discourse becomes personal. Hoping that God's good will, as manifested by handing the nation a victory over the Amorites, would be reflected in regard to his own destiny as well, Moses pleads with God to allow him to cross over the Jordan together with the rest of the nation, but his request is rejected and he is told to pass the scepter to Joshua (Deut. 3:23-29).

At this stage, the first discourse moves to its second section, from history to the present, the time of Moses' address. He urges the Israelites to be meticulous in their fulfillment of the Law. There is no need to add restrictions, just to carefully observe those which have been commanded, especially those relating to idol worship, for which there was apparently a strong attraction in those days. Unfortunately, the lure of paganism was apparently not even palliated by God Himself speaking to them from the midst of a fire, but with no visible image (Deut. 4:1-24).

The last part of the second section contains the negative prophecy that eventually the nation will become habituated to life in Israel and lose their fervor to the extent that they will worship idols. Although this will lead to exile, the consolatory message is that after reaching a nadir, the Jews will be moved to repent, and God will heed their prayers (Deut. 4:25-40). It is no wonder that this section is read on the morning of Tisha b'Av, the fast commemorating the destruction of the Temple and subsequent exile from the Land of Israel.

The narrative until this point—the first discourse—took place at one sitting. A brief interlude follows, in which Moses, rather than delivering a speech, designates three cities of refuge on the eastern side of the Jordan (Deut. 4:41-43). Since the first order to be given to Moses' successor was to cross the Jordan (Josh. 1:2), Moses wished to complete all unfinished business relating to the eastern bank.

Since the three discourses in the book of Deuteronomy took place over a two-month period, it may be assumed that they were separated by a number of weeks. According to how the Vilna Gaon divided the book, the second discourse, which is to continue through ch. 26 in *Ki Tavo*, and is initiated by the phrase: "And Moses called [*va-yikra*] all Israel and said to them" (Deut. 5:1), starts with a repetition of the Ten Commandments. The commandments are enveloped in a number of auxiliary messages, e.g., that the Israelites should feel as if they themselves participated in the receiving of the Torah on Mt. Sinai (Deut. 5:3-4), that they should be as awe-struck by the feeling that they are in the presence of God as their ancestors were (Deut. 5:26), that every Jew is required to learn and observe the commands (Deut. 5:1, 29), and that they will be rewarded if they do so (Deut. 5:30).

Chs. 5 through 11 continue to be predominantly historical in nature, although they do include the Ten Commandments. For the Vilna Gaon, that is sufficient to make them part of the second discourse, while Hartom includes them in the first discourse by virtue of their overall content.

Ch. 6 continues with exhortative messages stressing observance of the law (Deut. 6:1-2, 13, 17), leading to reward (Deut. 6:3, 10-11, 18-19) or, God forbid, punishment (Deut. 6:15). It also includes the *Shema* prayer (Deut. 6:4-9), which is said twice daily by observant Jews and highlights central aspects of Judaism, namely:

1. Monotheism
Paganism allows for more than one supernatural force in the world. The result is that those gods do not transmit a unique code of behavior to human beings, for they frequently contradict each other, nor do

they serve as role models, since they have generally been depicted as behaving in a highly immoral fashion. On the other hand, the Torah and its commandments can endure and flourish only if the belief in the oneness and uniqueness of God is sufficiently strong for Israel to loyally adhere to His code of behavior, and not to that of any other god. The code that God wants Israel to fulfill is one that engenders love among mankind, as Rambam says: "the entire Torah was given to make peace in the world" (*Hilchot Chanukah* 4:14).

2. Interpersonal Laws

A God Who encourages peace, love, and harmony among mankind is Himself very easy to love, making it easy to fulfill the next verse of the *Shema*: "And you should love the Lord your God with all your heart and with all your soul, and with all your means" (Deut. 6:5). Loving God is fulfilled by loving his creatures. Loving God enables one to develop an instinctive sense of morality, which allows one to intuit behavior that meets with God's approval, as explicated in a later verse in this chapter: "And you should do what is proper and good in the eyes of the Lord" (Deut. 6:18).

3. Laws between Man and God

The main purpose of the ritual-oriented and God-oriented laws, as well as those restraining sexual and culinary appetites, is to train us in self-control, so that when one must control himself and his emotions in dealing with others, he will be well prepared to do so.[5] Additionally, some of these laws—such as binding the *tefillin* on one's hand and one's head, and fixing the *mezuzah* on the doorpost—serve as constant reminders to fulfill all of the *mitzvot*, each having its own specific goal, but also meshing with others to compose a unified whole. Accordingly, the *Shema* includes the command that:

> These words, which I command you today, should be in your

---

5. Eliezer Berkovits, *God, Man, and History* (1965), p. 109.

heart... And you should bind them as a sign on your hand, and they will be ornaments between your eyes. And you are to inscribe them on the doorposts of your house and your gates (Deut. 6:6,8-9).

4. Transmitting the Message to the Next Generation

A Jew believes that God created him and all other human beings for a purpose, and because he trusts Him and knows He is beneficent and has created the universe for the benefit of mankind, he has reason to be happy. It follows that Jews should experience and radiate *joie de vivre* and live up to the directive formulated by R. Nachman of Breslov: "It is a great mitzvah to be happy at all times" (*Likkutei Moharan* 2:24). Since living is meant to be a positive experience, a Jew delights in creating, nurturing, and educating the next generation, and this important task is also referred to in the words of the *Shema*: "These words, which I command you today, should be in your heart, and you must teach them to your sons" (Deut. 6:6-7). Further reinforcement appears at the end of the chapter, where adults are coached regarding how to respond to the questions of the younger generation (Deut. 6:20-25).

The second discourse (according to the Vilna Gaon) continues into ch. 7, where, as a holy nation, the Israelites are told not to tolerate idol worship in their homeland because of the adverse effects previously described, and are commanded to destroy any group that insists on maintaining that lifestyle (Deut.7:2). According to Rambam (*Hilchot Melachim* 6:1) and Ramban (Deut. 20:10), violence is to be resorted to only if a kingdom refuses to accept the seven Noahide laws, based on the verse: "When you approach a city to wage war against it, you should first propose peace to it" (Deut. 20:10).[6] The prerequisite for a peace treaty is the creation of a moral society by observing the Noahide laws.

---

6. Rashi (Deut. 20:10) disagrees and says the verse refers only to wars of conquest outside of the borders of the Land of Israel.

Va'etchanan

Sabbath Observance

As part of his farewell summary, Moses repeats the Ten Commandments, saying: "These are the testimonies, statutes, and ordinances which Moses spoke to the Children of Israel" (Deut. 4:45). However, Moses does not reiterate them word for word, but rather makes minor changes, and even small differences can be the source of important insights.

Regarding Sabbath observance, the fourth commandment in Exodus states: "Remember the Sabbath day and sanctify it… For [in] six days the Lord made the heaven and the earth, the sea and all that is in them, and He rested on the seventh day" (Exod. 20:8, 11). In other words, by resting on the Sabbath the Jew recalls that God too did so when creating the world, thus imprinting in a Jew's mind an image of God as the Creator. In Deuteronomy, however, the Sabbath is declared to be a means of remembering the Israelites' servile past, as the verse says: "And you should remember that you were a slave in the land of Egypt, and that the Lord your God took you out from there with a strong hand and with an outstretched arm; therefore, the Lord, your God, commanded you to observe the Sabbath day" (Deut. 5:15). Apparently, by not working on the Sabbath, one is reminded that there was a time when, as slaves, the Israelites were required to work on the Sabbath, leading to the alternate image of God as the Redeemer.

The dual themes of the Sabbath are referred to in the Friday evening sanctification over wine (*kiddush*), which thanks God for bestowing upon Israel "His holy Shabbat, in love and favor, as a heritage, *in remembrance of the work of creation*; the first of the holy festivals, *commemorating the exodus from Egypt*" (Jewish Prayer Book).

The Slonimer Rebbe, R. Shalom Noach Berezovsky (*Netivot Shalom*, vol. 2, pp. 86-88), asks three questions regarding these two remembrances.

The Ethics of Deuteronomy

1. The Torah is not a history book. It does not record information for the purpose of documenting the past, but only inasmuch as it can affect our behavior in the present or the future. Is the *kiddush* to be reduced to a reenactment of historical events?
2. Even if it is important to recall certain historical occurrences, the Talmud (BT *Berachot* 58b) states that memory loss does not take effect until twelve months have passed. *Torah Temimah* (Deut. 25:200) states that for that reason, recalling the treachery of Amalek is required only once a year. This is also the period of time after which one gives up hope (*yi'ush*) of ever finding lost articles. Following this line of reasoning, why should creation and slavery have to be remembered every week? Once a year should suffice.
3. How do all the restrictions and even the festive dress and meals which characterize the Sabbath remind one specifically of creation and the redemption from slavery? Some would say that the former are more reminiscent of the slavery itself than the redemption therefrom.

The Slonimer Rebbe bases his answer on the view of *Or ha-Chaim* (Gen. 2:3, s.v. *achen*), who explains that when the Torah states: "For [in] six days the Lord made the heaven and the earth, the sea and all that is in them, and He rested on the seventh day" (Exod. 20:11), it means not only that the universe was created in six days, but also that it was created with just enough energy to last six days. If the Sabbath is observed properly, God injects a new dose of spiritual energy that enables it to last another six days, without which the universe would revert to a state of emptiness and vacuity (*tohu va-vohu*). Therefore, the Sabbath must be celebrated at the highest level of spirituality, which only a truly righteous person (*tzaddik*) is capable of doing. Fortuitously, from the time of the original creation until this very day, each generation has been privileged enough to be blessed with such a person. The Midrash (*Shocher Tov*, Ps. 92) speaks of Adam

Va'etchanan

as observing the first Sabbath, and he was followed by his righteous descendants, Seth, Methuselah, Noah, Abraham, and so on. Even during their enforced slavery in Egypt, the Midrash (*Exod. Rabbah* 1:28) relates that Moses pleaded with Pharaoh to let the people rest on the Sabbath. *Or ha-Chaim* utilizes this concept to explain the Talmudic statement:

> Anyone who prays on the eve of the Sabbath and recites *va-yechullu* ["and the heaven and the earth were completed" (Gen. 2:1)] is considered by the written law as if he is a partner with the Holy One, blessed be He, in the creation (BT *Shabbat* 119b).

How can man be a partner in creation if he only came into being afterwards? On the basis of the concept that the world is recreated as a result of his behavior every Sabbath, man may indeed be considered to be a catalyst in the creation process.

The Slonimer Rebbe answers his questions by elucidating that the emphasis when saying *kiddush* and remembering the work of creation is not historical, but rather futuristic. The Jew prays that through his meticulous observance of the Sabbath, he will be able to achieve the heights of spirituality and righteousness which would qualify him to partner with God in the act of creation.

To some, this explication will seem too mystical to be taken seriously. However, one may look upon the idea of regeneration as being metaphorical. As such, one may relate this concept to his own life situation. A person may be depressed because he has lost the strength of his youth, or because he is unemployed and financially challenged, or perhaps he was injured in an accident or in the military and now feels incomplete, or maybe he feels lonesome and isolated as the result of the demise of a close friend or relative. By utilizing the Sabbath to renew his faith in God and observe His commands, he figuratively wipes the slate clean and is reinvigorated to energetically face his undiminished challenges with determination and resolution.

Moving on to the second theme, commemorating the exodus from Egypt, the Slonimer Rebbe once more draws inspiration from *Or ha-Chaim*'s exegesis of the following words taken from the prophecy of Balaam: "God Who brings them out [*motzi'am*] of Egypt with the strength of His loftiness" (Num. 23:22). The word "brings" is in the present tense. *Or ha-Chaim* notes that the verse should have said: "God Who brought them out [*hotzi'am*] of Egypt," in the past tense, since the text is referring to an event which occurred long before. He answers that the redemption from Egypt is a constantly recurring process, in accordance with the instructions of R. Gamliel (*Pesachim* 10:5) as to how one is to approach the Passover Haggadah, and which are now incorporated therein:

> In every generation a person is obligated to regard himself as if he had come out of Egypt, as it is said: "You are to tell your child on that day, it is because of this [Rashi: to fulfill His commands, e.g., (the eating of) the paschal lamb, *matzah*, and bitter herbs] that the Lord did for me when I left Egypt" (Exod. 13:8).

This Mishnah bases its proof on the phrase "the Lord did for me *when I left Egypt*." Although spoken to the congregation about to leave Egypt, it is directed at parents who will be among those who enter the Land of Israel (see Exod. 13:5), and thus did not physically leave Egypt, yet they are to consider themselves as if they did. The Haggadah formulates this idea explicitly, citing a pronouncement made by Moses to the next generation, but which ostensibly includes them among those who departed from Egypt:

> The Holy One, blessed be He, not only redeemed our fathers, but us as well, for it says: "It was *us* that He brought out from there, so that He might bring us [here] to give us the land

Va'etchanan

that He swore to our fathers" (Deut. 6:23).

Of course, the question which arises is why did they need to be redeemed if they were never in Egypt in the first place? The answer appears earlier in the Haggadah:

> If the Holy One, blessed be He, had not taken our fathers out of Egypt, then we, our children, and our children's children would have remained enslaved to Pharaoh in Egypt.

R. Menachem Kasher (*Land of Israel Haggadah*) explains that all tyrants are being referred to (the Hebrew etymology of "Egypt" [*Mitzrayim*] and "tyrants" [*metzeirim*] is similar). Having tasted freedom after escaping from Egypt and receiving the Torah, the Israelites could never again be enslaved spiritually, even if they were persecuted physically.

Rambam (*Hilchot Chametz u-Matzah* 7:6) has a slightly different rendition of the Mishnah. Instead of the phrase "a person is obligated to regard himself as if he had come out of Egypt," his version states: "a person is obligated to present himself as if he had come out of Egypt." Instead of passively mentioning the simile, one must actively display it, and he implies in the following paragraph (7:7) that this is the source of the rabbinical decree to exhibit royal behavior at the Passover Seder by partaking of a festive meal and drinking four glasses of wine in a reclining position.

In short, on Passover the Israelites were permanently redeemed as individuals both physically and spiritually. More importantly, as a result of the exodus and the ensuing revelation, they coalesced into a nation endowed with a sense of freedom and independence. Israel's nationhood and characteristic traits are refreshed every year during the season of Passover, when Jews collectively engage in Passover spring-cleaning, preparing *matzot*, buying specially prepared Passover foods, and preparing for the Seder, but most significantly retelling the story of their redemption from slavery. According to the Pew Research Center, over 70% of American Jews attend a Seder.[7]

If reenactment of national redemption is done on a yearly basis, the Slonimer Rebbe suggests that individual redemption is done on a weekly basis. He notes that it states in holy writings that the delivery from Egypt is mentioned in the Torah 50 times, corresponding to the 50 weeks of the Jewish lunar calendar. On the six weekdays, a Jew feels comparatively distant from God, as if he were in exile. On the Sabbath, he feels closer, as if he has entered the Promised Land. What causes this transformation?

The Midrash (*Gen. Rabbah* 22:13) states that on the first Sabbath after creation, when Cain said: "My iniquity is too great to bear" (Gen. 4:13), he meant to say that his iniquity was greater than that of his father Adam, since he had sinned against his fellow man in a way that cannot be undone, while Adam had sinned against God in a manner suitable for repair. God accepted his anguish as a form of repentance and cancelled half of his punishment. Adam, who had been unaware of the possibility of repentance, and feeling overcome with emotion, wrote the psalm: "A song [with musical accompaniment] for the Sabbath day. It is good to give thanks to the Lord, and to sing to Your name, O Most High" (Ps. 92:1-2). The Rabbis noted that in Hebrew, both "Sabbath" and "repentance" have the same root (*shuv*), while the Hebrew word for "thanking" (*le-hodot*) can also mean "admitting" (*Yefei Toar, Gen. Rabbah* 22:13). Adam thus declared the Sabbath to be a day fit for both his own repentance and, in the future, for that of the rest of mankind. Sabbath is a day when one desists from his mundane activities and devotes time and effort to spiritual pursuits, such as prayer, study, and contemplation, as well as social interaction. The former represents God-oriented *mitzvot*, while the latter represents interpersonal *mitzvot*. Practicing both elevates one spiritually, and

---

7. Michael Lipka, "Attending Seder Is Common Practice for American Jews," Internet, April 14, 2014. The author was manager of religious research at the Pew Research Center.

Va'etchanan

repenting on the Sabbath for transgressions in either area enables one to start off the next week with a clean slate, as the verse states: "Return us to You, O Lord, that we may be returned; renew our days as of old" (Lam. 5:21).

It is true that self-flagellating repentance is out of character on the Sabbath, as it will likely lead to painful recollections. However, the Rebbe believes that low-key repentance, through spirituality and fellowship, is quite appropriate, and is in fact the order of the day.

Summarizing the answer of the Slonimer Rebbe, remembrance of creation and of the exodus do not refer as much to the past as to the future. Remembering creation stimulates one to figuratively renew oneself each week as if newly created physically, while remembering the exodus symbolizes undergoing a spiritual and religious catharsis every Sabbath in preparation for the next week.

Is There a Command to Work?

The first topic dealt with was based on a minor difference between the versions of the Ten Commandments presented in the portion of *Yitro* in the book of Exodus and in *Va'etchanan* in the book of Deuteronomy. In this section, the focus will be on one and a half verses whose wording is identical in both sets of commands, namely:

> Six days you will work and perform all of your labor, and the seventh day is a Sabbath to the Lord your God; you may not perform any labor, neither you nor your son or daughter... (Exod. 20:9-10; Deut. 5:13-14).

The question that arises is whether the first part of the text—which says that one should work for six days—is merely an introduction to the Sabbath legislation which follows, or whether two separate laws are being presented, one requiring a person to work during the week, and a second requiring him to desist from doing so on the Sabbath.

The Ethics of Deuteronomy

The answer may be found in the following saying:

> Great is labor, for just as Israel was commanded to observe the Sabbath, so were they commanded concerning labor, for it says: "Six days you will work and perform all of your labor" (*Avot de-Rabbi Natan* 2:21).

What should be done by an independently wealthy person who really has no financial need to work? A second Mishnah relates to that situation:

> R. Yehuda b. Beteira says: "He who has no labor to perform, what should he do? If he has an arid yard or field, he should go and attend to it, for it says: 'Six days you will work.' And why does it [also] say: 'and perform all of your labor'? To include one who has arid yards or fields, let him go and attend to them" (*Avot de-Rabbi Natan* 11:1).

As previously pointed out, the Midrash states:

> When Moses saw that no rest time was allocated to the Hebrew slaves, he approached Pharaoh and said: "He who has a slave, if he does not rest one day a week, he will die. And so your slaves, if you do not set aside one day a week [to rest], they will die." He said to him: "Go and do for them as you said." Moses went and instituted for them the day of Sabbath [as a day] to rest (*Exod. Rabbah* 1:28).

Chatam Sofer[8] uses this Midrash as a means of support for the previous citations from *Avot de-Rabbi Natan*. He says that he who is idle all week uproots an important principle of the Sabbath, namely that it memorializes the exodus from Egypt, for our ancestors rested

---
8. Cited in Yisrael Brody, *Nefesh Chaya* (2009), p. 546.

Va'etchanan

on the Sabbath only after six days of arduous, backbreaking work. In other words, intrinsic in the commemoration is the transition from grueling work to blissful rest. Without the former, the symbolism is lacking.

The importance of work is threefold: first, to prevent boredom (even if one is independently wealthy), which frequently leads to sin; second, to provide sustenance; and third, to integrate and apply Torah law to daily existence, as hinted in the Biblical verse: "It [the Torah] is not in heaven" (Deut. 30:12) or, in Talmudic parlance: "The Torah was not given to ministering angels" (e.g., BT *Berachot* 25b). These verses stress the importance of attuning Torah values and laws to our earthly existence.

The first two of these points may be observed in the following Mishnah:

> (A) Torah study together with a worldly occupation [*derech eretz*] is excellent, for achieving both of them causes sin to be forgotten, (B) and Torah [study] without a worldly occupation will come to naught and cause the spread of sin (*Avot* 2:2).

Part (A) stresses the importance of both Torah study and work in the life of a Jew. Bartenura explains that immersion in Torah weakens one's evil inclination, while physical labor deprives one of his strength, so that combining the two fills one's day productively and negates both the will and the ability to sin. Hence the first point (preventing boredom).

Part (B), according to Bartenura, provides the answer to a potential question on Part (A). Since Torah study is so rewarding, perhaps one should devote all of his efforts to doing so? The Mishnah answers that if one does not work, he will lack a source of income and eventually turn to crime, consequently losing his taste for Torah study. Hence the second point (providing sustenance).

The third point (application of the law) follows from another Mishnah, which states: "Where there is no worldly occupation [*derech eretz*], there is no Torah" (*Avot* 3:21). Of course, this phrase could be explained to simply mean that if one does not work, he will have no means of sustaining himself to learn Torah. However, the Mishnah would then be redundant, since that message has been conveyed by the previously quoted Mishnah. A more appropriate interpretation would thus be that if one does not work, the moral principles outlined in the Torah will remain in the theoretical realm exclusively, since there will be no opportunity to apply them in any real-life situation.

If one works for a living, his integration in the work force satisfies the *derech eretz* requirement. If one is a paid religious functionary, his communal involvement satisfies the *derech eretz* requirement. However, studying Torah privately with no public interface would not fulfill the requirement.

A more thorough treatment of the Jewish work ethic is found in *The Ethics of Genesis*.[9]

Summary

This chapter has focused on the centrality of the Sabbath in the Jewish religion. On the one hand, it emphasizes Judaism's most basic axiom, belief in God as the Creator of the world. On the other hand, it highlights God's concern for the Children of Israel and for humanity as a whole, by recalling the redemption of the Israelites from slavery, followed by the giving of the Torah, which was designed to inculcate the sacred values of physical and spiritual freedom. Finally, as a day of rest, the Sabbath indirectly affirms the importance of individual and communal productivity during the remaining six working days of every week,

---

9. Abba Engelberg, *The Ethics of Genesis* (2014), Appendix 4, pp. 245-254.

Ekev

The exhortative part of Moses' second discourse in the book of Deuteronomy (according to the Vilna Gaon's subdivision) continues in this portion with some of the classical motifs, such as the description of God's beneficence (Deut. 8:1-18, 9:1-6, 11:1-12); the imperative to fulfill the commands (Deut. 7:17-26, 10:12-22, 11:18-21), coupled with an enumeration of the associated rewards (Deut. 7:12-16, 11:13-15, 11:22-25); and a listing of the potential punishments for disobeying the law (Deut. 8:19-20, 11:16-17). The sinful behavior of the nation at the time of the golden calf is also referenced (Deut. 9:7-10:11).

A parallel exists between the portion of *Ekev* and the portion of *Vayeitzei* in Genesis. The latter portion depicted a new stage in the life of Jacob. According to Jewish tradition, until then Jacob had lived in his parents' house, perhaps sharing a bit in the household chores, but devoting most of his time to religious studies. In the portion of *Vayeitzei*, he took his first steps towards setting up a family and making a living. Of course, Jacob did not dissociate himself from the words of wisdom which he had imbibed in the yeshiva of Shem and Ever. When he transitioned from a life of Torah-learning to one of work, he was expected to integrate his Torah knowledge with his daily work and to set aside time for daily study.

Similarly, the portion of *Ekev* describes the end of one stage and the beginning of a new stage—not in the life of an individual, but in the life of the nation. The portion tells of the culmination of a miraculous existence—starting from the ten plagues and continuing with Miriam's well, the clouds of glory, and the descent of manna from heaven. The narrative transitions to a more natural life-style, as reflected in the verse: "And the Lord, your God, will drive out those nations from before you, little by little. You will not be able to destroy them quickly, lest the beasts of the field outnumber you" (Deut. 7:22). Many of the miracles recorded in the Israelites' history surpassed what would have been involved in protecting the nation from wild beasts. However, since the intensity of the miraculous is to be drastically reduced, the nation is informed that it will no longer be able to rely on such intervention.

Certainly, God has not totally withdrawn His assistance, as indicated by the promise: "And also the hornet the Lord your God will incite against them" (Deut. 7:20), which Rashi, based on BT *Sotah* 36a, interprets to be "a species of flying insect which injected poison into them [the Canaanites], making them impotent and blinding their eyes wherever they hid."

The condition to be fulfilled, in order to ensure God's continued assistance even after they arrive in the Land of Israel, is to obey the commandments, as the verse states:

> Every commandment that I command you this day you must be careful to do, so that you may live and multiply, and arrive [in Israel] and possess the land that the Lord promised to your forefathers (Deut. 8:1).

What will help stimulate the nation to properly observe the *mitzvot* is the constant remembrance of the miracles which the Lord performed for the sake of the Children of Israel, for example:

> Your clothing did not get worn out [Rashi, based on *Pesikta de-Rav Kahana* 11:21, s.v. *va-yehi be-shalach*: the clouds of glory would rub their clothes and clean them so that they looked like freshly laundered clothes; and also, as their

Ekev

children grew, their clothes grew along with them, like a snail's shell, which grows along with it], nor did your foot swell [Rashi: like dough, as usually happens with those who walk barefoot, that their feet swell] these forty years (Deut. 8:4).

Interestingly, some of the most wondrous miracles, such as the ten plagues and the splitting of the Reed Sea, are not explicitly mentioned. On the other hand, the miracle of the manna is mentioned twice in the following verses:

1. "And He afflicted you and starved you, and then fed you with manna... in order to make you aware that man does not live by bread alone, but rather by all that comes out of the mouth of the Lord does man live" (Deut. 8:3).
2. "Who fed you with manna in the desert... in order to afflict you and in order to test you, to benefit you in your end" (Deut. 8:16)?

Why did the Torah choose to highlight the miracle of the manna over other miracles? A possible answer is that more important than the miraculous aspect of the manna was the fact that it played a role in developing the habits and attitudes incumbent upon Jews to fulfill their future mission. Three aspects of manna will be referred to: the affliction, the manna itself, and the halachic details.

Manna: A Means of Affliction

As noted, in the present portion, manna is referred to more as a form of affliction than as a miracle. The first question which may be asked is, in what sense can being fed without having to labor for one's sustenance be considered distressing? The answer follows from a cursory reading of the verses describing the introduction of manna:

The Ethics of Deuteronomy

> They journeyed from Elim... on the fifteenth day of the second month after their departure from the land of Egypt. The entire community of the Children of Israel complained against Moses and against Aaron in the desert. The Children of Israel said to them: "If only we had died by the hand of the Lord in the land of Egypt, when we sat by pots of meat, when we ate bread to satisfaction. For you have brought us to this desert to starve the entire congregation to death" (Exod. 16:1-3).

Rashi explains that the community complained because at that point, exactly one month after their departure from Egypt, the extra *matzah* which they had brought with them from Egypt was depleted. By this comment, Rashi wishes to indicate that the nation's aggravation was completely understandable, since they were unaware of any alternative source of nourishment. The Talmud as well justifies their peeve when it states: "Bread for which they asked properly [justifiably] was given to them properly [in an honorable manner]" (BT *Yoma* 75b).

It is thus clear that the initial appearance of manna was as the follow-up of a painful ordeal. However, when the verse speaks of God having "fed you with manna in the desert... in order to afflict you" (Deut. 8:16), the implication is that suffering was associated not only with the preliminary waiting period, but with the very consumption of the manna itself (Rif, *Ein Ya'akov, Yoma* 74b). Furthermore, the travail associated with the manna is said to have persisted throughout the entire "forty years in the wilderness" (Deut. 8:2), and it is with respect to the latter phrase that the Talmud wonders, in the following extract, how being fed without having to labor for one's sustenance can be considered distressing:

> "Who fed you with manna in the desert... in order to afflict you." R. Ammi and R. Assi [argue with respect to this]. One said: You cannot compare one who has bread in his basket

Ekev

to one who has none [Rashi: one eats today and worries about tomorrow (the lack of certainty is anguishing)]. The other said: You cannot compare one who sees what he eats to one who does not see what he is eating [Rashi: when eating manna, one chooses the (desired) taste, but he only sees manna; *Iyun Ya'akov* notes that the requirement to light candles on Friday evening may be for the purpose of making the food visible]. R. Yosef says: This is an allusion to [the reason] why blind people eat without satisfaction [R. Chananel: as if in agony]. Abaye said: Therefore, one who has a meal should eat it only in the day [Maharsha: or at night by candlelight, as was done with respect to the paschal lamb]. R. Zeira said: What verse [indicates this]? "Better is what he sees with his eyes than what satisfies his appetite" (Ecc. 6:9). Reish Lakish said: Better is the pleasure of looking at a woman than the act itself, as it says: "Better is what he sees with his eyes than what satisfies his appetite" (BT *Yoma* 74b)

According to *Iyun Ya'akov, in situ*, the affliction associated with the manna ("in order to afflict you") readied the nation emotionally to exert themselves and even toil in their Torah studies, and these are his words: "Acquiring Torah comes about specifically by minimizing pleasures, and they had to therefore afflict and starve themselves [to inure themselves in preparation for their task], as they say: 'he who increases knowledge, increases pain' (Ecc. 1:18)." *Iyun Ya'akov* apparently understands the latter verse to be applicable in both directions. On the one hand, possessing more knowledge makes one more susceptible to pain, but on the other, in order to obtain more knowledge, one has to be willing to endure a certain level of discomfort and self-discipline. The affliction improved their intellectual abilities and turned the generation of the desert into a knowledgeable one. *Tzeror ha-Mor* (*Ekev*, ch. 8) supplies a logical explanation for this phenomenon: "For they came from Egypt fat with a full belly from unhealthy foods, to the point that they were obtuse in their minds from eating fish and squash and onions, and in order to enter the service of the Lord and to learn the Torah and the commandments, they had to fast and starve themselves."

Ba'al ha-Turim claims that the manna itself made them wiser, which he derives from the words in Deut. 8:3, "in order to make you aware," as well as from a verse in the book of Nehemiah: "And You provided them with Your good spirit to enable them to understand, and You did not withhold Your manna from their mouth" (Neh. 9:20).

Manna: A Stimulus to Repent

In the portion of *Ki Tavo*, a series of blessings are recorded, which are to take effect if the nation observes the commandments (Deut. 28:1-14), and a much longer series of curses which will occur in the event that Israel misbehaves and fails to fulfill the *mitzvot* (Deut. 28:15-69). The next portion, *Nitzavim*, reinforces these blessings and curses by presenting the nation with a covenant to concretize them as a binding contract. The portion opens with the words: "You are all standing this day before the Lord" (Deut. 29:9), which the Midrash (*Tanchuma Nitzavim* 29:1, cited by Rashi, Deut. 29:12) explicates as follows:

> Why is this portion [*Nitzavim*] juxtaposed to the curses? Because when Israel heard ninety-eight curses delineated in this portion [*Ki Tavo*], besides the forty-nine stated in Leviticus (26:14-38), they turned pale and said, "Who can possibly endure these?" [Thereupon,] Moses began to appease them [by saying, "You are all (still) standing this day, as opposed to the non-Jews who lived at the time of the deluge (Gen. 7:23), the tower of Babel (Isa. 14:22), Sodom (Gen. 19:25), and the Egyptian enslavement (Exod. 14:28), who were either destroyed or vanished].

Ekev

The Midrash notes that Israel continues to exist in spite of having seriously sinned:

> But you did not listen to My voice, and you expressed thoughts before Me for which you were deserving of destruction, but I did not destroy you, as it says: "Our forefathers in Egypt did not appreciate Your wonders; they did not remember the multitude of Your kind deeds, and they were rebellious by sea, at the Sea of Reeds" (Ps. 106:7). And not only that, but you addressed the [golden] calf saying: "These are your gods, O Israel, who have raised you up from the land of Egypt" (Exod. 32:4).

The Midrash proceeds to ask why Israel was afforded special treatment, while the Gentiles were annihilated, and supplies the following answer:

> Because when punishment is visited upon them, they reject it and do not utter the name of the Holy One, blessed be He, as it says: "Pour out Your wrath upon the nations that do not know You and upon the kingdoms that did not call out in Your name" (Ps. 79:6). But Israel, when punishment is meted out to it, accedes [to its message] and prays, as it says: "[When] ropes of death surrounded me, and the straits of the nether-world befell me, [and] I found trouble and grief, then I called out in the name of the Lord: 'Please, O Lord, deliver my soul'" (Ps. 116:3-4). Therefore, the Holy One, blessed be He, said: "Even though those curses devolve upon you, they strengthen you," and so it says: *"Who fed you with manna in the desert... in order to afflict you and in order to test you, to benefit you in your end"* (Deut. 8:16). Similarly, Moses said to Israel: "Although this punishment befalls you, you remain upright. For this reason, it says: 'You are all standing this day'" (Deut. 29:9).

The Midrash implies that the fear of hunger and other inconveniences associated with the manna led the nation to engage in self-examination and repentance for their sins, a lesson which became part of their permanent outlook on life and an essential element of the Jewish religion.

Another Midrash (*Yalkut Shimoni*, Ecc. 974) applies the phrase "to benefit you in your end" not only on the national level, but on the individual level as well, in order to answer the perennial question of theodicy: Why do the righteous suffer? The Midrash compares life decisions to the case of one who stands at the intersection of two paths: one paved at the beginning, but overlaid with thorns afterwards, and the second encumbered with thorns at the start, but very smooth the rest of the way. The beginning of the path represents the present world, in which the righteous frequently suffer while the wicked prosper. The remaining majority of the path represents the world to come, where the righteous of this world will thrive. The Torah encapsulates the situation when God is quoted as saying: "I have set before you life and death" (Deut. 30:19). Life (in the world to come) will be granted to those who manage "to love the Lord your God, to listen to His voice, and to cleave to Him… [and] to dwell on the land which the Lord swore to your forefathers, to Abraham, to Isaac, and to Jacob, to give to them" (Deut. 30:20). God urges every Jew to "choose life, so that you and your offspring will live" (Deut. 30:19). In other words, one is entreated to act properly even if the reward is not immediate, since, as Kohelet says: "The end of a thing is better than its beginning" (Ecc. 7:8).

In review, the hardship associated with relying on manna for sustenance nurtured the qualities of diligence (necessary for mastery over Biblical and Talmudic literature), repentance, and acceptance of worldly adversity as a prelude to metaphysical pleasure in the world to come.

Ekev

MANNA: THE FREQUENCY OF ITS DESCENT

There were two stages associated with the manna—its falling from heaven and its being gathered by the congregation. Regarding the latter, there were numerous laws, which God informs the Children of Israel that He had given them "to afflict you in order to test you, to know what is in your heart, whether you would keep His commandments or not" (Deut. 8:2). One of these laws required the manna to be gathered daily. However, the Talmud asks why the manna had to fall daily, even if it was important that it be gathered daily. It could have fallen once a year, with each family gathering the appropriate amount daily (Rif, *Ein Ya'akov, Yoma* 76a). The Talmud reports the following conversation:

> R. Shimon b. Yochai was asked by his disciples: Why did the manna not come down to Israel once annually [instead of daily]? He replied: I will give you a parable: It may be compared to a flesh and blood king who had one son. He provided him with maintenance once a year, and he would only visit his father once a year. He then decided to supply him daily, and he visited him every day. The same [is what God did] with Israel. One who had four or five children [Maharsha: for smaller families, food could be purchased from the nearby nations] would worry, saying: Perhaps no manna will come down tomorrow, and all will die of hunger. As a result, they all turned their attention to their Father in Heaven. Another answer: They could thus eat it while it was still warm. Another answer: Because of the burden of the way [carrying it would greatly hamper them on their journey to Israel] (BT *Yoma* 76a).

The very dependence on God certainly stimulated and habituated the nation to trust in the Lord. In addition, the daily waiting for the family's portion served as a basis for daily prayer and led to a feeling of continuous communication between each individual Jew and the Creator of the universe, i.e., to acknowledging the presence of Divine Providence in the private life of every individual.

Concerning the second answer, that it fell daily so that it could be eaten warm, Maharsha asks why this should present a problem, since in any case the congregation was in the habit of warming up the manna, as God had told them: "Bake whatever you wish to bake, and cook whatever you wish to cook" (Exod. 16:23). He answers: "This [benefit] was directed at the righteous, who ate the manna as it was upon its descent, but with respect to the mediocre and sinful, who needed to bake the manna [as has been noted], it was indeed warmed up when baked." This phenomenon provided another important lesson to the young nation, namely that individuals are rewarded for their good deeds and punished for their bad deeds, since the righteous received their food ready to eat, while the less virtuous had to toil in its preparation. In short, God demonstrated the concept of reward and punishment for the Children of Israel.

R. S.R. Hirsch commented that the manna strengthened the nation's belief in God, discouraged blind pursuit of material wealth, and cleared time for spiritual growth, all in addition to its introduction of the new idea of *hashgachah pratit* (Divine Providence), i.e., Divine supervision over each individual.

In the following excerpt, R. Hirsch relates to the concept of *mitzvah ha-ba'ah be-aveirah* (a mitzvah accomplished by first performing a transgression), claiming that such behavior occurs as a result of the attitude expressed in the Biblical verse: "And you will say to yourself: 'My strength and the might of my hand have accumulated this wealth for me'" (Deut. 8:17). No matter how much effort a person expends in supporting himself and his family, he will still not succeed unless he realizes that any achievement of his results only from the nurturance of the Almighty. Only then will he be able to thrive in a moral and religiously sanctioned manner. Acknowledging, and to some extent

Ekev

relying on, God's participation in his sustenance will induce him to set aside time for Torah study and spiritual development. As a prerequisite to making these points, R. Hirsch provides a novel interpretation of the word *lechem*, meaning "bread":

> *Lechem* is the food wrested [i.e., that man fights for (*nilcham alav*)] from Nature and the competition of your fellow men. Bread is the product of human intelligence mastering Nature and the world, so that bread represents human intelligence creating the continuance of its existence by mastering Nature in social cooperation. Now the illusive idea that this creative power of man is the sole condition for his existence on earth and forgets God's ruling [as] being the first factor of the provision of man's food—although His providing care is shown by every tiny piece of bread by which we sustain one minute of our existence—this illusive idea is the most dangerous rock on which our faithful attention to duty founders. The worry to provide bread for wife and child is in itself such a justified incentive for our activities that it easily tends to drive all other considerations out of sight as soon as we believe that we, and we alone, have to provide for the existence of ourselves and those dependent on us. As soon as we believe that every acquisition that we wrest from Nature and our contemporaries ensures our and their existence, no matter how that acquisition had been obtained—whether thereby we had cared for the laws of God and kept to the paths He had indicated, or whether only by clever deft handling we had secured the bread without giving a thought as to whether God would agree with these means [then we have embraced a dangerous approach]. And where this looking on one's own human powers alone having to provide bread does not lead us from the path of what is right and where our duty lies, it is still inclined to make us think of providing

beyond the immediate necessities towards an ever-widening future. We think we have never done enough to satisfy our imagined duty, and talk ourselves into believing we have not discharged it unless we have acquired beforehand the means of existence of the whole of the future and for that of our children and grandchildren, and so we make the worry of providing bread into an unlimited breathless chase after income, which denies any time for interest in purely spiritual and intellectual matters (R. S.R. Hirsch, Deut. 8:3).[10]

R. Hirsch proceeds to show how the gift of manna served as a means of inculcating the centrality of *hashgachah pratit* in the Jewish religion and to interpret the phrase: "man does not live by bread alone, but rather by whatever comes forth from the mouth of the Lord does man live" (Deut. 8:3) as indicating that as important as it is to work for one's living, he will not succeed unless he also obeys all of the other directives which God has transmitted in the Written and Oral Law and relies on God to complete any part of his sustenance which he fears may be lacking.

That is why God led us into the great school of a forty-year wandering in the wilderness, where all the factors were lacking which otherwise grant men their bread out of Nature and human powers, and made the one factor which, in normal conditions, tends to become pushed more and more into the background and so easily forgotten, viz. the Divine Providential solicitude—[He] made that factor come visibly into the foreground. Instead of bread, bearing the stamp of human achievement, *He fed us day by day in such a manner, modified for each soul in our huts, that it demonstrated in the most striking clarity the most specific care of God for each*

---

10. Translations of R. S.R. Hirsch's commentary are by Isaac Levy, published by Judaica Press (1971).

soul, and each tiny soul, individually. And in this preparatory school for the course of our lives we learned that not on bread alone—not on what bread represents of the support of man and Nature—is man directed to seek means for his existence; but on *everything* that God ordains—bread too that man makes by his own skill is naught but such a one—can man live. He can be quite sure that he will not be lost if, in order to keep faithful to God's commands, he has to give up what normally he would get from Nature and man, and in the midst of the richest abundance of the gifts of Nature and man, it is only the most special care of God that will feed him (R. S.R. Hirsch, Deut. 8:3).

THE HALACHIC DETAILS

The halachic details concerning the distribution of the manna served as a source for important principles in Judaism. The Israelites' daily necessity to gather the manna on their own nurtured diligence (Exod. 16:16) and the limitation of the daily allotment discouraged hoarding and encouraged consideration of others (Exod. 16:16-18), while the prohibitions of leaving remnants (Exod. 16:19) and collecting manna on the Sabbath (Exod. 16:26) habituated them to following orders and obeying the *mitzvot*. Only the unruliest violated these rules, namely Dathan and Abiram, the "usual suspects" (*Tanchuma Shemot* 20; Rashi, Exod. 16:20). R. Hirsch learns from the Sabbath laws which forbade collecting the manna, but required festively partaking of it, that Judaism does not condemn relaxation nor does it disdain bodily pleasures, rather it sanctifies them. In his words:

> For this inactivity is no wrong, self-chosen laziness. It is ordered by God and dedicated to God, and therefore has as high, as positive a value as any activity ordered by God. Also, this makes eating on Sabbath itself a mitzvah, an act ordered by God, directed to God, an ennobling and happiness-bringing

deed. The fact that man is to submit his efforts to gain his living to the direction of God is not to lessen or do away with enjoyment of his earthly existence. On the contrary, it is to enhance the enjoyment of his material existence and to raise the enjoyment of even sensual pleasures into the sphere of free, moral, God- serving acts, so that even by the enjoyment of his senses, his eating, his drinking, etc., he feels himself near to his God. *This elevation of the enjoyment of one's senses into a God-serving act, dedicated to God, constitutes one of the most characteristic marks of the difference between Jewish teachings and others* (R. S.R. Hirsch, Exod. 16:25).

Summary

The miracle of the manna hints at the following basic guidelines of the Jewish religion:

1. Affliction inculcated the precepts of repentance and theodicy, as well as the necessity of toiling in one's studies and in observance of the laws of the Torah.
2. The manna itself symbolized faith in God, reward and punishment, and Divine Providence.
3. The halachic details stimulated the traits of diligence, generosity, and consideration, while simultaneously demonstrating the sanctification of pleasurable actions by transforming them into ritual ceremonies that form an integral subset of the laws of the Torah, which constitute the Jewish religious heritage.

Re'eh

The Dietary Laws

Since the dietary laws were initially broached in the portion of *Shemini* in the book of Leviticus, a short review of that material is in order as an introduction to the portion of *Re'eh*, which also deals with those same laws (Deut. 14:3-21). Ch. 11 in the portion of *Shemini* starts out by enumerating the dietary laws, non-observance of which leads to a state of impurity through consuming (or even touching the carcasses of) unclean creatures, as indicated by the following verses:

> This is the law of the beast, and of the fowl, and of every living creature that moves in the waters, and of every creature that swarms upon the earth; to make a difference between the impure and the pure, and between the living thing that may be eaten and the living thing that may not be eaten (Lev. 11:46-47).

Non-kosher food is described throughout ch.11 in *Shemini* as being either *tamei*[11] (impure) or, mainly regarding birds and reptiles, *sheketz*[12] (detestable).

Actually, the idea that some animals are *tahor* (pure) and others are *tamei* is already alluded to in the story of the flood, where Noah was told to take only two sets (male and female) of the unclean

---

11. Lev. 11:4-8, 26-29, 31, 20:25; Deut. 14:7-8, 10, 19.
12. Lev. 11:10-13, 23.

animals, and seven sets of the clean animals (Gen. 7:2-3), and Rashi explains that more were needed of the clean animals, since some of them (as opposed to the unclean animals) would be sacrificed afterwards, which indeed occurred (Gen. 8:20). Interestingly, this distinction existed at a time when it was still prohibited for mankind to eat meat (BT *Sanhedrin* 59b).

Purity and Holiness

The purpose of observing the laws of purity is to allow each Israelite as an individual, and the congregation as a whole, to achieve holiness, which is (roughly) how the name of the portion *Kedoshim* in Leviticus is translated. Transitioning from purity to holiness is reflected in the following verses:

> You should not make your souls detestable with [eating] any creeping thing, neither should you make yourselves impure through them, thereby defiling yourself. For I am the Lord your God; sanctify yourselves and be holy, for I am holy (Lev. 11:43-44).[13]

In the portion of *Re'eh*, the charge to be a holy nation (Deut. 14:2) is followed immediately by an enumeration of the non-kosher creatures, after which the goal of attaining holiness is again recorded (Deut. 14:21).

The first cursory mention of the dietary laws is actually in Exodus, where it is already stipulated that their goal is to enable one to become holy: "And you shall be *holy* men unto Me; therefore, you should not eat any flesh that is torn from beasts in the field; you should cast it to the dogs" (Exod. 22:30). Rashi explains: "If you are holy and abstain from carrion and the flesh of animals torn by wild beasts, then you will be Mine; otherwise, you will not be Mine."

In short, obeying the dietary laws leads to purity, which leads to

---

13. See also Lev. 20:25-26.

Re'eh

holiness. However, because holiness is such a nebulous concept, the following questions are still relevant:

1. Why does God desire that Israel observe the dietary laws?
2. What is the meaning of holiness?

ANSWERING THE FIRST QUESTION: WHY OBSERVE THE DIETARY LAWS?

Regarding the verse "And you should guard all of My statutes and all of My ordinances, and do them; I am the Lord" (Lev. 19:37), Rambam explains:

> The Sages said to guard and do the statutes, just as [is required for] the ordinances. The doing is well known—i.e., to perform the statutes; and as regards the guarding, one should be cautious and not imagine that they are of less importance than the ordinances. The ordinances are the commandments whose reasons are revealed, and the benefit of doing them in this world is known; for example, the prohibition to steal and spill blood, and [the command] to honor one's father and mother. The statutes are the commandments whose reasons are not known. The Rabbis said: [There are] statutes that I legislated for you, and you are not permitted to cast doubt on them. A person's evil inclination anguishes him [makes him question] and the nations of the world denigrate them—for example [partially based on BT *Yoma* 67b], the prohibition to eat pig, and meat and milk, and the calf whose neck is broken; the red heifer, and the scapegoat (*Hilchot Me'ilah* 8:8).

The answer to the question is thus that the dietary laws are statutes that Jews are expected to observe for no reason other than that

God commanded them to do so. Furthermore, it was noted that observing them helps one attain holiness, which is a state that each Jew is commanded to realize, as indicated by the second verse in the portion of *Kedoshim*: "You should be holy, for I, the Lord your God, am holy" (Lev. 19:2).[14] Holiness is thus a characteristic of God which is achievable by man.

The following Mishnah seemingly supports the view that one should not try to rationalize the *mitzvot*: "If one [when praising the Lord] says 'Your mercy extends [even] to the bird's nest'... he is silenced" (*Berachot* 5:3), which the Talmud elucidates as follows: "because he presents the measures taken by the Holy One, blessed be He, as springing from compassion, whereas they are but decrees" (BT *Berachot* 33b). In other words, the only reason to obey God's law is because He commanded one to do so, and it is pointless and even misleading to claim otherwise, because once the field is open to rationalization, one will be tempted to make exceptions to the rules on the basis of the proposed reasons.

Ba'al ha-Akeidah

Ba'al ha-Akeidah (*Akeidat Yitzchak*, sha'ar 60, *Shemini*) apparently also adopts the view that the dietary laws are statutes. He claims that by disobeying them, one pollutes his soul, as is written: "neither should you make yourselves *impure* through them, thereby defiling yourself" (Lev. 11:43). He concludes by saying that consuming non-kosher food will "blunt the intellectual powers and generate confused opinions and strange, ravenous and brutish appetites [among men], which destroy them and defeat the purpose of their creation."

How a person's eating habits affect his spiritual life is clearly beyond human comprehension, so these commands remain in the realm of unexplained edicts.

---

14. The portion of *Kedoshim* may be looked upon as a continuation, or perhaps culmination, of the ideas presented in the earlier portion of *Shemini*, with the focus transferred from animal-related to interpersonal laws, but with the common goal of achieving holiness.

Re'eh

Ba'al ha-Akeidah cites a Midrash (*Lev. Rabbah* 13:2) to bolster his view:

> R. Tanchum b. Chanilai said: It is comparable to a doctor who visits two patients, one who will survive, and one who will die. He told the one who would survive: "This you can eat, and this you cannot." Concerning the one who was not to live, he says: "Whatever he wants, give him." So, with regard to idol worshippers who are not destined to reach the next world, it says regarding them: "Every moving thing that lives may serve as food for you; as the green herb [Rashi: already permitted to Adam] have I given you all" (Gen. 9:3). But [He says to] Israel, who are destined to reach the next world: "These are the living things which you may eat from among all the beasts that are on the earth" (Lev. 11:2).

The Midrash seems to be saying that there is no salvation for non-Jews. Such an approach is problematic for a number of reasons. Since similar claims have been made concerning the Christian and Muslim religions, and many have died as a result, it would seem especially dangerous to posit the same exclusivism with regard to Judaism.

From a purely logical point of view, the God of mercy would not have created human beings who from the onset have no chance of ultimate success. The following points will accordingly be considered:

1. Although the Midrash seems to be precluding entry of Gentiles into the next world, it is possible that its main intent is to encourage Jews to expend the strenuous efforts needed in adhering to the minutiae of the dietary laws, and the negative implication regarding Gentiles is not to be taken literally.
2. Note that the term used for non-Jews is "idol worshippers." Pagans believe that there is more than one supernatural force in the world. The result is that their gods do not transmit a code

of behavior to human beings, for each god can contradict the opinions of the others. In addition, they do not serve as role models, because they themselves are embroiled in arguments with each other and do not behave in a moral fashion. They exhibit traits of hedonism and selfishness, with no consideration for others.[15] It is unlikely that people possessing such beliefs can ever achieve the level of morality advocated by the Noahide commandments, so that in the end, they will not be deserving of eternal life. Those non-Jews, however, who behave in accordance with the Noahide code, do indeed have a portion in the world to come (*Peirush ha-Mishnayot, Sanhedrin* 10:2) and are termed *chasidei ummot ha-olam* (*Mishnat R. Eliezer* 6).

3. Even if taken literally, the Midrash does not represent the mainstream view. The Mishnah in *Sanhedrin* (10:2) says that Balaam (who incited the nation to engage in prostitution)[16] will not have a portion in the world to come, whereupon the Talmud notes: "Balaam will not enter [the future world], but other [Gentiles] will enter" (BT *Sanhedrin* 105a). This is the view of R. Yehoshua, while R. Eliezer holds the view reflected in the Midrash. Since the opinion of R. Yehoshua is quoted anonymously in the *stam* Mishnah, it is assumed to be the favored opinion. Rambam, as well, decides in accordance with R. Yehoshua (*Hilchot Melachim* 8:11).

4. There is a Talmudic text which actually implies that non-Jews might be more deserving of eternal reward than Jews. The Talmud states: "A Tanna taught in the name of R. Meir: Why was the Torah given to Israel? Because they are intense" (BT *Beitzah* 25b). Rashi (as quoted in *Ein Ya'akov*) explains the implication of the word "intense" as follows: "They are intense in their wickedness, and the Torah was given to occupy them, and it weakens their strength and subdues their drives."

---

15. Abba Engelberg, *The Ethics of Exodus* (2014), pp. 26-33.
16. BT *Sanhedrin* 106a; Rashi, Num. 25:1.

Re'eh

The Sanzer Rebbe, R. Chaim Halberstam, amplifies Rashi by explaining that, unfortunately, Jews are more prone to commit serious sins such as haughtiness, adultery, and embezzlement than non-Jews. As a result, the Torah had to legislate many laws in order to discipline the Israelites and reduce their tendency to sin. Gentiles, on the other hand, are less driven to transgress, and accordingly, the seven Noahide laws suffice for them. He proceeds to state: "God forbid one believe that honoring the nations is taken lightly, because we appreciate their beneficence to us, and when God will redeem us, He will also reward them for their goodness."[17]

SEFER HA-CHINUCH

The author of *Sefer ha-Chinuch* (a compendium of *mitzvot*) claims that the crux of the sin of mixing meat and milk is the actual mixing process, which he proves by noting that it is forbidden to do so even if one does not partake of the mixture (*Sefer ha-Chinuch*, mitzvah 92). He compares this command to that forbidding sorcery (*Sefer ha-Chinuch*, mitzvah 62), where he explains that at the time of creation, the nature of all items was determined, as well as the effect of mixing them with each other. Some of the results were to have positive effects, while others were to be deleterious, and it was hence commanded not to engage in such mixtures, which were called sorcery. Other examples of forbidden mixtures of animals (*kilayim*), grains, and even clothing (*shaatnez*), are reflected in the following verse:

> You must keep My statutes. You must not allow your cattle to gender with a diverse kind; you may not sow your field with two kinds of seed; neither should you wear a garment of two kinds of fibers mingled together (Lev. 19:19).[18]

---

17. Cited by Yehudah Levi, *Mul Etgarei ha-Tekufah* (1993), p. 48.
18. These laws are repeated in Deut. 22:9-11.

Although the *Sefer ha-Chinuch* attempts to provide some form of explanation, the arbitrary nature of the forbidden mixtures classifies them as statutes. It is also clear that he accepts the validity of sorcery as referred to in the Torah, just not its permissibility. Rambam, on the other hand, speaks out forcefully against the efficacy of necromancy in any of its forms (Deut. 18:10-11) and considers them to be sleight of hand, which are punishable only because of their false and misleading claims (*Hilchot Avodat Kochavim* 11:16), not because they actually work. Rambam accordingly feels that any Aggadic reference to such phenomena are to be understood metaphorically (Introduction to *Chelek*). It should be noted that the Vilna Gaon (*Yoreh De'ah* 179, note 13), as well as many others,[19] accept the position of the author of *Sefer ha-Chinuch*.

Proposed Reasons for the Dietary Laws

Although Rambam classifies the dietary laws as statutes whose reasons are unknown, he apparently merely means that one cannot determine with absolute certainty why they were instituted, and accordingly cannot draw conclusions based on their surmised purpose. He does not mean to prohibit conjectures, as long as they are not accepted as definitive, as will be seen from the citations below.

Rambam explains the previously cited Mishnah (*Berachot* 5:3), which seems to state that God's laws are decrees and not based on human understanding, as follows:

> When in the Talmud those are chastised who use in their prayer the phrase, "Your mercy extends [even] to the bird's nest" (BT *Berachot* 33b), it is the expression of one of the two opinions mentioned by us, namely, that the precepts of the Law have no other reason but the Divine will. We follow the other opinion (*Guide for the Perplexed* 3:48).[20]

---

19. Ran in *Derashot ha-Ran*, end of *Derush* 4 and *Derush* 12; Ramban (*Kitvei Ramban*, p. 380); Rashba in *Shu"t ha-Rashba* 1:413.
20. Translations of *Guide for the Perplexed* are by M. Friedlander.

Re'eh

The other opinion cited in the Talmud takes the exact opposite approach by explaining that one should not speak of God's mercy with respect to the bird's nest "because [by doing so] he creates jealousy among God's creatures." In other words, the quoted slogan could be understood to imply that God has mercy only on birds and not on any of His other creatures, while in reality He is merciful to all of His creations.

Utilitarian Explanations—Health Benefits

Rambam feels that Jewish dietary restrictions are meant to engender a healthy lifestyle. In his own words: "I maintain that the food which is forbidden by the Law is unwholesome" (*Guide for the Perplexed* 3:48). Regarding meat and milk, he claims that "meat boiled in milk is undoubtedly gross food, and makes one overfull" (ibid.). As far as pig and forbidden fat, he has the following to say:

> There is nothing among the forbidden kinds of food whose injurious character is doubted, except pork (Lev. 11:7) and fat [of the internal organs and entrails] (Lev. 7:23). But also in these cases the doubt is not justified. For pork contains more moisture than necessary [for human food], and too much of superfluous matter. The principal reason why the Law forbids swine's flesh is to be found in the circumstance that its habits and its food are very dirty and loathsome. It has already been pointed out how emphatically the Law enjoins the removal of the sight of loathsome objects, even in the field and in the camp; how much more objectionable is such a sight in towns. But if it were allowed to eat swine's flesh, the streets and houses would be dirtier than any cesspool, as may be seen at present in the country of the Franks. A saying of our Sages declares: "The mouth of a swine is as dirty as dung itself" (BT *Berachot* 25a). The fat of the intestines makes us

full, interrupts our digestion, and produces cold and thick blood; it is more fit for fuel [than for human food].

Apparently, Rambam, many years before John Wesley coined the phrase, felt that "cleanliness is next to Godliness." However, he was not the only one to propose a utilitarian explanation. Rashbam states:

> All of the animals and beasts and fowl and fish and types of locust and creeping creatures which the Lord prohibited to Israel are disgusting, and they destroy and heat the body, and [they are therefore] called impure, and even outstanding doctors say as much. And it is even mentioned in the Talmud [BT *Shabbat* 86b] that the bodies of non-Jews who eat creeping creatures degenerate (Lev. 11:3).

Similarly, Ramban discusses the reason that the Torah only permits fish having fins and scales:

> The reason for [the requirement of] fins and scales is that those [fish] which have them always dwell in the upper transparent waters, and they develop using the air that enters there. Therefore, their bodies contain some heat which negates the abundance of moistness, just as wool, hair, and nails do in man and beast. Those [fish] which have no fins and scales always dwell in the lower dirty waters, and [because of] much moistness and gathering of water, do not repel anything. Hence, they contain cold, sticky fluid, which easily causes death, and it [the cold fluid] causes death in some waters, such as stagnant lakes (Lev. 11:9).

Other aspects of *kashrut* which lead to a healthier lifestyle are:[21]

---

21. Milton Steinberg, *Basic Judaism* (1947), pp. 126-127.

Re'eh

1. Swine meat is derived from an unsanitary creature which is also a carrier of trichinosis (although the latter can be eliminated by thorough cooking).
2. Shellfish deteriorate rapidly and dangerously.
3. The lungs of a slaughtered animal must be examined meticulously, and it is rejected if there is any sign of tuberculosis.

These explanations should be looked upon in a general manner as expressing God's concern with the health of mankind, His most outstanding creation. Clearly, not all details match the hypothesis, as noted by Abravanel (Lev. 11:1). For example, all fruits and vegetables are permitted, even those which are poisonous. Furthermore, some clean animals cause disease, such as sheep, which transmit tape worms, and cows, which transmit liver worms. Finally, Abravanel notes that the empirical evidence contradicts the assumption that non-kosher food affects one's health, since Gentiles appear to be no less strong and healthy than fully observant Jews.

Akeidat Yitzchak (*sha'ar* 60, *Shemini*) adds that by giving a health-based reason one has reduced the Torah to the level of a medical textbook. If in fact non-kosher animals are harmful to one's health, it is probably possible to develop an antidote to cancel the negative effect. Would these animals then become kosher?

Symbolic Reasons

The Torah has defined the requirements for an animal to be kosher as follows: "Any [animal] which parts the hoof and is wholly cloven-footed and chews the cud, among the beasts, those you should eat" (Lev. 11:3). R. S.R. Hirsch[22] introduces his analysis of the subject as follows:

> Just as the human spirit is the instrument which God uses to make Himself known in this world, so the human body

---

22. Samson Raphael Hirsch, *Horeb* (1962), par. 454, trans. I. Grunfeld.

is the medium which connects the outside world with the mind of man, and *vice versa*.... Thus, the task of the body should be to act as the messenger of the world to man, and of man to the world. Moreover, the body of man should be the servant of his spirit. This task the body can best perform if it is not too active in a carnal direction, if it is passive and indifferent to its own desires, and if it is submissive to the demand of the soul... the ideal quality of the body would be utter dependence on the mind and a kind of quiescent neutrality.

Based on this approach, R. Hirsch goes on to say that plants are the most passive substance, and are therefore permitted without limit. Next come animals which are herbivorous and thus nearer to the vegetable world; namely, cattle, sheep, and goats, which show little vivacity, passion, and activity. He goes on to say:

Among animals that chew the cud, only those that also have cloven hoofs have four stomachs. After the food consumed has passed through two stomachs, it is driven up the gullet again, and chewed for a second time, and then led through two stomachs one after the other. Thus, these animals spend a great deal of time in the absorption of food, which may be termed the vegetative activity of animals. In contrast to herbivorous animals, carnivorous animals have short intestines and little time is wasted on the more passive and plant-like function of digesting the food.... The cloven hoofs of the permitted animal also seem to have been created more for the mere purpose of standing than for being used as weapons or tools.

The birds forbidden for food are the birds of prey; the gay, lively, and singing birds; those which show a special artistic instinct in the building of their nests.... No bird with cruel habits is permitted for food.... The sign of cleanliness with birds is again several stomachs.

...[T]he remaining animals, such as amphibians, insects, worms, are most of them very active in their spheres, especially insects, with their mechanical instinct and skill.

As far as forbidden substances, namely blood and fat (*chelev*), R. Hirsch looks upon blood as representing "utmost activity... the body in flow." On the other hand, he characterizes *chelev*, which he calls a "dulling substance," as: "bare of all movement, having become alien in the organism itself, nourished by inactivity."

In summary, R. Hirsch divides all food substances into three categories: Passive (permitted foods), too active (non-kosher animals, birds, reptiles, insects), and too dull (*chelev*; carcasses, i.e., *nevelah*; and mortally wounded, i.e., *treifah*). In order to enable the human body to be subservient to the soul and implement its values in this world, it is necessary for the body to be as submissive as possible and allow the soul's spiritual message through, without interference from any competing agendas on the part of the body. On the other hand, the body must not be so dull and isolated that it is not even able to relate to the important tasks which the soul imposes upon it.

SELF-DISCIPLINE

A Jew is not required to refrain from enjoying the pleasures of life. In fact, quite the contrary, he is forbidden to do so, as implied by the following Talmudic dictum: "In the future world, every man will be held accountable for everything (kosher) that his eyes saw and he did not eat" (JT *Kiddushin* 4:12). *Meshech Chochmah* posits that enjoying the fruit of the land is actually a Biblical requirement, based on the verse: "And the Lord God commanded the man, saying: 'Of every tree of the garden you may eat freely'" (Gen. 2:16). Furthermore, on holidays, the Jew is enjoined to engage in culinary delights, as indicated by the following ruling: "Included in 'You shall rejoice on your holidays' (Deut. 16:14) is that which they also said: Rejoice in all kinds of pleasure. Namely, eat meat on holidays and drink wine and wear new clothing and distribute fruits and sweets to children and women" (Rambam, *Sefer ha-Mitzvot*, positive command 54).

In spite of encouraging one to enjoy the pleasures which the world has to offer, the Jewish belief is that the purpose of creation is not to engage exclusively in physical gratification, but rather to continuously advance in the hope of attaining spiritual perfection. What is spiritual perfection? Rambam writes (*Hilchot Megillah ve-Chanukah* 4:14): "Great is peace, since the entire Torah was given to make peace in the world, as it says: 'Her ways are ways of pleasantness, and all her paths are peace'" (Prov. 3:17). In other words, the Torah was given in order to perfect inter-personal and inter-communal deportment. That spirituality relates to the way one behaves toward others is evident in a maxim attributed to R. Israel Salanter: "One attains [his own] spirituality by satisfying the material [and social] needs of the other."

Relating in a positive manner to others requires one to limit his own enjoyment at times, and such an attitude is inculcated by observing the dietary laws. R. Eliezer Berkovits has suggested that they serve the same purpose as war games (*God, Man and History*, p. 109). One creates such games to teach the soldier how to both attack and defend himself in a real war. The experience that he gains is not as good as in a real war, but it serves, at a low cost, to reduce the casualty rate when soldiers are ordered into combat. Similarly, laws restraining the appetite serve to train one in self-control, so that when it is necessary to curb one's emotions in dealing with compatriots, he will be well prepared.

It is for this reason that the following Midrash (*Sifra Kedoshim* 9:4) discourages one from developing a phobia towards unclean creatures:

Re'eh

> R. Elazar b. Azariah stated: How does one know that he should not say… "Eating pig meat is disgusting,"… but rather [he should say] "I would [probably] enjoy [eating] it. What should I do if my Father in heaven has decreed against doing so?"

Only by maintaining one's drives, yet regulating them, does one achieve optimal self-control.

Rambam cites another law, not related exclusively to one's diet, which is designed to inculcate self-control, namely the requirement to fulfill one's vows. He states:

> In addition to the things prohibited by the Law, we are also commanded to observe the prohibitions enjoined by our own vows (Num. 30). If we say, "This bread or this meat is forbidden for us," we are not allowed to partake of that food. The object of that precept is to train us in temperance, that we should be able to control our appetites for eating and drinking. Our Sages say accordingly, "Vows are a fence for abstinence" (*Guide for the Perplexed* 3:48).

Ramban believes that man was created in order to be God-directed, and not people-directed, as is evident from the following quotation:

> The purpose of all of the commands is that we believe in our God and thank Him for creating us, and this is the intention of creation… and the Supreme Being has no need for [creatures in] the world below other than that man should know [of the existence of] his God and thank Him for creating him (Ramban, Exod. 13:16).

Ramban clearly disagrees with Rambam's people-oriented view concerning the purpose of creation. Nevertheless, unless one has tasted the pleasures of life to some extent, he has no knowledge of what he is being thankful for. It is thus evident that according to both Ramban and Rambam, it is important to enjoy oneself, either in order to appreciate what God has bestowed upon human beings (Ramban) or to appreciate what human beings bestow upon each other (Rambam and R. Israel Salanter). However, it is also necessary to bridle one's pleasures, and this is a lesson to be learned from the dietary laws. By controlling one's drives rather than allowing them to control him, one develops the moral strength needed to face both social and spiritual crises as they arise.

Paradoxically, the dietary rules do not necessarily bestow a feeling of limitation, but rather of release from the enslavement to one's instincts and desires.[23] Man was created with three drives, in order of diminishing intensity: food, sex, and acquisition. The Torah does not seek the repression of these impulses, but rather their regulation and sanctification. The first command given to man, "Of every tree of the garden you may eat freely" (Gen. 2:16), legislates a minor restriction on the primary drive, but formulates it in a positive manner, thereby showing that pleasure may be cherished but not overdone. As far as sex is concerned, the first limitation is in the Noahide laws (BT *Sanhedrin* 56a), and these laws are extended in the Ten Commandments (Exod. 20:13) and enlarged upon in Leviticus (chs. 18, 20). Never was there any attempt to forbid sex; on the contrary, one of the first commands was to be fruitful and multiply (Gen. 9:1). As stated in *Iggeret ha-Kodesh* (*The Holy Letter*), a 13th-century treatise on sexuality often ascribed to Ramban, "One should know that sexual union is holy and pure when it is done as it should be, at the proper time, and with proper intent. A person should not imagine that proper sexual union is shameful or ugly, God forbid."

Finally, the proper means of acquisition (i.e., the prohibition to steal) is also among the Noahide laws, and is extensively detailed in the portion of *Mishpatim* (Exod. 21-23). Judaism has never deprecated

---

23. Isidor Grunfeld, *The Jewish Dietary Laws* (1972), p. 12.

Re'eh

the significance of adequately supporting oneself, as indicated in Mishnah *Avot*:

> Torah study together with a worldly occupation is excellent, for achieving both of them causes sin to be forgotten, and Torah [study] without a worldly occupation will come to naught and cause the spread of sin (*Avot* 2:2).

MORALITY AND ETHICAL VALUES

The dietary laws preach morality in two ways. First, the slaughtering process must be performed in the most humane way. Second, the animals considered unclean are those whose traits are thought to be repulsive; by not eating such animals, one distances himself, figuratively, from such behavior.

A. The slaughtering process

The ritual slaughterer or *shochet* must be a devout and educated person who realizes that the act he is about to commit is frowned upon in principle, and is allowed only because the exigencies of life justify it. Because of his background, it is assumed that he will perform his task in a merciful manner. The slaughtering knife must be razor sharp and free of notches, so that its incision is as painless as possible, and the act of slaughtering must be done with a steady hand. The details of ritual slaughter ensure that the animal meets its death in a swift, humane, and efficient way. In the words of Rambam: "It is not allowed to torment the animal by cutting the throat in a clumsy manner [or] by poleaxing" (*Guide for the Perplexed* 3:48). The special consideration required of the slaughterer, far from eliciting callousness or brutality, induces the soul to be gentle and pure.[24]

As explained in the Talmud (BT *Sanhedrin* 59b), initially only a vegetarian diet was permitted for man (Gen. 1:29), and only after man had internalized the seven Noahide laws, which would hopefully

---

24. *Gen. Rabbah* 44:1.

prevent this predilection from badly affecting his personality, was he permitted to eat meat (Gen. 9:3).

Dayan Grunfeld[25] explains the transition in man's diet. Antediluvian man had sunk to very low depths and long life spans had enabled the wicked to solidify their control of the world. By shortening the length of life, it was possible to more easily renew the ethical culture. But shorter lifetimes intensified the process of life, demanding food more energizing than vegetables, leading Rambam to describe the healthiest diet as consisting "of vegetables and of the flesh of animals" (*Guide for the Perplexed* 3:48). To prevent the re-emergence of man's animal nature, the seventh Noahide law (the prohibition of tearing a limb from a live animal—*ever min ha-chai*) was added to the previous six (*Hilchot Melachim* 9:1). When the Torah was given and it was determined that the Jews were destined to instruct the world in the realm of ethics, a stronger safeguard was needed, and so they were prohibited from consuming blood altogether, inasmuch as "the blood is the life [soul], and you should not eat the life with the flesh" (Deut. 12:23).

In spite of all the precautions, the Sages still feared that a ritual slaughterer would be affected negatively and eventually become a cruel person, as stated in the Mishnah: "The worthiest of butchers is the partner of Amalek" (*Kiddushin* 4:14). *Tosafot Yom Tov* explains that Amalek was the first nation to attack Israel after its escape from Egypt. All of the other nations were afraid to attack the Israelites, who had heretofore been saved miraculously, destroying their enemies in the process. The Amalekites were so viciously antagonistic that they were willing to overlook their own well-being in order to harm the Israelites. This added measure of cruelty is now ascribed to the *shochet*. Ramban (Deut. 22:6) testifies from his own experience that slaughterers of large oxen and donkeys are especially cruel "men of blood," who do not hesitate to decapitate human beings when they believe it is called for.

---

25. Isidor Grunfeld, *The Jewish Dietary Laws* (1972), p. 8.

Re'eh

B. Characterizing the unclean animals

None of the permitted creatures is carnivorous, as the Mishnah (*Chullin* 3:6) states explicitly regarding kosher birds. One might say that creatures of prey are (metaphorically) committing murder and enjoying it, which they do by instinct. However, man is expected to avoid doing this and also to overcome any craving he may have to do so, even in the direst of circumstances.

Similar sentiments are expressed in the *Letter of Aristeas*, written by a courtier of Ptolemy II Philadelphus (who reigned from 281-246 BCE) to his brother, Philocrates, twenty Greek copies of which are known to survive. In the letter, Aristeas explains that the dietary laws "were made for the sake of righteousness, to aid the quest for virtue and the perfecting of character." The relevant section appears below:

> For all the birds that we use are tame and distinguished by their cleanliness, feeding on various kinds of grain and pulse, such as for instance pigeons, turtle-doves, locusts, partridges, geese also, and all other birds of this class. But *the birds which are forbidden you will find to be wild and carnivorous*, tyrannizing over the others by the strength which they possess, and cruelly obtaining food by preying on the tame birds enumerated above and not only so, but they seize lambs and kids, and injure human beings too, whether dead or alive, and so by naming them unclean, He gave a sign by means of them that those for whom the legislation was ordained must practice righteousness in their hearts and not tyrannize over any one in reliance upon their own strength nor rob them of anything, but steer their course of life in accordance with justice, just as the tame birds, already mentioned, consume the different kinds of pulse that grow upon the earth and do not tyrannize to the destruction of their own kindred. Our Legislator taught us therefore that it is by such methods as these that indications are given to the

wise, that they must be just and effect nothing by violence, and refrain from tyrannizing over others in reliance upon their own strength. For since it is considered unseemly even to touch such unclean animals as have been mentioned on account of their particular habits, ought we not to take every precaution lest our own characters should be destroyed to the same extent? Wherefore all the rules which He has laid down with regard to what is permitted in the case of these birds and other animals, He has enacted with the object of teaching us a moral lesson (*Letter of Aristeas*, 145-151).

Some of the signs which the Talmud (BT *Chullin* 65a) formulates in characterizing the mean nature of the non-kosher birds are that "they seize prey and eat it," they place three toes on one side and one on the other when perched on a cord (showing dexterity when clawing), and they catch food and eat it in the air.

The unsavory traits that Aristeas describes in non-kosher birds, *Ba'al ha-Akeidah* notes with regard to non-kosher animals as well, referring to their razor-sharp teeth and nails, and the incessant greed and constant prowling of those animals that do not store their nourishment and chew their cud (*Akeidat Yitzchak, Shemini, sha'ar* 60). Ralbag adds that animals which do not have split hoofs have either fingers or a round hoof which enable them to more easily prey and brutally attack (Lev. 11:1). They accordingly say that God has required of Israel to distance itself from such creatures. Unlike Aristeas, however, *Ba'al ha-Akeidah* does not propose that eating such animals would influence a person negatively, but rather that doing so would corrupt the soul and produce future generations of violent and depraved people who victimize the indigent,[26] of the type described as follows by Agur in the book of Proverbs: "A generation whose teeth are as swords, and their great teeth as knives to devour the poor from

---

26. *Ba'al ha-Akeidah* is therefore classified among those who look upon the dietary laws as being statutes, whose positive effect is mystical in nature.

Re'eh

off the earth, and the needy from among men" (Prov. 30:14). And when such people become leaders, *Ba'al ha-Akeidah* relates to them, using the words of the prophet Micah, as follows:

> ... [P]rophets who mislead my people, who decree [that there will be] "peace" when their teeth have been given something to bite [i.e., when bribed]; and [regarding those] who do not put anything into their mouths [i.e., bribe them], they [declare that the people should] prepare [for] war against him (Mic. 3:5).

With regard to the prohibition to imbibe blood, the Bible states: "For the life of the flesh is in the blood" (Lev. 17:11), so that consuming blood parallels depriving a creature of his life. In the book of Ezekiel (33:25), the prophet rebukes the nation by saying: "You eat [meat] with blood, and lift up your eyes to your idols, and shed blood; and [with this behavior] you expect to possess the land?" The verse implies that neglecting the prohibition to consume blood can lead to murder, while distancing oneself from it may instill revulsion to violence and bloodshed.[27]

Judaism views hunting for sport disdainfully. This follows from the injunction to avoid causing unnecessary pain to any living creature, which is based on the Biblical law requiring even a bystander to help unload an overburdened animal (BT *Bava Metzia* 32b). Certainly, shooting an animal and abandoning it to writhe in pain or be maimed for life is included in the prohibition. The enjoyment that accompanies the blood-lust when hunting for sport is foreign to Judaism and totally repugnant to its values.

As far as hunting for sustenance, clearly shooting to kill cannot be a source of meat for Jewish people, since ritual slaughter is obligatory. However, it is possible to trap or otherwise temporarily disable the prey, and then slaughter it. There is a law that when slaughtering

---

27. *Encyclopedia Judaica*, "Dietary laws."

kosher beasts or birds, one must cover their blood (Lev. 17:13). Perhaps one can explain this rule as being an attempt to stress the intrinsic cruelty of the act, which is being done of necessity, and not for entertainment, as is the practice of less sensitive people.

C. Severing limbs

It is no surprise that Rambam saw cutting off part of a living animal as an act which "would produce cruelty" (*Guide for the Perplexed* 3:48), since tearing off a limb from an animal while it is alive causes great pain, and doing so would induce one to desensitize himself to the agony of other living beings, in complete opposition to what the Torah wishes to inculcate.

D. Meat and milk, mother animal and child, mother bird and young

The most powerful type of love is that of a parent (especially a mother) for its child. On the animal level, such instinctual love ensures that the physical needs of a young creature will be satisfied. On the human level, it also lays the foundation for the child's emotional development. Three of the dietary laws prohibit torturing animals by harming their offspring in their presence, either metaphorically or actually. Ibn Ezra (Exod. 23:19) states:

> It is dire cruelty to cook the kid in its [own] mother's milk, similar to "it [a female animal] with its young [may not be slaughtered] on the same day" (Lev. 22:28). Also "do not take the mother with its young" (Deut. 22:6).

Regarding the latter two (slaying mother and child on the same day and taking the young in the presence of the mother), Rambam (as well as Ramban on Deut. 22:6) is in full agreement with Ibn Ezra, as seen from his reasoning for these laws:

There is no difference in this case between the pain of man and the pain of other living beings, since the love and tenderness of the mother for her young ones is not produced by reasoning, but by imagination, and this faculty exists not only in man but in most living beings.

The same reason applies to the law which enjoins that we should let the mother fly away when we take the young. The eggs over which the bird sits, and the young that are in need of their mother, are generally unfit for food, and when the mother is sent away, she does not see the taking of her young ones, and does not feel any pain. In most cases, however, this commandment will cause man to leave the whole nest untouched, because [the young or the eggs], which he is allowed to take, are, as a rule, unfit for food (*Guide for the Perplexed* 3:48).

Most importantly, Rambam stresses the direct effect of these laws on the human condition:

If the Law provides that such grief should not be caused to cattle or birds, how much more careful must we be that we should not cause grief to our fellowmen (ibid.).

Ecological Extension

The author of *Sefer ha-Chinuch* explains that taking the mother with its young symbolizes the decimation of an entire species, which contradicts God's will in creating that species. He goes on to say that "no species has ever been destroyed and lost, from lice eggs to the horns of the wild ox" (*Sefer ha-Chinuch*, mitzvah 545) from the time of creation.[28] The command thus indicates that not only must one have mercy on the mother bird, but, in a sense, also on God, Who created

---

28. Of course, it is now known that unfortunately, since that time (and perhaps before) many species have become extinct.

that bird. The additional lesson for mankind is: "When a person fulfills the commands of his Creator and walks in a straight way, and is clean-handed and pure of heart, then the Lord's protection will be extended to him [as it is to all creatures], and his [physical] body will last for a long time in this world, and his [spiritual] soul forever in the world to come" (ibid.). The author of the *Sefer ha-Chinuch* looks upon the command not to slaughter a mother animal and its offspring on the same day in a similar fashion (*Sefer ha-Chinuch*, mitzvah 294).

Although the author does not say so, the message of not cooking a kid in its mother's milk can be explained likewise. In short, the message of all three of these *mitzvot* may be that Jews should be merciful towards all living creatures, and in return, God will be merciful to them.

DISTINGUISHING THE JEWISH NATION
According to Prof. Yehudah Levi,[29] the Jewish nation has a mission, namely to influence the Gentile world to accept the dominion of the Lord and to obey His laws, which means observing the seven Noahide commands, i.e., to live a moral life. Although it might sound presumptuous of Israel to look upon itself in this way, Prof. Levi quotes a Talmudic maxim which states: "Do you imagine that I offer you rulership? It is servitude that I offer you" (BT *Horayot* 10a-b). In other words, Israel's efforts aim to perfect mankind as a whole, which is the ultimate beneficiary of the nation's exertion, and by no means should its members look upon themselves as superior to the rest of humanity.

According to Prof. Levi, Israel's message cannot be promulgated on an individual basis, by each Jew guiding the non-Jews with whom he makes contact, for two reasons. First, Israel is relatively small in size, as the Bible states: "You are the fewest of all peoples" (Deut. 7:7). A small group is more likely to assimilate in a larger population than to have an effect on it. Second, if the Jewish nation is not isolated,

---

29. Yehudah Levi, *Mul Etgarei ha-Tekufah* (1993), pp. 14, 48-50.

it will be unable to properly educate its own members. Accordingly, God tells the Jewish people: "You will be to Me a kingdom of priests and a holy nation" (Exod. 19:6). Each individual has a function, but only in the context of the mission of the entire nation.

Interestingly, Netziv, although Zionistically inclined, felt that Israel could significantly influence the world "only when scattered throughout the Diaspora," and he saw this task as a justification for their many years of exile (*Harchev Davar*, Gen. 47:28). Of course, such an effect is possible only if the Jews are accorded all of the rights of citizenship, which has not always occurred in the past.

Abraham was already aware of the importance of building a cohesive family unit when he told his servant: "Do not take a wife for my son from the daughters of the Canaanites… but go to my country and my birthplace" (Gen. 24:3-4), as was Isaac when he told Jacob: "You should not take a wife from the daughters of Canaan. Arise, go to Paddan-aram, to the house of Bethuel your mother's father" (Gen. 28:1-2). As if reminding the Lord of the importance of having an exclusive domain, after the sin of the golden calf, Moses requests of God "that we be distinguished, I and Your people, from all the people that are upon the face of the earth" (Exod. 33:16), and God later acquiesces by saying, specifically with regard to the dietary laws: "I have set you apart from the peoples, so that you should be Mine" (Lev. 20:26). The necessity of separation is formulated as the explicit command "you should be holy" (Lev. 19:2), upon which the Midrash comments: "You should be separated" (*Sifra Kedoshim*, portion A, Introduction to ch. A). Israel can maintain its unique holiness only by creating a well-defined entity. Even the Gentile prophet Balaam realized the necessity of Israel having a clearly distinguishable habitat, as is clear from his words: "They are a people that must dwell alone" (Num. 23:9).

The Talmud (BT *Avodah Zarah* 36b) states that one should not eat non-Jewish bread and oil because it may lead to drinking wine with non-Jews, which will in turn lead to intermarriage and the worshipping of foreign gods. Similarly, by obeying the dietary laws, a Jew protects himself from assimilation and remains mindful of his mission and destiny in life, which is to enhance his own personality and serve as a prototype for others.

It has been suggested that the division between clean and unclean animals corresponds to the distinction between Israel and the nations.[30] This observation is actually explicit in the text, where it first says: "You must separate between the clean beast and the unclean" (Lev. 20:25), followed in the next verse by: "I have set you apart from the peoples." On the phrase from Song of Songs (1:3), "Your oils [ointments] have a pleasant fragrance," the Midrash (*Song of Songs Rabbah* 1:2) comments that just as oil does not dissolve in other liquids, so Israel does not mix with the other nations, but rather rises to the top.

As previously noted, however, the Jew was not meant to develop a loathing for non-kosher products, but rather to look upon them as tempting but off limits for himself. Similarly, a Jew is meant to respect non-Jews, but to temporarily look upon them as inaccessible on a personal level until the Jewish nation is able to fulfill its responsibility.

REJECTING IDOLATROUS RITES
Rambam in the *Guide for the Perplexed* (3:48) has the following to say about the prohibition of mixing meat and milk:

> Meat boiled in milk is undoubtedly gross food, and makes [one] overfull; but I think that most probably it is also prohibited because it is somehow connected with idolatry, forming perhaps part of the service, or being used on some festival of the heathen. I find a support for this view in the circumstance that the Law mentions the prohibition twice after the commandment given concerning the festivals:

---

30. Gordon J. Wenham, "The Theology of Unclean Food," *Evangelical Quarterly* 52:1 (Jan-Mar 1981) 6-15.

Re'eh

"Three times in the year all of your males must appear before the Lord God" (Exod. 23:19, 34:26), as if to say: "When you come before Me on your festivals, do not seethe your food in the manner as the heathen used to do." This I consider as the best reason for the prohibition; but as far as I have seen [in] the books on Sabean rites, nothing is mentioned of this custom.

R. Menachem Kasher (*Torah Shleimah, Mishpatim*, appendix 21) realized that Rambam's conjecture was correct. He notes that in 1928, ancient Ugaritic tablets dating back to the time of revelation[31] were found in Ras Shamra, which describe how a kid was cooked in its mother's milk as a means of praying to the gods to bless the land with a fruitful yield, a custom still extant among the Beduins. Maharal (*Gevurot Hashem* 46) points out that the three pilgrimage festivals are agriculturally based, with Passover celebrating the ripening of the grain, Pentecost its harvesting, and Tabernacles its ingathering from the fields after it dried out over the summer. These are times when it is especially appropriate to warn the nation against adopting pagan fertility rituals. It is also not surprising that in two of the three recordings of the prohibition to mix meat and milk (Exod. 23:19 and 34:26, but not in the portion of *Re'eh*—Deut. 14:21), the same verse mentions bringing the first fruits to the holy Temple, rather than to a house of idol worship, as noted by Sforno (Exod. 23:19) in the Middle Ages.

According to Rambam, the prohibition of cutting off a limb of a live animal, like cooking an animal in its mother's milk, was also "a kind of idolatrous worship" (*Guide for the Perplexed* 3:48).

Similarly, Rambam felt that eating blood "leads to a kind of idolatry, to the worship of spirits" (*Guide for the Perplexed* 3:46). He

---

31. According to Wikipedia. R. Kasher had thought that they dated back to the time of the patriarchs. It is possible that the customs reported were in fact from an earlier period.

also describes others who did not actually eat the blood as follows:

> There were, however, people who objected to eating blood, as a thing naturally disliked by man; they killed a beast, received the blood in a vessel or in a pot, and ate of the flesh of that beast, whilst sitting round the blood. They imagined that in this manner the spirits would come to partake of the blood which was their food, whilst the idolaters were eating the flesh; that love, brotherhood, and friendship with the spirits were established, because they dined with the latter at one place and at the same time; that the spirits would appear to them in dreams, inform them of coming events, and be favorable to them.

How God counteracted this form of spirit worship is described as follows by Rambam (ibid.):

> The blood was sprinkled upon the altar, and in the whole service it was insisted upon pouring it out, and not upon collecting it. Compare: "And he should pour out all the blood at the bottom of the altar" (Lev. 4:18); "And the blood of your sacrifices must be poured out on the altar of the Lord your God" (Deut. 12:27). Also, the blood of those beasts that were killed for common use, and not for sacrifices, must be poured out, "You should pour it upon the earth as water" (Deut. 12:24). We are not allowed to gather and have a meal round the blood, "You shall not eat round the blood" (Lev. 19:26).

Being that the people at the time of the exodus were still quite primitive, the only way to avoid such pagan festivities was to prohibit the eating of meat altogether during the desert period, as Rambam (ibid.). states:

Re'eh

As the Israelites were inclined to continue their rebellious conduct, to follow the doctrines in which they had been brought up, and which were then general, and to assemble round the blood in order to eat there and to meet the spirits, God forbade the Israelites to eat ordinary meat during their stay in the wilderness: they could only partake of the meat of peace offerings. The reason of this precept is distinctly stated, viz., that the blood should be poured out upon the altar, and the people do not assemble round about. Compare: "To the end that the Children of Israel may bring their sacrifices, which they offer in the open field, even that they may bring them to the Lord… And the priest will sprinkle the blood upon the altar… and they will no more offer their sacrifices to the spirits" (Lev. 17:5-7).

Finally, Rambam (ibid.) uses this background material to rationalize the covering of the blood of birds and beasts, but not domesticated animals, after they have been slaughtered:

Now there remained to provide for the slaughtering of the beasts of the field and birds, because those beasts were never sacrificed, and birds did never serve as peace offerings (Lev. 3). The commandment was therefore given that whenever a beast or a bird that may be eaten is killed, the blood thereof must be covered with earth (Lev. 17:13), in order that the people should not assemble round the blood for the purpose of eating there. The object was thus fully gained to break the connection between these fools and their spirits.

The Ethics of Deuteronomy

Answering the Second Question: What Is the Meaning of Holiness?

The opening verse of the portion of *Kedoshim* (which literally means "holiness") in the book of Leviticus is: "Speak to all of the congregation of the Children of Israel, and say to them: You should be holy; for I, the Lord your God, am holy" (Lev. 19:2). In the preceding portion of *Shemini*, holiness was associated with properly obeying the dietary code (Lev. 11:44), as it was towards the end of *Kedoshim* (Lev. 20:25-26) and as it is in the present portion of *Re'eh* (Deut. 14:2, 21). In *Kedoshim*, holiness is associated with successful fulfillment of a number of other commands, namely those connected to correct sexual behavior (Lev. 19:29, 20:10-22) and to the attainment of a philosophical understanding of Jewish theology (Lev. 19:4; 20:1-7, 27), as well as to those social laws which enable the proper functioning of a just society (Lev. 19:32-36).

From a global point of view, holiness may be said to be composed of three elements:

1. Separation of the Jewish Nation from all others by their observance of ritual laws which apply to them exclusively, as previously presented (Distinguishing the Jewish Nation).
2. Perfecting themselves as individuals who unite to form a model nation which strives for holiness—this was dealt with extensively in *The Ethics of Leviticus* in the portion of *Kedoshim* (pp. 194-229).
3. Serving as a light to other nations, as described in numerous places in the book of Isaiah (42:6, 49:6, 60:3), and previously described in this chapter (Distinguishing the Jewish Nation).

Re'eh

SUMMARY

The topic dealt with in this portion is the dietary laws, a basic tenet of Judaism, whose observance characterizes religious Jews. Although Rambam classifies these laws as statutes, apparently he means only to say that there are so many proposed reasons and justifications (by him as well as by others), that they must all be treated as mere conjecture, with the bottom line being that Jews are expected to obey them punctiliously, whether or not any particular explanation seems relevant at the moment.

The suggested reasons range from the mystical (pollution of the soul and alienation from the natural order) to the utilitarian (health hazard and ecological damage), and their observance is said to positively influence one's character and emotional development by inculcating discipline and self-control. Interestingly, the Torah itself imparts a moral justification when it stresses the dire cruelty of cooking a kid "in its own mother's milk" (Deut. 14:21).

The many approaches to the dietary laws, which are said to engender purity, together with various other Biblical references, enable an enhanced understanding of the concept of holiness.

Shoftim

The portion of *Shoftim* is divided into two basic sections. The first (Deut. 16:18-19:21) deals with the implementation of civil government, which necessitates defining the status of judges, kings, priests, and prophets; as well as prohibitions against idol worship and laws relating to crime. The second section stretches from ch. 20 until the end of the portion, and relates to the waging of war, generally establishing a higher moral standard than that which was prevalent in the ancient world. The section actually continues into the next portion, where the laws concerning female captives of war are laid out.

Shoftim commences with the following verses:

> **18** You should install judges and law enforcement officials for yourself in all your cities and they are expected to judge the people [with] righteous judgment. **19** You may not pervert justice; you may not show favoritism, and you may not take a bribe, for bribery blinds the eyes of the wise and perverts just words. **20** Justice, justice you should pursue, so that you may live and possess the land which the Lord, your God, is giving you (Deut. 16).

The first verse is directed at the community and its leaders, who are expected to set up and maintain a court system. Rambam (*Hilchot Sanhedrin* 2:8), based on the Talmud (BT *Sanhedrin* 88b), explains:

From the Supreme Sanhedrin, they would send emissaries throughout the entire Land of Israel to seek out judges. Whenever they found a person who was wise, sin-fearing, humble, modest, with a good reputation, and beloved by the populace, they had him appointed as a judge in his own city. From there, they promoted him to [the court which holds sessions at] the entrance to the Temple Mount. From there, he was promoted to [the court which held sessions at] the entrance to the Temple Courtyard, and from there, to the Supreme Sanhedrin.

In other words, the Sanhedrin chose qualified people, and they moved up in the hierarchy in accordance with their merit. However, Rambam indicates in another location (*Hilchot Sanhedrin* 3:8, based on BT *Sanhedrin* 7b) that kings and exilarchs were authorized to make such appointments. R. Yehuda Zoldan[32] has explained that representatives of the Sanhedrin vetted a candidate's personality and professional level, but final approval had to be issued by the reigning ruler. There was also a mechanism in place for enabling a court to remove a judge who acted improperly (*Hilchot Talmud Torah* 7:1, based on BT *Mo'ed Katan* 17a).

The next verse (v. 19) focuses on the judges themselves, who are told not to pervert justice by accepting bribes. Regarding the phrase "you may not show favoritism," *Sifrei* (*Devarim* 16) interprets a similar phrase (Deut. 1:17) to be referring to those who appoint the judges, so that verse 19 may be commanding both the king and Sanhedrin not to accept bribes or show favoritism, as well as the individual judges.

Regarding the phrase in v. 20: "Justice, justice you should pursue," Rashi, based on BT *Sanhedrin* 32b, states: "Seek out a good court,"

---

32. Yehuda Zoldan, "*Minui Shoftim ve-Dayanim*," http://www.dintora.org/print_page/articles/362. Also appeared in *Mussaf Tzedek, Mekor Rishon*, Issue 718.

meaning one whose judges have a good reputation. The focus shifts to the litigant, so that the three verses refer serially to the appointing body, the judges themselves, and finally the litigants. However, it was noted that v. 19 might also refer to the appointing body; by the same token, v. 20, which refers to pursuing justice, may do so as well. In fact, Rashi implies that this is the case in his commentary on the continuation of the verse, "so that you may live and possess the land," where he says: "The appointment of fitting judges is sufficient merit to keep Israel alive and settled in their land."[33]

The classical question with regard to v. 20 is why the word "justice" is repeated. The simple answer is that when seeking justice, an extra dose of diligence and thoroughness is in order. When Rashi speaks of looking for a good court, what he means to say is that it is not enough to take the dispute to court, but one must make efforts to find the court having the best reputation for honesty and neutrality.

Ramban believes that according to Rashi, the word "justice" is repeated to exhort both the judges themselves as well as the litigants, who must seek a trustworthy court. As a second answer, Ramban says that a judge who acts justly in this world will be treated justly in the next one. Ibn Ezra, on the other hand, applying v. 20 to the litigants exclusively, takes the repetition to stress that they must strictly adhere to the truth, whether it is to their benefit or their detriment.

The Talmud presents two explanations for the repetition that relate to the judges themselves, rather than their appointment or their litigants. The first is that the repetition stresses that at times extra efforts are needed when interrogating disputants. The Talmud states:

> It says: "You should judge your neighbor justly" (Lev. 19:15), and it also says: "Justice, justice you should pursue" (Deut. 16:20). How does this work [why is justice stated once in the first verse, twice in the second]? The latter refers to a suspicious suit [or one brought by a plaintiff known to be

---

33. Based on *Sifrei* (Malbim, Deut. 16:20).

dishonest, which requires a more thorough investigation], the former to an [apparently] genuine claim [which does not require an exhaustive investigation] (BT *Sanhedrin* 32b).

The second explanation is that the word is repeated to teach that not only must legal decisions be just, but even when the litigants reach a compromise decision on their own, the judge should intervene to assure that both are getting a fair deal. The Talmud presents the following elucidation:

It has been taught: "Justice, justice you should pursue" (Deut. 16:20). The first [mention of justice] refers to a decision based on strict law, the second to a compromise [where the most just compromise must also be sought]. How does this work? Imagine that two boats sailing on a river meet [in a narrow strait]. If both attempt to pass simultaneously, both will sink [after colliding]. If one passes after the other, both can pass [without mishap]. Likewise, if two camels meet each other while on the ascent to Beth-Horon [which is steep and narrow].[34] If they both ascend [at the same time], both may fall down [into the valley]; but if [they ascend] after each other, both can go up [safely]. How then should they act? If one is laden and the other is not laden, the unladen should give way to the laden. If [they are both laden, but] one is near [to its destination] and the other is not near, the nearer should give way to the not nearer. If both are [equally] near or far [from their destination,] make a compromise between them, and each pays a fee to the other (BT *Sanhedrin* 32b).

---

34. The following note appears in the Soncino Talmud, *Sanhedrin*, p. 203: Beth Horon the Upper stands on the summit of a conical hill, while a short distance west of this point, on a rocky eminence, stands Beth Horon the Lower. The deep valley between the two places may account for the name "the house of the hollow." The road winds up the mountain in zig-zag line, and is in many places cut in the rock. It is rugged and difficult.

The Ethics of Deuteronomy

Yad Ramah explains that in the latter situation, each is asked what monetary compensation he would be willing to take to allow the other to proceed first. The one who had asked for the larger compensation goes forward, and he pays the smaller fee to the second one. The basic principle is that the one who is less inconvenienced by waiting allows the other to go first, and if they are both equally inconvenienced, a monetary compensation should be forthcoming.

THE ENDS DO NOT JUSTIFY THE MEANS

R. Simcha Bunim of Peshischa[35] interprets the repetition of the word "justice" to indicate that it is not sufficient that one's activities are directed toward a just goal, it is also necessary that those activities themselves be just. In modern parlance, the means must be just, as well as the ends, because the ends do not justify the means. The most blatant violation of this principle took place during the 20th century with the development of communism in Russia and other countries. The goal of communism was laudable in that it attempted to give all citizens an equal opportunity to find suitable employment and to share in the country's wealth. However, to achieve these goals, the Russian communist government, for example, permitted itself to oppress religious people (since communism had despaired of organized religion), to murder its political opponents, and to send problematic intellectuals (from their standpoint) to the gulag. Vladimir Lenin attempted to justify what he called the inevitable collateral damage when he allegedly said: "You cannot make an omelet without breaking eggs,"[36] and he was echoed by Mao Tse-tung, who said "a revolution is not a dinner party." The persecutions carried out by the communist regimes are the best proof of the importance and relevance of R. Simcha Bunim's exegesis. In R. Kook's words: "A

---

35. Cited by R. Shmuel Alter, *Likkutei Batar Likkutei* (1950).
36. Actually, the parallel Russian saying is: "To chop down a forest, splinters will fly," so it probably was not Lenin who originated the phrase.

person must always sanctify and purify his goal and the means by which he plans to realize it, that they also be holy and pure" (*Olat Ra'ayah* 2:257).

In 1927, R. Yosef Yitzchak Schneersohn (the *frierdiker* Lubavitcher Rebbe, 1880-1950) was imprisoned and sentenced to death in communist Russia for setting up a secret network for teaching Torah and supplying religious needs, such as *tefillin*, *etrogim*, etc., and only as a result of international pressure was he released. Similarly, R. Isser Zalman Meltzer (1870-1953) was arrested numerous times until he was able to escape to Kletsk in Poland. Had he not succeeded, Torah study and Jewish practice in future generations would have greatly suffered, as R. Isser Zalman was the mentor of many of the greatest Sages and halachic decisors of the 20th century.[37]

The Talmudic idiom parallel to "the ends justify the means" is *mitzvah ha-ba'ah be-aveirah* (a precept whose fulfillment was enabled by performing a transgression), which is not permitted. In other words, it is prohibited to perform a mitzvah if doing so is only possible as the result of the previous commission of a sin. The source of the prohibition is the explanation proffered by the Talmud for the Mishnaic statement: "A stolen or withered *lulav* is invalid" (*Sukkah* 3:1). The Talmud bases this law on the exposition of the verse: "And you brought that [animal] which was stolen, and the lame and the sick. And [when] you bring an offering [from these], will I accept it from your hand?" (Mal. 1:13), upon which the Talmud comments:

> The "stolen" is thus compared with the lame. Just as the lame can never be rectified [to become a valid offering], similarly that which is stolen can never be rectified,

---

37. His students include R. Shlomo Zalman Orbach (Yeshivat Kol Torah), R. Chaim Ya'akov Goldvicht (Kerem be-Yavneh), R. Shlomo Goren (Chief Rabbi of Israel), R. Yosef Eliyahu Henkin (Ezrat Torah, USA), R. Moshe Feinstein (Metivta Tifferet Yerushalayim, New York), R. Yitzchak Kulitz (Chief Rabbi, Jerusalem), and R. Elazar Menachem Shach (Ponevezh Yeshiva, Bnei Brak).

irrespective of [whether the stolen animal] is used before *yi'ush* [abandonment of hope of recovery by the owner] or after *yi'ush*. Now it is understandable [that the stolen animal may not be used] before *yi'ush*, since the Torah said: "When any man *from among you* brings an offering to the Lord" (Lev. 1:2) ["from among you" implies that the sacrifice is of an animal belonging to him] and this [animal] is not his, but [why should the law apply] after *yi'ush* [its abandonment by the rightful owner], since he [the thief] has acquired it by [virtue of] *yi'ush*? The reason must then be that it is a *mitzvah ha-ba'ah be-aveirah* (BT *Sukkah* 30a).

The situation is completely parallel to that of the *lulav* (a palm branch), concerning which the verse states: "And you should take *for yourselves* on the first day the fruit of a goodly tree, branches of palm trees, a branch of a braided tree, and willows of the brook" (Lev. 23:40). Here too the phrase "for yourselves" means that these four species must be owned by you. Even if the true owner has given up hope of finding them (*yi'ush*) after they were stolen, they are still unacceptable, because they have been obtained in a disgraceful manner and as such are a *mitzvah ha-ba'ah be-aveirah*.

The Jerusalem Talmud is even harsher in its condemnation of one who performs a *mitzvah ha-ba'ah be-aveirah*, concerning whom it states:

> R. Levi said: To whom is one who uses a stolen *lulav* compared? To one who honors the sultan with a delicacy, which it transpires he actually stole from the sultan. They say [regarding that person]: "Woe unto this one, whose defender became his prosecutor" (JT *Sukkah* 3:1).

The implication of this text is that in using a stolen *lulav*, not only has one not fulfilled the mitzvah, but he has performed a second sin in addition to that of stealing the *lulav* in the first place.

The previous citation from the Babylonian Talmud continues with the following parable:

> R. Yochanan in the name of R. Shimon b. Yochai further said: [The purport of] that which is written: "For I am the Lord, Who loves justice, hates robbery in a burnt offering" (Isa. 61:8) is as follows: Consider a human king who passed through a custom-house and said to his attendants: "Pay the tax [for the goods I am carrying] to the tax-collectors." They said to him: "Does not the whole tax belong to you?" He answered them: "All travelers will learn from me not to evade their payments of tax." So the Holy One, blessed be He, said: "I am the Lord Who.... hates robbery in a burnt offering. From Me My children will learn to distance themselves from robbery" (BT *Sukkah* 30a).

That "the Lord... hates robbery in a burnt offering" may have served as the basis for *Minchat Chinuch* (325:9), who rationalized the concept of *mitzvah ha-ba'ah be-aveirah* as follows: "he has not fulfilled the mitzvah because that [enabling it through a sin] is not the desire of the Creator, and accordingly he has not fulfilled the mitzvah."

Tosafot (BT *Sukkah* 30a, s.v. *mi-shum*, and Maharam thereon) are of the opinion that *mitzvah ha-ba'ah be-aveirah* is a Torah-level principle to the extent that there is no need for a specific word or phrase to indicate that objects involved in performing various *mitzvot* must be legally acquired, although Tosafot in a different location (BT *Sukkah* 9a, s.v. *ha-hu*) hold that it is a rabbinical enactment.

Clearly, cheating in financial matters for personal gain, whether with respect to business or governmental income tax, is considered to be an intrinsically immoral act. Since the ends do not justify the means, even such a positive goal as distributing charity to the poor is not acceptable if the source of the wealth is ill-gotten, implying that the deeds of the English folk-hero Robin Hood would not pass muster according to Jewish law.

In a university setting, a student may justify copying on tests by maintaining that he knows the material quite well, but he gets nervous and does not succeed on tests. Furthermore, he may claim that he wishes to make a great contribution to society as a doctor who plans to travel to Africa to supply medical service to the native populations. Similarly, a student may justify such actions by noting that a law degree is a prerequisite to obtain employment in his uncle's firm, but he never intends to actually serve as a lawyer. Nevertheless, since the ends do not justify the means, in all of the previously mentioned situations, one is permitted to utilize only halachically-sanctioned methods to achieve his goals.

Mesillat Yesharim (ch. 11) discusses the topic of "stealing time," referring to one who spends work-time (the means) to give charity or learn Torah (the ends):

> Even if one performs a mitzvah during his working-time, he is not credited with righteousness, but charged with a transgression. A transgression cannot be a mitzvah…. Our Sages of blessed memory have said (BT *Bava Kamma* 94a): "One who steals a measure of wheat, grinds it, bakes it, and pronounces a blessing over it, is not blessing, but abusing, as it is written: 'And the thief who blesses, abuses God.'" (Ps. 10:3)…. Stealing an object is stealing, and stealing time is stealing. As with a stolen object that is used for a mitzvah, so with stolen time that is similarly used, one's defense attorney becomes his prosecutor.

It goes without saying that stealing money or any physical object in order to perform one of the above-mentioned *mitzvot* is indeed odious and negates the word and spirit of the law.

Shoftim

BIBLICAL PRECEDENTS

The last five portions in the book of Exodus deal mainly with the construction of the Tabernacle (which accompanied the Israelites in their travels through the wilderness), the vessels that were to be found in it, and the garments to be worn by the priests. However, this train of thought is broken three times, once with the story of the golden calf, and twice with a warning to properly observe the Sabbath—in the portion of *Ki Tisa* (Exod. 31:13-17) and in the portion of *Vayakhel* (Exod. 35:2-3). In the latter case, the Midrash (*Mechilta, Vayakhel parsha* A) states:

> Why is this section stated? Because it says: "And they should make Me a sanctuary, so that I may dwell among them" (Exod. 25:8), from which I might understand [that it should be made] both on weekdays and the Sabbath… and this should be true *a fortiori*. If the Temple service, which is only possible as a result of the existence of the preparatory items [the Tabernacle and its vessels] supersedes the Sabbath, certainly [producing] the preparatory items, which themselves make the service possible, should *a fortiori* supersede the Sabbath; for example, if the horn of the altar fell off or the [slaughtering] knife was blemished, I would think they could be fixed on the Sabbath. [Therefore,] the Torah says: "Six days work may be done, but the seventh day will be holy, a day of complete rest to the Lord" (Exod. 35:2).

If the desired end is the proper functioning of the Tabernacle, and the means is constructing its edifice and manufacturing its vessels, the Torah is stating emphatically that the ends do not justify the means. One may ask: if that is the case, why is the Temple service permitted on the Sabbath, as it involves performing some of the 39 *melachot* (categories of labor forbidden on the Sabbath)? The answer is that those Sabbath prohibitions never applied to the Temple in the first place.

A second instance in which the Torah prohibits unjust means to achieve a desirable end is with regard to punishment for transgressions, concerning which the Torah states: "Fathers may not be put to death because of sons, nor may sons be put to death because of fathers; a man may be put to death for his own transgression [only]" (Deut. 24:16). Ezekiel reinforced this approach when he said: "The soul that sins will die; a son will not bear the iniquity of the father, and a father will not bear the iniquity of the son; the righteousness of the righteous will reflect upon himself, and the wickedness of the wicked reflect upon himself" (Ezek. 18:20). If it were to be known that a man's wife and descendants would be punished for his offenses, this might deter some people from committing a crime, since one may be willing to risk his own life, but when he realizes that his entire family may suffer, he might think twice. However, even though diminishing the prevalence of sin is a worthy end, it is not permitted to harm innocents for the sole purpose of achieving that goal.

The Talmud questions the claim that children may not be punished for their fathers' sins:

> Are not children then to be put to death for the sins committed by their parents? Is it not written: "God visits the iniquities of fathers on their children" (Exod. 20:5, 34:7)? There, the reference is to children who follow in their parents' footsteps. As it has been taught: "[And those of you who survive will rot away because of their iniquity in the lands of your enemies;] moreover, they will rot away because the iniquities of their fathers are still within them" (Lev. 26:39); [i.e.,] if they hold fast to the evil doings of their fathers… But do they [really] not [suffer for the sins committed by others]? Is it not written: "And they will stumble one upon another" (Lev. 26:37), meaning: "One [will stumble] through the sin of

the other," which teaches that all are held responsible for one another [and will suffer for their sins]? There, the reference is to those who had the power to restrain [their fellow men from evil], but did not (BT *Sanhedrin* 27b).

Rashi traces the Talmud's limitation of punishment of future generations to cases where the children also practice evil, to the last four words of the phrase "God visits the iniquities of fathers on their children, on the third and the fourth generation of those who hate Me" (Exod. 20:5), the implication being that they are only punished if they too are included in the category of "those who hate Me."

But what exactly does it mean to say that iniquities will be visited upon the fourth generation if that generation maintains the evil way of their forebears? Ibn Ezra (Exod. 20:5) understands this to mean that God will not necessarily punish a wicked person, because perhaps his son, grandson, or even great-grandson, will be righteous. Apparently, having a righteous descendant implies that the sinner has repented a bit and served as a good influence on his descendants, or maybe God is willing to retroactively reward an ancestor because of the virtues of his descendant. If, however, all four generations are ignoble, they are all punished simultaneously. Alternately, each generation is only punished when the following three generations are sinful. Ramban *in situ*, however, has a different take on the subject. He believes that the earlier generations are only mildly punished, since "their measure [of evil] is not yet full." Each generation suffers more than the previous one, since they are punished for the cumulative sins of their ancestors. However, if wickedness continues, by the fourth generation the measure is full and its members are punished severely. At this stage, the slate is wiped clean and the next generation starts afresh and does not suffer for the sins of earlier generations.

In spite of the harmonization of the verses proposed by the Talmud, in Deuteronomy Ibn Ezra explains the contradictory verses differently:

> "Fathers may not be put to death because of sons" is a commandment to the Israelites [when passing judgment in a court of law], and regarding "God visits the iniquities of fathers on their children" (Exod. 20:5), it is He who does the visiting (Ibn Ezra, Deut. 24:16).

In other words, a human court may only penalize the perpetrator, but God Himself works in mysterious ways and we do not have the right to question them. After all, the entire concept of *tzaddik ve-ra lo* (suffering of the righteous) highlights the suffering of the innocent. Clearly, God does occasionally punish innocents. The question arises: Is only God allowed to punish innocents, but man may never do so, or does God occasionally even command man to do so?

The answer may be derived from the case of the *ir ha-nidachat* (idol-worshipping city), concerning which the Torah states:

> **15** Then you must inquire, investigate, and ask thoroughly, and, behold, it is true, *the matter is certain, that such abomination has been committed in your midst.* **16** You must surely strike down the inhabitants of that city with the edge of the sword. Destroy it with all that is in it and its livestock, with the edge of the sword… **18** And nothing that is doomed to destruction may cling to your hand, so that the Lord may return from His fierce wrath, *and grant you compassion, and be compassionate with you,* and multiply you, as He swore to your forefathers (Deut. 13).

V. 16, which even commands the destruction of the animals in the city, certainly implies that minors are to be killed as well. On the other hand, v. 15 stresses that only those concerning whom it is certain that they committed an abomination deserve capital punishment, and v. 18 speaks of God being compassionate, which would certainly imply that innocent children are to be spared.

Shoftim

Not surprisingly, the contradictory messages in the text led to differing opinions in its exegesis. *Midrash Tanna'im* (Deut. 13:15) exempts children, based on the phrase saying that the inhabitants are only killed if it is certain that the abomination has been committed. Abba Chanin, in *Sifrei* (Re'eh par. 94), exempts them, based on the simple meaning of Deut. 24:16: "nor may sons be put to death because of fathers." R. Akiva, cited in Tosefta *Sanhedrin* 14:3, ascribes their exemption to God's promise in v. 18 to be compassionate. On the other hand, both *Sifrei* and Tosefta cite dissenting opinions which take the text literally and mandate the death penalty for children as well. Rambam also favored the latter view when he wrote:

> If the entire city was led astray, all of the inhabitants, including the women and the children, are slain by the sword. If a majority of the inhabitants were led astray, the transgressors' wives and children are slain by the sword (*Hilchot Avodah Zarah* 4:6).

Rambam says explicitly that children were to be killed. The distinction he makes between the entire city sinning, as opposed to a majority, is explained by R. Nachum Rabinovitch in *Yad Peshutah* (apparently based on R. Menachem Krikovsky in *Avodat ha-Melech*) as follows: If every adult sinned, the children were also to be executed. If only a majority of the adults sinned, those who did not sin, whether man or woman, were spared, while children who sinned were killed only if their mother also sinned. Perhaps Rambam's logic was that if all the adults are executed, who would take care of the children? On the other hand, if a child's mother was not punished because she did not worship idols, then she can bring up her child and set him on the right path, even if he sinned.

Migdal Oz understands Rambam to be saying that in the case of the majority sinning, the wives and children of those who engaged in idol worship would be slain irrespective of whether they themselves were guilty. Ramban, in Deut. 13:16, says that women are presumed to be sympathetic to their husbands, while *Migdal Oz* says that the children, whom the fathers dote on, were killed in order to increase the suffering of their fathers. It would seem that *Migdal Oz* considers the potential execution of the children to be a deterrent, implying that in this case he allows the ends to justify the means.

In review, it is clear that God does not necessarily obey the rule that innocents never suffer while, on the other hand, a *beit din* (Jewish court) is never allowed to make a decision calling for innocents to be punished. The disputed case is whether God would ever give a direct order to a human court to disobey the rules, and that explains the two opinions in the *Sifrei* and the Tosefta.

This argument can be utilized to explain a difference of opinion with regard to the story of Achan, who had taken silver and gold from the spoils which had been captured during the conquest of Jericho, and which were meant to be donated to God's treasury. God had decreed: "And it will be, he that is caught with the accursed thing will be burned with fire, he and all that he has" (Josh. 7:15). Achan's public ordeal is then described as follows:

> **24** And Joshua, and all Israel with him, took Achan the son of Zerah, and the silver, and the garment, and the wedge of gold, and his sons, and his daughters, and his ox, and his donkey, and his flock, and his tent, and all that he had; and they brought them up to the Valley of Achor. **25** And Joshua said: "Why have you troubled us? The Lord will trouble you this day." And all Israel stoned him with stones, and burned them with fire, and stoned them with stones (Josh. 7).

Interpreting v. 24 literally, one would say that he (Achan) was stoned, but they (his children, animals, and belongings) were burned and stoned. Indeed, a Midrash cited in *Yalkut Shimoni* (Josh. 18) states:

Shoftim

And they stoned him with stones—he himself. And they burned them—the phrase refers to his sons and daughters, for God had told him: "he that is caught with the accursed thing will be burned with fire, he and all that he has." If that is so, why does it say "they stoned him"? It is to teach you that he admitted stealing [the items] on the Sabbath, so he was stoned for desecrating the Sabbath and burned for taking possession of the accursed items.

Another explanation for his punishment by stoning is that he had committed adultery with a betrothed damsel (BT *Sanhedrin* 44a). The Talmud, however, asks: "If he sinned, wherein did his sons and daughters sin?" and it answers that they were actually not punished. Rather, they were brought to witness the execution "to overawe them," i.e., to chastise them and deter them from disregarding God's instructions in the future. How then is the phrase "[they] burned them with fire, and they stoned them with stones" to be interpreted? The Talmud answers: "Those suitable for burning [the inanimate property] were burned, and those suitable for stoning [the livestock] were stoned."

In this case, the Midrash takes the approach that although innocent people cannot be punished by a court, they may be executed in response to a direct command of God, while the Talmud, which rejects the claim that his children were punished, holds that only God Himself can administer undeserved suffering, but not a human court, even if it is following God's instructions.

Of course, there are other incidents mentioned in the Bible where innocents are murdered for deterrence or some other end, but usually they are either completely implemented by God or by unscrupulous people. For example, with respect to Korah's rebellion, the verse states: "The earth beneath them opened its mouth and swallowed them and their houses [Ibn Ezra: an inclusive term denoting their wives, children, and even infants; see also Ibn Ezra on Deut. 11:6], and all the men who were with Korah and all the property" (Num. 16:32). Innocents were certainly slain together with the guilty, but that was God's doing.

Similarly, with regard to one who sacrifices his children to Molech as part of the blood-thirsty rite associated with him, the Bible states: "Any man… who gives any of his offspring to Molech must surely be put to death; the people of the land will pelt him with stones" (Lev. 20:2). *Sifra* (Malbim, *Kedoshim* 91:4) explains the two stages of execution as follows: Initially, he is to be tried by the court. If the court is not physically powerful enough to kill him, then the people perform the execution in an orderly fashion. What happens if neither the earthly court nor the populace execute the death penalty? The text proceeds:

> But if the people of the land ignore that man when he gives of his offspring to Molech, not putting him to death, I will set My attention upon that man, *and upon his family,* and I will cut him off, and all who stray after him to stray after Molech, from amidst their people (Lev. 20:4-5).

Once again, as a deterrent, it seems that members of the man's family are being made liable to punishment for a crime that they did not commit. On the other hand, the punishment is to be implemented by the Almighty, and it has been noted that He is given more leeway. However, the Talmud and Midrash apparently felt that even God needed justification for his behavior, when both stated:

1. R. Shimon says: [In] what [way] did the family sin [that they are punished]? However, this teaches you that there is no family in which there is an [unfair] tax collector which does not consist entirely of tax collectors… for they all cover up for him (BT *Shavuot* 39a; *Sifra*, Malbim, *Kedoshim* 95:13).
2. What does it teach us [by saying "I will cut him off" rather than "I

Shoftim

will cut them off"]? Because it says, "[I will set My attention upon that man] and upon his family," one might think that his entire family is included in [the punishment of] excision. It therefore says "him"—he will be excised, but the entire family will not be punished with excision, but rather with suffering (*Sifra*, Malbim, *Kedoshim* 96).

The Midrash is elucidating the family's punishment in two ways. First, it emphasizes that although the master of the household might have been the one to actually sacrifice a child to Molech, it would not have happened without the active support and acquiescence of the rest of the family. Therefore, the entire family is guilty to some extent. Second, since the level of guilt is nevertheless not equivalent among the family members, they will not suffer excision, but rather some weaker form of punishment, presumably proportional to each one's level of guilt. The Midrash has accepted the view of the previously cited Talmudic text (BT *Sanhedrin* 27b) that even God-enforced collateral punishment should conform to ethical standards.

Finally, it should be noted that a story from the book of Judges (chs. 19-21) describes a case where a large population consisting of many innocent people was wiped out. The concubine of a Levite traveler, passing through Gibeah in the territory of Benjamin, was abused by the town's people to the point of death. The Levite informed the remaining tribes of what had happened, and it was decided to ask the tribe of Benjamin to deliver the perpetrators of the crime to representatives of the nation, who subsequently sentenced the villains to death. When the Benjaminites refused to deliver the convicted men, a battle ensued, and with the exception of 600 soldiers, their army was decimated. Afterwards, a very regretful event occurred, as described in the following verse:

> And the men of Israel turned upon the children of Benjamin and smote them with the edge of the sword, [destroying]

from the city all of its inhabitants, even the cattle, even all that was found (Judg. 20:48).

In addition to killing as many Benjaminites as possible—men, women, and children, the tribes had also sworn not to give their daughters in matrimony to the surviving members of the tribe. At this point, the nation realized that with only 600 male members of Benjamin remaining alive, and with the entire female population having been destroyed, the tribe of Benjamin was effectively wiped out. Since losing an entire tribe was considered to be a great tragedy and a more severe retribution than initially contemplated, a plan to regenerate the tribe of Benjamin was desperately needed.

The plan which was devised contained two elements. It would first be determined whether there was any city which had failed to heed the call to participate in the battle. All the inhabitants of such a town, other than potential brides, would be slain, and the remaining maidens would be paired off with the 600 male Benjaminites for the purpose of rebuilding the tribe.

Jabesh-gilead, just over the Jordan, had in fact shirked its military duty and refrained from joining the fight. The plan was then implemented as described below:

> And the congregation sent there twelve thousand of the valiant men, and commanded them saying: "Go and strike the inhabitants of Jabesh-gilead with the edge of the sword, including the women and the children. And this is the thing that you must do: Destroy every male, and every woman that ever had relations with a male." And they found among the inhabitants of Jabesh-gilead four hundred virgin girls that had not had relations with any man (Judg. 21:10-12).

Of course, the desired goal of this narrative (termed *pilegesh be-Giv'ah*—the concubine in Gibeah) is a very worthy one, but the

Shoftim

means of accomplishing that end involved two wholesale slaughters of innocents, one of the civilian Benjaminites and a second of the citizens of Jabesh-gilead.[38] One might consider this story as a demonstration of how the ends may indeed justify the means, but it must be remembered that nowhere in the Biblical account is this behavior justified. On the contrary, a very blatant condemnation may be understood by the concluding verse of this episode and the entire book of Judges: "In those days there was no king in Israel; every man did what was right in his eyes" (Judg. 21:25). The implication is that "what was right in his eyes" was nowhere near what was right in God's eyes.

TALMUDIC SOURCES FOR THE END NOT JUSTIFYING THE MEANS: The Talmud (BT *Shevuot* 31a) discusses the following question:

> How do we know that if three persons [together] have a claim of a hundred *zuzim* against one person, one should not be the plaintiff and the other two the witnesses, in order that they may extract the hundred *zuzim* and divide it? Because it is said: "Distance yourself from a false matter" (Exod. 23:7).

It should be noted that although the traditional mitzvah-counters (Rambam and *Sefer ha-Chinuch*) do not count the verse cited as one of the *mitzvot*, *Sefer Yerei'im* (ch. 235) considers the verse to be the source of a Torah-level prohibition to lie concerning financial matters, while *Sefer Charedim* (ch. 6) goes further and understands it to prohibit all falsehoods, independent of the consequences.

The goal in the hypothetical case described is to retrieve the 100 *zuzim* owed to the threesome (33 to each). However, if one denies a financial claim in the absence of either witnesses or a signed contract, there is no way for the plaintiff to get his money back. In order to

---

38. Marital arrangements for the overage of 200 male Benjaminites was accomplished in a much more benign manner (Judg. 21:16-23).

extract the money from the borrower, the claimants devise a plan. Only one will claim to have lent 100 *zuzim*, and the other two will serve as witnesses to verify that the loan took place. Their testimony is sufficient to require the borrower to repay the loan. The problem is that in order for this plan to work, a number of lies have to be told. First, the plaintiff has to claim that he lent the entire sum of 100, when he only lent 33. Second, the two witnesses have to claim that they were present when the loan was made to the plaintiff, which is not necessarily true. The text emphasizes that although the ends are worthy, namely that the lenders receive the rightful amount owed to them, the forbidden means used to achieve that end are not justified.

Furthermore, not only is lying not permitted in order to obtain the money that one is lawfully entitled to, but even to save a life there is a case where it is not permitted. The Talmud states:

> R. Kahana said: If the Sanhedrin unanimously finds [the accused] guilty, he is acquitted. Why? Because we have learned by tradition that sentencing must be postponed [until the next day] in hope of finding new points in favor of the defense, but this cannot be anticipated in this case [an effort will not be made, since it seems hopeless] (BT *Sanhedrin* 17a).

Suppose all but one of the 23 judges feel that a person accused of murder is guilty. The judge who feels he is innocent might say to himself: "If I express my true opinion, which is that he is innocent, there will be 22 who feel he is guilty and one who feels he is innocent, and the verdict will be guilty. On the other hand, if I say in court that he is guilty, then all 23 judges will have voted to convict, in which case (according to the Talmudic extract cited above) the final verdict will be not guilty, which is what I desire."

Or ha-Chaim, in his commentary on the verse "You should not follow the majority for evil" (Exod. 23:2), states as follows:

Shoftim

Do not agree with their opinion of "guilty," the opposite of what you think, in order that he should be exonerated in accordance with your view, but rather express your opinion according to your understanding of the laws of the Torah, and do not try to supersede the law.

Once more, the goal of pardoning a person who is wrongly being sentenced to death may seem like an end which is worth striving for, but transgressing the prohibition to lie is not justified as a means of achieving that end.

MIDDLE AGES

Akeidat Yitzchak (*Bereishit, sha'ar* 20, *Vayera*) refers to the practice, which apparently existed in Spain in the 15th century, of allowing young single women to be intimate with bachelors or even married men who were seeking promiscuous sexual encounters. The justification was that, assuming these women immersed in a ritualarium (*mikveh*), as the Torah requires of menstrual women, having relations with single women was considerably less of a sin than doing so with married women, and significantly less dangerous to the continued existence of the Jewish nation than doing so with non-Jewish women (see **Appendix III: The Sanctity of Marriage**). Communities which defended this practice were clearly basing themselves on the belief that the end justifies the means. *Akeidat Yitzchak* roundly excoriated this practice, implying that he strongly disputed the claim that the ends might ever justify the means.

One might note that it is hard to imagine that women of ill-repute would actually be punctilious with respect to the intricate laws of purification through immersion. Since having relations in an impure state is punishable by excision, it is not an appreciably less serious offense than adultery. However, this aspect did not seem to be the main concern of *Akeidat Yitzchak*. Rather, it was the certification of a mode of behavior which is antithetical to the Torah way of life, albeit with the intention of achieving a worthy objective.

Akeidat Yitzchak compares tolerance for such brothels to the case of *pilegesh be-Giv'ah*, where some of the city residents attempted homosexual rape. Had the local court handed over the malefactors to the remaining tribes, then the sins would have been of individuals, and the story would have ended. When they refused to do so, the entire community was implicated, it became a form of public fornication, and the entire community was held responsible. This is an exact replication of what happened in Sodom. Homosexual rape, as well as neglect and abuse of the downtrodden, transitioned from a personal sin to a communal sin, for which the entire community was culpable and eventually destroyed. The case brought to the attention of the *Akeidat Yitzchak* was similar. As improper as the behavior of these young men and women was, they were still only acting as misguided individuals. Allowing the suggested prostitution to become institutionalized, however, makes the entire community guilty and liable to destruction. It is therefore preferable that individuals sin and be punished, even if it be a sin carrying a death penalty, than that the community offer illegitimate options for satisfying sexual lust, even if the transgressions involved are of a lower grade.

THE ENDS JUSTIFY THE MEANS

In spite of the many proofs that have been mobilized to indicate that the ends do not justify the means, there are many Biblical occurrences which seem to indicate the opposite. Certainly, being truthful is an important value in Judaism, in keeping with the phrase: "Distance yourself from a false matter" (Exod. 23:7). Nevertheless, in the book of Genesis, starting with claims by Abraham and Isaac that their wives were actually their sisters; continuing with Jacob's pretense when he claimed he was Esau, and Leah's when she claimed she was Rachel (according to the Midrash); and culminating with the sons of Jacob fabricating a discussion which they never had with their father

Shoftim

Jacob, the Torah ascribes a series of lies, i.e., improper means, which were used to achieve what were considered to be worthwhile ends. The Talmud implies that God acquiesced to this behavior and even Himself acted in this manner on certain occasions.[39]

Moving on to the book of Exodus, ch. 32 tells the story of the golden calf, whose production was organized by Aaron. In trying to understand how such a righteous person could encourage idol worship, the Talmud (BT *Sanhedrin* 7a) explains that Aaron himself was a true believer in God, but he realized that the paganism of the masses was so intense that they would have murdered him, had he opposed them. Killing a prophet was considered to be an unforgivable sin, while worshipping foreign gods, as terrible as it is, is subject to repentance. Aaron was willing to sacrifice his own immaculate reputation in order to maintain the option of repentance on the part of the Children of Israel.

Did Aaron make the right decision? According to Rashi he did not, since one cannot compromise with respect to the laws of the Torah. One cannot transgress a law in order to prevent others from transgressing a more serious prohibition. *Tosafot*, on the other hand, feel that to ensure the future of the entire nation, Aaron was permitted to violate a lesser proscription.[40] *Tosafot* believe that Aaron's unblemished reputation was maintained in this particular case by allowing the end to justify the means.

Aaron focused on the end rather than the means not only on the national level, but on the personal level as well. The Midrash (*Avot de-Rabbi Natan* A:12) describes how Aaron in cases of interpersonal disputes would privately tell each party how distraught his antagonist is, since he realizes that it is actually he who is at fault, just that he is too embarrassed to step forward and openly confess his guilt. When the disputants would meet, they would lovingly embrace and forget

---

39. See Abba Engelberg, *The Ethics of Genesis* (2014), pp. 94, 219-220, 270-281 (Appendix 8).
40. For a thorough treatment of this subject, see: Abba Engelberg, *The Ethics of Exodus* (2014), pp. 355-364.

that they had ever argued. In order to achieve peace and brotherly love, Aaron was willing to slightly modify the truth. Perhaps Aaron felt that he was reflecting the true opinions of each disputant, just that due to weakness of their character, they were unable to externalize their innermost feelings.

In Leviticus, the following general exhortation is found: "You must observe My statutes and My ordinances, which a man should do in order to live by them" (Lev. 18:5). The Talmud expounds the last phrase as follows: "to live by them and not to die by them" (BT *Yoma* 85b). Once more, there is an end and there are means of reaching that end. The verse has clearly stated what that end is, namely to fulfill as many *mitzvot* as possible. Clearly, one cannot fulfill any *mitzvot* at all if he is dead. What happens if, in order to be able to continue fulfilling *mitzvot*, one has to desecrate a specific mitzvah in order to remain alive. Does the worthy end of fulfilling many *mitzvot* justify the unworthy means which involve transgressing one of those very commands? The Talmud in *Yoma* is stating that in such a case, the ends do indeed justify the means. Exactly why this should be so is elucidated in the following Talmudic extract:

> For a day-old infant the Sabbath is desecrated [to enable him to do *mitzvot* in the future]. The Torah ordered: "Desecrate one Sabbath on his account so that he may keep many Sabbaths." If David, King of Israel, dies [on the other hand], the Sabbath may not be desecrated. Once man dies, he is free from [all] obligations, and thus R. Yochanan interpreted: "Among the dead I am free" (Ps. 88:6). Once a man is dead, he is free from religious duties (BT *Shabbat* 151b).

Although the means involve the transgression of one or more commands, because the desired end is to preserve the life of an individual who will be able to observe so many more *mitzvot*, the ends do indeed justify the means. Therefore, if desecrating the

Shoftim

Sabbath, eating non-kosher food, or not circumcising on the eighth day will enable the saving of a life (*piku'ach nefesh*), those acts may be performed. If action is required, not only is one permitted to act, one is required to, based on the verse: "You may not stand by [the shedding of] your fellow's blood" (Lev. 19:16; *Sefer ha-Mitzvot*, negative command 297). Even if it is possible that the person will survive without these heroic efforts (*safek piku'ach nefesh*), it is still obligatory to perform these acts (BT *Arachin* 7b, *Hilchot Shabbat* 2:1). The *Shulchan Aruch* (*Orach Chaim* 328:2) even prohibits one to ask a Rabbi when in doubt, because time is of the essence.

The Talmud lists three exceptions to the permit to transgress in order to save life:

> R. Yochanan said in the name of R. Shimon b. Yehotzadak: By a majority vote, it was resolved in the upper chambers of the house of Nitza in Lod that regarding every law of the Torah, if a man is told: "Transgress in order to be spared from death," he may transgress and not suffer death, excepting idolatry, incest and adultery, and murder (BT *Sanhedrin* 74a).

In these three cases, then, one may say the end does not justify the means, although *Ba'al ha-Maor* (Rif, *Sanhedrin* 18a) notes that if the incest or adultery is being done for the benefit and pleasure of the (non-Jewish) assaulter, rather than because he wishes to force a Jew to transgress a cardinal law, then one must not sacrifice his life.

One of the laws adjudicated in the book of Deuteronomy also takes the approach that the ends justify the means. The text describes the case of the rebellious son as follows:

> **18** If a man has a stubborn and rebellious son, who does not obey his father or his mother, and they chasten him, and [he still] does not listen to them, **19** his father and his mother should take hold of him and bring him out to the elders of his

city, and to the gate of his place. **20** And they will say to the elders of his city, "This son of ours is stubborn and rebellious; he does not obey us; [he is] a glutton and a drunkard." **21** And all the men of his city will pelt him to death with stones, so that he dies. And you will [thus] clear out the evil from among you, and all Israel will hear and fear (Deut. 21).

V. 20 indicates that in addition to being disobedient, the rebellious son is "a glutton and a drunkard." The Mishnah provides exact measurements of these attributes:

> When does he become liable [to punishment]? When he eats a *tartemar* [a large amount at one time] and drinks half a *log* of Italian wine [in one gulp—a volume equivalent to the space taken up by three eggs] (*Sanhedrin* 8:2).

The Talmud comments on this Mishnah:

> R. Yosi the Galilean said: Did the Torah decree that the rebellious son should be brought before *beit din* and stoned merely because he ate a *tartemar* of meat and drank a *log* of Italian wine? But the Torah predicts the final state of the rebellious son. For at the end, after dissipating his father's wealth, he will [still] seek to satisfy his accustomed [gluttonous] wants, but being unable to do so, go forth at the crossroads and rob passers-by. [Therefore,] the Torah said, "Let him die while yet innocent, and let him not die guilty." For the death of the wicked benefits themselves and the world; of the righteous, injures themselves and the world (BT *Sanhedrin* 72a).

In the concise wording of the Mishnah: "A stubborn and rebellious son is judged based on his ultimate destiny" (*Sanhedrin* 8:5).

Shoftim

Here we have a law of the Torah which carries the death penalty, with the Mishnah admitting that a child's punishment is totally disproportionate to the crime he has committed, yet since the end justifies the means, and in the end this child would have grown up to be both a dangerous criminal and a bad influence on others, we can therefore utilize the unjust means of stoning him while he is still innocent. Ramban (Deut. 21:18) notes that his severe punishment is meant to be a deterrent to others, and this is stressed by the phrase in v. 21, "and all Israel will hear and fear."

Ramban proceeds to cite other cases in which the Torah metes out disproportionate punishment just for the purpose of benefiting the congregation, under the assumption that the end (powerful deterrence) justifies the means (overly harsh penalty). The first example is that of *zaken mamrei*, a rebellious elder who promulgates an edict contradictory to the decision of the Sanhedrin, whom the Torah describes as "the man who acts intentionally, not obeying the *kohen* [ecclesiastical president of the Sanhedrin] who stands there to serve the Lord your God, or [not obeying] the judge" (Deut. 17:12). The verse continues: "that man must die, and so you will abolish evil from Israel. And all of the people will hear and fear, and they will [as a result of experiencing the elder's castigation] no longer act wantonly." In other words, seeing an overly harsh death penalty imposed will have a sobering effect on the nation, and that explains the recurrence of the phrase "the people will hear and fear," since their presence is the main purpose of the chastisement. In fact, the public exhibition of the punishment is such a central aspect of the law that the Talmud (BT *Sanhedrin* 89a) posits that execution is delayed until the next festival, when all of Israel appears in Jerusalem. As unfair as is the means in this case, the ultimate end is to unify observance of *mitzvot* and avoid numerous parallel and diverse interpretations of the law (Ramban, Deut. 17:11).

With regard to false witnesses (*eidim zomemim*, literally "plotting witnesses"), the Torah states: "If a false witness rises up against a man, to bear perverted testimony against him" (Deut. 19:16). The Mishnah (*Makkot* 1:4) explains the definition of false witnesses as follows: "They [another set of witnesses] say to them: 'How can you testify to that, since you were with us on that day in a particular place?'" Their punishment is described as follows: "then you will do to him as he plotted to do to his brother, and you will [thus] abolish evil from among you" (Deut. 19:19). What this means is that if the false witnesses intended to accuse the person of murder, which carries the death penalty, even though the murder was not actually carried out, the false witnesses are executed, since that is what they plotted to do to their brother. Once again, Ramban (Deut. 21:18) highlights the unfairness of this retribution, since the witnesses are being killed in compensation for a murder which never occurred. However, once more the end—creating a trustworthy legal system and deterring those who would have it otherwise—justifies the disproportionate means. And once more Ramban points out the public nature of the punishment, as emphasized in the verse: "And those who remain [the congregation] will listen and fear, so that they will no longer continue to commit any such evil thing among you" (Deut. 19:20).

Interestingly, if as a result of their testimony the person falsely accused of murder is actually executed, then the Talmud (BT *Makkot* 5b, *Chullin* 11b) exempts the plotting witnesses from execution, based on an analysis of the phrase "then you will do to him as he plotted to do," from which it may be derived: "as he plotted to do, but not as he actually did [i.e., if the accused was actually executed]" (Rashi, Deut. 19:19; BT *Chullin* 11b, s.v. *ein neheragim*). This strange anomaly may be explained as follows.[41] If the accused is executed, the public will assume that the court made a thorough investigation and arrived at the appropriate conclusion, which was then implemented. If the false witnesses are executed, the public will make the same assumption about the court and the false witnesses. However, if both the accused and the false witnesses are executed, it will be apparent that the court

---

41. Nachum Rakover, *Encyclopedia Yehudit* (Internet), see: *Eidim zomemim*.

Shoftim

has erred, and this could lead to a loss of confidence in the entire legal system. The law was designed to avoid such an inference on the part of the public.

The final example cited by Ramban is the case of once who incites others against God. The Bible states:

> 7 If your brother, the son of your mother, tempts you in secret... saying, "Let us go and worship other gods, which neither you nor your forefathers have known"... 11 You must stone him with stones so that he dies... 12 And all Israel will listen and fear, and they will no longer do any evil such as this in your midst (Deut. 13).

Again, Ramban stresses that the inciter is killed for what he said alone, even if those incited did not worship idols or allow themselves to be influenced in the least. V. 7 records what the inciter said, v. 11 stipulates his punishment, and v. 12 once more presents the exhortatory nature of the sentence, which is meant mainly as a deterrent.

As in the case of *zaken mamrei* (the rebellious elder), since the extreme punishment is mainly meant to forewarn the populace, R. Akiva decreed that the execution be delayed until the next holiday and take place at the ingathering of the nation in Jerusalem. In fact, the Talmud (BT *Sanhedrin* 89a; *Hilchot Mamrim* 3:8) applies this approach to all of the cases mentioned by Ramban:

> Our Rabbis taught: Public announcements [which would take place in Jerusalem at the next festival] must be made for four [malefactors]: an inciter against God, a rebellious son, a rebellious elder, and false witnesses (*eidim zomemim*).

In each of these four occurrences, the Bible clarifies that the harsh punishment is being imposed in order that the congregation "listen and fear" (Deut. 13:12, 17:13, 19:20, 21:21).

The Ethics of Deuteronomy

Summary

Biblical and Talmudic precedents have been cited showing that sometimes the approach taken was that the ends do not justify the means, but at other times it was assumed that they indeed justified the means. So, which one will it be? It is suggested that neither approach should be taken as definitive. Rather, the method which should be adopted is the systems approach, which is defined as follows: when attempting to achieve a particular goal, one must determine all of the means needed to achieve that goal, as well as all of the byproducts of the means used, and additionally all subsidiary goals which may be attained when applying those means and achieving that goal. A value should be associated with each action and result (positive if desirable, negative if not). If the sum of all the values is greater than zero, the means to achieve the end should be implemented, and in that case the ends do indeed justify the means, while if the sum is less than zero, the means do not justify the ends and no action should be taken.

One may ask why the expression "the ends do not justify the means" is very widespread, since it is not necessarily true. The answer may be that when a person is making an individual decision, of which he is the main benefactor, he will frequently minimize the damage caused by the means and exaggerate the benefit of the ends. For example, consider the case of a pre-med student who cheats on tests, which he justifies by declaring that his intention is to make a great contribution to the poverty-stricken by supplying medical treatment to indigent societies. He rationalizes his means (i.e., his cheating) by claiming that nobody is hurt, because the good students will still get the grades they deserve. However, he ignores the following repercussions of his behavior:

a. Since many tests are marked on a curve, some deserving students will get lower grades.
b. Since he will become a mediocre doctor, he will certainly damage

the school's reputation, which will impinge negatively on all of the past and future alumni.

c. As an unqualified doctor, he may frequently make mistakes and fail to cure his patients, and at times may cause their degeneration and even their demise.

In short, the means are not as harmless as he believes, nor is the end as beneficial as he claims.

Similarly, consider the case of a dishonest law student who justifies his cheating by explaining that he has no intention of ever practicing, but just seeks the prestige associated with having a law degree. If he ever practices, he will certainly only be able to provide mediocre service, possibly resulting in considerable financial loss or undeserved incarceration. Even if he never practices, since universities are non-profit organizations, he has wasted the school's resources and likely deprived some deserving young person of the opportunity to develop a respectable career, and of society to benefit from that career.

If the means cause no harm, then even if the end is not as worthy as it is made out to be, there is no loss in attempting to achieve it. Because of the tendency to exaggerate positive and minimize negative effects of one's course of action, demanding that the means have no negative side-effects serves as a method of damage control and was formulated as a "rule of thumb."

On the other hand, very few people would say that if a dog is seen attacking an infant, one should refrain from killing the dog, since the ends do not justify the means. Clearly that end does indeed justify the means. To summarize, then, one must strive to attain the most possible good in whatever way it can be achieved.

Determining the value associated with a particular means or end is not always easy, and this topic is dealt with in **Appendix IV: The Value Attached to Life**.

Ki Teitzei

The three consecutive portions of *Re'eh, Shoftim,* and *Ki Teitzei* contain the greatest concentration of *mitzvot* in the entire Torah, specifically 171 of the 613 *mitzvot*, or more than 25%. *Ki Teitzei* itself contains 74, more than any other portion. Most of the laws in *Ki Teitzei* deal with relations between man and his fellow man, and in particular between man and his immediate family, i.e., his wife and children. In addition, it contains laws between man and animals, as well as some statutes. Some of these laws appear below:

BETWEEN MAN AND HIS IMMEDIATE FAMILY:
- Marriage with a captive of war (21:10-14)
- The right of the first-born (21:15-17)
- The rebellious son (21:18-21)
- Preserving the holiness of marriage (22:13-23:9)
- Laws of divorce (24:1-4)
- Law of a newlywed (24:5)

BETWEEN MAN AND HIS FELLOW MAN:
- Restoring lost property (22:1-3)
- Lifting a fallen beast (22:4)
- Not returning a fugitive slave (23:16-17)
- Not taking interest (23:20-21)
- Permitting workers to eat the produce (23:25-26)
- Prohibition to take a millstone as a pledge (24:6)
- Prohibition of kidnapping (24:7)

Ki Teitzei

- Fair treatment of workers (24:14-15)
- Being fair in judgment (24:16-18)
- Generosity to the poor (24:19-22)

BETWEEN MAN AND ANIMALS:
- Not taking a mother bird with its young (22:6-7)
- Placing a railing on the roof of a house (22:8)
- Not yoking an ox with a donkey (22:10)
- Not muzzling an ox (25:4)

STATUTES:
- Distinction of sex in apparel (22:5)
- Not mixing seeds (22:9)
- Not wearing garments made of wool and linen interwoven (22:11)
- Laws of leprosy (24:8-9)

Clearly, the majority of these laws relate to how a person deals with those surrounding him whether they be family, friend, or any living creature. The rest of this chapter will be devoted specifically to the third category.

TZA'AR BA'ALEI CHAIM

Tza'ar ba'alei chaim means literally "the pain of creatures," and it refers to a prohibition to cause such pain. Even though Jewish law permits one to deprive animals of their lives, as long as they are living, and even during the slaughtering process, Jews must make every effort to ensure that they do not suffer. Whether the prohibition is because of a God-given soul, which animals possess as well as humans, or because cruelty to animals could adversely affect one's relationship to his fellow human beings, may be dependent on the difference of opinion between R. Yosef Albo and R. Kook (see **Appendix II:**

The Ethics of Deuteronomy

Vegetarianism). Whether the law was initially legislated by the Torah (*mi-de-oraita*) or a later rabbinical decree (*mi-de-rabanan*) may also be dependent on the same difference of opinion, with R. Kook's view that animal life is no less holy than human life fitting in with the *mi-de-oraita* approach, while R. Albo's—that cruelty is to be avoided because of its potentially bad influence on inter-human relationships—is more suited to the *mi-de-rabanan* approach. At any rate, the Talmud discusses this question without arriving at a clear-cut conclusion.

If *tza'ar ba'alei chaim* is in fact prohibited by the Torah, what is the source of the prohibition? A number of possibilities have been suggested.

Unloading and Reloading

The Torah relates to the case of an overloaded animal that is overcome by its burden. The verse states: "If you see your enemy's donkey lying under its burden, would you refrain from helping him? [Of course not!] You should certainly help [unload it] together with him [the donkey's owner]" (Exod. 23:5). In the phrase "helping him," the pronoun in Hebrew may refer either to the animal or to its owner. The animal is suffering, and by helping it one prevents *tza'ar ba'alei chaim*. The owner, on the other hand, is not suffering physically but rather financially or emotionally, because he is in the process of transporting the load to a location that will benefit him in some manner, and he will certainly be upset at being delayed. Note that the verse stresses that this is the proper thing to do even if the victim is one whom the helper had previously disliked. R. Joseph Hertz (*The Pentateuch*, 1938, p. 316) points out that the best way to turn an enemy into a friend is by performing deeds of loving-kindness, as the Bible states: "If your enemy is hungry, feed him bread, and if he is thirsty, give him water to drink" (Prov. 25:21).

A second instance dealing with a discomfited animal owner is found in the present portion, which states: "You should not see

Ki Teitzei

[i.e., look on without offering to help] your brother's donkey or his ox fallen [with its load] on the road, and ignore them. [Rather,] you must pick up [the load] with him" (Deut. 22:4).

Rambam looks at the verse in *Ki Teitzei* as being complementary to that in Exodus, presenting them as a unit:

> When a person encounters a wayfarer who is on a journey and his animal has fallen with its load, he is commanded to unload the burden from it… This is a positive commandment, as it says: "You should certainly help [unload it] together with him." One should not unload the animal and depart, leaving him in panic. Instead, one should lift it up and reload the animal's burden upon it, as it says: "you must pick up [the load] with him." This is another positive commandment, and if he leaves him in panic without unloading or reloading, he has cancelled [the observance of] a positive commandment and violated a negative commandment, as it says: "You should not see [i.e., look on without offering to help] your brother's donkey or his ox fallen [with its load] on the road, and ignore them" (*Hilchot Rotzeach* 13:1-2).

There is a difference between unloading and reloading. In the former case, the Talmud (BT *Bava Metzia* 32a) explains that the helper must perform the mitzvah gratis, while in the latter case he is entitled to receive minimum wages.[42] Although in both cases the owner will sustain a financial loss if he does not receive help (with respect to the animal if it is not unloaded, and regarding his ability to market the merchandise the animal is carrying if it is not reloaded), only in the case of unloading is there also *tza'ar ba'alei chaim*. Rosh (BT *Bava Metzia* 2:28) holds that even in the case of unloading, if one is employed, he is not obliged to lose money. Rather, he may request

---

42. R. Shimon says both are to be done gratis, but his view is not accepted (*Hilchot Rotzeach* 13:7).

his normal wages and the animal owner will decide if he wishes to benefit from his help under those conditions. This was the approach taken with regard to returning lost objects as well (Deut. 22:1-3; *Bava Metzia* 2:9). Ran (cited in *Nimukei Yosef, Bava Metzia,* Rif 17b, s.v. *lifrok*), however, says that unloading must always be done gratis, since this is not merely a monetary matter but also a moral one, and only reloading is handled in a manner parallel to that for lost objects.

Sources of *Tza'ar Ba'alei Chaim*

Ran (BT *Shabbat* 51a, in Rif) says that, based on the view of Rava (BT *Bava Metzia* 32a), the law of unloading is based on the principle of *tza'ar ba'alei chaim*, and is thus the source for the application of that principle to any situation where living creatures suffer.

Muzzling

The Torah states: "You may not muzzle an ox when it is threshing [grain]" (Deut. 25:4), and the Midrash (*Sifrei Devarim* 287) extends this to all creatures and all forms of labor. The straightforward reason for this law is that it is cruel to expect the beast to perform hard labor when there is food before its eyes which it cannot eat, and Rashi (BT *Shabbat* 128b, s.v. *tza'ar*) and Me'iri (BT *Bava Metzia* 32b) thus see it as a prototype which serves to prohibit all manifestations of cruelty toward animals, as reflected in the verse: "A righteous man has regard for the desire of his beast" (Prov. 12:10).

Halachah le-Moshe mi-Sinai

Both Ritva (s.v. *taida*) and Rabbeinu Peretz (s.v. *mi-chlal*), on BT *Bava Metzia* 32b, consider *tza'ar ba'alei chaim* to be a *halachah le-Moshe mi-Sinai*. Such laws are not formulated in the written law, but rather are believed to have been transmitted orally to Moses at Mt. Sinai and to possess an equal status in Jewish law. Similarly, the requirement and basic details of slaughtering meat are nowhere explicated in the

Torah. That such laws even exist is hinted at by the usage in Deut. 12:21: "you may slaughter… as I have commanded you."

Balaam

Rambam sees the Biblcal source of *tza'ar ba'alei chaim* in the words of rebuke which God directed at Balaam for striking his donkey three times. In his words:

> There is a rule laid down by our Sages that it is directly prohibited in the Law to cause pain to an animal, and is based on the words: "Why have you beaten your she-donkey these three times?" (Num. 22:32). But the object of this rule is to make us perfect, that we should not assume cruel habits, and that we should not uselessly cause pain to others; that, on the contrary, we should be prepared to show pity and mercy to all living creatures, except when necessity demands the contrary: "When… your soul desires to eat meat" (Deut. 12:20). We should not kill animals for the purpose of practicing cruelty, or for the purpose of play. It cannot be objected to this theory: "Why should God select mankind as the object of His special Providence, and not other living beings?" For he who asks this question must also inquire: Why has man alone, of all species of animals, been endowed with intellect? The answer to this second question must be, according to the three aforementioned theories: It was the will of God, it is the decree of His wisdom, or it is in accordance with the laws of Nature (*Guide for the Perplexed* 3:17).

Of course, Rambam does not include *tza'ar ba'alei chaim* among the 613 *mitzvot*, since he does not count generalized categories of *mitzvot* (*Sefer ha-Mitzvot, shoresh* 4).

The Ethics of Deuteronomy

Other Laws Which Legislate Merciful Behavior to Animals

A number of other Torah laws stress the importance of being merciful to all creatures. One is not allowed to slaughter a female animal with its young on the same day (Lev. 22:28). In addition to stressing the importance of preserving all species, which this prohibition emphasizes, it is intended to prevent suffering on the part of the mother. In the words of Rambam (as previously noted in *Re'eh*):

> It is also prohibited to kill an animal with its young on the same day in order that people should be restrained and prevented from killing the two together in such a manner that the young is slain in the sight of the mother, for the pain of the animals under such circumstances is very great. There is no difference in this case between the pain of man and the pain of other living beings, since the love and tenderness of the mother for her young ones is not produced by reasoning, but by imagination, and this faculty exists not only in man but in most living beings. This law applies only to ox and lamb because, of the domestic animals used as food, these alone are permitted to us, and in these cases the mother recognizes her young (*Guide for the Perplexed* 3:48).

Targum Yonatan (Lev. 22:28) generalizes the verse when it states: "My nation the Children of Israel, just as our Father in heaven is merciful, so should we be merciful on earth—a cow and a sheep should not be slaughtered on the same day as their child."

Another law which may be placed in the same category is the requirement to send away the mother bird before taking her young or her eggs (Deut. 22:6-7), termed *shiluach ha-ken*. Concerning this law, Rambam states:

The eggs over which the bird sits, and the young that are in need of their mother, are generally unfit for food, and when the mother is sent away, she does not see the taking of her young ones and does not feel any pain. In most cases, however, this commandment will cause man to leave the whole nest untouched, because [the young or the eggs] which he is allowed to take, are, as a rule, unfit for food. If the Law provides that such grief should not be caused to cattle or birds, how much more careful must we be that we should not cause grief to our fellowmen (*Guide for the Perplexed* 3:48).

Ramban similarly rationalizes both laws as follows:

The reason for both is so that we not have a cruel heart and be unmerciful, or [alternatively] that the Torah does not wish to permit the destruction and uprooting of a species even though it permitted slaughtering that species, for he who kills the mother with the children on the same day or takes them when they are free to fly away, it is as if he annihilated that species (Deut. 22:6).

Along the same lines is the prohibition to "plow with an ox and a donkey together" (Deut. 22:10). Ibn Ezra explains that "the strength of a donkey does not equal that of an ox," implying that the former would have to over-exert itself in order to keep up with the latter, causing it severe pain. *Ba'al ha-Turim* notes that an ox chews its cud. The donkey, seeing the ox digesting food, might think that the ox had just been fed and that he (the donkey) was being neglected, not realizing that the ox was merely regurgitating food that had been freely distributed at feeding time. *Ba'al ha-Turim* generalizes the lesson not to generate ill feelings in others to human beings as well. Additionally, *Sefer ha-Chinuch* (550) comments that it is unpleasant for animals of a given species to be in the company of those of another species, and it is even more upsetting when they are required to work together. *Sefer ha-Chinuch* concludes that people who differ in outlook should not be hired to work together on the same project, since if the Torah considers the well-being of insensate creatures, certainly one must be considerate of more perceptive ones.

Finally, another set of laws which accentuates the emphasis placed on dealing mercifully with animals is the set of commands not to sever limbs from living animals (*Sifrei* 76, referring to Deut. 12:23) and to slaughter animals in the prescribed manner (Deut. 12:21). *Sefer ha-Chinuch* (452) explains that there is nothing crueler than to cut off the limb of a living animal and eat it in its presence. It is understandable that in ancient times, when there was no refrigeration, removing a limb provided a way to obtain a small quantity of meat at a time, rather than killing the animal and allowing most of its meat to spoil. Nevertheless, although it was permitted to eat meat, causing unconscionable pain was not to be permitted.

Similarly, regarding *shechitah* (kosher slaughtering), Ramban (Gen. 1:29) explains that the specific details were given in order to minimize the animal's pain, which he considers to be a Torah-level prohibition. *Sefer ha-Chinuch* (451) understands Ramban to be referring to the fact that the animal is killed by sliding the knife across the neck, the most vulnerable location, leading to the most instantaneous death. Furthermore, Rambam notes that "in order to ensure an easy death, our Sages insisted that the knife should be well sharpened" (*Guide for the Perplexed* 3:26).

Interestingly, not only is the Jew commanded not to cause pain to animals, he is even required to provide social benefits, based on the phrase with respect to the Sabbath: "On the seventh day you must rest, in order that your ox and your donkey may rest."

An Apparent Contradiction

A previously mentioned Mishnah states: "If one [when praising the Lord] says: 'Your mercy extends [even] to the bird's nest'... he is

Ki Teitzei

silenced" (*Berachot* 5:3). In answer to a query as to what impropriety was committed, the Talmud answers:

> Two Amoraim in the West, R. Yosi b. Abin and R. Yosi b. Zebida, give different answers; one says it is because he creates jealousy among God's creatures [as the verse refers only to birds], the other, because he presents the measures taken by the Holy One, blessed be He, as springing from compassion, whereas they are but decrees (BT *Berachot* 33b).

In his *Guide*, Rambam states:

> Our Law is only concerned with the relations of men, but the idea that irrational living beings should receive a reward has never before been heard of in our nation.... Divine Providence [*hashgachah pratit*] does not extend to the individual members of species except in the case of mankind. It is only in this species that the incidents in the existence of the individual beings, their good and evil fortunes, are the result of justice, in accordance with the words: "For all His ways are judgment" (Deut. 32:4). But I agree with Aristotle [who does not believe in Divine Providence at all] as regards all other living beings, and *a fortiori* as regards plants and all the rest of earthly creatures (*Guide for the Perplexed* 3:17).

Based on this viewpoint, Me'iri (BT *Berachot* 33b) explains that the law requiring sending away the mother bird would seem to imply that Divine Providence devolves upon birds but not other creatures, possibly generating jealousy in the animal kingdom, when in reality it applies only to humans. His second answer is that although the law seems to be based on being merciful to creatures, it should be looked upon as merely a Divine decree with no capability of being extrapolated to other situations. Therefore, the second answer would seem to negate the possibility of using *shiluach ha-ken* or any of the other animal-oriented laws as a source for *tza'ar ba'alei chaim*.

Rambam (*Guide for the Perplexed* 3:48) simply says that he follows the first opinion in *Berachot*, and therefore feels comfortable assigning rational reasons to the commandments and even generalizing their lessons to other situations.

Ramban (Deut. 22:6), on the other hand, says that even the second view in the Talmud allows interpretation of the *mitzvot*. However, the Mishnah wishes to censure those who believe that God wishes to be merciful to birds, since, as Rambam himself says (*Hilchot Tefillah* 9:7), if that were the case, why does He permit ritual slaughter of birds? In fact, *shiluach ha-ken* is required not to be merciful to the bird (and in that sense it is a decree), but rather so that people will not develop bad traits by becoming hardened to the suffering of living creatures and, by extension, cruel to human beings and insensitive to their travails.

A third answer is based on Rashi's gloss on the phrase: "If one [Rashi: as part of his prayers] says: 'Your mercy extends to the bird's nest'... he is silenced." *Tosafot Yom Tov* explains that one is allowed to analyze the command and draw appropriate conclusions. The only prohibition is to declaim in an absolute sense that the only reason for this mitzvah is as a reflection of God's mercy. The danger of such an approach is that when one arbitrarily determines the rationale behind a mitzvah, he may easily be led to propose its cancellation when his own explanation seems to no longer be relevant. However, realizing that one's suggested reason is not definitive does not mean one cannot extract important lessons, especially when a series of commands seem to all be pointing in the same direction, and that is what the various exegetes have done with respect to the concept of *tza'ar ba'alei chaim*.

Finally, it should be noted that in his *Guide* (3:26), Rambam says that all commands, even those called statutes, have reasons. However, he does admit that many of the details were given merely

Ki Teitzei

to inculcate obedience. In *Hilchot Me'ilah* (8:8), however, he makes no mention of any rationale being associated with statutes. Perhaps the contradiction may be resolved by distinguishing between what may be said in prayer or accepted as dogma, and lessons which may be derived, as was noted with respect to *shiluach ha-ken*. In other words, in prayer, one should look at certain laws as statutes, since many of the details of their observance belong to that category, even though the overall command is purposeful. Taken in this sense, the two answers of the Talmud regarding *shiluach ha-ken* may be taken to be complementary rather than contradictory. Since by saying "Your mercy extends [even] to the bird's nest" one might get the wrong impression, either according to Me'iri's explanation of the first Talmudic opinion or Ramban's elucidation of the second, and also one might lose sight of the fact that many of the details of observance are indeed Godly decrees, it is preferable, at least when praying, not to mention it in conjunction with any of the proposed justifications.

Distinctions between the Torah and Rabbinical Approaches to *Tza'ar Ba'alei Chaim*

In general, if *tza'ar ba'alei chaim* is considered to be a Torah-level requirement (*mi-de-oraita*), it must be adhered to in all situations, while if it is only rabbinical (*mi-de-rabanan*), the rabbis have the right not to enforce it if they have other overriding considerations. According to *Tosafot ha-Rosh* (BT *Bava Metzia* 32b, s.v. *mi-chlal*), the rabbinical decree was only on one's own animals, while according to *Minchat Chinuch* (mitzvah 80), the rabbis only prohibited causing pain manually, but did not require intervention to prevent pain stemming from other sources.

Even according to the view that *tza'ar ba'alei chaim* is *mi-de-oraita*, if causing the animal pain is beneficial to mankind, it is permitted. The most obvious example is the killing of animals for dietary purposes, although ritual slaughter is designed to be as painless as possible. Another example mentioned in the Mishnah (*Bava Metzia* 2:10) is the exemption of old people from unloading an animal, since it is considered to be dishonorable for them to do so (*Nimukei Yosef, Bava Metzia* Rif 17b, s.v. *mi-shum*). Similarly, the Talmud (BT *Bava Metzia* 32b) notes that one should load his enemy's animal before he unloads his friend's (although unloading should have priority) in order to subdue his evil inclination, i.e., to enable him to reconcile with his enemy. As *Minchat Chinuch* (mitzvah 80) says, if it is permitted to pain an animal for human physical benefits, it is certainly permitted to do so for spiritual gain.

The Mishnah (*Bava Metzia* 2:10) mentions that according to R. Yosi ha-Glili, there is no obligation to help unload if the animal was overloaded, and apparently his disputant, the first opinion (*tanna kamma*), believes that even so the bystander must help. The assumption is that if the law is *mi-de-oraita*, help must be given in all circumstances, since the animal suffers even more with an oversize burden, while if rabbinic, it can be limited, since the verse states "under its burden," which can be interpreted to mean its normative burden. If the owner was careless and overloaded his animal, the Rabbis might not have taken *tza'ar ba'alei chaim* into account, since his predicament was self-imposed (BT *Bava Metzia* 32b).

The same Mishnah states that if the owner sat down and told the passer-by to do all the work because he has an obligation, the latter is exempt, since the verse says: "You should certainly help [unload it] together with him," implying no obligation if it is not to be done together. If *tza'ar ba'alei chaim* is *mi-de-oraita*, even if the owner misbehaves, the animal is still suffering. The Talmud explains that according to the view that the law is *mi-de-oraita*, indeed the passer-by must help even in that case, just that he is exempt in the sense that he is not obligated to do it gratis, but has a right to insist on being paid for his efforts (Rashi, BT *Bava Metzia* 32b, s.v. *avid*).

Another distinction between the Torah and rabbinic level is with respect to a non-Jew. Three situations may arise:

Ki Teitzei

1. The animal and its burden are owned by a non-Jew. If *tza'ar ba'alei chaim* is *mi-de-oraita*, unloading is always required (even if the burden is associated with idol worship), since it is certainly not the animal's fault that its owner is not Jewish. If it is rabbinic, even unloading the non-Jew's animal is intrinsically optional, although the Rabbis might have decreed it to be necessary in order to avoid enmity. Reloading would not be required according to either opinion.
2. The animal is owned by a non-Jew, and its burden by a Jew. If *tza'ar ba'alei chaim* is *mi-de-oraita*, unloading is required. If it is rabbinic, unloading is not required. Reloading would not be required according to either opinion.
3. The animal is owned by a Jew, and its burden by a non-Jew. All agree that unloading is required. Reloading may also be required, so as not to inconvenience the Jewish driver of the animal he owns by causing him to wait.

The halachic decision process and the final verdict are presented in **Appendix X: The Halachic Decision Regarding *Tza'ar Ba'alei Chaim*.**

Distinction between Jews and Gentiles

Why are Gentiles discriminated against? If it is important to be kind—and it most certainly is—should not that behavior be exhibited in one's dealings with others independent of race, religion, or sex? Why is one exempt from unloading and reloading a Gentile's donkey? The question may be reinforced based on another verse in the present portion: "You may lend with interest to a Gentile, but to your brother you may not lend with interest" (Deut. 23:21). Again, why should a distinction be made?

First, it must be pointed out that all human beings are created with the same degree of spirituality. Second, all human beings possess equal potential to achieve salvation.

The Ethics of Deuteronomy

The first point follows from the following Mishnah (*Avot* 3:14):

> Beloved is man, for he was created in the image [of God]; still greater was this love in that it was made known to him that he was created in the image, as it says: "For in the image of God He made man" (Gen. 9:6).

Rambam, in his Mishnaic commentary, interprets the image of God as being "the rational faculty which distinguishes man and whose goal is knowledge of God to the extent of man's capacity and intelligence." One can get to know God through philosophy, natural science, social science, art, music, etc. Rambam's innovation is that humans were placed in the world not to exclusively satisfy their physical drives, which is what animals do, but rather to utilize the intelligence that God endowed them with to understand their Creator and His universe. The Mishnah continues by stressing that in explicitly recording that man is made in His image, God displays more love than one who favors another but does not inform him of it. Finally, *Tosafot Yom Tov* notes that by the Mishnah's citing a verse said to Noah before the emergence of the Nation of Israel, its contents must apply to all of mankind.

As far as the second point is concerned, the Mishnah mentions that Balaam will have no portion in the world to come, upon which Rambam comments:

> It mentions Balaam, who is not an Israelite, because the devout of the nations of the world will have a portion in the world to come, and the Mishnah notes that Balaam is among the wicked of the nations of the world, and [therefore] he has no portion in the world to come (*Peirush ha-Mishnayot*, *Sanhedrin* 10:2).[43]

---

43. The Mishnah is in accordance with the view of R. Yehoshua (BT *Sanhedrin* 105a; Tosefta *Sanhedrin*, Tzukermandel 13:2).

Ki Teitzei

How can a Gentile be devout? Rambam answers that the term refers to: "everyone who accepts the seven Noahide laws and is careful to observe them" (*Hilchot Melachim* 8:11). Those laws are, in principle, moral laws which prohibit theft and murder, and demand the institution of civil law, as summarized by *Torah Temimah*:

> All of these commands are built for and are the basis of the existence of the world, the habitation of countries in a manner that allows a secure life, maintenance of possessions, and merciful and empathetic feelings toward other creatures, as is obvious to all (Exod. 21, note 277).[44]

Furthermore, Jewish communities are obligated to supply social services to non-Jews, as is evident from the following Talmudic excerpt:

> We support the poor of the heathen along with the poor of Israel, and visit the sick of the heathen along with the sick of Israel, and bury the poor of the heathen along with the dead of Israel [but not in the same cemetery] in the interests of peace (BT *Gittin* 61a).

Rambam (*Hilchot Melachim* 10:12) notes that this segment refers to all non-Jews, even those who do not observe the Noahide laws, based on the following Biblical verses: "The Lord is good to all, and His mercy extends to all of His works" (Ps. 145:9); "her ways are ways of pleasantness, and all her paths are peace" (Prov. 3:17).[45]

To answer the original question, one can look upon the Jewish Nation as a kind of club whose members have made certain commitments upon joining. Examples of commitments are to provide

---

44. For a thorough discussion of these laws, see: Abba Engelberg, *The Ethics of Exodus* (2014), pp. 287-291.
45. Abba Engelberg, *The Ethics of Leviticus* (2018), p. 351.

interest-free loans to each other and to help other members with their donkeys (cars) whenever they misbehave. Non-members of the club do not expect to receive these benefits, nor do they contribute their time and energy to provide them; they do not expect to receive interest-free loans, nor do they plan to make interest-free loans to club members. However, as shown above, although members do not provide financial benefits to non-members, they highly respect non-members, especially those who exhibit admirable behavior.

Modern Questions

Road Assistance

R. Ovadia Yosef was asked whether one driving on an inter-city highway is required to stop if he sees a stranded motorist whose car has broken down, if the former is indeed capable of helping (*Yechaveh Daat* 5:65). R. Ovadia points out that at the very least, Jews are commanded to be benevolent. According to Rambam (*Sefer ha-Mitzvot*, shoresh 2; *Hilchot Evel* 14:1), the requirement of benevolence is a rabbinic extension of the mitzvah to love one's neighbor as oneself.

However, R. Ovadia tries to relate such help to the mitzvah associated with loading and unloading, as well as *tzaar baalei chaim*. This is not simple for a number of reasons. First, a car is not a living creature which can suffer from pain. Second, the original law relates to transfer of a burden, not transporting human beings.

He answers these questions by noting that Rambam (*Hilchot Rotzeach* 13:9) requires helping load the burden of a Gentile placed on an animal owned by a Jew because of the distress caused to the Jew, who would otherwise have to wait a long time. He notes that Sma (R. Yehoshua Falk, *Choshen Mishpat* 272:13) holds that this is because of *tzaar baalei chaim* since, if it is forbidden with respect to animals, it applies all the more so to humans.[46] In short, although the

---

46. In agreement with Rashba (*Teshuvot* 1:252), but in disagreement with *Chavot Ya'ir* (191) and Radbaz (*Teshuvot* 2:728), who say that an animal

car does not suffer, its driver does and the *halachah* takes that into consideration.

As far as the second objection, which relates to broadening the realm of application, R. Ovadia found support in the *Aruch ha-Shulchan* (*Choshen Mishpat* 272:8), who speaks of a horse-drawn wagon that became mired in mud. In such a case, a passer-by must help unload the wagon (the mitzvah of unloading) in order to dig it out, and then reload it. The law has been generalized from the animal's back to a wagon, even though *tza'ar ba'alei chaim* is not necessarily involved. Furthermore, if the wagon's wheel fell off, the passer-by is required to repair it if he knows how, and even to accompany it for a while in order to ascertain that the wheel has been fixed. If the wagon is empty, the situation hardly differs from that of a car which essentially carries its passengers only.

Hunting

R. Yechezkel Landau (1713-1793) was asked by a wealthy man who owned forests in which wild animals roamed freely, whether there is anything wrong with him hunting the animals for sport (*Noda be-Yehudah, Mahadurah Tanyana, Yoreh De'ah* 10). In his answer, he distinguishes between the letter of the law and recommended moral behavior.

The Talmud (BT *Avodah Zarah* 11a) says that at the death of a king, one may mutilate his animals by cutting the tendons above the hoofs so that they become unusable in the future, which is a form of honoring the dead king. Tosafot in *Avodah Zarah* (s.v. *okrin*) implies this is permitted only because by glorifying the king one honors the entire nation, and the needs of the nation supersede the prohibition of *tza'ar ba'alei chaim*. However, both *Piskei Tosafot* (BT *Avodah Zarah, Lifnei Eideihen* 11) and Tosafot (BT *Bava Metzia* 32b, s.v. *mi-divrei*) imply that even if the benefit is only to an individual, it is

---

may be overloaded, but a person should have enough sense to avoid such a situation.

permitted. This approach was adopted by R. Yisrael Isserlein (1390-1460), who states that animals were only created to satisfy man's needs (*Kiddushin* 4:14, based on Gen. 1:26), and even to cut the tongue of a chicken to enable it to speak, or the ears and tail of a dog to beautify it, are permitted. His proof is from the Talmud, which permits one to overload one's donkey (BT *Bava Metzia* 32b) and to castrate various animals (BT *Shabbat* 110b, BT *Chagigah* 14b), as the necessity arises (*Terumat ha-Deshen*, *Pesak* 105). Furthermore, *Noda be-Yehudah* notes that killing is not included in *tza'ar ba'alei chaim* altogether, since kosher slaughter is obviously permitted, although he seems to be unaware that frequently when hunting, the beast is "only" injured or maimed in a way which does indeed cause serious and permanent pain (*Chelkat Ya'akov*, *Choshen Mishpat* 34:4).

From a moral point of view, *Noda be-Yehudah* arrives at quite the opposite conclusion. He starts by pointing out that only two Biblical characters are mentioned as being hunters: Nimrod is mentioned as being "a mighty hunter before the Lord" (Gen. 10:9) and Esau is characterized as "a man acquainted with hunting" (Gen. 25:27). The former, whose name is derived from the Hebrew word for "rebellion" (BT *Pesachim* 94b), was one of the leaders in the construction of the tower of Babel (BT *Chullin* 89a), who later cast Abraham into a burning furnace (BT *Eruvin* 53b) and introduced military battles to mankind (Maharsha, BT *Eruvin* 53b) as Amraphel (Gen. 14:1). Esau, in addition to the Biblically-enumerated sins of disgracing the tradition of the birthright by selling it for a bowl of red lentil soup (Gen. 25:29-34) and planning to murder Jacob (Gen. 27:41), is described in the Talmud as a rapist, heretic, and serial murderer (BT *Bava Batra* 16b).

Moving from *aggadah* (narrative) to *halachah*, Rema (*Orach Chaim* 223:6) cites Mahari Veil (1385-1456), who says not to say the blessing *she-hecheyanu* (normally said upon purchasing new clothing) on garments made from animal skins, and *Mishnah Berurah* (223:25) adds that this is the case even if they are from non-kosher animals.

Ki Teitzei

Apparently, the thoughts aroused by such apparel are quite disgusting and clash with the moral principle that "the Lord is good to all, and He is merciful to all of His creations" (Ps. 145:9). Although Rema finds the reasoning to be quite weak, since if that approach were to be taken literally, Judaism would insist upon vegetarianism, he notes that many do indeed observe this custom.

Noda be-Yehudah proceeds to stress the level of respect which is displayed even toward wild animals such as wolves, lions, bears, leopards, and panthers. Even if they killed a person, they may be put to death only by a court of 23, if they are domesticated and are owned. According to R. Akiva (whose view Rambam accepts, *Hilchot Sanhedrin* 5:2), only a snake which has bitten someone may be killed on the spot (*Sanhedrin* 1:4). If not domesticated, animals may be killed for safety reasons, but only if they enter an inhabited area. There is no intent to allow one to enter a forest and seek out animals if there is no danger that they will wander into a settlement, and in such a case "there is no mitzvah and one is merely pursuing his heart's lust."

Noda be-Yehudah does, however, make an exception with regard to furriers and trappers who support themselves by hunting, whose behavior is not designated as being cruel, for how is killing non-kosher animals for their skins any different from slaughtering kosher animals for sustenance? All creatures were given to man to fulfill his needs. Only when such activities are engaged in to provide entertainment, rather than for the purpose of providing a livelihood, are they termed "cruelty."

Noda be-Yehudah proceeds to say that the dissuasion offered until this point was of the meta-halachic variety, which could perhaps be associated with the command to "do what is proper and good in the eyes of the Lord" (Deut. 6:18). He then transitions to the clear-cut halachic requirement of not endangering oneself. Note that Esau, who is described as "a man acquainted with hunting," in justifying his flippant relinquishing of his entitlement, says: "Behold, I am going to die, so why do I need this birthright" (Gen. 25:32). Although Rashi cites *Midrash Aggadah* (p. 64), according to which Esau feared the many prohibitions punishable by death if he were to serve as a priest (as the priesthood was originally intended for the first-borns), *Noda be-Yehudah* says that the verse retains its simple meaning, which is that his profession, which involves circulating among ferocious beasts, endangers him daily, as explained by Rashbam.

Noda be-Yehudah then asks another question. If it is prohibited for a Jew to risk his life, how could one be a professional hunter? From his answer, one sees the great importance Judaism attaches to making a living rather than taking money from charity, even if a degree of peril is involved. He bases himself on the verses in this portion that prohibit withholding the wages of a day laborer, which state:

> You may not withhold the wages of a poor or destitute hired worker… you must give him his wage on the day [of his work] and not let the sun set over it, for he is poor and he risks his life for it (Deut. 24:14-15).

With respect to the phrase "he risks his life for it," the question that arises is to what does the word "it" refer? Ramban understands that it alludes to his wages, when he explains: "If you do not pay him immediately when he leaves his job, he will go home and his wages will remain with you until the morning, and he will die of starvation during the night." The Midrash (*Sifrei Ki Teitzei* 279; *Midrash Tannaim*, Deut. 24:15; BT *Bava Metzia* 112a), cited by Rashi, believes that "it" relates to the risk involved in performing his task, which may well have required climbing up a ramp or suspending oneself from a tree, thus implying that one is allowed to endanger his life in order to make a living.

The only additional exception to the prohibition of risking one's life is the requirement to serve as a soldier to protect one's nation, as clearly indicated in the book of Numbers (32:6).

Ki Teitzei

In conclusion, although there are opinions which hold that animals were created to pleasure humans, and if one enjoys hunting it should be permitted, nevertheless *Noda be-Yehudah* posits that the element of danger involved is sufficient to prohibit it as unnecessary life endangerment, based on the Talmudic exegesis of the verse stating that one should live according to the laws of the Torah (Lev. 18:5), and not allow himself to die in their fulfillment (BT *Yoma* 85b), and *a fortiori* he may not endanger himself for a lesser purpose. In addition, he considers hunting to be grossly inappropriate from a moralistic point of view and most certainly in conflict with the commandment to do only what is proper in the eyes of the Lord (Deut. 6:18).

MEDICAL EXPERIMENTATION

Noda be-Yehudah has laid the basis for dealing with the question of whether one may subject animals to pain if medical knowledge relevant to humans can be derived thereby. On the one hand, *tza'ar ba'alei chaim* is a very important principle. On the other hand, since animals were created to aid mankind, if political or financial benefit can be gained, there are no constraints, as long as all relevant procedures are performed in the least oppressive manner.

Even before *Noda be-Yehudah*, Rema had posited (based on the previously cited *Terumat ha-Deshen*):

> Anything needed for healing or other [beneficial] purposes is not subject to the prohibition of *tza'ar ba'alei chaim*. Accordingly, one may pluck the feathers of live geese without worrying about *tza'ar ba'alei chaim*. Nevertheless, the public refrains [from doing so], since it is cruel (Rema, *Even ha-Ezer* 5:14).

Chelkat Ya'akov's understanding (*Choshen Mishpat* 34:4) of this comment of Rema is that according to the letter of the law, *tza'ar ba'alei chaim* is permitted if it satisfies any particular need, but as an act of piety (*midat chasidut*), one should not cause pain to animals. He implies that those who wish to act beyond the letter of the law would refrain from medical experimentation.

Even according to *Chelkat Ya'akov*, however, the degree of need must be taken into account. For example, if a person's life might be saved by removing an animal's organ, he would probably have permitted doing so, even if the operation or its after-effect is painful to the animal. *Chelkat Ya'akov* himself cites the case of Samson, upon whom the Holy Spirit rested (Judg. 13:25), and whom the Talmud considers to be righteous to the extent that he never mentioned God's name in vain (BT *Sotah* 9b). Nevertheless, in fighting the Philistines, Samson tied torches to the tails of 150 pairs of foxes, which must have been exceedingly agonizing to them. *Chelkat Ya'akov* explains that this was permitted as part of a war by commandment (*milchemet mitzvah*—a war required by the Torah), and for such a war, Samson would actually be required to risk his own life and expose himself to potential pain as well. Similarly, with regard to the case at hand, since the preservation of life overrides virtually every other religious consideration (Lev. 18:5; BT *Yoma* 84b), one may pain an animal in order to save a person's life.

However, *Chelkat Ya'akov* distinguishes between an immediate threat and long-term potential benefit (which is itself subject to debate),[47] where he allows personal piety to play a role *(Choshen Mishpat* 35:3). R. Yechiel Ya'akov Weinberg (*Sridei Eish* 3:7), on the other hand, believes that personal piety is not relevant in such a situation, since the public may not be deprived due to the desire of a particular person to act piously. One may be strict only when the result of the stringency affects himself alone.

---

47. "Experts Debate Jewish View on Use of Animals in Medical Experimentation," JTA, Sept. 14, 1994.

Ki Teitzei

Summary

Ki Teitzei contains seventy-four *mitzvot*, a larger number of the 613 traditionally considered to be contained in the Torah than in any other portion. These laws include those between man and his immediate family, man and his fellow man, and man and animals, as well as straightforward statutes.

We focused on one specific directive, that of preventing pain to animals—*tza'ar ba'alei chaim*. After a detailed halachic discussion, it was noted that although most of humanity live today in a non-agrarian society, there are numerous opportunities to behave mercifully, or God forbid, cruelly, in dealing with animals, whether in a recreational (hunting) or scientific (medical experimentation) context. Furthermore, the command to interact with animals compassionately has been extended to inter-human activity as well. In this sense, there is a degree of reinforcing overlap between the various categories of laws described in this portion.

Ki Tavo

The portion of *Ki Tavo* deals with two main topics. The first relates to agricultural gifts which were to be bestowed upon the priests, the Levites, and the needy after the Land of Israel is divided among the tribes, while the second focuses on the centrality of Torah law in Jewish life, and the rewards and punishments associated with its fulfillment or lack thereof.

First fruits, called *bikkurim*, were to be brought to the Holy Temple by representatives of every household, where a prayer thanking God for His beneficence was conducted by the priests, who were then presented with those very fruits.

A number of tithes were to be brought from agricultural produce, and were to be distributed to the priests (*terumah, bikkurim*), the Levites (*ma'aser rishon*), and poor people (*ma'aser ani*). Other tithes were to be eaten by the farmer himself and his family in Jerusalem (*ma'aser sheini* and the produce of trees in their fourth year of growth—*neta revai*). Some of these tithes were given yearly, while others followed a three-year cycle. After two three-year cycles came the Sabbatical year. *Ki Tavo* contains the formal declaration which the farmer was to make after each three-year cycle (on the day before Passover of the fourth and seventh years of the seven-year cycle, each of which is called *shnat ha-bi'ur*).

Ki Tavo

The Ceremony on Mt. Gerizim and Mt. Ebal

The Three Sets of Stones

The second topic opens with a reminder of the initial covenant between God and Israel (Exod. 24:7), which established their mutual chosenness, and continues with a command to engrave the entire Torah "very clearly" (Deut. 27:8) on a set of twelve stones. The Torah (Deut. 27) states:

> **2** And it will be, on the day that you cross the Jordan to the land that the Lord your God is giving you, that you are to set up for yourself huge stones and plaster them with lime. **3** And you must write upon them all the words of this Torah when you cross… **4** And it will be, when you cross the Jordan, that you are to set up these stones, [regarding] which I command you this day, on Mount Ebal… **5** And there, you are to build an altar to the Lord… **7** And you are to slaughter peace offerings, and you will eat there, and you will rejoice before the Lord your God. **8** You are [then] to write upon the stones all the words of this Torah, very clearly.

These verses are a bit repetitive and somewhat confusing. However, based on their actual implementation as described in the book of Joshua (4:1-9, 20-24; 8:30-32), the Talmud (BT *Sotah* 35b) is able to piece together the following explanation:

> In consequence [of what is related in the Scriptures], you must conclude that there were three sets of stones: one which Moses caused to be erected in the land of Moab, for it says: "On that side of the Jordan, in the land of Moab, Moses commenced to explain this Law" (Deut. 1:5)… and one (the second set) which Joshua erected in the midst of the Jordan [to commemorate the miraculous drying up of the river to

enable the congregation to cross], for it says: "And Joshua set up twelve stones in the midst of the Jordan" (Josh. 4:9), and one (the third set) which he erected in Gilgal [Rashi: after building the altar at Mt. Ebal, he dismantled (the stones) and brought them to Gilgal, and installed them there], for it says: "And these twelve stones, which they took out of the Jordan, Joshua set up in Gilgal [where the Tabernacle resided for fourteen years]" (Josh. 4:20).

R. Eliyahu Mizrachi (Deut. 27:2) further elucidates that twelve stones were set up in the Jordan to commemorate the miracle, while another twelve stones were extracted from the Jordan to be taken to Mt. Ebal, to be used in the construction of an altar. The Torah would be engraved on those stones, which would then be dismantled and taken to Gilgal, where they were to be reassembled. He parses vv. 2-3 as follows: "you are to set up for yourself huge stones" refers to the stones mounted in the bed of the Jordan River; "and plaster them with lime. And you must write upon them all the words of this Torah" refers to the stones which were extracted from the river, used as an altar at Mt. Ebal, and as slates upon which the Torah was written before they were transferred to Gilgal.

The Mishnah (*Sotah* 7:5) explains the words "very clearly" in v. 8 to mean that the entire Torah was to be engraved on them in the seventy languages known to the Rabbis. But how could one fit the entire Torah with seventy translations onto a few stones? Ramban (Deut. 27:3) concludes that either the stones were enormous, or this was one of the miraculous occasions when "the smaller contained the larger." Abravanel says that only the book of Deuteronomy was inscribed; *Tosafot Yom Tov* cites Saadiah Gaon, who says that it was only the list of the 613 commands; and Ralbag says it was the blessings and curses which appear immediately afterwards. *Torah Temimah* (Deut. 27:8, based on Rashi, Exod. 24:12, s.v. *va-yomer*) goes even further, saying that only the Ten Commandments were

Ki Tavo

written, which he derives from the wording of the verse which speaks of writing "all of the words [commands] of the Torah," rather than all of the Torah. A second point in favor of the view of *Torah Temimah* is the Talmud's claim (BT *Sotah* 35b) that the stones were engraved in seventy languages to make their contents accessible to the nations of the world, since it was their duty to be conversant with them. However, it is known that Gentiles are only commanded to observe the seven Noahide laws. Only if the writing corresponded to the Ten Commandments, which roughly overlap the Noahide laws, may one say that it was required reading for non-Jews.

The Ceremony

After describing the stones, altar, and sacrifices, the Torah portrays an elaborate ceremony in which twelve blessings and curses would be pronounced before the entire congregation. These blessings and curses were hinted at in the first three verses of the portion of *Re'eh*, which opens with the verse: "Behold, I set before you today a blessing and a curse" (Deut. 11:26), upon which Rashi comments: "those that would be stated, [respectively,] on Mount Gerizim and on Mount Ebal." Details of the ceremony were explicated, apparently on the same day, in the portion of *Ki Tavo*, where the Torah states:

> The following will stand on Mt. Gerizim to bless the people when you cross the Jordan: Simeon, Levi, Judah, Issachar, Joseph, and Benjamin. And the following will stand on Mt. Ebal for the curse: Reuben, Gad, Asher, Zebulun, Dan, and Naftali. The Levites will speak up, saying to every individual of Israel in a loud voice: "Cursed be the man...." And all the people will respond, saying "Amen" (Deut. 27:12-26).

The Midrash (*Tanchuma Balak* 12) notes the difference in phraseology used regarding those who were "to bless the people," as opposed to those who stood on Mt. Ebal "for the curse." The former implies an active eagerness, while the latter implies a passive displeasure. This message is highlighted later in the portion with respect to the more intensive blessings and curses, where God displays His involvement when blessings are to be endowed, using such phrases as: "The Lord your God will place you higher than all the nations of the earth" (Deut. 28:1); "The Lord will order the blessing to be with you in your granaries" (Deut. 28:8); "The Lord will establish you as His holy people, as He swore to you " (Deut. 28:9); "The Lord will open up for you His good treasury" (Deut. 28:12); and "The Lord will set you at the head, and not at the tail" (Deut. 28:13). God distances Himself, on the other hand, from the curses, using such phrases as: "All these curses will come upon you [as if by themselves]" (Deut. 28:15).

The implementation of the ceremony is described in the book of Joshua (8:33-35), and elaborated upon in the Mishnah (*Sotah* 7:5):

> How were the blessings and curses delivered? When Israel crossed the Jordan and came to Mt. Gerizim and Mt. Ebal, which are in Samaria… six tribes ascended to the summit of Mt. Gerizim and six tribes ascended to the summit of Mt. Ebal, and the priests and Levites and the Ark were stationed below in the center, with the priests surrounding the Ark and the Levites [surrounding] the priests, and all Israel on this side and that side, for it says: "And all Israel, and their elders and officers and their judges, stood on this side of the Ark [and on that side, opposite the priests the Levites, the bearers of the Ark of the covenant of the Lord; the stranger as well as the native-born, half of them facing Mt. Gerizim and half of them facing Mt. Ebal, as Moses the servant of the Lord had commanded, to bless the people of Israel first]" (Josh. 8:33). They [the Levites] turned their faces towards Mt. Gerizim and opened with the blessing: "Blessed is the man who does not make a graven or molten image," and both parties [on both mountains] respond "Amen." They then turned their faces

towards Mt. Ebal and opened with the curse: "Cursed is the man who makes a graven or molten image," and both parties respond "Amen" (Deut. 27:15). [They continued] until they completed the blessings and curses. After that they brought the stones [which had been extracted from the Jordan], built the altar, and plastered it with plaster, and inscribed on it all of the words of the Torah in seventy languages, as it says: "very clearly." Then they took the stones [from Mt. Ebal] and went and spent the night in their place [i.e., they set up the altar in Gilgal (Josh. 4:20)].

Ibn Ezra (Deut. 27:12) notes that on Mt. Gerizim, the sons of Jacob's wives, Leah and Rachel, stood. However, since there were eight of them, Reuben and Zebulun, as the oldest and youngest of Leah's sons, joined the four sons of the concubines on Mt. Ebal. R. S.R. Hirsch on this verse says that the Torah went out of its way to ensure that the tribes descended from the concubines would not be considered inferior, and that is why they were joined by the eldest and youngest of Leah's sons. The Levites, who proclaimed the blessings and curses, represented all of Israel, and everyone answered "Amen." Nevertheless, just to reinforce the feeling of equality, when the Levites faced Mt. Ebal for the curses, it was as if the tribes on Mt. Ebal were directing the curses at those tribes standing on Mt. Gerizim, while the blessings, which seemingly emanated from Mt. Gerizim, were metaphorically directed at the tribes on Mt. Ebal. The universality and democratic nature associated with the ceremony is stressed by the concluding verse in the description of the ceremony: "There was not a word of all that Moses commanded which Joshua did not read before all the congregation of Israel, with the women, and the little ones, and the strangers that walked among them" (Josh. 8:35).

Chizkuni (Deut. 27:12, based on BT *Shabbat* 55b) explains that it was important for the tribe of Reuben to be on the side which the Levites faced when they said: "Cursed is he who sleeps with his father's wife" (Deut. 27:20), and to say "Amen" while staring at the Levites, to emphasize that the suspicion that Reuben slept with his father's concubine Bilhah was baseless. On the other hand, R. Bachya comments that it was important that the tribe of Simeon be included in the group toward whom the blessings were directed, since Moses did not intend to bless that tribe before his demise, as punishment for the incitement of its prince, Zimri b. Salu, who had led the tribe in sin. Had the tribe of Simeon been placed on Mt. Ebal, the curse would have had no blessing by Moses to counterbalance it.

The Talmud notes that the Levites are listed in the Bible as one of the tribes which stood on Mt. Gerizim, but the Mishnah states that they stood below. How is this possible? The Talmud cites three answers:

> R. Eliezer b. Ya'akov says:... The elders of the priests and Levites were below and the rest above. R. Yoshiyah said: All [the Levites] who were qualified to serve [Rashi: to carry the Ark; i.e., between the ages of thirty and fifty] were below, and the rest above. Rebbi says: Both these [the priests and Levites] and also these [the Israelites] were standing below.... What is [the meaning of] "on" [the mountain]? [It means] "near to" [Rashi: as it says in Josh. 8:33] (BT *Sotah* 37a).

The Talmud summarizes the order of events at the ceremony (BT *Sotah* 36a):

> After that they brought the stones, built the altar, and plastered it with plaster, and inscribed thereon all the words of the Torah in seventy languages.... Then they sacrificed burnt offerings and peace offerings, ate and drank and rejoiced, pronounced the blessings and the curses, and came and lodged in Gilgal, as it is said: "Carry them over with you and lay them down in the lodging place" (Josh. 4:3).

Ki Tavo

This order corresponds to that appearing in *Ki Tavo* (Deut. 27) and the book of Joshua (8:30-35). Surprisingly, however, the Mishnah in *Sotah* reverses the order, placing the blessings and curses before the construction of the altar and the writing of the Torah on its stones. *Tiferet Yisrael* (*Boaz*) answers that of course the altar at Mt. Ebal was built first; however, the writing on the stones took place only after the stones reached their semi-permanent resting place, which was Gilgal. Although the writing is mentioned both in the Torah and the book of Joshua before the blessings and curses, it must be remembered that the stones used at Ebal and Gilgal were the same, so the fact that the writing is mentioned earlier does not mean that it could not have been done after the stones reached their final "lodging place" (Josh. 4:3). When the Mishnah says: "After that they brought the stones, built the altar, and plastered it with plaster," it is referring not to the original construction on Mt. Ebal, but to the second time at Gilgal, when the writing was engraved on the stones.

The Vilna Gaon (Soncino *Sotah*, p. 177, note 4) corrected the Talmudic text so that instead of saying "pronounced the blessings and the curses," it says "pronounced the blessings," which is said to refer to grace after meals, and not the blessings and curses at the mountains, which took place earlier. However, although that change reconciles the Mishnah and the Talmud, it does not explain why they differ from the two Biblical texts which place the reciting of the blessings only after the altar had been built. It would have been more logical to emend the Mishnah so that it is in agreement with the Talmudic text and the two Biblical references.

THE BLESSINGS AND THE CURSES

As noted, there are twelve blessings and twelve curses. Although the text only contains the formulations of the curses, that there are parallel blessings is clear from the previously cited first verse of the portion of *Re'eh*. The twelve curses relate to: (1) idolatry, (2) dishonoring parents, (3) removing boundaries, (4) misleading the blind, (5) dishonestly judging the weak, (6-9) sexual immorality, (10) murder, (11) bribery, (12) violation of Torah law.

Clearly, the last curse is all-inclusive, while the first eleven stress particular sins. In fact, for that reason, some commentators consider there to have only been eleven curses. Rashbam (Deut. 27:15) says there were twelve, one corresponding to each tribe, while Rashi (Deut. 27:24) says there were eleven for the same reason, just that the tribe of Simeon was not included in the count, since Moses did not intend to bless that tribe as part of his farewell address. Perhaps the symbolism is that just as all of the tribes compose the Nation of Israel, similarly refraining from all of the enumerated sins characterizes the true nature of the nation.

However, the question remains: Why were these specific laws chosen out of the entire group of 613 *mitzvot*? Rashbam (ibid.) says that all of the sins enumerated are generally transgressed privately, with the exception of idolatry and murder, and for that reason the related verses (27:15, 24) state explicitly that the reference is to when those sins are transgressed secretly. Publicly transgressed sins are punishable in court, but those listed here will never be brought before a court, so that chastisement is left to God Himself. This is the import of the verse in the portion of *Nitzavim*: "The hidden things belong to the Lord our God [to avenge], but the revealed things apply to us and to our children forever, [namely] that we must fulfill all the words of this Torah [by administering the accepted disciplinary measures—lashes, stoning, burning, beheading, and strangulation]" (Deut. 29:28). As an example, Rashbam states that committing adultery is not mentioned, because it is publicly noticeable if a man enters the house of a married woman. However, disrespecting one's parents or having relations with one's father's wife (27:20), an animal (20:21), or a sister (20:22) occur in places to which the sinner has free access, and hence do not arouse suspicion.

The twelve curses may be looked upon in another way. As

previously noted, the entire Torah, or perhaps all of the 613 commands, were written on stones extracted from the Jordan. Such a work would have been a delight for the scholarly-oriented, especially at a time when written material was at a premium. However, the Torah was meant to be observed by the entire populace, even the uneducated and non-intellectuals. Seeing the entire Torah engraved in stone might have been too much for such people to digest. Interestingly, as an alternative interpretation, *Torah Temimah* (Deut. 27:8) explains the "seventy languages" that appeared on the stones as the seventy faces of the Torah, i.e., the many different ways of interpreting the contents of the Torah, certainly a challenging intellectual exercise. The blessings and curses, however, focus on a much smaller number of extreme cases of irreligion and immorality, and could certainly be much more easily absorbed by the masses. The idea is similar to that proposed by R. Yosef Zvi Rimon (*Haggadah mi-Mekorah*, 2013) to explain different sections of the Haggadah, where one segment appeals to text-oriented scholars, while another targets children and adults who learn best by illustration and demonstration. A shortened version would suffice to elucidate to the entire congregation exactly what was expected of them, so that they would be cognizant of the reward that awaited them for observing the commands and the punishment to be meted out for disobedience.

As important as observance of the law is, it must be recalled that Judaism is based on three pillars: Torah, Divine service, and acts of kindness (*Avot* 1:2). Accordingly, the inscription of the Torah on the altar stones was accompanied by Divine service, namely the bringing of sacrifices (Deut. 27:7), which served not only as a catalyst for prayer, but as an occasion for merriment and refreshments. Finally, the positive formulation of three of the curses—honoring parents, helping the disadvantaged, and acting fairly and considerately toward the weak—certainly emphasize the centrality of *chesed* (acts of kindness) in Judaism. Thus, the ceremony at Mt. Gerizim and

Mt. Ebal presented the nation with a microcosm of what the Jewish religion is about, and what it expects of its members.

FOUR QUESTIONS ABOUT LATER TRAGEDIES

The remainder of the portion is devoted to the subject of reward and punishment. First, the bountiful blessings, which are the reward of every individual who observes the laws of the Torah, are listed, followed by the *tochachah*, the curses which are the punishment of those who ignore and violate those commandments. A parallel presentation appears in the portion of *Bechukotai* at the end of the book of Leviticus, and a comparison of the two treatments of the same subject may be found in *The Ethics of Leviticus* (pp. 288-298). *Ki Tavo* concludes with a short summary of the miracles which the nation had already experienced in its short history, which should provide adequate motivation for accepting and observing Israel's part of the covenant.

The two versions of the *tochachah* provide material which can be helpful in answering the following questions, which have arisen in the few generations that have elapsed since the Holocaust, specifically:

1. How could God have allowed the occurrence of the many tragedies which visited the Jewish people, culminating in the Holocaust?
2. If God was in fact involved in later tragedies, why did He conceal His involvement?
3. If God was in fact involved, what were the Jews being punished for?
4. How can the Jewish people attempt to avoid future tragedies?

Ki Tavo

ANSWERING THE FIRST QUESTION: HOW COULD GOD HAVE ALLOWED THE OCCURRENCE OF THE MANY TRAGEDIES WHICH VISITED THE JEWISH PEOPLE, CULMINATING IN THE HOLOCAUST?

The Sages applied relevant verses from *Ki Tavo* to the various calamities that have dotted Jewish history. Consider the following verses:

> The Lord will bring you, and the king whom you set over yourselves, to *a nation that you have not known*, neither you nor your fathers; and there you will serve other gods of wood and stone (Deut. 28:36).

According to Abravanel (Deut. 28:15), "you, and the king whom you set over yourselves" refers to the last of the Judean Kings, who was carried away to Babylonia in the waning days of the first Temple. This approach is consistent with the view of the Talmud (BT *Yoma* 52b) that when the Torah was rediscovered by Hilkiah the priest, it was open to the above verse, which the righteous King Josiah interpreted as referring to the destruction of the First Temple and the exile of the Jewish nation.[48]

R. Yitzchak Arama (1420-1494), in his *Akeidat Yitzchak* (*sha'ar* 98, *Ki Tavo*), points out that although the leaders of the nation were exiled with King Jehoiachin in 598 BCE, the "poorest peasants" remained (2 Kings 24:14). Even at the time of the Temple's destruction in 586 BCE, Jeremiah encouraged the Israelites to remain in Jerusalem and pay their respects to Nebuchadnezzar (Jer. 27:17). Accordingly, the verses from Deuteronomy which follow relate to people who owned land and engaged in agriculture, but continued to execute the three cardinal sins which brought on the destruction of the First Temple:

---

48. For a more extensive treatment of this subject, see Abba Engelberg, *The Ethics of Exodus* (2014), pp. 379-381. For background history with respect to the destruction of the two Temples, see: Abba Engelberg, *The Ethics of Leviticus* (2018), pp. 356-366.

idol worship, immorality, and bloodshed:

> You will take much seed out to the field, yet you will gather in little... You will plant vineyards and work [them], but you will neither drink of [their] wine, nor gather [the grapes].... You will have olive trees throughout all your boundaries, but you will have no oil for anointing.... You will bear sons and daughters, but you will not have them, because they will go into captivity. All your trees and all the fruit of your soil the locust will make destitute. *The stranger who is among you will rise above you, higher and higher...* All these curses will befall you, pursuing you and overtaking you to destroy you because you *did not obey the Lord*, your God, to observe His commandments and statutes (Deut. 28:38-45).

The phrase "a nation that you have not known" in Deut. 28:36 seems inappropriate, since the Babylonians had occupied Israel for many years and their beliefs were quite familiar to its inhabitants. However, *Akeidat Yitzchak* explains that the reference here is to the tens of thousands of Jews who had already been exiled (as indicated by the beginning of the verse) and had adopted the idol-worshipping habits of their neighbors. He transposes the phrases of the verse as if to say, "you will serve other gods of wood and stone that you have not known, neither you nor your fathers" or, in its original order, "you will be brought to a nation that you did not know in the sense of accepting its beliefs."

The same message, stressing the futility of their efforts while they were still indulging in sin, was contained in the prophecy of the contemporary prophet Haggai, who said: "You have sown much, but you bring in little; you eat without being satiated; you drink without getting full; you dress, but it does not warm you; and he who profits, profits into a bag with holes [through which his profits slip]" (Hag. 1:6).

Ki Tavo

Finally, the text speaks of "the stranger who is among you," namely the Babylonians who lived among them in the Land of Israel, according to *Akeidat Yitzchak*, who ruled them harshly, and all this because they "did not obey the Lord."

Ramban (Lev. 26:16, Deut. 28:42), on the other hand, says that the entire *tochachah* which appears in *Ki Tavo* refers to events that occurred at the end of the Second Temple period and after its destruction, as opposed to the events described in *Bechukotai*, which took place at the time of the destruction of the First Temple. In Lev. 26:16, Ramban states that Deut. 28:36 refers specifically to King Agrippa I, a grandson of Herod. Ramban derives this by analyzing the words: "The Lord will bring you, *and the king whom you set over yourselves*, to a nation that you have not known." Agrippa was brought to Rome, home of a nation not known to the Jews, where he partied with the insane emperor Caligula, who eventually appointed him governor over the Land of Israel. Ramban attributes the destruction of the Second Temple to Agrippa's behavior in Rome. Furthermore, Ramban explains that the verse speaks of a "king whom you set over yourselves," as opposed to "a king who rules over you [based on Torah law]." Agrippa was crowned illegally, since he was not even Jewish (his mother was not Jewish). His father, although Jewish (son of Mariamne), was certainly not of the tribe of Judah. Finally, Babylonia could not be considered to be "a nation that you have not known," since it was quite well known to the Jews because of its proximity and the constant state of warfare which existed between Israel and Babylonia.

In Deuteronomy 28:42, Ramban suggests that the king being referred to might have been King Aristobulus II, whom Pompey defeated and took back with him to Rome in chains, in order to participate in a victory march. Historical details are provided in **Appendix V: The Last Years of the Second Temple.**

The *tochachah* continues: "The Lord will bring upon you *a nation from afar… a nation whose language you will not understand, a brazen nation*" (Deut. 28:49-50). All of the commentaries relate these verses to the Roman period. Ramban (Lev. 26:16) points out that the reference could not be to Babylonia or Assyria, because those countries are not far away, and apparently the intelligentsia spoke their language, as indicated by the request of Hezekiah's officers that Sennacherib's generals converse with them in Aramean so that the populace would not understand the interchange (2 Kings 18:26, Isa. 36:11). Abravanel (Deut. 28:49) explains that each of the three repetitions of the word "nation" in vv. 49-50 refer to a different event in the Roman period. The first was when Pompey took Aristobulus II back to Rome with him; the second was when Herod defeated Antigonus, the son of Aristobulus II, by joining with the Romans and massacring the residents of Jerusalem to the point that Herod feared that there would be nobody left for him to govern; and the third was in the time of Agrippa II (son of Agrippa I, great-grandson of Herod), when Titus besieged Jerusalem, breached its walls, and burned the Second Temple.

Abravanel believes that v. 36 relates to the Judean king being exiled, while v. 49 speaks of the arrival of an enemy from a great distance. Had v. 36 been referring to the Roman period, why would it speak of the population being exiled before it even mentions the enemy's arrival in v. 49? He thus rejects Ramban's view and relates v. 36 to a First Temple occurrence.

Akeidat Yitzchak points out that the siege imposed by Titus was so devastating that the verses which follow the reference to Titus truly characterize the catastrophic conditions which prevailed, namely:

> And during the siege and the desperation which your enemies will bring upon you, you will eat the fruit of your womb, the flesh of your sons and daughters, whom the Lord your God gave you. The most tender and delicate man among you will begrudge his own brother and the wife of his embrace, and the rest of his children whom he will leave over, of giving

Ki Tavo

any one of them of the flesh of his children that he is eating [he will not share the meat of the dead children with the remaining children] (Deut. 28:53-55).

In the verses which follow, *Akeidat Yitzchak* sees a prophetic prediction of his own experiences during the Inquisition. Although the Jews were integrated among their non-Jewish neighbors, they did not achieve tranquility, but rather were constantly being disgraced, suspected of proselytizing, and subject to persecution. He felt that this second (present) exile, when the Jews live among the Gentiles and are a constant target of assault, is far more insufferable than the first, when although the Jews were subject to heavy taxation and onerous obligations, they were permitted to live as a group within their own communities. He further notes that a third of the Jews of his time were burned at the stake, a third escaped from Spain and Portugal or were in hiding, and the remainder lived in constant fear, as described in the following verses:

> And among those nations, you will not be calm, nor will your foot find rest. There, the Lord will give you a trembling heart, dashed hopes, and a depressed soul. And your life will hang in suspense before you. You will be in fear night and day, and you will not believe in your life. In the morning you will say, "If only it were evening!" and in the evening you will say, "If only it were morning!" because of the fear in your heart which you will experience and because of the sights that you will behold (Deut. 28:65-67).

According to R. Dovid Zvi Hoffman (Deut. 28:68), the phrase "and the Lord will bring you back to Egypt in ships," which appears in the next verse, refers to another historical event which occurred toward the end of the Second Temple period, during the tenure of Titus. As part of his efforts to quell the rebellion, he packed 17,000 Jews into ships and sent them to Egypt, the location of their past enslavement.

Finally, it is clear that the possibility of a holocaust was predicted in the Torah. One of the maledictions included in the *tochachah* of the portion of *Ki Tavo* is:

> And you will serve your enemy, whom the Lord will send against you, in hunger, and in thirst, and in nakedness, and in want of all things; and he will put a yoke of iron upon your neck, until he has destroyed you (Deut. 28:48).

This verse comes surprisingly close to describing the abominable conditions prevalent in concentration camps: starvation, nakedness, backbreaking work, and eventual death.

Answering the Second Question: If God Was in Fact Involved in Later Tragedies, Why Did He Conceal His Involvement?

If God had revealed His acquiescence to the catastrophes of the Holocaust and other tragedies, it would certainly have enhanced their function as punishment for straying from the ways of the Torah, if that was the intention, and prevented countless people from losing their faith. So why did He not do so?

It seems that with the exception of Revelation, God's way is to minimize His blatant intervention in Nature. Ramban (Gen. 6:19) notes with regard to Noah's ark that we know of thousands of species of animals, birds, and fish. How could they all fit into the ark? In addition, Noah had to store enough food to feed his entire family as well as all the other creatures for an entire year. He answers that only by a miracle was everything able to fit in. But then, he asks, why trouble Noah to make a huge ark that was 300 by 50 cubits? Two by four cubits would have sufficed.

Ramban's first answer is that God wished the ark to be so large that it stood out and became a conversation piece. When people became aware of its purpose, they might be stimulated to introspection and eventually to repentance. His second answer is that with regard to all of the miracles mentioned in the Bible, God's approach is to allow man to accomplish as much as he is capable of, and only then to intervene. Today, in the absence of manifest miracles, God's way is to camouflage His worldly involvement, and even His existence (*hester panim*). For modern man, belief in God cannot be patently obvious, for that would deprive man of his freedom of choice.

R. Jonathan Sacks[49] notes that even with regard to the splitting of the Reed Sea, the supernatural aspect, described as God telling Moses to "raise your staff and stretch out your hand over the sea and split it" (Exod. 14:16), is coupled with a scientifically sound explanation, when the Torah states: "And Moses stretched out his hand over the sea, and the Lord caused the sea [to go back] with a strong east wind all night, and He made the sea into dry land and the waters divided" (Exod. 14:21). Even to the extent that the splitting of the sea was miraculous, the Sages did not look at it as an *ad hoc* supernatural event, but rather as a pre-programmed occurrence dating from the time of the creation of the world, as indicated by the following Midrash:

> R. Yonatan said: The Holy One, blessed be He, made a condition with the sea [at the time of creation] that it should be split for the Israelites. This is the meaning of what is stated: "The sea returned to its full strength [*le-eitano*]" (Exod. 14:27). [Read this as] *le-tena'o* [to the condition] which had been agreed upon. R. Yirmiyah b. Elazar said: Not only did the Holy One blessed be He make conditions with the sea, but rather with everything that was created in the six days of creation. That is [the meaning of] what it says: "My hands stretched out the heavens and I commanded all

---

49. Jonathan Sacks, "The Divided Sea: Natural or Supernatural," *Covenant and Conversation, Beshalach,* 5779.

of their occupants" (Isa. 45:12).... I commanded the sun and the moon to stand [still] before Joshua... the ravens to sustain Elijah... the fire not to injure Hananiah, Mishael, and Azariah... the lions not to injure Daniel... the fish to vomit forth Jonah (*Gen. Rabbah* 5:5).

R. Harold Kushner wrote a book called *When Bad Things Happen to Good People* (1981). In reality, bad things can *only* happen to good people. Suppose one shoots a man who is trying to kidnap a child or molest a young girl. In that case, a bad thing happened to a bad person, and that is a good thing. However, if one shoots that same person when he is walking calmly down the street, a bad thing happened to a good person, which is a bad thing. What happens is called bad only if it happens to good people. By the principle of freedom of choice, God allows people to be bad, which in turn enables bad things to occur.

If a bell-shaped curve were to be constructed to describe people's quality, with Hitler's name appearing at a very negative value on the x-axis and Moses' name at a very positive value, with almost everyone falling between those two extremes, then most people's "goodness score" would hover around the hump at zero, but every once in a while there would be someone really good or really bad, whose "goodness score" would be in the tails. In fact, there were ten genocides in the twentieth century with more than one million victims, and fifteen with over half a million victims. The largest was perpetrated by Mao Tse-Dong; between 50 and 75 million innocent Chinese were killed under his aegis. Previously, Hideki Tojo, the Japanese general turned prime minister, who initiated the Second Sino-Japanese War in 1937, was responsible for the deaths of over 20 million Chinese. So almost 100 million Chinese non-combatants were killed in the twentieth century.[50] Of course, percentage-wise,

---

50. https://www.scaruffi.com/politics/dictat.html. Although this source only lists eight genocides of over one million, and associates "only" five million genocidal deaths with Hideki Tojo, other sources hold the latter responsible for twenty million deaths, and charge both Kim Il Sung of North Korea and

Ki Tavo

the Jews still suffered more, but unfortunately the Holocaust was not unique and accordingly illustrates how God's worldly intervention is attired in natural vestments.

ANSWERING THE THIRD QUESTION: IF GOD WAS IN FACT INVOLVED, WHAT WERE THE JEWS BEING PUNISHED FOR?
Clearly, direct guilt for the occurrence of the Holocaust falls on the shoulders of Hitler and his many willing executioners, just as guilt for the enslavement of the Israelites in Egypt falls on the shoulders of Pharaoh in spite of the fact that God had told Abraham many years earlier: "Your seed will be strangers in a land that is not theirs, and they will enslave them and oppress them for four hundred years" (Gen. 15:13). Similarly, responsibility for the destruction of the Temples must be placed on the shoulders of Nebuchadnezzar and Titus. Nevertheless, the Talmud (BT *Yoma* 9b) associates the destruction of the First Temple with idolatry, immorality, and bloodshed; and that of the Second Temple with groundless hatred (*sinat chinam*). *Ha'amek Davar* (Introduction to Genesis) explains that although the Jews in the Second Temple era were quite religious, they took different approaches in their observance of the *mitzvot*. Instead of accepting this diversity, they labeled members of alternate camps to be apostates, and this *sinat chinam* led to strife and sometimes even bloodshed. This behavior was so disturbing to God that He eventually allowed evil pagan forces to destroy the Temple.

One of the verses in the *tochachah* provides the following justification for the predicted tribulations: "because you did not serve the Lord your God with joyfulness and with gladness of heart, by reason of the abundance of all things" (Deut. 28:47). Rabbeinu Bachya understands the verse to be rebuking the Jews for not serving

---

Mengistu Haile Mariam of Ethiopia with killings of over one million innocent people. See: https://www.moreorless.net.au/killers/tojo.html; https://www.moreorless.net.au/killers/kim-il-sung.html; https://www.independent.co.uk/news/world/africa/mengistu-found-guilty-of-ethiopian-genocide-428233.html.

God with a sense of euphoric joy. Certainly, being able to do so would add an element of Divine energy to one's blessings and prayers. Unfortunately, many are overwhelmed by the vicissitudes of life and find it hard to mobilize the requisite enthusiasm to achieve true ecstasy; but is God so demanding that He deems such a deficiency sufficient to justify a holocaust? R. Jonathan Sacks[51] has put the stress on the last words of the verse, "by reason of the abundance of all things." He says that it is amazing that the Jews maintained their faith and observance in spite of expulsions, forced conversions, blood libels, and *autos da fé*; yet, when they attained democracy and freedom to behave as their hearts desired, many abandoned their piety and uniqueness in favor of the prevailing culture.

R. Sacks does not mean to rail against enjoying "the abundance of all things." On the contrary, he states:

> Asceticism is the denial of pleasure; hedonism is the worship of it. Judaism rejects both and instead invites us to sanctify pleasure: food, by the laws of *kashrut* and pronouncing blessings over enjoyment; drink, through *kiddush* at sacred times; sex, through the disciplines of marriage and *taharat ha-mishpachah* [family purity]. To be a Jew is to celebrate life, to see God in life, and to make a blessing over life. It is to find joy in family and community, to find meaning through constant study of Torah, and to share one's blessings with others.

The same idea is brought out by *Beit ha-Levi* in his interpretation of the verse in Genesis, in which Jacob beseeches God to save him "from the hand of my brother, from the hand of Esau" (Gen. 32:12) after the messengers whom he had sent to greet Esau reported that they had arrived "at your brother, at Esau" (Gen. 32:7). *Beit ha-Levi*,

---

51. Jonathan Sacks, "Judaism's Greatest Challenge," *Covenant and Conversation, Ki Tavo*, 5767.

in situ, interprets the twice-repeated phrase to stress that the Jewish nation looks upon itself as God's messenger to spread belief in God and moral behavior to all nations of the world. Since these principles are often hard to accept, Esau related to Israel in two distinct ways. One is manifested in his aggressively approaching Jacob's camp with 400 men (Gen. 32:7), and that is what is meant by the "hand of Esau." The other way is reflected in Esau's suggestion that they travel in tandem (Gen. 33:12), and that is what is meant by the "hand of my brother." Esau acts like a brother, but the ultimate result (if not the purpose) of his fraternization is to corrupt Jacob morally and divert him theologically from the desired path.[52]

Destruction of the Temples:

Akeidat Yitzchak (*sha'ar* 98, *Ki Tavo,* based on *Yossipon*) notes that both Temples were destroyed as a result of not heeding the words of the prophets and the Sages. Before their destruction, the religious leaders had urged the populace not to rebel against the ruling powers. Jeremiah had declared: "If you fight against the Babylonians, you will not succeed" (Jer. 32:5). R. Shimon b. Gamliel[53] and R. Yochanan b. Zakkai[54] had urged the nation to accept the offer of Titus that he would allow the Jews to remain in their land and observe their religion if they would be loyal to Rome.

The two approaches mentioned—that the Temples' destruction was a result of closeness to the Gentile world and accepting their hedonistic life-style, and that it resulted from not accepting the views of the prophets and Sages—are not contradictory. Judaism does not oppose enjoying life's pleasures. On the contrary, Judaism is in favor of maximizing one's physical enjoyment in this world, as may be understood from the Talmudic maxim: "In the future [world], man will be accountable for everything [edible] that his eye saw and he did

---

52. See Abba Engelberg, *The Ethics of Genesis* (2014), pp. 94, 134-137.
53. Mordechai Margolioth, *Encyclopedia le-Chachmei ha-Talmud ve-ha-Geonim*, p. 850.
54. See: Jewish Encyclopedia, Johanan b. Zakkai.

not eat" (JT *Kiddushin* 4:12). Also, in the spring, when one sees trees blossoming, the Talmud records the blessing over trees in bloom, which praises God, "Who has withheld nothing from His world and has created beautiful creatures and beautiful trees in it so that men may delight in them" (BT *Berachot* 43b). The two approaches, when synchronized, stress that although man is encouraged to enjoy worldly pleasures, he is urged to do so in a manner which harmonizes with the Torah's commandments as interpreted by the Sages and the prophets.

The Talmud cites another reason for the destruction:

> R. Yochanan said: Jerusalem was destroyed only because they gave judgments in accordance with Biblical law. Were they then to have judged based on torture and force? But say thus: because they based their judgments [strictly] upon Biblical law, and did not go beyond the requirements of the law (BT *Bava Metzia* 30b).

A number of questions arise:

A. What is the exact meaning of going "beyond the requirements of the law"?
B. How can there be a requirement to go "beyond the requirement"?
C. Even if there can be such a requirement, can failing to do so be so severe as to justify the destruction of the Second Temple?
D. In another location, does not the Talmud associate the destruction of the Second Temple with *sinat chinam*?

Answering Question A: What is the exact meaning of going "beyond the requirements of the law"?
The classical meaning of this concept is to be stricter with oneself than the law demands. The Talmud (BT *Bava Metzia* 24b) cites the view of Shmuel that if one found a purse with an identifying sign in

a busy marketplace, he should return it to its owner, even though the latter has certainly given up hope of finding it, in which case the finder is technically exempt from seeking the loser. Similarly, the father of Shmuel saw some donkeys in the desert, and noticed them again a year later. Once more, the assumption is that after such a long period, the owner despairs of ever finding them, and so the finder is permitted to keep them. Nevertheless, Shmuel's father sought the owner and returned them. In another case (BT *Bava Metzia* 30b), R. Yishmael b. R. Yosi, an older man, was asked to help another person with a load. Although the Torah generally requires a positive response in such a situation (Deut. 22:4), older people, for whom such behavior is considered undignified, are exempt. Nevertheless, R. Yishmael acted as if he were required, but in order not to embarrass himself, bought the entire load so that it would then be his.

If an expert craftsman performs a service gratis, but makes a costly mistake, he is exempt from compensating the client. Nevertheless, R. Chiya (BT *Bava Kama* 99b) reimbursed a client in such a situation, beyond the requirement of the law. At times, Rabbis even ruled that it was required to act beyond the requirements of the law, e.g., when Rav required Rabbah b. Bar Chana to pay his workers for moving a barrel of wine, even though they had negligently broken the barrel, causing all of its contents to be lost, nor was he permitted to demand compensation for the wasted wine (BT *Bava Metzia* 83a).

However, "going beyond the requirements of the law" can sometimes lead to being more lenient. Consider the famous story of Kamtza and Bar Kamtza:

> A certain man had a friend Kamtza and an enemy Bar Kamtza. He once made a party and said to his servant, "Go and bring Kamtza." The man went and brought Bar Kamtza. When the man [who gave the party] found him there he… took him by the hand and put him out. Said the other [Bar Kamtza]: "Since the Rabbis were sitting there and did not

stop him, this shows that they agreed with him. I will go and malign them at the king's palace." He went and said to the Emperor: "The Jews are rebelling against you." He said: "Who can confirm this?" He said to him: "Send them an offering and see whether they will offer it [on the altar]." So he sent with him a fine calf. While on the way, he made a blemish… in a place where for us it is [considered] a blemish but for them it is not. The Rabbis intended to offer it in order not to offend the king. R. Zechariah b. Avkulas said to them: "People will say that blemished animals may be offered on the altar." They then considered killing Bar Kamtza, so that he should not go [to the king] and tell him [that they had not offered his sacrifice]. R. Zechariah said to them: "They will say: 'He who makes a blemish on consecrated animals is to be put to death?'" R. Yochanan thereupon remarked: "The modesty of R. Zechariah b. Avkulas caused the destruction of our House, the burning of our Temple, and our exile from our land" (BT *Gittin* 55b-56a).

R. Shlomo Dichovsky (*Psikat Halachah u-Mediniut Pesikat ha-Halachah*, *Techumin* 38) notes that from a purely technical point of view, R. Zechariah b. Avkulas is one hundred percent correct. One does not sacrifice a blemished animal, nor is one who inflicts a blemish liable to the death penalty. However, *Magen Avraham* (*Orach Chaim* 256:8) rules that one is permitted to transgress a negative command if one fears the reaction of the authorities, although *Eshel Avraham*, *in situ*, limits that ruling to life-threatening situations. Rashi explains the word "modesty" as meaning "tolerance," in the sense that R. Zechariah refrained from killing Bar Kamtza. *Maharatz Chayot* (*Gittin* 56a) explains that R. Zechariah was accused of being overly modest, since he did not invoke his position as a great Sage to make an *ad hoc* decision which took into account the great danger that the nation was facing. *Tiferet Ya'akov* (*Gittin* 56a) explains that the least

Ki Tavo

learned generally express their opinions first, since greater scholars would not feel obligated to accept the view of the less learned. R. Zechariah spoke first because he considered himself the least learned. However, everyone else considered him the greatest scholar and they refused to contradict his opinion.

R. Dichovsky is providing a new interpretation of going "beyond the requirements of the law." A great scholar must take into account the political ramifications of his decisions, and sometimes rule more leniently if adhering to the letter of the law might lead to the occurrence of a calamity. According to Tosafot in *Sanhedrin* 7a (s.v. *ke-neged*), Aaron similarly acted "beyond the requirements of the law" by being lenient and allowing the construction of the golden calf, because not doing so would have endangered the future of the nation.[55]

Answering Question B: How can there be a requirement to go "beyond the requirement"?

After examining the true meaning of going "beyond the requirement of the law," it is clear that in most cases, doing so is a personal decision. On the other hand, when observing the letter of the law can lead to undesirable consequences, one must go further by either being stricter, as in the case of Rabbah b. Bar Chana, or more lenient, as in the case of Kamtza and Bar Kamtza, and that of the golden calf.

Answering Question C: Even if there can be such a requirement, can failing to do so be so severe as to justify the destruction of the Second Temple?

The commentaries explain that certainly there were other reasons as well, e.g., *sinat chinam*. However, *Ben Yehoyada* (BT *Bava Metzia* 30b, s.v. *ella*) notes that had the nation been more particular and observed the law beyond the basic requirement, God would also have

---

55. For a thorough discussion of this matter, see Abba Engelberg, *The Ethics of Exodus* (2014), pp. 355-364.

not held as strictly to the letter of the law when He meted out their punishment, and He would have spared the Temple and not exiled them.

Answering Question D: In another location, does not the Talmud associate the destruction of the Second Temple with *sinat chinam*?
This question has been asked by *Tosafot* (BT *Bava Metzia* 30b, s.v. *lo*). *Torat Chaim, in situ,* answers that in dealing with others, going "beyond the requirement of the law" generally means conceding to one's friend even if the latter is not entitled to benefit financially according to the letter of the law. However, because there was much groundless hatred, people were not willing to relinquish their rights by compromising and going "beyond the letter of the law." The two concepts are thus inextricably related.

Answering the Fourth Question: How Can the Jewish People Attempt to Avoid Future Tragedies?

Two points are relevant. Firstly, one need not be a *Litvak*—i.e., the proverbial ascetic. As previously noted, one is permitted to enjoy food and drink, as long as the dietary laws are observed and the appropriate blessings are recited. In fact, the Talmud (BT *Ta'anit* 11a) states that a person is not allowed to habitually fast, noting that if a Nazirite is considered a sinner because he deprives himself of wine, surely a person who voluntarily deprives himself of all food is a sinner. As previously noted, sexual gratification is also not proscribed, as long as it takes place within the proper framework and in accordance with the regulations of family purity.

The second point is that although enjoyment is permitted and even encouraged, it should be experienced vertically rather than horizontally. One should make the most of what he is blessed with, rather than frenetically scout for more exotic pleasures. With regard to the blessings in the present portion, it is stated: "And all these blessings will come upon you and overtake you" (Deut. 28:2). If the blessings devolve upon a given person, what do the words "overtake you" add? According to R. Yissocher Frand (*Rabbi Frand on the Parshah*, pp. 280-282), the first words refer to experiencing the blessings, while the last words refer to being satisfied and satiated by those blessings. Similarly, in the Grace after Meals, one says, "And you will eat and be satisfied" (Deut. 8:10). Eating is only half of the blessing, while being satisfied is the more important half. As written in *Avot* 4:1: "Who is a rich man? He who is satisfied with his lot." It has been pointed out that the Hebrew word for a rich man, *ashir*, is actually an acronym for the four Hebrew words: *einayim* (eyes), *shinayim* (teeth), *yadayim* (hands), and *raglayim* (feet). The message being conveyed is that one should first be happy that he has his health and vital organs. Afterwards, one should make an inventory of his financial, spiritual, familial, and social assets, and endeavor to rejoice in them to the maximum, and only then seek out new challenges. Many of the vices which led to the destruction of the Second Temple resulted from greed and unbridled ambition.

One can explain the approach to pleasure—satisfaction with the existing, as opposed to the constant striving for the newer and greater—as the intrinsic difference between the characters of Jacob and Esau (Natan Slifkin, *Focus*, p. 199). Esau was born with a full head of hair (Gen: 25: 25), and Rashi bases the etymology of the name Esau, meaning ready-made, on this detail. Rather than struggle and invest in order to produce, Esau preferred ready-made products, so that he could swiftly re-focus on his next conquest. When asked to supply his father with a meat meal, Esau went "to hunt for venison, and to bring it" (Gen. 27:5), prompting Rashi to explain the redundancy "to bring it" to indicate that if he was not successful in the hunt, Esau would not hesitate to steal. Jacob, on the other hand, struggled on numerous occasions: at the time of his birth (Gen. 25:26), with a messenger of God (Gen. 32:25-30), to acquire his wife (Gen. 29:8), and to earn his living (Gen. 30:32). His pleasure was derived by appreciating each hard-earned acquisition. When Jacob proffered a gift to Esau, he at first turned it down, saying "I have plenty" (Gen. 33:9), but Jacob insisted that Esau keep the gifts, replying "I have everything [*kol*]" (Gen. 33:11). *Kli Yakar* explains that when Esau said he had plenty, the clear implication is "plenty—but I can certainly handle a little more." However, when Jacob said that he had everything, he meant that he had no interest in obtaining anything else. He was completely enthralled with what he had, and had no craving for further conquests. Basking in the pleasures of the present, rather than foraging for new thrills, is a lesson which may be learned from Jacob.

Summary

1. How could God have allowed later tragedies to occur? It was clearly predicted in the present portion.
2. If God was in fact involved in later tragedies, why did He conceal His involvement? God has always camouflaged His imprint on humanity.
3. If God was in fact involved, what were the Jews being punished for? Although there were many righteous individuals, they were being punished as a nation for straying from their beliefs and heritage. This mode of behavior had already been associated by the Sages with the destruction of both Temples. In the foremath of the Holocaust, many Jews seized the first available opportunity to assimilate, when it was provided by the Gentiles.
4. How can the Jewish people attempt to avoid another holocaust? Religious Jews believe that history is directed by God. The hope is that by being meticulously observant of His laws, the chance of suffering future tragedies can be minimized. This task may be eased by realizing that on the whole, the Jewish religion prescribes a pleasurable life, and that each individual's happiness may be maximized by being content with those pleasures which God grants him.

Nitzavim

As noted in the introduction to Deuteronomy, its third and last section is mainly devoted to the concept of reward and punishment. After presenting in *Ki Tavo* a short and a long version of the rewards and punishments which await the Jewish nation depending on their behavior, the Torah makes the case once more in a four-part prose segment, which actually starts at the end of *Ki Tavo* and carries on until the end of *Nitzavim*.

In the first part (Deut. 29:1-8), Moses recalls the miraculous sustenance with which God provided the Israelites in their travels in terms of nourishment (manna) and clothing, as well as the military support which enabled them to defeat their enemies. Did they appreciate it? Moses tells them: "Until this day, the Lord has not given you a heart to know, eyes to see, and ears to hear" (v. 3). According to Rashi, only on that day, after forty years of benefiting from those miracles, were they able to internalize the special relationship between God and Israel. However, according to Saadiah Gaon, even on that day they were still unable to comprehend the *quid pro quo* expected by God; namely, that it was the immoral behavior of the Egyptians which had led to their downfall, and the same measuring stick would be applied to Israel as well.

The second part (Deut. 29:9-28) describes the covenant that God wishes to make with the nation as they enter into the Land of Israel. The last time a covenant was made was with a previous generation at the time of revelation (Exod. 24:7), the expanded version of which may have included the last two portions of Leviticus.[56] On the last day of his life (according to Rashi), Moses, in a completely democratic manner, gathered all elements of the population—men, women, and children—from the most senior members (the elders and leaders) to the most menial laborers (the woodcutters and water drawers). The purpose of the covenant was to establish the Israelites as God's exclusive nation: "to establish you this day as His people, and that He will be your God" (v. 12). Furthermore, the covenant is being made not only "with those standing here with us today before the Lord our God, but [also] with those who are not here with us this day" (v. 14).

What are the contents of the covenant? It contains a warning not to be tempted by the idolatrous lifestyles of the Egyptians and other sundry nations through which they passed in the course of their travels. Moses warned Israel of the dire consequences which would befall the individual, family, or tribe who ignores the curses mentioned in *Ki Tavo* as a result of disobeying the cardinal laws. In the case of an entire tribe, the punishment would be the decimation of its land, depicted by the Torah as follows: "Sulfur and salt will burn up its entire land. It will not be sown, nor will it grow [anything], and no grass will sprout upon it" (v. 22). Eventually, they would be exiled from their land (Ibn Ezra, vv. 18, 20), and in response to foreign nations amazed at the resulting desolation, it would be clarified that it happened because "they went and served other deities… and the Lord's fury raged against that land… and the Lord uprooted them from upon their land with fury, anger and great wrath, and He cast them to another land [as happened first to the ten tribes and then to the remaining tribes]" (vv. 25-27).

In the third part (Deut. 30:1-10), Moses informs the Israelites of what would occur after the suffering and exile in consequence of their sins. Within their state of exile, they would eventually wholeheartedly return to God, as stated in v. 2, "with all your heart and with all your soul, and you will listen to His voice according to all

---

56. See Abba Engelberg, *The Ethics of Leviticus* (2018), pp. 282-283.

Nitzavim

that I am commanding you this day." God would then respond in kind by collecting the nation from the furthest reaches, inspiring Moses to wax poetic and declare: "Even if your exiles are at the end of the heavens, the Lord your God will gather you from there... and bring you to the land which your forefathers possessed... and He will make you more numerous than your forefathers" (vv. 4-5).

As wonderful as these tidings were, the Israelites may have been asking themselves what guarantee there would be that after the ingathering, individuals or even a significant fraction of the nation would not sin again and cause another upheaval. It would seem that this was the same question that the family of Noah asked themselves after experiencing the flood. At that stage, God had anticipated their fears, which He allayed by stating: "I will no longer curse the earth because of man, for the inclination of man's heart is evil from his youth, and I will no longer smite all living things as I have done. So long as the earth exists, seed-time and harvest, cold and heat, summer and winter, and day and night will not cease" (Gen. 8:21-22). God's goal in creating the world was that good prevail over evil. On the other hand, God had created man with an evil inclination because He wanted man to be good not because he was unable to be bad, but rather because he chose to be so. However, before the flood, evil elements were so predominant that there was no chance that righteous people could thrive. The flood served as a filter to remove the wicked people and restore the equilibrium. This is not to say that Noah's descendants were all angels, as is demonstrated by the post-diluvian behavior of Noah and one of his sons, not to mention the other villains that populate the Pentateuch. Nevertheless, the playing field was cleared and the opportunity to achieve ethical and moral superiority was restored.

Similarly, in this section, after exposing Israel to the travails of exile, God would make an adjustment to the challenges facing them, as expressed in the following message: "And the Lord your God will circumcise your heart and the heart of your offspring, [so that you may] love the Lord your God with all your heart and with all your soul, so that you may live" (v. 6). Ibn Ezra explains that unlike physical circumcision, which is done by man, God Himself will open the hearts of Israel to make them more accepting of spiritual and moral teachings, and more submissive to God's law. Sforno adds that He will also make the nation more perceptive and endow them with greater understanding, which will prevent them from being misled in their search for truth. On the other hand, perhaps the verse describes a natural process. The years of suffering in exile will nurture within the Jews a strong motivation to improve, and as the Talmud says: "He who comes to purify himself will be helped [by God]" (BT *Yoma* 38b, *Avodah Zarah* 55a, *Menachot* 29b).

Ramban feels that Divine intervention in human behavior in the present world, which is based on freedom of choice, is inappropriate. He therefore relates v. 6 to Messianic times, when man would be instinctively righteous, and his evil inclination would be dormant, as was the case in primeval times, before Adam sinned.[57] Ezekiel prophesied: "I will give you a new heart… and I will put My spirit within you and bring it about that you will walk in My statutes and you will keep My ordinances and do [them]" (Ezek. 36:26-27). Ramban maintains that this too is a reference to Messianic times. The "new heart" refers to a physical change in which the evil inclination will be extinguished, while God's spirit is associated with a desire to assimilate the quintessence of the Torah and pro-actively fulfill its laws—a situation described by Jeremiah as well, when he says: "In those days, God would place His law in their midst and inscribe it in their hearts" (Jer. 31:32).

In the fourth part (Deut. 30:11-20), the text clarifies that even after God's intervention and positive stimulation, the nation will still face challenges. Two points are made. First, that it is within the reach of every Jew to fulfill the *mitzvot*, as described in the following words of encouragement:

---

57. A more detailed account appears in Abba Engelberg, *The Ethics of Genesis* (2014), pp. 22-23.

Nitzavim

> For this commandment which I command you this day is not concealed from you, nor is it far away. It is not in heaven, that you should say: "Who will go up to heaven and take it for us, and allow us to hear it, so that we can do it?" Nor is it beyond the sea, that you should say: "Who will cross to the other side of the sea and take it for us, and allow us to hear it, so that we can do it?" Rather, it is very close to you; with your mouth and your heart you can do it (Deut. 30:11-14).

The last verse refers either to repentance, which involves regretting in one's heart followed by confessing with one's mouth (Sforno); or to obeying the commands, whose ultimate goal is to affect one's heart, which is accomplished by orally referring to them, which is in turn reinforced by actually performing them (Ibn Ezra). Of course, from an external point of view, one would say the reverse: first one resolves in his heart to observe a law, then he speaks of his intentions and learns its details, and only after that prelude does he finally perform the mitzvah.

The second point is that even though man will be instinctively righteous in Messianic times (as he was before Adam and Eve sinned), in the present world he still has freedom of choice. God has endowed him with the ability to choose between the fleeting pleasures of sensual gratification in the short run but suffering and tribulations in the long run, as opposed to eternal salvation in the long run coupled with less glowing, but deeper-seated satisfaction in the short run. God summarizes the situation succinctly, when He says: "I call upon the heaven and the earth this day as witnesses [to the fact that I have warned you]. I have set before you life and death, the blessing and the curse. You should choose life, so that you and your offspring will live" (Deut. 30:19). In other words, God has presented both alternatives and has clarified the ramifications of each. He urges every Jew to choose the path leading to eternal life, but leaves the final decision to each individual.

The Ethics of Deuteronomy

Messianic Times

It was noted that Ramban believes that the third part of *Nitzavim* relates to Messianic times. Rambam (*Hilchot Melachim* 11:1) considers the following verse in that part to be the foundational text regarding the Torah's promise of such an event:

> And the Lord your God will return [with you from] your exile, and He will have mercy upon you, and He will return and gather you from all the nations where the Lord your God dispersed you (Deut. 30:3).

The first returning mentioned refers to God Himself returning from exile, while the second refers to His bringing back the entire nation, as amplified in the Talmud:

> Come and see how beloved are Israel before God, for to every place where they were exiled, the *Shechinah* [Divine Presence] accompanied them. They were exiled to Egypt and the *Shechinah* was with them, as it says: "Did I [not] reveal Myself to the house of your father when they were in Egypt" (1 Sam. 2:27) [Rashi: Did you know that I gave Aaron this favor and greatness? From here (we deduce) that Aaron prophesied in Egypt. What was the prophecy? It is that which is stated: "And I said to them: Each man, cast away the detestable things upon which his eyes gaze, and with the idols of Egypt do not defile yourselves" (Ezek. 20:7).] They were exiled to Babylon and the *Shechinah* was with them, as it says: "For you I went to Babylon" (Isa. 43:14). And when they will be redeemed in the future, the *Shechinah* will be with them, as it says: "And the Lord your God will return [with you from] your exile" (Deut. 30:3). It does not say here "and He will bring back" but "and He will return." This

Nitzavim

teaches us that the Holy One, blessed be He, will return with them from the places of exile (BT *Megillah* 29a).

Maharsha explains that sometimes God speaks to prophets, but at other times He actually makes His presence felt. In 1 Sam. 2:27, the word "reveal" is repeated *(ha-niglo nigleiti)*, indicating His commiseration with the Israelites in their suffering in Egypt. Alternatively, Maharsha notes that the Hebrew words for "reveal" (*niglah*) and "exile" (*golah*) sound similar to each other, once more indicating a high degree of empathy. As for the verse from Isaiah, it is interpreted allegorically to refer to Nebuchadnezzar's harassment of the nation as they were led into exile. In order to maximize their suffering, he had them carry vessels filled with sand. The Midrash states that in order to alleviate their anguish, both the ministering angels, as well as God Himself, helped lift their burdens. Instead of interpreting the Hebrew as "For you I sent [Cyrus] to Babylon [*Metzudat David*: in order that you should return from exile, I sent Cyrus to destroy Babylon]," it is interpreted as "For you I went to Babylon," i.e., to ease your agony, once more indicating the presence of God in their time of sorrow (*Shocher Tov*, Ps. 137:3).

The Messianic Environment

Rambam adduces another strong hint in the Torah of the future advent of Messianic times from a promise made by God which is certainly destined to be fulfilled:

> With regard to the cities of refuge, He states: "And when the Lord your God expands your boundary, as He swore to your forefathers... then you will add three more cities for yourself, in addition to these three [Mizrachi: in the land of Canaan]" (Deut. 19:8-9). This command was never fulfilled. Surely, God did not give this command in vain (*Hilchot Melachim* 11:2).

The Ethics of Deuteronomy

Israel had been told to set aside six cities of refuge, three in Transjordan and three in Canaan (Num. 35:14), and in Deuteronomy they were informed of another three to be added in the future, obviously in Messianic times.

Rambam describes the state of affairs that will prevail in Messianic times:

> All the statutes will return to their previous state [Rashi: the four forms of capital punishment will be reinstated (BT *Sanhedrin* 51b, s.v. *hilchata le-meshicha*)]. We will offer sacrifices and observe the Sabbatical and Jubilee years according to all their particulars, as described in the Torah (*Hilchot Melachim* 11:1).

Will nature change in Messianic times? It has been noted that Ramban believes that man's personality will change drastically, as he will be instinctively righteous. A simple reading of the prophets would seem to reinforce this approach, with one of the most famous passages being:

> And a wolf will live with a lamb; and a leopard will lie down with a kid; and a calf, a young lion, and a fattened lamb [will lie] together, and a little child will lead them. And a cow and bear will graze [in the pasture], their young will lie down together, and a lion, like cattle, will eat straw. And an infant will play on a cobra's hole, and a weaned child will stretch forth his hand into a viper's nest (Isa. 11:6-8).

Rambam, on the other hand, interprets these verses as reflecting a natural occurrence:

> Do not presume that in the Messianic age any facet of the world's nature will change or there will be innovations in the

Nitzavim

work of creation. Rather, the world will continue according to its pattern. Although Isaiah states: "And a wolf will live with a lamb; and a leopard will lie down with a kid," these words are a metaphor and a parable. The interpretation of the prophecy is as follows: Israel will dwell securely together with the wicked Gentiles who are likened to a wolf and a leopard, as in the prophecy: "A wolf from the wilderness will spoil them [Israel] and a leopard will stalk their cities" (Jer. 5:6). They will all return to the true faith and no longer steal or destroy. Rather, they will eat permitted food at peace with Israel, as Isaiah states: "a lion, like cattle, will eat straw." Similarly, other Messianic prophecies of this nature are metaphors. In the Messianic era, everyone will realize which matters were implied by these metaphors and which allusions they contained (*Hilchot Melachim* 12:1).

The difference of opinion between Ramban and Rambam is actually based on a Talmudic precedent (BT *Berachot* 34b, *Sanhedrin* 99a):

R. Chiya b. Abba also said in the name of R. Yochanan: All the prophets prophesied [miraculous events] only for the days of the Messiah, but as for the world to come, "no eye has seen, oh God, beside for You [it cannot be described to humans]" (Isa. 64:3). These Rabbis differ from Shmuel, for Shmuel said: There is no difference between this world and the days of the Messiah except [that in the latter there will be no] bondage of foreign powers, as it says: "For there will never cease [not even in Messianic days] to be needy in the land" (Deut. 15:11).

Clearly, Ramban, who forecasts a miraculous existence in Messianic days, has adopted the view of R. Yochanan, while Rambam accepts the opinion of Shmuel. Rambam in fact cites the exact formulation of Shmuel, "There is no difference between this world and the days of the Messiah except bondage of foreign powers," twice (*Hilchot Melachim* 12:2, *Hilchot Teshuvah* 9:2). The complicating factor is that Rambam (*Hilchot Teshuvah* 8:7) also cites the words of R. Yochanan verbatim, "All the prophets prophesied only for the days of the Messiah," a discrepancy pointed out by *Kesef Mishneh, in situ*. *Lechem Mishneh, in situ,* posits that Rambam actually holds like R. Yochanan, just that he believes that even according to R. Yochanan, nature will not change, only human behavior, to the extent that poverty will be wiped out in a completely natural manner; while Shmuel holds that even such blights as destitution will persist, with the only outward change being that Israel will overthrow the yoke of the nations. *Lechem Mishneh* points out, however, that the Talmud says in two places (BT *Pesachim* 68a, *Sanhedrin* 91b) that in R. Yochanan's view decidedly supernatural events will occur in Messianic times, to which it applies the verse: "And the light of the moon will be as the light of the sun, and the light of the sun will be seven times as [intense as] the light of the seven days" (Isa. 30:26). Perhaps one could take the reverse approach and say that Rambam actually accepts the opinion of Shmuel, just that he cites the words of R. Yochanan that prophets prophesied for the days of the Messiah to stress that even Shmuel has to accept the words of the prophets, which Shmuel believes can be interpreted in a natural fashion (including the verse from Isaiah).

Another way of answering Rambam's contradictory statements is suggested by *Shlah* (*Toldot Adam Beit David* 51), who says that when Rambam speaks of natural occurrences, he refers to the pre-Messianic period up to and including the lifetime of Mashiach b. Yosef (see **Appendix VII: Mashiach ben Yosef**). For this reason, Bar Kochba, whom R. Akiva (JT *Ta'anit* 4:5) thought might be the Messiah (i.e., Mashiach b. Yosef), was not expected to perform miraculous deeds (*Hilchot Melachim* 12:3). According to *Shlah*, this period will last through the first six millennia of the world's existence. During

Nitzavim

the seventh, Mashiach b. David will make his appearance, and at that point many supernatural events will occur.

THE MESSIAH

The previously cited source in *Nitzavim* for the belief in Messianic times does not mention a human savior who will become the leader and implement the changes predicted for the Messianic period. However, Rambam does proclaim the future appearance of such a person as one of the fundamentals of Jewish faith.

> In the future, the Messianic king will arise and renew the Davidic dynasty, restoring it to its initial sovereignty. He will build the Temple and gather the dispersed of Israel… Anyone who does not believe in him or does not await his coming, denies not only the statements of the other prophets, but those of the Torah and Moses our teacher (*Hilchot Melachim* 11:1).[58]

THE NAME

The name Messiah derives from the Hebrew word *mashiach*, meaning "anointed," and refers to a person who was anointed with specially prepared oil (Exod. 30:22-33) upon assuming a high position, such as high priest (Exod. 30:30) or king (Saul: 1 Sam. 10:1, David: 1 Sam. 16:13, Solomon: 1 Kings 1:39). It is also used figuratively with respect to people who have been designated by God to perform a particular function, such as the prophet Isaiah (Isa. 61:1) and Cyrus, who was chosen to enable the building of the Second Temple (Isa. 44:28-45:1).

In Jewish sources, in addition to being called Mashiach (BT *Pesachim* 5a, *Megillah* 12a, *Sanhedrin* 98b, etc.), the Messiah has also

---

58. This belief composes the twelfth of Rambam's *Thirteen Principles of Faith*. See Rambam's *Introduction to Perek Chelek* and the Daily Prayer Book after *shacharit*.

been called *Melech ha-Mashiach* (Messianic king, e.g., in the above citation), Mashiach b. David (BT *Sotah* 48b, *Sukkah* 52a; *Gen. Rabbah* 97:10; *Tanchuma Toldot* 14, *Vayishlach* 6; etc.) or simply Ben David (BT *Yevamot* 62a, *Yoma* 10a, *Megillah* 17b, *Samhedrin* 97a, *Avodah Zarah* 5a, *Eruvin* 43a, etc.).

The Talmud even suggests personal names for the Messiah (BT *Sanhedrin* 98b):

> What is his [the Messiah's] name? The school of R. Shila said: His name is Shiloh, for it is written: "until Shiloh [will] come" (Gen. 49:10). The school of R. Yannai said: His name is Yinnon, for it is written [concerning King Solomon, and applied to the Messiah]: "Let his name endure forever. All the days of the sun let his name be Yinnon [magnified; Rashi: an expression of kingdom and dominion]" (Ps. 72:17). The school of R. Chaninah maintained: His name is Chaninah, as it is written [in the last verse of Jeremiah's malediction before his words of comfort: "And I will cast you off this land to a land that you and your fathers did not know] and I will show you no *chaninah* [favor]" (Jer. 16:13). Others say: His name is Menahem b. Hezekiah [the name of a contemporary leader of a *beit midrash*], for it is written: "for the *menachem* (comforter) to restore my soul is far from me" (Lam. 1:16).

Note that the Sages found names similar to their own (Shila vs. Shiloh, Yannai vs. Yinnon, and Chaninah). Also, the acronym for the four names: Menachem, Shiloh, Yinnon, and Chaninah, is in fact *mashiach*.

The text concludes with one more suggested name:

> The Rabbis said: His name is "the leper scholar," as it is written: "Surely he has borne our griefs, and carried our sorrows: yet we did consider him a leper, smitten of God, and afflicted" (Isa. 53:4).

Nitzavim

REFERENCES IN THE TORAH

Interestingly enough, the Biblical source cited by Rambam for the Messiah is from the prophecy of the non-Jewish prophet Balaam, as he proceeds to describe in *Hilchot Melachim* 11:1:

> Reference [to the Messiah] is also made in the portion of Balaam; there, he prophesied with regard to two Messiahs: the first Messiah, David, who saved Israel from its oppressors; and the final Messiah, who will arise from his descendants and save Israel in the end of days. And there (Num. 24:17-18) it says: {1} "I see it, but not now"—this is David; "I perceive it, but not soon"—this is the Messianic king. {2} "A star will step forth from Jacob"—this is David; "and a scepter will arise in Israel"—this is the Messianic king. {3} "Crushing the corners of Moab"—this is David, and so it says: "He smote Moab and measured them with a line" (2 Sam. 8:2); "decimating all of Seth's descendants"—this is the Messianic king, about whom it says: "He will rule from sea to sea" (Zech. 9:10). {4} "Edom will become a possession"—this is David, and so it says: "Edom became the servants of David" (2 Sam. 8:6); "Se'ir will become a possession of his enemies"—this is the Messianic king, and so it says: "Saviors will ascend Mount Zion to judge the mountain of Esau" (Ovad. 1:21).

Rambam's sources are various *Midrashim* which were known to his predecessors as well. The exegesis of {1} appears *in situ*, in *Midrash Aggadah*, written around the time of Rambam, but based on earlier Midrashic sources such as R. Moshe ha-Darshan and *Midrash Lekach Tov*; of {2} in Onkelos *in situ*; and of {4} in *Midrash Aggadah*. The reference of the first part of {3} to David appears in Rashi, while the second part's reference to the Messiah is cited by Rashbam. The comments of R. Bachya *in situ*, which he claims to be based on *Midrashim*, are almost identical to what appears in *Hilchot Melachim*.

The Ethics of Deuteronomy

Of course, it is not known to which specific *Midrashim* Rambam had access, but he was clearly aware of their general contents.

Perhaps Rambam chose the verses pronounced by Balaam because of the repeated allusions to King David and the Messianic king, or perhaps because it was prophesied by a non-Jew, implying recognition by the Gentile world as well. At any rate, the future royalty of David and the Messiah were already predicted in the blessings which Jacob bestowed on his son Judah: "The scepter will never depart from Judah, nor a lawgiver from between his feet, until Shiloh comes, and to him will be a gathering of peoples" (Gen. 49:10). Onkelos and *Targum Yonatan* relate the first phrase to stewardship in general. According to Radak and Ibn Ezra, the reference is to the leadership displayed by the tribe of Judah from the very beginning. Judah was designated as the first tribe to offer sacrifices at the inauguration of the Tabernacle (Num. 7:12), was the tribe whose flag marched first (Num. 10:14), and it was Judah who was given the task of initiating battle both in the case of the Canaanites (Judg. 1:3) and the Benjaminites (Judg. 20:18). *Gen. Rabbah* (99:8), on the other hand, relates the scepter specifically to kingship, and this is the view adopted by Rashi, and the implication is that starting from the time of the Judean David, the divinely inspired royal dynasty were his descendants.

After the destruction of the First Temple, the kingship, when it existed, was usurped by the priestly Hasmonean dynasty of the tribe of Levi, so how can the verse maintain that it never departed from Judah? The following Talmudic excerpt attempts to reconcile the situation:

> "The scepter will never depart from Judah": this refers to the exilarchs [from the third century CE] of Babylon who rule over Israel with scepters; "nor a lawgiver from between his feet": this refers to the descendants of Hillel [in the Land of Israel] who teach the Torah in public (BT *Sanhedrin* 5a).

Nitzavim

Traditionally, the exilarchs were deemed to be of Judaic origin (JT *Yoma* 7:1, *Sotah* 7:6), as were the *nesi'im*, the princes who headed Torah academies and possessed religious, but not political, authority (*Gen. Rabbah* 98:8). Rashi actually took this into account, as his exact words are: "[even] after the house of David [ceases to reign]—this refers to the exilarchs in Babylon" (Gen. 49:10).

The verse in Genesis concludes by saying that Judah's leadership will persist "until Shiloh will come, and to him will be a gathering of peoples." Rashi, in accordance with his approach in the first half of the verse, takes Shiloh to refer to the Messiah. Ibn Ezra and Radak, on the other hand, understand Shiloh to refer to King David, with the word Shiloh meaning his (*she-lo*) son or descendant—David being of the tribe of Judah. Finally, "to him will be a gathering of peoples," because many nations became subservient to King David and his son Solomon. According to Ibn Ezra and Radak, the verse thus states that from the time of Jacob until that of David, leadership would not depart from the tribe of Judah, and from that point on, Judean royalty would commence.

Rashbam agrees with Ibn Ezra and Radak as to the beginning of the period referred to, but differs with respect to the proper translation of Shiloh, which he believes refers to the name of the town where the Tabernacle was located for 369 years. It was nearby, in Shechem, that Rehoboam became ruler of the Kingdom of Judah (1 Kings 12:1) and, soon after, the ten tribes seceded under Jeroboam to establish the Kingdom of Israel (1 Kings 12:20). At that stage, Judah lost its role as the unique ruling tribe, and the message of the verse is that Judah's exclusive rulership lasted until the division of the monarchy in Shechem, near Shiloh, following Rehoboam's coronation. At that event, the tribes of Judah and Benjamin were joined by the nations previously subdued by David and Solomon. Rashbam consequently translates the verse as follows: "The scepter will not depart from Judah, nor lawgivers from between his feet, until he [Judah, i.e., Rehoboam] will come to Shiloh, and to him will be a gathering of peoples."

According to Rashbam, the previously asked question—how it can say "the scepter will never depart from Judah," when in fact Judean kings did not reign after the destruction of the First Temple—is answered. The verse speaks only of the period until King David or perhaps King Rehoboam, and no later.

Although the interpretations of Ibn Ezra, Radak, and Rashbam are quite reasonable, and indeed a good fit for the text, the more traditional interpretation of Shiloh is that it refers to the Messiah (*Targum Yonatan*, Onkelos, *Gen. Rabbah* 99:8). The Midrash interprets Shiloh as standing for *oto she-ha-malchut she-lo* (he for whom dominion is his), while Rashi sees it as a combination of the two words *shai lo* (a present [is deserved by] him). Interestingly, the numerical value of the letters composing *mashiach* (358) equals that of the Hebrew words in Gen. 49:10, *yavo Shiloh* ("Shiloh will come").

The question referred to previously, namely that leadership was not continuously in the hands of the tribe of Judah, was asked explicitly by the Midrash, according to the interpretation of *Etz Yosef*:

> "The scepter will never depart from Judah": This is the throne of kingship… When? "A lawgiver from between his feet," i.e., when the one for whom kingship is designated arrives (*Gen. Rabbah* 99:8).

In other words, kingship will indeed not depart from Judah, but that situation will only occur after the arrival of the Messiah. The verse is thus to be understood as follows:

> The scepter will never depart from Judah, [starting from when] a lawgiver [will issue] from between his feet, which is when Shiloh [Messiah] comes, and to him will be a gathering of peoples (Gen. 49:10).

Nitzavim

REFERENCES IN THE PROPHETS

References to a Messiah are plentiful in the Prophets. In the words of Rambam, "all their books are filled with mention of this matter" (*Hilchot Melachim* 11:2). Perhaps the most explicit, which specifies the Messiah as a descendant of David, is from the chapter in Isaiah cited previously for its vivid description of Messianic times:

> And a shoot will spring forth from the stock of Jesse, and a twig will sprout from his roots. And the spirit of the Lord will rest upon him, a spirit of wisdom and understanding, a spirit of counsel and might, a spirit of knowledge and fear of the Lord. And his delight will be in the fear of the Lord; and he will not judge by the sight of his eyes, neither will he chastise by the hearing of his ears; and he will judge the poor justly, and he will chastise with equity the humble of the earth, and he will smite the [*Metzudat David*: villains of the] earth with the curses [literally: rod] of his mouth and with the breath of his lips he will put the wicked to death. And righteousness will be the girdle of his loins, and faithfulness the girdle of his reins.... And it will come to pass on that day, that the root of Jesse will stand as a banner for peoples—nations will inquire of him, and his resting place will be magnificent (Isa. 11:1-10).

A verse from Jeremiah establishes the Messiah as a descendant of David:

> Behold, days are coming, says the Lord, when I will set up from David a righteous shoot, and he will reign as king and prosper, and he will execute judgment and righteousness in the land. In his days Judah will be saved, and Israel will dwell safely; and this is his name by which he will be called: The Lord is our righteousness (Jer. 23:5-6).

The Ethics of Deuteronomy

Both Malachi 3 and Psalms 72 are taken to refer to the Messiah, while Micah 4 and Daniel 12 are considered to be descriptive of Messianic times.

ATTRIBUTES OF THE MESSIAH

The following attributes are associated with the Messiah:

1. Wisdom:

Rambam states that he will be "a greater master of knowledge than Solomon" (*Hilchot Teshuvah* 9:2), based on the previously cited phrase: "And the spirit of the Lord will rest upon him, a spirit of wisdom and understanding" (Isa. 11:2).

2. Prophecy:

Rambam states that he will be "a great prophet, close to the level of Moses our teacher" (*Hilchot Teshuvah* 9:2), based on the phrase: "He will be exalted and lifted up" (Isa. 52:13).

3. Modesty:

The prophet describes him as being "humble and riding on a donkey" (Zech. 9:9). According to *Pirkei de-Rabbi Eliezer* (ch. 31), Mashiach will arrive on the same donkey used by Abraham at the binding of Isaac (Gen. 22:3) and by Moses when he brought his family to Egypt (Exod. 4:20). However, according to the Gemara, this is not necessarily the case:

> R. Yehoshua asked: It is written: "And behold with the clouds of the heaven, one like a man was coming" (Dan. 7:13), while [elsewhere] it is written: "Your king will come to you. He is just and victorious, humble, and riding a donkey" (Zech. 9:9). [These verses are contradictory, the first implying a glorious arrival, the second a lowly one]. If they are meritorious, [he

Nitzavim

will come] with the clouds of heaven [Rashi: swiftly]; if not, lowly and riding upon a donkey (BT *Sanhedrin* 98a).

The Talmud forecasts two possible scenarios. In the first, Israel achieves a high spiritual level independent of the Messiah, and the latter's arrival coincides with Israel successfully overcoming its enemies. In the second, the nation is still morally and spiritually lacking, and the Messiah's outstanding qualities are meant to initiate, by example, a process of self-improvement, which starts by stressing the attribute of humility. This bifurcation is explicated in the same Talmudic discussion:

> R. Yochanan also said: The son of David will come only in a generation that is either altogether righteous or altogether wicked. "In a generation that is altogether righteous," as it is written: "And your people, all of them righteous, will inherit the land forever" (Isa. 60:21). [Or] "altogether wicked," as it is written: "And He saw that there was no [Rashi: righteous] man, and He was astounded that there was no intercessor, and His arm saved him, and His righteousness supported him [Rashi: even though we are not worthy of salvation]" (Isa. 59:16); and it is [elsewhere] written: "For My sake, for My sake I will do [redeem Israel], for how can I allow it [Rashi: My name] to be profaned? And My honor I will not give to another [god who will be praised by My enemies]" (Isa. 48:11).

However, if Israel has not risen to the occasion, God will prolong the pre-Messianic period in the hope that they will eventually see the light, as stated in the continuum of the Talmudic segment:

> R. Alexandri said: R. Yehoshua b. Levi asked: It is written "in its time [will the Messiah come]," while it is also written

[immediately afterwards] "I [the Lord] will hasten it [implying before its scheduled time]" (Isa. 60:22). [The answer to the contradiction is:] If they are worthy, I will hasten it. If [they are] not, [he will come] at the due time.

If even after receiving an extension, the nation has not repented and subsequently reached the desired level, God will still send the Messiah, and the spiritual awakening will occur after his arrival.

4. A teacher of Jew and Gentile:
Rambam states that "he will teach the entire nation and instruct them in the path of God, and all the Gentile nations will come to hear him" (*Hilchot Teshuvah* 9:2), based on the prophetic description of Messianic times:

> And many peoples will go, and they will say, "Come, let us go up to the Lord's mount, to the house of the God of Jacob, and let Him teach us of His ways, and we will go in His paths, for out of Zion will the Torah come forth, and the word of the Lord from Jerusalem" (Isa. 2:3).

5. A judge and moral mentor:
Isaiah describes his activities as follows:

> And he will judge between the nations and reprove many peoples, and they will beat their swords into plowshares and their spears into pruning hooks; no nation will lift its sword against another nation, neither will they [need to] learn war anymore (Isa. 2:4).

6. An eternal king:
As previously noted, Rambam termed the Messiah "the Messianic king" (*Hilchot Melachim* 11:1), based on a text in the book of Daniel:

Nitzavim

And He gave him dominion and glory and a kingdom, that all peoples, nations, and tongues should serve him; his dominion is an eternal dominion, which will not be removed, and his kingdom is one which will not be destroyed (Dan. 7:14).

7. He is not capable of performing miracles.

In the words of Rambam:

> One should not imagine that the Messianic king must be able to perform miracles and wonders, create new phenomena in the world, resurrect the dead, or perform other similar deeds. This is definitely not true, since R. Akiva, who was one of the great Sages of the Mishnah, was one of the supporters of Bar Koziva the king [leader of the third war against Rome (132-135 CE) in the reign of Hadrian, which terminated disastrously at Beitar], and he would say of him that he was the Messianic king. He and all the Sages of his generation considered him to be the Messianic king until he was killed because of sins. Once he was killed, they realized that he was not the Messiah. The Sages did not ask him for any signs or wonders (*Hilchot Melachim* 11:3).

However, Ra'avad objects, relying on a Talmudic text that describes the Messiah's qualities, based on the descriptive verse: "And he will be filled (*va-haricho*) with the fear of the Lord, and neither with the sight of his eyes will he judge, nor with the hearing of his ears will he chastise. And he will judge the poor justly, and he will chastise with equity the humble of the earth" (Isa. 11:3-4). The Talmud discusses the exact meaning of the Hebrew word *va-haricho*:

> R. Alexandri said: This teaches that He will fill him with good deeds and [cause him] suffering [which will atone for Israel's sins; see Isa. 53], like a mill [is laden with grain; the

spelling of *va-haricho* in Hebrew is close to that of *reichayim*, meaning "mill"]. Rava said: He smells [a man; *va-haricho* in Hebrew means to smell] and is capable of passing judgment [accurately], as it is written: "And neither with the sight of his eyes will he judge, nor with the hearing of his ears will he chastise" (BT *Sanhedrin* 93b).

Rava's implication is that since he will use neither his eyes nor his ears, he must judge through his sense of smell, which is a miraculous phenomenon. The Talmudic extract continues:

Bar Koziva reigned two and a half years, and then said to the Rabbis: "I am the Messiah." They answered: "Of Messiah it is written that "he smells and is capable of passing judgment. Let us see if he [Bar Koziva] can do so." When they saw that he was unable to judge by the scent, they slew him.

Ra'avad claims that it is clear from this segment that the Messiah will indeed be able to perform miracles, and that is why Bar Koziva (also known as Bar Kochva) was killed. However, *Kesef Mishneh* notes that according to earlier sources (*Eichah Rabbah* 2:4 and JT *Ta'anit* 4:5), the Romans killed him. Accordingly, he says that Rava clearly disagrees with the previously quoted view of Shmuel that there is no difference between this world and the days of the Messiah. Rambam agrees with Shmuel and also accepts the Midrashic report of how Bar Koziva died. *Lechem Mishneh* goes further than *Kesef Mishneh*, and says that the Talmud in *Sanhedrin* 93b also believes that it was the Romans who killed him, rather than the Rabbis, who obviously did not feel he was required to have supernatural powers. For this reason, the Talmud cites the view of R. Alexandri that *va-haricho* does not imply that the Messiah will possess miraculous abilities.

Nitzavim

ALTERNATE OPINIONS

As universally accepted as the concept of the Messiah would seem to be, the Gemara (BT *Sanhedrin* 99a) still cites a differing opinion, perhaps attesting to the open-minded approach of the Talmud:

> R. Hillel [grandson of R. Yehudah ha-Nassi and brother of Yehudah Nessiah] said: There will be no [future] Messiah for Israel, because they have already enjoyed him in the days of Hezekiah. R. Yosef said: May God forgive him [for saying so]. Now, when did Hezekiah flourish? During the First Temple. Yet Zechariah, prophesying in the days of the Second Temple, proclaimed: "Rejoice greatly, O daughter of Zion; shout, O daughter of Jerusalem; behold, your king will come to you. He is just and victorious; humble, and riding a donkey" (Zech. 9:9).

Rashi (BT *Sanhedrin* 98b, s.v. *ein mashiach*) explains that R. Hillel is not gainsaying the Jewish concept of Messiah. He is just saying that Hezekiah, the righteous king, has already played that role, and references to the Messiah (Mic. 5:3) and Messianic times (Ezek. 29:21) have been fulfilled already in the person of Hezekiah and during his lifetime. Accordingly, R. Yosef queried R. Hillel from a verse in Zechariah, who lived after Hezekiah and yet prophesied about a Messiah who was to come in the future.

R. Hillel's view would actually seem to be well-founded, based on the Gemara's lavish praise of Hezekiah and his generation. The Talmud states:

> Hezekiah [had eight names], as it is written: "For a child is born to us, a son is given to us; and the authority [of God] is upon his shoulder; and He will call his name: [i] Wonderful, [ii] Counsellor, [iii] Mighty, [iv] Judge, [v] Everlasting, [vi] Father, [vii] Prince of [viii] Peace" (Isa. 9:5). But is there not

The Ethics of Deuteronomy

> Hezekiah too [i.e., a ninth name]? [That is a mere appellation meaning] "whom God strengthened." Alternatively, Hezekiah [denotes] "Who strengthened" Israel [in their devotion] to their Father in heaven (BT *Sanhedrin* 94a).

The name Hezekiah is said to derive from the Hebrew word *chazak* (strong), hence the last two explanatory comments. Hezekiah is seen to be an outstanding judge and counsellor, a symbol of strength and peace, who positively influenced Israel and inculcated in them the depths of Torah knowledge, as follows from the continuation of the Talmudic extract:

> R. Yitzchak the Smith said: The yoke of Sennacherib was destroyed on account of the oil of Hezekiah, which burned in the synagogues and schools. What did he do? He planted a sword by the door of the schoolhouse and proclaimed: "He who does not study Torah will be pierced with this sword." They searched from Dan [in the north] to Beersheba [in the south], and did not find an uneducated person; from Gabbath [in the north] to Antipris [in the central region], and no boy or girl, man or woman was found who was not thoroughly versed [even] in the [very complex] laws of cleanliness and uncleanliness (BT *Sanhedrin* 94b).

Hezekiah developed an egalitarian system which bestowed a high-grade education universally, independent of one's class or gender, truly a worthy goal for a Messianic figure.

Understanding R. Hillel

Did R. Hillel really not believe that Messiah is yet to come? *Anaf Yosef, in situ*, explains that R. Hillel had good reason to believe that Hezekiah was the Messiah, being that that was God's original intention, as described in the Gemara:

Nitzavim

The Holy One, blessed be He, wished to appoint Hezekiah as the Messiah, and Sennacherib as Gog and Magog [According to Ezek. 38-39, King Gog would lead the armies of Magog (against Israel) to defeat, thus ushering in the Messianic era], whereupon the [hypostasized] Attribute of Justice said before the Holy One, blessed be He: "Sovereign of the Universe! If You did not make David King of Israel the Messiah, who uttered so many hymns and psalms before You, will You make Hezekiah, for whom You performed all of these miracles, the Messiah? [The reference is to the salvation from Sennacherib's siege (2 Kings 19:35-36) and Hezekiah's miraculous cure from a life-threatening illness (2 Kings 20:5-6).].... Immediately, the earth exclaimed: "Sovereign of the Universe! Let me utter song before You instead of this righteous man [Hezekiah], and make him the Messiah." So it broke into song before Him, as it is written: "From the end of the earth we heard songs: 'Fulfill the wish of the righteous [(Hezekiah).' And I (God) said, 'It is My secret, it is My secret.']" (Isa. 24:16). Then the Prince of the Universe [Rashi: an angel into whose hands the whole world is given] said to Him: "'Sovereign of the Universe! Fulfill the wishes of this righteous man [Hezekiah, since the earth has sung songs of praise on his behalf]." A heavenly Voice cried out, "It is My secret, it is My secret [i.e., the delay in the advent of Messiah]" (BT *Sanhedrin* 94a).

Anaf Yosef comments that on the basis of the preceding narrative, R. Hillel may very well have erred in his understanding of the text. S. Mendelsohn, in the *Jewish Encyclopedia* (vol. 6, p. 401), implies that R. Hillel may have not actually believed his own statement. He claims that R. Hillel was known to be a great scholar who may have even been the Hillel referred to in *Avot* 2:4 (see *Tosafot Yom Tov, in situ*), as well as a very modest person, and it was unlikely that he would have taken issue with the prevailing attitude. However, an early Christian, Origen, was in the habit of consulting him on difficult Biblical passages. He realized that Origen was claiming that some of the verses in the Bible predicted the advent of the founder of Christianity, in particular the very verse in Isaiah (9:5) cited previously, which the Talmud (BT *Sanhedrin* 94a) applies to Hezekiah. Therefore, R. Hillel is telling Origen that indeed that verse may be referring to the Messiah, but not the one he had in mind. Rather it refers to Hezekiah—a Messiah who has already come, and there will be no other one.

On the other hand, R. Yosef Albo (*Sefer ha-Ikkarim* 1:1) takes R. Hillel literally to be saying that the Jewish nation is awaiting neither a Messiah nor a Messianic age. On the basis of the statement of R. Hillel, he even wonders how Rambam could include belief in the Messiah as one of his Thirteen Principles of Faith, since according to Rambam, whoever does not believe in all of his principles is called a heretic and has no portion in the world to come (*Peirush ha-Mishnayot, Sanhedrin* 10:1). Would the Talmud include heretical opinions? And even if one says they are included in order to refute them, would the one who espouses them be addressed with the appellation of Rabbi (BT *Sanhedrin* 98b, 99a)? He conjectures that R. Hillel actually accepted the belief in the Messiah, and his only intention was to show that this belief is based exclusively on the oral tradition and does not follow from the Biblical references, which can all be related to King Hezekiah rather than a future Messiah. Even the citation from Zechariah does not have to relate to an as of yet unfulfilled event, since it may be referring to one of the leaders during the Second Temple period, such as Zerubabel; Nehemiah; one of the princes, such as Judah the Prince; or one of the Hasmonean kings (*Sefer ha-Ikkarim* 4:42). However, R. Albo rejects this hypothesis based on R. Yosef's harsh reply: "May God forgive him [for saying so]," which would have been far too brusque if the only argument was concerning the technical origin (Oral or Written Law) of belief in the Messiah.

Nitzavim

This is not to say that R. Albo accepts the opinion of R. Hillel. On the contrary, he says explicitly that it is obligatory for every religious Jew to believe in a future Messiah (*Sefer ha-Ikkarim* 1:23, 4:42). The point R. Albo is trying to make is that believing in the future Messiah is not a principle whose disbelief makes one a heretic; it is rather a corollary of the second of his three basic principles: belief in God, reward and punishment, and the divinity of the Torah (*Sefer ha-Ikkarim* 1:4). Life in the Messianic era is one form of reward, but not the only possible form. Rejection of the entire concept of reward and punishment, on the other hand, would indeed be heretical, and such a person will have no portion in the world to come.

It should be noted, however, that *Chatam Sofer* (Responsa *Yoreh De'ah* 356) disagrees with R. Albo and holds that since the view of R. Hillel is a minority opinion which is not accepted, and since Rambam has posited that the Messiah is indeed a human being and not a metaphor for God's administration of the Messianic era, anyone who maintains the view of R. Hillel, as interpreted by any of the different commentators, is considered to be an apostate who denies the sanctity of the message of the Jewish prophets.

Rashi's View of R. Hillel

Rashi, who lived a hundred years before Rambam and experienced the first Crusade, apparently considered the possibility of R. Hillel negating the unfulfilled yearning of the Jewish people for the arrival of the Messiah to be too heretical to imagine. He accordingly comments on R. Hillel's proclamation, "There will be no Messiah for Israel," as follows: "Rather, the Holy One, blessed be He, will Himself reign and redeem them by Himself." In other words, there will definitely be a Messianic age, and even a Messianic figure, just that the Messianic figure will not be a person, but God Himself. Alternatively, one may say that there will be a Messianic era with no Messianic figure, but rather it will be under the control of God, Who will serve as chief administrator.

The Ethics of Deuteronomy

Rema, in *Torat ha-Olah* (1:19), explains Rashi's view as being related to the previously cited passage from the Talmud: "R. Yochanan also said: The son of David will come only in a generation that is either altogether righteous or altogether wicked" (BT *Sanhedrin* 98a). The proof adduced in the Talmud is from two verses which imply that if there were no righteous people, God Himself would intervene and initiate the Messianic era in order not to be shamed, since by not redeeming His own people, He would indirectly be bestowing credence, superiority, and even divinity to the false gods of the Gentiles. As Ezekiel cites in God's name: "Not for your sake do I do this, O house of Israel, but for My Holy Name, which you have profaned among the nations in which you have sojourned" (Ezek. 36:22).

Apparently, R. Hillel believed that a human Messiah would only emerge from the nation if they were sufficiently worthy. Perhaps one will say, if not for their sake, then for the sake of their great patriarchs Abraham, Isaac, and Jacob. To answer this query, Rema cites a Talmudic passage (BT *Shabbat* 55a) which states that the merit of the patriarchs (*zechut avot*) was no longer present from the time of Hezekiah (it was exhausted after being utilized to allow the miraculous defeat of Sennacherib, 2 Kings 19:35-36). Thus, the only remaining option was that God Himself accompany His nation into the Messianic era.

Lest one ask why Hezekiah himself, who nurtured an entire generation of Torah-infused Israelites, was not deemed worthy of being the Messiah who would inaugurate the Messianic era, it should be recalled that although he had succeeded in arranging for all citizens to learn, he had accomplished it only by threatening to pierce those who did not do so with a sword. Perhaps, from God's point of view, the populace would be worthy of the arrival of Messiah only when each member is self-motivated to live a full Torah life, not when he does so as a means of self-preservation.

R. Yosef, on the other hand, felt that it was premature to condemn

Nitzavim

the nation as irremediable. He cited the verse from Zechariah (9:9), implying that the Messianic king would appear when the nation merited his coming, and Israel was accordingly encouraged to rejoice upon his arrival (certainly inappropriate if the Messiah had arrived as a result of the generation being altogether wicked). Furthermore, the verse points at a specific human Messiah, as opposed to the view of R. Hillel.

ABRAVANEL

Abravanel (*Yeshuot Meshicho* 2:1, ch. 3) rejects R. Albo's elucidation of R. Hillel's view as being too heretical, which is probably the way that Rashi would have viewed it as well. Abravanel cites one commentator who translates R. Hillel's saying: "There will be no Messiah for Israel," to mean: "There will be no Messianic era before the revival of the dead." Since R. Eliezer had said that forty years would elapse between these two events (BT *Sanhedrin* 99a), R. Hillel's differing opinion is that there is not necessarily any period of time during which the Messianic age will not co-exist with the ingathering of exiles and the revival of the dead.

However, for a number of reasons, Abravanel does not find this interpretation acceptable. First, throughout this section, the Talmud discusses "the days of the Messiah," mentioning it four times on this very page. So why would R. Hillel have used a shortened form (saying "Messiah" rather than "Messianic era"), especially since it is liable to be misinterpreted. Second, the continuation of R. Hillel's statement— "because they have already enjoyed *him* in the days of Hezekiah"— would not be accurate, since if the *days* of the Messiah are being discussed, it should have said "they have already enjoyed *them*." Accordingly, Abravanel finds Rashi's exegesis the most reasonable.

The Ethics of Deuteronomy

Summary

The focus in the portion of *Nitzavim* is on the renewal of the covenant between God and the Jewish people. The initial covenant had been made at Sinai, forty years earlier, with a different generation—all of whose males between the ages of twenty and sixty had not lived to enter the Holy Land, in punishment for their rebellious behavior upon hearing the pessimistic report of the spies. The portion makes it quite clear that the maledictions embedded in the covenant would in fact take place at some point in the future in consequence of Israel's backsliding. However, this inauspicious message is coupled with the propitious tidings that the nation would eventually repent and return from its exile to its homeland, and could look forward to the advent of a Messiah and a Messianic era.

Various views regarding the details of the Messianic experience are presented. The centrality of the belief in a specific Messianic figure is examined, including an Amoraic claim that the Messiah has already arrived and the effect of that opinion on Jewish philosophy. Additional events which are meant to occur in the end of days are discussed in **Appendix VI: The War of Gog and Magog, Appendix VII: Mashiach Ben Yosef,** and **Appendix VIII: Birthpangs of the Messiah.**

Vayeilech

The portion of *Vayeilech* describes the events of the last day in the life of Moses. Although the Torah states that "his eye had not dimmed, nor had he lost his freshness" (Deut. 34:7), Moses explains that he is nevertheless no longer able to attend to the activities demanded of a leader ("I can no longer go or come," Deut. 31:2). He adds that he will not even be able to accompany the nation as a simple citizen, since God had expressly told him that he would not be permitted to cross the Jordan (Deut. 31:2). He proceeds to inform the people that they would not have to fend for themselves, as Joshua would be taking over as leader. More importantly, they would be able to rely on the help of God, Who would intervene on their behalf in conquering the Canaanite nations, just as He had done in the battle against the Amorites. Moses continues by giving similar encouragement to Joshua himself in the presence of the entire nation (Deut. 31:3-8).

The *Hakhel* Ceremony

At this stage, Moses had received all the laws of the Torah, and he had completed his review of those laws and the history of the sojournings of the Israelites in the desert, which make up the book of Deuteronomy. He was then able to commit the entire Torah to writing, and without wasting a moment, God commanded Moses to make it clear to the entire nation that the Torah scroll is not meant to be hidden away in the Ark inside the Tabernacle (and eventually the Temple), but rather to be studied and to become the intellectual heritage of the entire nation. This was to be accomplished by instituting a public reading of the Torah scroll, called *hakhel* (literally, "gathering"), every seven years. Moses relays the following instructions to the nation:

> **10** ... At the end of [every] seven years, at the time of the *shemittah* year, on the festival of Sukkot, **11** when all of Israel comes to appear before the Lord your God in the place He will choose, you are to read this Torah before all of Israel, in their ears. **12** Assemble the people—the men, the women, and the children, and the convert in your cities, in order that they hear, and in order that they learn to fear the Lord your God, and [consequently] they will observe and obey all the words of this Torah. **13** And their children, who have not known, will hear and learn to fear the Lord your God, all the days that you live on the land (Deut. 31).

WHO ATTENDED THE *HAKHEL* CEREMONY?
V. 12 says explicitly that the attendees are "the men, the women, and the children, and the convert in your cities," and the purpose of their attendance is so "that they learn to fear the Lord your God, and [consequently] they will observe and obey all the words of this Torah." The first question that arises is that it is understandable that the men, women, and converts will learn at this event, but what can babies gain from being present? Ramban (v. 12) says that the children mentioned are not infants, but rather those who have reached an age at which they are educable, as indicated in v. 13, which states: "And their children, who have not known, will hear and learn to fear the Lord," i.e., the children referred to in the previous verse are those who did not know until now, but are capable of hearing and learning from what they hear. Maharsha (BT *Chagigah* 3a), on the other hand, claims that specifically because the next verse speaks of older children, it must be that v. 12 is speaking of children who are too young to learn. He then asks why the men, women, and younger children are referred

Vayeilech

to in the earlier verse, and the older ones in the later verse. His answer is that v. 12 specifies "observing and obeying," which is only relevant to adults who are obligated to hear, and to obey by bringing along their infant children. V. 13, on the other hand, mentions "hearing and learning," which are appropriate for older children, who are capable of learning, but not yet required to observe the laws.

The question that then arises is: what is the purpose of bringing infants, especially since their presence is likely to negatively affect the concentration of those capable of learning? The Talmud (BT *Chagigah* 3a) answers this question by saying that the children are brought not because they will benefit from the experience, but rather to reward their parents for obeying the command to bring them. The Midrash (*Mechilta de-Rabbi Yishmael, Bo, Masechta de-Pascha* 16) cites numerous cases where the Torah rewards one for seemingly unnecessary actions, such as when the Torah states: ""Sanctify to Me every first-born… among man and among animals; it is Mine" (Exod. 13:2). Actually, the first-born is holy whether the individual sanctifies it or not, but one is rewarded for doing so. Similarly, with respect to the covenant in the portion of *Nitzavim*, the Bible states: "You are all standing this day before the Lord your God, the leaders of your tribes, your elders and your officers, every man of Israel, your young children, your women, and your convert" (Deut. 29:9-10). Again, children are included to reward their parents for bringing them. *Tosafot* (BT *Chagigah* 3a, s.v. *kedai*) note that the practice of bringing toddlers to the *hakhel* ceremony serves as a precedent for doing the same when attending synagogue.

Kli Yakar (Deut. 31:12) explains that the *hakhel* ceremony is a form of communal repentance, coming after the High Holy Days, which are directed at individual repentance. One of the verses in the *Avinu Malkeinu* prayer recited during the Ten Days of Repentance is: "Our Father, our King! Have compassion upon us, and upon our children and infants," while in the *selichot* (communal forgiveness) service, one asks God to "act for the sake of weaned children, who have never sinned." Displaying the children before God is a means of enhancing and personifying the accompanying prayers.

R. Zalman Sorotzkin (*Oznayim la-Torah*, Deut. 31:12) suggests that even infants can benefit from exposure to words of wisdom. He cites R. Dosa, who recalled how the mother of R. Yehoshua b. Chananya would take him in his cradle to the *beit midrash* in order that he might overhear Torah discussions (JT *Yevamot* 1:6). It is known that R. Yehoshua became a great scholar as a disciple of R. Yochanan b. Zakkai, who said of her: "Happy is she who gave birth to him" (*Avot* 2:8). It is not clear whether R. Sorotzkin means that the child benefits in a mystical manner, or whether he means to say that although he cannot understand the import of the Torah dialogue, he may imbibe the spiritual atmosphere and recall it nostalgically as he ages. Indeed, *Akeidat Yitzchak* (*sha'ar* 102) points to the active participation of royalty at *hakhel* and the warm and kindly expressions on the faces of the participants as being capable of leaving an indelible impression on even the youngest of children.

Details Added by the Mishnah

The Mishnah (*Sotah* 7:2) lists the *hakhel* Torah reading as one to be done in Hebrew, not in translation, since it is important that the entire community be familiar with the original language in which the Torah was written. A later Mishnah (*Sotah* 7:8) discusses four aspects of *hakhel*:

1. Where was the ceremony performed?

The Mishnah states that a wooden platform was constructed in the courtyard of the Temple, and it was from that platform that the Torah was read to the community. The question that arises, however, is that building such a structure would seem to be Biblically forbidden. The Torah states: "You shall not plant for yourself an *asherah* of any tree, near the altar of the Lord" (Deut. 16:21). Any tree planted or even a pole set up is called an *asherah*, which was a heathen practice and

Vayeilech

symbolized Astarte, the goddess of fertility. Ramban, *in situ,* explains that the custom was to place such trees near the entrance of idolatrous houses of worship and near altars, as reflected in God's message to Gideon: "Destroy the altar of the Baal which belongs to your father, and the *asherah* which is next to it you must cut down" (Judg. 6:25). Rambam (*Hilchot Avodah Zarah* 6:9) says the tree indicated where people should gather, and of course provided shade for those who did so.

The Talmud (BT *Tamid* 28b) extends the prohibition to even building an exedra (a covered wooden structure open at one end), understanding the phrase "an *asherah* of any tree" to be saying "an *asherah*, or anything made of wood," since the Hebrew word for tree and wood are the same. *Sefer ha-Chinuch* 492 notes that although the Torah-level prohibition only refers to a tree that grows in the ground, and not to wood used for building purposes, the Sages instituted this measure as a "fence around the Torah." Rambam, in two locations (*Hilchot Beit ha-Bechirah* 1:9, *Hilchot Avodah Zarah* 6:10), posits according to the Talmudic extension, and by saying that it is "an extra restriction," would seem to be agreeing with the *Chinuch* that it is of rabbinic origin. *Minchat Chinuch*, however, *in situ*, cites a view that Rambam actually considers the extension to be a Torah-level prohibition, just that, unlike the initial prohibition, it is not punishable by lashes.

Ra'avad, in both locations, notes that there are examples of wooden structures which were in fact built in the Temple courtyard, namely the office of the high priest (*Middot* 5:4), the balcony constructed on Sukkot at the time of the rejoicing at the place of the water-drawing (which is the source of the modern *mechitzah*), and of course the platform built for the king at *hakhel*. In *Hilchot Beit ha-Bechirah*, Ra'avad answers that the wooden structures referred to were all made in the women's court, which was to the east and fifteen steps below the entrance to the Temple, hence not included in the prohibition. In *Hilchot Avodah Zarah*, Ra'avad answers that the high priest's office was a completely enclosed "house" and not an exedra, which is open from one side, and thus was neither included in the prohibition nor in its extension. The other two structures were of a temporary nature, thus also not included in the ban. *Kesef Mishneh* understands Ra'avad's intention when calling the high priest's office a "house" to be that it was actually made of stone, and when the Mishnah in *Middot* says it was made of wood, it means only that it once held wood (or, perhaps, it was paneled with wood). He continues that it is unlikely that it was actually made of wood, since why would its construction have differed from that of the other offices mentioned in the Mishnah in *Middot*?

2. Who reads the Torah "before all of Israel?"

The Mishnah (*Sotah* 7:8) calls the portion to be read "the king's chapter," and further states that the king received the Torah from the high priest while he was standing, and then sat down to read it. The question is, what is the source of the Mishnah? The text of the Torah states:

> **7** And Moses called Joshua and said to him in the presence of all Israel, "Be strong and courageous!".... **9** Then Moses wrote this Torah, and gave it to the priests.... and to all the elders of Israel. **10** And Moses commanded them, saying, "At the end of [every] seven years.... **11** When all Israel comes to appear before the Lord.... you are to read this Torah before all Israel" (Deut. 31: 7-11).

The commandment seems to be directed at the priests and the elders (v. 10), not the king, although the only person actually mentioned by name is Joshua (v. 7). R. Yosef Bechor-Shor says that the command was indeed meant for Joshua, whose authority paralleled that of a king.

Vayeilech

Sefer Yerei'im (ch. 266) derives that the intended reader is the king from a Biblical precedent. As noted in the introduction, King Josiah had asked the high priest Hilkiah to gather silver from the Temple to pay for renovations (2 Kings 22:4). While doing so, he accidentally found the Torah which had originally been placed by Moses either in the Ark (R. Meir) or on an abutting shelf (R. Yehudah, BT *Bava Batra* 14a), but had then been removed from its original location and concealed (*Metzudat David*, 2 Kings 22:8). According to Rashi in 2 Kings, the wicked King Ahaz (father of Hezekiah) had burned several copies of the Torah, and in order to protect this specially valuable copy, written by Moses himself, it had been hidden away.[59] Upon its discovery, King Josiah ordered the elders, priests, prophets, and inhabitants of Jerusalem to gather together, and he publicly read the Torah to them. Ralbag (2 Kings 23:3) points out the similarity of the king's behavior to that which occurs during *hakhel*.

According to both *Bechor-Shor* and *Sefer Yerei'im*, the requirement that the king read the selected portions is Torah-level (*mi-de-oraita*). In fact, *Sefer Yerei'im* counts the king's requirement to read and the congregation's requirement to listen as two separate commands (ch. 266 and ch. 433). *Tiferet Yisrael* (*Sotah* 7:52), on the other hand, considers the king's obligation to be rabbinical in nature, and it was instituted as a means of honoring the Torah and stressing to the congregation that even the king is subject to the Torah and its *mitzvot*.

---

59. Rashi's Midrashic source is unknown, and Radak, *in situ*, claims that the righteous Hezekiah would certainly have uncovered it. He therefore assumes that the Torah was simply neglected during the reign of the wicked Manasseh (Hezekiah's grandson), and was found in its proper location. Alternatively, the Talmud (BT *Sanhedrin* 103b) mentions that Manasseh cut out God's name from the Torah, and his son, the wicked King Amon, burned it, and it would be quite reasonable to assume that during one of their reigns (which immediately preceded Josiah) Moses' Torah was hidden. In fact, Abravanel, *in situ*, says that it was during the reign of Manasseh that it was found hidden between two rows of stones, when Hilkiah was searching the Temple's entire premises in order to determine what repairs were needed.

3. When precisely is the Torah to be read to everyone?

The Mishnah explains that it is to be read in the eighth year, after the completion of the seven-year *shemittah* cycle, on the first of the intermediate days (*chol ha-mo'ed*) of Sukkot. The timing is derived from the fact that the verse says: "At the end of [every] seven years, at the time of the *shemittah* year, on the festival of Sukkot, when all of Israel comes to appear before the Lord" (Deut. 31:10-11). Analyzing these verses, the first two phrases seem contradictory. The first phrase speaks of the end of the seven-year cycle, i.e., after *shemittah*, while the second speaks of being in the *shemittah* year. The Talmud (BT *Rosh Hashanah* 12b), cited by Rashi on the verse, explains that even in the eighth year, some of the restrictions of the seventh year still apply, namely harvesting the grain that grew in the seventh, so the eighth year can still be termed "the time of the *shemittah* year."

The phrase "when all of Israel comes to appear before the Lord" implies that it should be at the beginning of the holiday, which is when the Israelites arrive in Jerusalem. Rashi (BT *Sotah* 41b, s.v. *me-eimat*) asks, if that is the case, why not make it on the first day? He answers that one may not construct the wooden platform on the holiday itself, only on the intermediate days. Rashi then asks, why not construct it the day before the holiday, and answers, basing himself on JT *Megillah* 1:4, that doing so would cause the courtyard to be cluttered at a time when many people would be crowding into it to bring their holiday sacrifices (pilgrimage, festal, and jubilation offerings). Tosafot (BT *Sotah* 41a, s.v. *katav*), however, disagrees with Rashi's logic for the following reasons:

a. The Torah does not mention a platform altogether. Accordingly, the requirement to build it could not have been a reason not to perform the mitzvah on the first day of Sukkot. Rather, one would suspend with building it altogether.
b. Indeed, construction of a platform is prohibited on the first day of Sukkot, but it is prohibited on the intermediate days as well.

c. It would have been possible to build the platform modularly, and only assemble it on the first day of Sukkot, if the construction were the problem.

Tosafot concludes that the real reason that *hakhel* is done on the first intermediate day is because the verse should be transposed as follows: "At the end of the seventh year of *shemittah*, at the time of the festival of Sukkot." Reading the verse in that manner, the phrase "at the time of (*be-mo'ed*)" is an extra phrase, which implies that it should be read during the holiday. But the phrase "when all of Israel comes" implies it should be read at the beginning of the holiday. By reading it on the first intermediate day, both requirements are fulfilled.

Exactly when on the first intermediate day (*chol ha-mo'ed*) should *hakhel* be done? Following the logic of Tosafot, it should be done as soon as possible, i.e., on the night after the first day of Sukkot, and this is stated explicitly by *Tiferet Yisrael* (*Sotah* 7:48). On the other hand, Rambam, in his *Peirush ha-Mishnayot*, says that it was to take place on the second day of Sukkot, and Rashash, *in situ* (s.v. *katav*), says explicitly that it is not reasonable to assume that it was to be read at night, possibly because young children were expected to attend.

Why was this specific time chosen? *Akeidat Yitzchak* (102) enumerates a number of reasons. First, being the year immediately after *shemittah*, the people have rested physically; they are not engaged in the ingathering of crops, since none were harvested during the Sabbatical year, and their dietary needs have been satisfied, as the Torah states: "I will command My blessing for you in the sixth year, and it will yield produce for three years" (Lev. 25:21). R. Zalman Sorotzkin (*Oznayim la-Torah*, Deut. 31:10) points out that after the Sabbatical year, the population is also refreshed spiritually, having been able to devote more time to Torah learning and observance, and they are thus adequately prepared for the spiritual gathering which *hakhel* is. Another reason for the timing, according to *Akeidat Yitzchak*, is the pleasant fall weather, which is even superior to spring weather, when there may remain a few vestiges of the cold and damp winter weather.

The phrase in v. 11, "when all Israel comes to appear before the Lord," stresses that for the sake of convenience, *hakhel* takes place when the entire community is already gathered at the Temple, so as not to burden the nation by requiring an additional trip (R. Zalman Sorotzkin, *Oznayim la-Torah*, Deut. 31:11).

4. How is it possible to publicly read the entire Torah in one standing?

The Mishnah explains that in fact the entire Torah was not read, only certain sections from the book of Deuteronomy—in particular, those which summarize the principles of the religion. It will be recalled that R. Yosef Albo had chosen the three cardinal Jewish principles to be belief in God, in Divine Providence (*hashgachah pratit*, including reward and punishment), and in the divinity of the Torah. It has also been claimed that among the 613 commandments in the Torah, those between man and his fellow man have special significance.[60] The Mishnah enumerates the sections which were read at *hakhel*:

a. Deut. 1:1-6:3—basic history, including revelation, the giving of the Ten Commandments, and the threat of exile if they are disobeyed.
b. Deut. 6:4-9—the *Shema*, in which the Jew accepts God's sovereignty (Albo's first principle).
c. Deut. 11:13-21—reward and punishment, as reflected in agricultural yield (Albo's second principle and second paragraph of the *Shema*).
d. Deut. 14:22-29, 26:12-15—laws of the annual first tithe for the Levite; the second tithe, which is given in the first two years of each of the three-year cycles of the seven-year cycle, and is eaten

---

60. A more detailed account appears in Abba Engelberg, *The Ethics of Genesis* (2014), pp. 223-234.

Vayeilech

by the landowner on the pilgrimage festivals in Jerusalem; and the tithe for the poor, given in the third year of the two three-year cycles (Rashi, Deut. 14:29). Rashi (BT *Sotah* 41a) explains that this is read because it is timely, since *hakhel* is performed on Sukkot at the time of ingathering. The Jerusalem Talmud (*Sotah* 7:8) explains that since *hakhel* takes place in the eighth year, and tithes are not given in the seventh Sabbatical year, the congregation had to be reminded that they would once more have to go back to giving tithes.

e. Deut. 17:14-20—the portion describing the appointment, requirements, and limitations of kings. The Mishnah records that when King Agrippa came to the verse: "You may not appoint a foreigner over you, one who is not your brother" (Deut. 17:15), tears rolled down his cheeks, whereupon the populace said to him: "Fear not, Agrippa, you are our brother, you are our brother, you are our brother." Rashi (BT *Sotah* 41a, s.v. *achinu*) says that Agrippa was actually Jewish, since his mother was Jewish. Although the Talmud itself implies that he was not Jewish, since it says on the next page (41b) that by the Jews saying Agrippa was their brother, they were actually flattering him, Rashi (BT *Sotah* 41b, s.v. *egrofa*) explains that even though he was technically a brother, he was not the kind of brother that is appropriate to be a king, being that his father was an Idumean slave. Tosafot (BT *Sotah* 41b, s.v. *oto*) go further by saying that the verse which prohibits "a foreigner" from being a king demands that both parents be full-fledged Jews, and by ignoring this requirement, the congregation committed the serious offense of respecting a human being more than God and His law. On the other hand, Tosafot in a different location (BT *Bava Batra* 3b, s.v. *kol*) take the Talmudic implication literally, and assume that his mother was not Jewish. This is apparently also the opinion of Rambam who, in his *Peirush ha-Mishnayot* (*Sotah* 7:8), states that the people only said he was Jewish to comfort him (and perhaps also to protect themselves), in spite of the fact that he was not a legitimate king, his kingship having been forced upon the Jews by the Roman emperor.

According to modern historians,[61] there were actually two Agrippas. Agrippa I (years of reign: 41-44 CE) was the son of Aristobulus IV, who was the son of Herod. However, his mother was Berenice, daughter of Salome, who was a sister of Herod. In other words, halachically, Agrippa I was the son of a Gentile mother, and hence not Jewish. Agrippa had been a gambler in Rome as a youth, but after being crowned, became quite humble and relatively religious, and was much loved by the people, who understandably chose to reassure him upon realizing that he was depressed. The Mishnah (*Sotah* 7:8) states that at the *hakhel* ceremony, a Torah scroll was taken from the synagogue located on the Royal Porch of the Temple Mount and given to the high priest, who passed it on to the king, who received it while standing up, but read it after sitting down. King Agrippa, however, behaved differently, as described by the Mishnah: "King Agrippa stood and received it [the Torah scroll] and read it while standing [in honor of God's word], for which act the Sages praised him" (*Sotah* 7:8). This respectful devout behavior, coupled with the fact that he cried when he realized that a foreigner could not be king according to *halachah*, would seem to support the view of Tosafot in *Bava Batra* that the Mishnah speaks of Agrippa I, who was not Jewish.

Agrippa II (years of reign: 50-100 CE) was actually Jewish, being the son of Agrippa I and his wife Cypros, daughter of Shlomzion, daughter of Mariamne the Hasmonean, wife of Herod, making Agrippa II a great-grandson of Herod. Rashi would then have been referring to Agrippa II, because in addition to claiming that he was Jewish, Rashi (BT *Sotah* 41a, s.v. *Agrippas*)

---

61. For a summary of the basic historical details, see Appendix V: The Last Years of the Second Temple.

says that he reigned at the time of the destruction of the Temple.

On the other hand, Agrippa II does not really fit the narrative of the Mishnah. First, he did not even reign in Jerusalem, but rather in a Syrian kingdom called Chalcis, although it is true that he was given responsibility to supervise the Temple in Jerusalem. Nevertheless, it is doubtful that he would have been in Jerusalem at the time of *hakhel* during the twenty years of his reign which overlapped the existence of the Temple. Second, the Mishnah praises his devotion, yet Agrippa II was actually quite irreligious, and in fact Josephus (*Antiquities of the Jews*, Book 20, ch. 7) accuses him of having an incestuous relationship with his sister Berenice. It is highly unlikely that he would have stood for the Torah reading out of respect. Third, Agrippa II was detested by the populace, since he sided with the Romans during the rebellion, so it is unlikely that they would have been eager to comfort him. Fourth, why would he have cried upon hearing that the king must be Jewish, if he was in fact Jewish? Finally, why was the congregation excoriated for using flattery when saying Agrippa II was a brother, if that were truly the case? Although answers have been offered to some of these questions, Rambam's explanation seems to better fit the simple meaning of the Mishnah and Talmud.

Women's Learning

V. 12 calls for the presence of men and women at *hakhel*, with no seeming distinction between the two, "in order that they hear and in order that they learn" the words of the Torah. R. Eliezer b. Azariah (BT *Chagigah* 3a), however, immediately qualifies the seemingly egalitarian aspect of Torah learning implied by the text, when he interprets the words: "in order that they hear" as referring to the women, and "in order that they learn" as referring to the men. What exactly is meant by this distinction?

The Ethics of Deuteronomy

The Talmud refers to the learning of Torah by women in a number of locations. The Mishnah (*Kiddushin* 1:7) states that fathers, but not mothers, have certain obligations with respect to their sons. The Talmud (BT *Kiddushin* 29a) cites various examples, one of which is derived from the verses: "And you must set these words of Mine upon your heart and upon your soul… And you must teach them to your sons" (Deut. 11:18-19). The Talmud understands that since the verse says "to your sons," as opposed to "to your children," it must be that daughters do not have to be taught. Through textual analysis, the Talmud proceeds to say that women, who do not have to be taught, also have no obligation to study.

Does this mean that women are not rewarded for studying Torah? Apparently they are, based on the Talmudic statement: "He who is commanded and fulfills [a mitzvah] is greater than he who fulfills it though not commanded" (BT *Kiddushin* 31a). *Tosafot* (s.v. *gadol*) explain that this is because one feels the pressure of having to fulfill the requirement, which is not felt by one who performs the mitzvah voluntarily. At any rate, the reward is less for those who are not commanded, but it still exists (*Chiddushei ha-Ramban, Kiddushin* 31a).

A second source which deals with women's learning is the Mishnah (*Sotah* 3:4), which discusses an adulterous woman who drinks the *mayim ha-me'ararim* (curse-bearing waters). The Mishnah states that if the woman is meritorious (by ensuring that her sons are taught Scripture and Mishnah, and by acquiescing to the prolonged absence of her husband when he learns Torah in a distant location, BT *Sotah* 21b), the punishment may be delayed for as long as three years. Ben Azzai says, on the basis of this occurrence, that a man must teach his daughter Torah, so that if she ever has to drink *mayim ha-me'ararim* and is indeed guilty of adultery, and if she does not immediately feel its effects, it is not necessarily because the waters are ineffective, but rather because she has some merit, and she will eventually be punished. R. Eliezer, on the other hand, adamantly

Vayeilech

objects to the propriety of teaching women Torah, claiming that one who does so may be compared to one who teaches his daughter *tiflut*. Rashi (BT *Sotah* 21b, s.v. *ke-ilu*) understands *tiflut* to mean sophistication, which will be utilized for conniving sexual advances. Rambam (*Peirush ha-Mishnayot, Sotah* 3:4) translates it as "worthless words and vanity," meaning that women will not appreciate its serious and holy message. In the Jerusalem Talmud (*Sotah* 3:4), R. Eliezer formulates his view more harshly, when he says: "Rather burn the Torah text than make it accessible to women."

The two previously cited sources appear on the surface to be contradictory. On the one hand, the text from *Kiddushin* seems to imply that Torah study for women is a recommended, reward-bearing activity, even if less so than for men. The Mishnah in *Sotah*, at least according to R. Eliezer, sounds as if it is saying that women should be prohibited from studying Torah. Nevertheless, Rambam (*Hilchot Talmud Torah* 1:13) attempts to reconcile them as follows:

(1) A woman who studies Torah will receive reward. However, that reward will not be [as great] as a man's, since she is not commanded [to study]. Whoever performs a deed which he is not commanded to do, does not receive as great a reward as one who performs a mitzvah that he is commanded to do.

(2) Even though she will receive a reward, the Sages commanded that a person should not teach his daughter Torah, because most women's minds are not directed to studying, and they transform the words of Torah into idle matters because of the weakness of their minds. Our Sages declared: "Whoever teaches his daughter Torah is like one who teaches her vanity."

(3) Where does this rule apply? With respect to the Oral Law. [With regard to] the Written Law: initially, one should not teach her. However, if he taught her, it is not as if he taught her vanity.

Note that part (1) follows directly from the *Kiddushin* text, while part (2) seems to reflect R. Eliezer's view in *Sotah*. Rambam reconciles them by saying that studying is a rewardable good deed for anyone, but he warns the father that since his daughter will probably not comprehend it or relate to it seriously, he may be wasting his time. In part (3), Rambam introduces a new distinction, and the question is on what he based himself.

Bach (*Yoreh De'ah* 246) says that Rambam realized that even R. Eliezer would not (and could not) have intended to contradict the explicit law in the Torah that women should (at least) hear the words of the Torah in order for them to become aware of the *mitzvot* they are commanded to fulfill. But then, why does Rambam himself say that they should not be taught the Written Law at the outset? Bach answers that the distinction that R. Eliezer b. Azariah makes with regard to the mitzvah of *hakhel* between women "hearing" as opposed to "learning" means to discourage formal textual teaching even of the Written Law, in favor of *ad hoc* oral exposure to its contents, as in fact occurred during *hakhel*. On the other hand, if women would consistently misinterpret the content of the Written Law as "worthless words and vanity," the Torah would not have sanctioned their presence at the ceremony altogether.

The Vilna Gaon (*Yoreh De'ah* 246:25) found an alternate source for Rambam's opinion that teaching women the Written Law is permitted. The Mishnah in *Nedarim* (4:3) says that if one (A) is prohibited by vow from deriving any benefit from his fellow (B), "he (B) may [still] teach his (A's) sons and daughters Scripture [since *mitzvot* were not given for pleasure, so even if B is fulfilling the mitzvah that A was obligated to do, he is not giving him pleasure by doing so]." At any rate, it is clear from the Mishnah that it was accepted that girls would be taught Bible. Interestingly, when Rambam cites this law (*Hilchot Nedarim* 6:7), he doesn't mention teaching A's daughter, apparently because he frowns upon doing so initially.

Vayeilech

PRACTICAL JEWISH LAW

R. Yehudah ha-Chasid (late twelfth century) allows women to be taught practical *halachah*, since otherwise they will not know how to perform *mitzvot*. He mentions *hakhel* and the covenant in the portion of *Nitzavim* (Deut. 29:10), both of which address women and men, as well as the historical precedent of King Hezekiah, during whose reign women were thoroughly versed with the most complex laws that were applicable to them (*Sefer Chasidim* 313).

Maharil (1360-1427), on the other hand, does not permit any type of formal learning for women. Rather, he holds that the basics necessary for performing *mitzvot* should be transmitted to them orally. He explains all Talmudic references to knowledgeable women as referring to cases in which the women, by dint of their questioning their fathers and Rabbis, achieved a high degree of expertise in laws relevant to them, such as those related to salting meat, menstruation, etc. (Responsum 199).

Rema seems to posit according to R. Yehudah ha-Chasid, in that he says: "A woman is required to learn the laws relevant to women" (*Yoreh De'ah* 246:6), which indicates formal learning as opposed to *ad hoc* instruction and the answering of questions.

SELF-STUDY

R. Yehoshua Falk (1555-1614) writes in his commentary on the *Tur*, *Perishah*, that although R. Eliezer forbade fathers to teach Torah to their daughters, he did not prohibit women from learning it on their own. R. Chaim Navon explains how this view can be derived from three expressions used by Rambam:

> First, Rambam notes that if a woman studies Torah, she is eligible for reward. Second, according to Rambam, the Sages directed that a man should not teach his daughter Torah (following Rabbi Eliezer's formulation), but they said nothing about her right to study Torah on her own. Finally, Rambam

writes that "the majority of women have not a mind adequate for its study," which implies that some women do indeed have the intellectual capacity for Torah study, and that they do not turn the words of the Torah into trivialities. [62]

MODERN TIMES

In the early twentieth century, many women were receiving a secular education, and with no parallel level of Jewish studies available to them, they would frequently become lax in their observance or even leave the fold. In response to this situation, Sarah Schenirer established the network of Bais Ya'akov schools, starting in Krakow in 1918. Although the negative viewpoint of R. Eliezer with regard to women's Torah learning was well known, the *posek ha-dor* (the generation's most accepted halachic decisor), *Chafetz Chaim*, came to the conclusion that "all of this applied in earlier times," but now, when many women have been taught "the script and language of the nations," he concluded:

> It is a great mitzvah to teach them the Pentateuch, and also the Prophets and the Writings and the ethical teachings of the Sages, such as *Avot* and *Sefer Menorat ha-Ma'or* and the like, so that our holy faith should become verified to them, for if not, they are liable to turn completely away from God's path, and transgress, God forbid, all of the foundations of the religion. (*Likkutei Halachot, Sotah* 3).

While *Chafetz Chaim* called women's Jewish education a great mitzvah, R. Zalman Sorotzkin termed it an absolute requirement (*Moznayim la-Mishpat* 42). Although *Chafetz Chaim* and R. Sorotzkin diverged from Rambam's decision that there should be no formal Torah study for women, they maintained his view that the appropriate course of study be confined to the Bible (the Written Law), with the additional

---

62. Chaim Navon, "Women and Torah Study," VBM Haretzion.

Vayeilech

caveat that they also accepted Rema's extension of the curriculum to practical *halachah*, including Jewish ethics.

R. J.B. Soloveitchik, on the other hand, came to the conclusion that in a day when women have achieved equality with men, both academically and employment-wise, in myriad secular fields, it is incumbent upon them to achieve a commensurate level of Jewish knowledge, which of necessity demands proficiency with regard to the Oral Law as well (*Peninei ha-Rav*, p. 167).

SUMMARY

The portion of *Vayeilech* introduces the *hakhel* ceremony, during which the entire community is exposed to the words of the Torah—men, women, and even children too young to comprehend their meaning, but old enough to retain a memory in the future of the grand occasion which they experienced. Mentioning the attendance of women at *hakhel* opened up a discussion of whether Torah study is demanded, expected, or even permitted for women in the same manner as it is for men. The answer is that historically, there was certainly a very clear differentiation between the education of men and women. While Maharil felt women were to be taught *halachah* only by example and by answering their questions as they arise, others felt that these areas could be conveyed to them in a more formal manner. While Rambam dissuaded formal study of Scripture for women, *Chafetz Chaim* approved of it and R. Zalman Sorotzkin demanded it in the modern era. According to R. J.B. Soloveitchik, all fields of Jewish endeavor should be made available to women as well.

Ha'azinu

The main topic in the portion of *Ha'azinu* is Moses' farewell poem. One of the highlights of the early years of his career had been the "*Az Yashir*" song of praise and triumph, sung after the successful crossing of the Reed Sea. In *Ha'azinu*, Moses composes another song, in which he predicts the future of the fledgling nation after his departure from the scene, including Israel's unfaithfulness and ingratitude, for which it would be severely punished, but notes that in the end, the nation would be redeemed from its suffering and achieve salvation. This forecast was already presented in prose form as the third segment in the portion of *Nitzavim* (Deut. 30:1-10).

The last three verses of *Vayeilech* contain the introduction to the poem of *Ha'azinu*. Here, Moses concisely summarizes one of the basic themes of the upcoming poem when he says:

> For I know that after my death, you will surely become corrupted, and deviate from the way which I had commanded you. Consequently, evil will befall you at the end of days, because you did evil in the eyes of the Lord to anger Him through the work of your hands (Deut. 31:29).

What is missing from Moses' introduction, but included in the poem, is the happy ending after the many ages of suffering.

Moses starts off in ch. 32 by noting the nation's ingratitude at some point in the future for the many acts of grace which God had performed for them, calling them a "stubborn and twisted generation"

Ha'azinu

(v. 5). He goes on (Deut. 32:7-14) to describe the loving protection which God provided the nation, which might be compared to an eagle "hovering over its fledglings" (v. 11), and the fertile land which He allocated to them, which was flowing with "the cream of cattle and the milk of sheep, with the fat of lambs and rams and he-goats, with the best grains of wheat, and it [Israel] would drink the finest red wine made from grapes" (v. 14).

Next, Israel's misbehavior and consequent punishment is described (Deut. 32:15-33). In spite of God's largesse, "Jeshurun (Israel) became fat and rebelled" (v. 15), which manifested itself by sacrificing "to demons which have no power, deities they did not know" (v. 17). This behavior would stimulate God's retribution, which would consist of famine, attacks by demons, animals, and snakes, as well as by terror-wielding enemies. In fact, their behavior would apparently be wicked enough to justify their complete annihilation, which God considered doing, but then who would replace them—certainly not the Gentile nations, who would credit their own gods for the downfall of Israel, saying: "Our hand was triumphant! The Lord did none of this" (v. 27).

Since there is no alternative, God will in the end avenge His people and destroy their enemies (Deut. 32:34-43). More specifically, "the appointed day of their reckoning is near" (v. 35), and accordingly, "I will bring vengeance upon My adversaries and repay those who hate Me. I will intoxicate My arrows with blood [of Israel's enemies], and My sword will consume flesh from the blood of the slain and the captives" (vv. 41-42).

THE CONCLUSION OF THE POEM

At the conclusion of the poem, the Torah states: "And Moses came and spoke all the words of this song into the ears of the nation, he and Hoshea the son of Nun" (Deut. 32:44). The verse would seem to be redundant, since an almost identical verse appears before the presentation of the poem in the portion of *Vayeilech*: "And Moses spoke into the ears of the entire assembly of Israel the words of the following song, until its completion" (Deut. 31:30).

Abravanel (Deut. 32:44) points out that there is even a third verse which hints at the transmission of the song of *Ha'azinu*: "And Moses wrote this song on that day, and taught it to the Children of Israel" (Deut. 31:22). He notes that Moses initially taught the poem only to those who were present when he received the inspiration (v. 22), and for that reason it states "to the Children of Israel," but not to all of them. Moses was then told: "Assemble to Me all the elders of your tribes and your officers, and I will speak these words into their ears, and I will call upon the heaven and the earth as witnesses against them" (Deut. 31:28), leading to v. 30, where the elders and officers were addressed. Finally, in 32:44, the nation at large was informed of God's message, and so it was spoken "to all Israel" (v. 45).

In the final rendition to the entire congregation, the elucidatory phrase "he and Hoshea the son of Nun" is included. Rashi (Deut. 32:44) attempts to explain the significance of this addition by combining a Talmudic statement with a Midrashic addendum. The Talmud states: "It was the Sabbath of transition [when] the authority was taken from one to be transferred to the other" (BT *Sotah* 13b). Although Sabbath might seem to be an inappropriate time for making civic appointments, it must be recalled that the main source of legislation in Judaism is Torah knowledge, which is traditionally imparted on the Sabbath. In fact, the Midrash states:

> God said to Moses: "Appoint an interpreter for Joshua, so that Joshua can ask [questions of a religious nature] and expound and teach [Torah] lessons in your lifetime, so that Israel would not say to him [Joshua]: 'During your teacher's lifetime you did not [dare to] speak, and [only] now do you speak!'" (*Sifrei Nitzavim* 305).

Ha'azinu

R. Meir Danon, in *Be'er ba-Sadeh*, explains that Moses and Joshua did not read the poem together, because then Moses would have continued to be looked upon as the leader, and Joshua as subordinate. Rather, Moses started, and he let Joshua continue on his own, for the purpose of endowing Joshua with an equal degree of spirituality, as indicated by first mentioning Moses ("And Moses came," v. 30), and only then Joshua, as opposed to writing: "And Moses and Joshua came," which would have implied that they acted jointly. The occasion was made indelible by virtue of the fact that not only did it take place on Sabbath, but it was the last day in the life of Moses (*Tosafot*, BT *Menachot* 30a, s.v. *mi-kan*). Finally, an interpreter was appointed, whose job was to explain the lesson to the people on a level that was understandable to them, just as was done for Moses' lectures.

A second point which Moses wished to emphasize was that Joshua was worthy not only intellectually, but personality-wise as well. In v. 44, Joshua is referred to by his original name "Hoshea" (Num. 13:16) rather than by "Joshua." The Midrash states:

> And why does Scripture say "he and Hoshea b. Nun"—to inform one of Joshua's righteousness. One might assume that he would become haughty [or corrupt] when he was designated for governance, [therefore] it says, "he and Hoshea b. Nun." Hoshea with his righteousness, even though he was appointed a governor over Israel, he is still [the same] Hoshea with his righteousness [and modesty] (*Sifrei Ha'azinu* 334).

Just as Moses was outstandingly modest (Num. 12:3), so was Joshua.

The Prescription for Salvation

After describing the rise and fall and eventual redemption of the nation, the Torah prescribes the perennial means of salvation, which is by obeying its laws: "Set your hearts to all of the words which I bear witness for you this day, so that you may command your children to observe to do all the words of this Torah" (Deut. 32:46). The second half of the phrase stresses observance of the law, while the first half—which speaks of setting one's heart to the words of the poem—refers to study, not only of this particular song, but of the entire corpus of Jewish law, as clarified by the Midrash cited by Rashi:

> A person must direct his eyes, his heart, and his ears to the words of the Torah… which are likened to "mountains suspended by a hair" [i.e., numerous laws derived from a single word of the Torah. Also, a hair-width distinction can affect halachic decisions] (*Sifrei Ha'azinu* 335).

Studying the laws in depth is clearly necessary for proper observance. However, beyond that necessity, there are two ramifications of study that play an important role in a Jew's daily life. The first is the development of an intellectual approach to life, both in general and to Judaism in particular, by grappling with God's message to mankind, even in conjunction with aspects of the Bible which do not relate to legislation. The second is with regard to the proper utilization of one's free time, as depicted by R. S.R. Hirsch:

> Only a way of life devoted to the pursuit of study as well as of economic independence can take up our time to such a degree that there will be no unoccupied hours during which we could indulge in thoughts that are far from good and that could make us drift away from the path of goodness (*The Hirsch Siddur*, p. 434).[63]

The final verse in connection with the poem of *Ha'azinu* (32:47) reinforces the message of the previous verse: "For it is not an empty thing for you, for it is your life, and through this thing, you will

---

63. For a more thorough treatment, see Abba Engelberg, *The Ethics of Genesis*, pp. 245-254.

lengthen your days upon the land to which you are crossing over the Jordan, to possess it." Rashi suggests two possible meanings for "empty." The first is "without reward," and the verse is saying that one will be rewarded for the performance of *mitzvot* with long life, if not in this world, then in the next. Although the emphasis here is on actively performing the commands, *Chizkuni* explains that a degree of study is also implied, since without knowledge one does not know which positive commands to do and which negative actions to refrain from. Although one should not focus on the reward when performing good deeds, justice demands that the righteous be compensated.[64]

A second explanation of "empty," based on the Midrash, is that it refers to the text of the Torah: "There is not one superfluous ['empty'] word in the Torah which, if [properly] expounded upon, will not be rewarded in this world, and the principal remains intact in the next world" (*Sifrei Ha'azinu* 336).

The Midrash proceeds to list *mitzvot*, in addition to Torah study, which the Bible explicitly rewards with long life, namely: honoring parents (Exod. 20:12), sparing the mother bird (Deut. 22:7), performing acts of lovingkindness (Prov. 21:21), and making peace between man and his fellow man (Ps. 34:15, Isa. 54:13).[65]

THE WORLD TO COME (*OLAM HA-BA*)

Based on the approach of v. 47 that there is much to be learned by analyzing every word of Scripture, Saadiah Gaon (*Emunot ve-De'ot* 7:1) examines one of the passages in the section of the poem dealing with the lot of Israel's enemies. The verse states: "There is no god like Me! I cause death and grant life. I wound and I heal, and no one can

---

64. Ibid., pp. 233-234.
65. The derivation of long life from Ps. 34:15 is explained in the Talmud (BT *Yevamot* 109b, *Kiddushin* 40a). The Midrash derives it from the verse in Isaiah which equates Torah study and making peace by contiguity (*hekesh*), and since Torah study is rewarded by long life, based on v. 47, so is making peace (*Toldot Adam*).

rescue from My hand" (v. 39). Regarding the phrase "I cause death and grant life," R. Saadiah notes that death is mentioned before life, which is the opposite of the natural order. Of course, the phrase could be taken to mean that nations recede and are replaced by others. However, the next phrase says "I wound and I heal," indicating that just as it is the same body which is wounded and healed, the previous phrase is referring to the same body when it says that it dies and is reborn—a clear reference to resurrection in some future world. That this will occur at the dawn of salvation is clarified by the phrases which follow: "When I raise up My hand to heaven… When I sharpen the blade of My sword… Sing out praise, O you nations, for His people [parallel to Jer. 31:6]! For He will avenge the blood of His servants, inflict revenge upon His adversaries, and appease His land [and] His people" (vv. 40-43).

Midrashically, the Talmud derives the existence of *olam ha-ba* from a verse in *Ki Teitzei* regarding the law of sparing the mother bird, which states: "You should send away the mother, and [then] you may take the young for yourself, in order that it should be good for you, so that your days be lengthened" (Deut. 22:7). The Talmud remarks: "'In order that it should be good for you' means on the day that is wholly good; and 'so that your days be lengthened' on the day that is wholly long" (BT *Kiddushin* 39b). The reference is clearly to the next world.

Rambam asserts the existence and appellation assigned to *olam ha-ba* as follows:

> It [the world to come] exists and is present, as implied by: "How great is Your goodness that You have hidden [implying it is already existent] for those who fear You, that You have worked for those who take refuge in You" (Ps. 31:20)… It is only called the world to come because that life comes to a man after life in this world, in which we exist as souls within bodies. This [physical type of existence] is what is available

Ha'azinu

to all men initially [only to be followed by the next world] (*Hilchot Teshuvah* 8: 8).

Exactly who will occupy the next world is discussed in **Appendix IX: Entitlement to the World to Come.**

Rambam's Description of *Olam ha-Ba*

Rambam's understanding of the next world is based on Biblical and Talmudic passages which he culls from various locations and weaves into a whole. The following six points, enumerated with citations from Rambam and his sources, summarize his approach:

1. Human beings are composed of three elements: the body, the soul (*neshamah*, close to *neshimah*, the Hebrew word for "breath"), and the form of the soul (*nefesh*). The existence of the first two elements is limited to the lifetime of a person on earth, but the last element, which is the abode of one's knowledge and understanding, lasts forever. Rambam defines the *nefesh* as follows:

   The soul of all flesh [*nefesh*] is the form which it was given by God. The extra dimension which is found in the soul of man is the form of man who is perfect in his knowledge. Concerning this form, the Torah states "Let us make man in our image and in our [spiritual] likeness" (Gen. 1:26)—i.e., granting man a form which knows and comprehends ideas that are not material, like the angels, who are form without body, until he can resemble them... It is not the soul found in all living creatures which allows them to eat, drink, reproduce, feel, and think (*Hilchot Yesodei ha-Torah* 4:8).

Rambam (*Hilchot Yesodei ha-Torah* 4:9) distinguishes the first two elements from the third:

> The form of this soul is not a combination of the fundamentals [fire, wind, water, and earth] into which it will ultimately decompose, nor does it come from the *neshamah* so that it would require the *neshamah,* as the *neshamah* requires the body. Rather, it is from God, from heaven.
>
> Therefore, when the matter [of the body]—which is a combination of the fundamentals—decomposes, the *neshamah* [also] ceases to exist, for it [the *neshamah*] exists only together with the body and requires the body for all its deeds; this form [the *nefesh*] will not be cut off, for this form does not require the *neshamah* for its deeds. Rather, it knows and comprehends knowledge which is above matter, knows the Creator of all things, and *exists forever*. This is what Solomon said in his wisdom: "The dust will return to the earth as it [originally] was, and the spirit [*ruach,* meaning *nefesh*] will return to God who granted it" (Ecc. 12:7).
>
> Note that according to Rambam, the *nefesh*—as opposed to the body and the *neshamah*—is eternal.

2. The world to come is populated by *nefashot* (forms of the souls). The Talmud (BT *Berachot* 17a) states:

> A favorite saying of Rav was: The future world is not like this world. In the future world, there is no eating and no drinking and no propagation and no business and no jealousy and no hatred and no competition, but [rather] *the righteous sit with their crowns on their heads delighting in the radiance of the Divine Presence,* as it says: "And they saw God, and they ate and they drank [Rashi: they were satiated by the brightness of the Divine Presence as if they had eaten and drunk]" (Exod. 24:11).

Ha'azinu

Based on the fact that there is no eating or drinking in *olam ha-ba*, Rambam was able to state: "In the world to come, there is no body or physical form, only the souls of the righteous alone, without a body, like the ministering angels" (*Hilchot Teshuvah* 8:2). Rambam further analyzes the Talmudic text as follows:

The phrase "the righteous sit" must be interpreted metaphorically, i.e., the righteous exist there without work or labor. Similarly, the phrase "their crowns on their heads" means [they will possess] the knowledge that they comprehended, which allowed them to merit the life of the world to come... What is meant by the expression "delighting in the radiance of the Divine Presence?" That they will comprehend the truth of Godliness, which they cannot grasp while in a dark and humble body (*Hilchot Teshuvah* 8:2).

3. Rambam initiates his discussion of *olam ha-ba* as follows:

The good that is hidden for the righteous is the life of the world to come (*olam ha-ba*). This will be life which is not accompanied by death, and good which is not accompanied by evil (*Hilchot Teshuvah* 8:1).

In other words, *olam ha-ba* serves as an eternal dwelling place for the soul. This paragraph is drawn almost verbatim from the Midrash, which bases itself on the following verse: "The dust will return to the earth as it [originally] was, and the spirit will return to God, who granted it" (Ecc. 12:7). The Midrash asks:

Which spirit is it that will return to God, who granted it? These are the spirits of the righteous and pious and repentants who stand before Him at the highest level, and this is the life which has no death, and the good which has no evil. This is what is written in the Torah: "in order that it should be good for you" (Deut. 22:7), forever. From the oral tradition we have learned: "in order that it should be good for you" means on the day that is wholly good; and "so that your days be lengthened" on the day that is wholly long [i.e., forever]. The reward of the righteous is that they will merit to take part in this good (*Tanchuma, Vayikra* 8).

After citing the Midrash, Rambam adds:

The retribution of the wicked is that they will not merit this life. Rather, they will be cut off and die… After these souls become separated from bodies in this world, they will not merit the life of the world to come. Rather, even in the world to come, they will be cut off (*Hilchot Teshuvah* 8:1).

4. Rambam posits that *olam ha-ba* is available to righteous people immediately after their demise (*Hilchot Teshuvah* 8:8). This paragraph as well is based on Midrash *Tanchuma, Vayikra* 8:

That the Sages called it "the world to come" was not to imply that it does not exist at present, or that the present realm will be destroyed and then that realm will come into being. [The term merely states that] for us, who are today in this world, it is yet to come. Therefore, one says the world to come, [because that life comes to a man] after a person leaves this. Regarding he who says that the present realm will be destroyed and then *olam ha-ba* will come into being, the matter is not so. Rather, when the righteous leave this world, they immediately ascend and stand at this great height, as it says: "How great is Your goodness that You have hidden [implying it already exists] for those who fear You, that You have worked for those who take refuge in You" (Ps. 31:20).

Ha'azinu

5. The Talmud (BT *Berachot* 34b) suggests that it is impossible for mortal man to even conceive the pleasure that awaits him in the world to come:

> R. Chiya b. Abba also said in the name of R. Yochanan: All the prophets prophesied only for the days of the Messiah [during which time nature will run its course (*Hilchot Melachim* 12:1)], but as for the world to come, "No eye has ever seen [the pleasures awaiting the soul in the world to come], oh God, other than You; [He will make them (occur) for one who awaits it]" (Isa. 64:3).

The previously cited Midrash elucidates:

> The Sages of the previous generations have already informed us that man does not have the potential to understand it and describe it, and does not know its greatness, beauty, and power, for it has no possible evaluation, comparison, or likeness [in this world].

Rambam describes man's inability to comprehend *olam ha-ba* graphically:

> Just as a blind person cannot conceive colors, nor a deaf person sounds, nor a eunuch sexual craving, similarly corporeal beings cannot conceive spiritual pleasures. Just as a fish cannot be aware of the secret of fire, since he is ensconced in its inversion, similarly one in this material world cannot be aware of the pleasures of the spiritual world (*Peirush ha-Mishnayot*, Introduction to *Sanhedrin* 10).

6. Rambam adduces a proof to his thesis that the body does not exist in the world to come by noting that if it did, since the Sages have

said (BT *Berachot* 17a) that in the next world one has no physical needs, "It is absurd that man would possess these organs in vain. Heaven forbid that God would produce [them] in vain, for if a person has a mouth, stomach, liver, and reproductive organs, and does not eat, drink, or reproduce, then their existence is absolutely futile" (*Ma'amar Techiyat ha-Meitim*). R. Meir ha-Levi Abulafia (1170?-1244), in his *Yad Ramah* (BT *Sanhedrin* 90a), however, claims that the continued existence of these organs emphasizes God's omnipotence by highlighting His ability to completely change their nature and associated drives by His very whim.

Summary of Rambam's View

Compensation for one's good deeds in this world begins immediately after a person passes away. According to Rambam, in the world to come, man exists as a *nefesh* (soul) without a *guf* (body), and is hence not susceptible to physical needs, nor to character flaws. The body disintegrates, but the soul (*nefesh*) of those who are worthy continues to exist eternally in the next world—*olam ha-ba*. The soul experiences never-ending spiritual pleasure which cannot be comprehended by human beings living in the present world. In short, according to Rambam, the world to come is populated by bodiless souls who experience spiritual enjoyment in that environment.

Questions on Rambam's View
Concerning Resurrection of the Dead

The Mishnah (*Sanhedrin* 9:1) states that one who says that "resurrection of the dead (*techiyat ha-meitim*) is not intimated in the Torah" is a heretic and has no portion in the world to come. After reading Rambam's words, namely that "in the world to come, there is no body or physical form" (*Hilchot Teshuvah* 8:2), Ra'avad concludes that Rambam was coming dangerously close to being a non-believer, since he is clearly denying physical resurrection.

Ha'azinu

Rambam's approach is contradicted by various Tamudic texts, such as: "In the future, the righteous will rise in their own clothes" (BT *Ketubot* 111b); "The righteous, whom the Holy One blessed be He will resurrect, will not revert to dust" (BT *Sanhedrin* 92a); and "They will rise with their defects and then be healed" (BT *Sanhedrin* 91b). In fact, R. Meir ha-Levi (a younger contemporary of Rambam and an older contemporary of Ramban) records that Jewish communities in Isfahan (in Iran) and Yemen, when faced with dissidents who denied the principle of resurrection of the dead, were unable to defend their belief when the latter cited the previously quoted passage, "In the world to come there is no body or physical form" (*Hilchot Teshuvah* 8:2), and so they were compelled to send Rambam a query requesting him to elaborate.

Kesef Mishneh (ibid.) attempts to reconcile Rambam and Ra'avad by saying that Rambam also believes in physical resurrection, just that he calls it *techiyat ha-meitim*, and it is this which he refers to in *Hilchot Teshuvah* 3:6 and in his introduction to ch. 10 of *Sanhedrin* (*Perek Chelek*), and it is distinct from *olam ha-ba*, which he describes in ch. 8 of *Hilchot Teshuvah*. What Rambam calls *techiyat ha-meitim*, Ra'avad calls *olam ha-ba*, but the difference between the two scholars is no more than semantics. However, this answer seems insufficient for a number of reasons:

1. It is not clear that Ra'avad has any entity parallel to Rambam's *olam ha-ba*.
2. Rambam states that *techiyat ha-meitim* is available only to the righteous (*Peirush ha-Mishnayot, Sanhedrin*, Introduction to ch. 10), while Ra'avad, who equates it with *olam ha-ba*, certainly believes that it is designated for every Jew other than those listed in the Mishnah (e.g., heretics, *Sanhedrin* 10:1), and even to deserving non-Jews (Tosefta *Sanhedrin* 13:1).
3. Rambam clarifies his view in his *Essay on Resurrection* (*Ma'amar Techiyat ha-Meitim*), stating that not only is it restricted to the

righteous, but it is also of limited duration, since "those whose souls will return to their bodies will eat, drink, marry, and procreate, and they will die after a very long life, like those who will live during the Messianic age." One may assume that Ra'avad most probably disagrees with this supposition.

In his *Essay on Resurrection*, written when he was fifty-six years old, Rambam notes that he had written in his commentary on the Mishnah (Introduction to *Perek Chelek*), more than twenty-five years earlier, that resurrection was one of the fundamental beliefs of Judaism, and one who rejects that belief has dissociated himself from the Jewish religion. Rambam admits that he frequently interprets Biblical verses metaphorically, but he continues:

> This resurrection, the return of the soul to the body after death, is mentioned by Daniel in a way that does not allow for reinterpretation, and he said: "And many who sleep in the dust of the earth will awaken—some for eternal life [and others for disgrace and for eternal abhorrence]" (Dan. 12:2), and the angel [then] told him: "And you, go to the end, and you will rest and rise to your lot at the end of the days" (Dan. 12:13).

In addition to these incontrovertible verses, Rambam notes that the Talmud (BT *Sanhedrin* 90b) cites numerous phrases which are potential sources for the belief in resurrection. Nevertheless, in his *Essay on Resurrection*, he clarifies that as central as it is in Jewish dogma, the ultimate goal is not resurrection but rather the world to come, citing his own description of *olam ha-ba* in *Mishneh Torah*: "This is the reward above which there is nothing higher and the good beyond which there can be no [other] good" (*Hilchot Teshuvah* 8:2), and it is this reward "which is not terminated by death."

The question that arises at this point, however, is that since

Ha'azinu

Rambam considers *olam ha-ba* to be significantly superior to *techiyat ha-meitim*, both in content and duration, why is resurrection needed altogether? To this question, Rambam answers in his essay:

> However, what we do deny, and dissociate ourselves before God from, is the assertion that "the soul will never return to the body, as this is impossible," for this denial will lead to the rejection of all wonders and miracles—a denial of God and a departure from the [Jewish] religion.

In other words, a central principle of Judaism is that God can, and does, perform miracles, and the archetype of such miracles is resurrection, so that one who does not believe in *techiyat ha-meitim* likely denies all of the Biblical miracles, from the splitting of the Reed Sea (Exod. 14:21-22) to the prophet Elisha's revival of the son of the Shunamite woman (2 Kings 4:33-36).

But if this is the purpose of resurrection, why is it confined to the righteous? One would assume that this lesson is even more imperative for the uneducated and non-believers. Ramban in *Sha'ar ha-Gemul* and R. Albo in *Sefer ha-Ikkarim* (4:30) answer this question by assuming that in Rambam's view, resurrection will occur in Messianic times. They perhaps base themselves on Rambam's claim in the *Essay on Resurrection* that those who are resurrected "will die after a very long life, like those who will live during the Messianic age," even though in another place in the same essay Rambam is unsure of its timing, saying only: "It will happen in the lifetime of the Messiah, or before him, or after he dies." They propose that the purpose of resurrection is to allow the righteous to achieve a higher level of knowledge and understanding than they were able to attain during their lives. Such scholars may have been disturbed in their studies by the vicissitudes of earthly life, not to mention war and persecution. As Rambam states in *Hilchot Melachim* (12:4-5), in Messianic times, peace will prevail and an environment conducive to self-improvement will predominate. Once the resurrected have accomplished this mission, their lives will end and they will be empowered to achieve the highest level of satisfaction in the world to come.

Sefer ha-Ikkarim even entertains the possibility that independent of self-improvement, the righteous may be entitled to compensation for the hard times they suffered in their earthly life. This implies that in addition to the spiritual reward enjoyed in *olam ha-ba*, Rambam believes in physical rewards as well at the time of resurrection.

SAADIAH GAON'S DESCRIPTION OF *OLAM HA-BA*

Saadiah Gaon's view of physical resurrection in the world to come has been adopted by Ra'avad, *Yad Ramah*, and Ramban. According to *Yad Ramah* (*Sanhedrin* 90a), the days of the Messiah (*yemot ha-Mashiach*) will be followed by *techiyat ha-meitim* and *olam ha-ba*, based on the following text:

> R. Kattina said: The world will exist six thousand years, and one [thousand, the seventh], it will be desolate, for it says: "And the Lord alone will be exalted on that day" (Isa. 2:11). [A day symbolizes a thousand years, based on the verse: "For a thousand years in Your eyes are but as yesterday" (Ps. 90:4).] Abaye said: it will be desolate two [thousand years], for it says: "After two days He will revive us; on the third day, He will raise us up, and we will live before Him" (Hos. 6:2)....
> The School of Eliyahu teaches: The world is to exist six thousand years. In the first two thousand there was desolation [Rashi: the Torah was not revealed to Abraham until he was fifty-two years old, which was two thousand years after the creation of Adam], two thousand years the Torah flourished [Rashi: from Abraham's fifty-second year until one hundred and seventy-two years after the destruction of the Second

Ha'azinu

Temple; this does not mean that the Torah would cease thereafter, but is mentioned merely to distinguish it from the next era], and the next two thousand years is the Messianic era [Rashi: Messiah will come within that period, and the exile will terminate, and the subjugation of Israel will end] (BT *Sanhedrin* 97a).

Yad Ramah explains that since mankind will be destroyed after six thousand years, the only possibility for life in the world to come is if there will be resurrection. For that reason, the Mishnah (*Sanhedrin* 10:1) teaches that he who does not believe in resurrection has no part in the next world, because he would have no basis for arriving there.

According to Saadiah Gaon, the world to come is preceded by the revival of the righteous Jewish dead (*techiyat ha-meitim*) in the present world (*Emunot ve-De'ot* 7:2, 7:6), which will occur when God decides to end the creation of new souls (ibid., 9:1). The resurrected will exist eternally (ibid., 7:5), as stated in the Talmud: "The righteous, whom the Holy One blessed be He will resurrect, will not revert to dust [but will retain their bodies]" (BT *Sanhedrin* 92a), and will be transferred to *olam ha-ba* (ibid., 7:6).

In the world to come, even those who were not revived in *techiyat ha-meitim* will be resurrected (ibid., 7:7). Each person will be reincarnated with his body and soul, and will receive his just deserts—the wicked will be punished with the excruciating heat of *gehenom* (hell), while the righteous will bask in the pleasurable warmth exuding from *Gan Eden* (the Garden of Eden). Since both the body and the soul cooperated in doing good or evil during the person's lifetime, they share the same fate in the world to come (ibid., 9:5).

The world to come will be a physical world, and the human body will be as perfect as that of Adam in the Garden of Eden before he sinned. The environment will be different from that of the present world, as implied in the Bible: "'For, as the new heavens and the new earth that I am making stand before Me,' says the Lord, 'so will your seed and your name stand'" (Isa. 66:22). The heavenly bodies will shine with exceeding brilliance, as reflected in the verse: "And the light of the moon will be like the light of the sun, and the light of the sun will be seven-fold as the light of the seven days, on the day the Lord binds the fracture of His people, and the stroke of their wound He will heal" (Isa. 30:26). Evil will not exist, and human drives will not prevent mankind from clinging to the Lord.

Some wonder how God can reconstruct human bodies from decayed flesh and bones, but Saadiah Gaon points out that if God is capable of *creatio ex nihilo*, how much more so is he able to return the existing to its initial form (*Emunot ve-De'ot* 7:1, *Yad Ramah, Sanhedrin* 90a). Others wonder how a human being—accustomed to eating, drinking, and marital relations—will suddenly be transformed into a being unhindered by such needs. Did not Moses our teacher undergo such a transition (Exod. 34:28) when he ascended Mt. Sinai for a period of forty days, as did Elijah when fleeing from Jezebel (1 Kings 19:8), after slaying the prophets of Ba'al (*Emunot ve-De'ot* 7:6, 9:5; *Yad Ramah, Sanhedrin* 90a)? Similarly, the Israelites in the desert ate manna, concerning which Scripture states: "And He afflicted and starved you… in order to let you know that man does not live by bread alone, but rather by whatever comes forth from the mouth of the Lord does man live" (Deut. 8:3). Rambam, however, rejects these parallels in his *Ma'amar Techiyat ha-Meitim*, noting that:

> The organs of Moses and Elijah, of blessed memory, were not in vain, because both of them existed in this world—they ate and drank before the miracle and after it. What kind of analogy can be drawn from that to continued existence in an eternal world that is, as described by those of blessed memory, "a world that is all good, a world that is forever lasting" (BT *Kiddushin* 39b).

Ha'azinu

Another proof brought by *Yad Ramah* is from the Mishnah, which states:

> The men of Sodom have no portion in the world to come, for it says: "And the men of Sodom were exceedingly wicked and sinful before the Lord" (Gen. 13:13), "wicked"—in this world, and "sinners"—in the world to come. But they will stand in judgment [after resurrection] (*Sanhedrin* 10:3).

Yad Ramah reasons that if the wicked are to be judged in the next world, it is for evil acts which were performed by their bodies as well as their souls. This is in concurrence with the Talmud, which states that at the time of judgment, God brings the soul, places it in the body, and judges them together (BT *Sanhedrin* 91b). However, according to Rambam, their bodies are no longer in existence, and will thus escape their well-deserved punishment. Rambam, of course, had defended himself against this criticism when he stated: "The retribution of the wicked is that they will not merit this life. Rather, they will be cut off and die" (*Hilchot Teshuvah* 8:1). Furthermore, Ramban in *Sha'ar ha-Gemul* explains that in Rambam's view, the degree of pleasure experienced in *olam ha-ba* is directly proportional to one's level of intellectual achievement and righteous behavior in his lifetime. In short, Rambam holds that retribution for the sins of the body are reflected in the fate of the soul in the next world.

Yad Ramah cites a number of verses quoted in the Talmud, all of which indicate that the body will be resurrected into a physical world, namely:

1. "So must you too set aside a gift for the Lord… and you will give of the Lord's gift to Aaron the priest" (Num. 18:28). The verse speaks of events that will occur upon entering the Land of Israel after Aaron's demise. It must be that Aaron will be resurrected, at which time he will receive the priestly gifts (BT *Sanhedrin* 90b).

2. God adjures Israel to observe the law "in order that your days and the days of your children will be increased, on the land which the Lord swore to give to your forefathers" (Deut. 11:21). God never gave the land to the forefathers, because they had long since passed away, unless one assumes that the forefathers would eventually be resurrected, at which point they too would be the recipients of God's bounty (BT *Sanhedrin* 90b).
3. "Then Joshua will build an altar to the Lord, God of Israel, on Mount Ebal" (Josh. 8:30). The simple meaning of the verse is that Joshua then built an altar, just as "then Moses and the Children of Israel will sing" (Exod. 15:1) means, on a simple level, that Moses and the congregation sang. Nevertheless, the Talmud interprets the verse Midrashically to refer to the time of *techiyat ha-meitim*, and certainly singing is not an activity which could be engaged in by pure souls (BT *Sanhedrin* 91b).
4. "Your watchmen [taken to mean prophets] will raise their voices, together they will sing, for eye to eye they will see when the Lord returns to Zion" (Isa. 52:8). The prophets will have died by then, but their bodies will return to participate in song (BT *Sanhedrin* 91b).

All of these proofs of the physicality of resurrection, however, do not refute Rambam's thesis, because he too accepts the fact that *techiyat ha-meitim* is physical in nature, as expanded upon in his *Essay on Resurrection*. He does, however, note *in situ* that the Biblical references are very weak indeed, as indicated by the lack of a consensus among the Sages as to which verse is the actual source. Rambam explains that it is not by chance that the first explicit reference to resurrection does not appear until the book of Daniel.

The Israelites in Egypt were initially quite skeptical of the veracity of prophets and the performance of miracles. It was this proclivity which stimulated God to implement the ten plagues, as He made clear to the Children of Israel when He told Pharaoh: "It was for this

Ha'azinu

[reason] that I have allowed you to stand, to show you My strength and to declare My name all over the earth" (Exod. 9:16). This is similar to God's not allowing the nation to conquer the Land of Israel immediately upon being redeemed from slavery, as it says: "God did not lead them [by] way of the land of the Philistines for it was near, because God said: 'Lest the people reconsider when they see war and return to Egypt'" (Exod. 13:17).

Only after experiencing and internalizing the miracles of Egypt, the voyage through the desert, and the conquest of Israel, and becoming acquainted with the predictive powers of a series of prophets, would the nation be receptive to the concept of the miraculous reincarnation of the righteous.

CONTROVERSY SURROUNDING RAMBAM'S VIEWPOINT

In the year 1174, the Babylonian exilarch Daniel, considered to be of the dynastic line of King David, passed away with no male descendants. R. Shmuel b. Eli the Levite,[66] a world-famed Talmudic scholar and self-proclaimed Gaon (the traditional gaonate had ended with the demise of R. Hai Gaon in 1038) usurped the exilarchy, ending its Davidic lineage and thus combining the positions of gaon and exilarch. In approximately the year 1190, R. Shmuel was asked to clarify the subject of resurrection, since Rambam had not elaborated on this issue in his *Mishneh Torah*. R. Shmuel answered that both body and soul would be reincarnated, and took advantage of the opportunity to attack Rambam's view of the disintegration of the body and the eternality of the soul alone in *olam ha-ba*. Rambam mentions in his *Ma'amar Techiyat ha-Meitim* that in 1191, he received a letter from one of his colleagues in Baghdad describing the Gaon's reply, and later he received the essay that R. Shmuel composed on the subject. Rambam relates to the Gaon's answer in his typically pleasant but satirical manner, mocking his simplistic philosophical outlook. Of course, in the essay, Rambam stresses that he too accepts bodily

---

66. H. Graetz, *History of the Jews*, vol. 3 (1894), pp. 438-440, 475-477.

resurrection in *techiyat ha-meitim* for a limited period, just not for eternity in *olam ha-ba*.[67]

Yad Ramah (R. Meir ha-Levi) [68] obtained Rambam's *Mishneh Torah* about the year 1200 and, as previously cited with respect to Ra'avad, disagreed strongly with Rambam's statement that "in the world to come, there is no body or physical form" (*Hilchot Teshuvah* 8:2), which he considered contradictory to the central Jewish belief in resurrection. He composed a letter in which he summarized his criticism and sent it to the great Tosafist, R. Yehonatan ha-Cohen of Lunel in Provence, with the intention that the latter pass it on to Rambam and rebuke him. However, the Sages of Lunel greatly admired Rambam and did not accept the criticism; R. Aharon b. Meshulem of Lunel even sent R. Meir ha-Levi a lengthy letter of rebuttal in defense of Rambam's position, leading to an exchange of letters and very hard feelings towards R. Meir on the part of the Provencal rabbis. R. Meir received a similar reaction from the scholarly community of Spain, with one of the Rabbis (Sheshet Benveniste) even questioning how a man whose name derives from the Hebrew word for "light" (Meir) could be so unenlightened, not to mention the impertinence of a young scholar taking on the older and highly revered genius of the entire generation.

However, R. Meir did not concede. Instead, he sent the entire correspondence with the school of Lunel to the northern Tosafists, led by R. Shimshon mi-Shantz (Sens) and his brother, R. Yitzchak b. Asher (Ritzba). Most of the northern scholars apparently declined to answer, possibly because they did not feel worthy of mediating between such great luminaries. R. Shimshon himself (but not necessarily his brother) leaned towards the opinion of R. Meir, but declined to join in the fray because of his great respect for Rambam.

In spite of their difference of opinion, R. Meir himself maintained

---

67. Simon Dubnov, *A General History of the Jewish People*, popular Hebrew edition prepared by Baruch Karu (1956), p. 317.
68. H. Graetz, *History of the Jews*, vol. 3 (1894), pp. 522-527.

highlights this distinction. The Talmud in *Menachot* notes that this requirement is to be enforced also according to the view of R. Shimon, since even if those verses were written by Moses, it was done in a non-normative fashion.

Based on Rashi's explanation, the *Shulchan Aruch* posits: "The last eight verses of the Torah may not be interrupted. Rather, one person reads all of them" (*Orach Chaim* 428:7).

Rambam, however, understood the Talmudic segment differently, as is clear from the following ruling:

> The eight verses at the end of the Torah may be read in a synagogue when fewer than ten people are present. Even though they are all Torah and were related to Moses by the Almighty, since they appear to be [written] after Moses' death, they are different, and therefore, it is permissible for an individual to read them (*Hilchot Tefillah* 13:6).

From this paragraph, one may derive the following with regard to Rambam's understanding of the Gemara in *Menachot*:

1. He adopts the view of R. Shimon, since he says explicitly that the entire Torah (including the last eight verses) was related by God to Moses.
2. He understands the phrase in *Menachot*, "The last eight verses of the Torah are read by one person," to mean that a *minyan* of ten is not required, and even a single person may read it. The words "are read" are to be interpreted as "may be read."

Ra'avad, however, prefers Rashi's interpretation of the Gemara, according to which the words "are read" are to be interpreted as "must be read." Furthermore, he cites the Jerusalem Talmud (*Megillah* 3:7), which states explicilty that the topic being discussed is the blessings to be said before and after reading these eight verses. Ra'avad notes that it would be strange for the Talmud to be indicating that a *minyan* is not needed for these verses, since it is certainly needed for the previous verses, so where did the people go? On the other hand, the Jerusalem Talmud speaks of a blessing before and after these verses to distinguish them from the rest of the Torah. But in today's *Chumashim* (Pentateuchs), the blessing is said at the beginning of ch. 34, which is *shevi'i* (the seventh *aliyah*), so these verses are not specially highlighted. The only relevant aspect of the law is to prohibit the subdivision of these verses for the purpose of allowing additional people to be called to the Torah (*hosafot*).

A third explanation, proposed by the Mordechai (*Menachot, Halachot Ketanot* 955), is that when the Talmud says the last verses are read by "one person alone [*yachid*]," it is actually referring to a scholar, who is termed a *yachid*. According to this interpretation, the last eight verses are being given a special status in a positive manner, as opposed to Rashi's and Rambam's reading, which singles them out as being inferior to the rest of the Torah.

THE BLESSINGS OF THE TRIBES

The second section in *Vezot Habrachah* contains the blessings which Moses, like his ancestor Jacob, bestowed on the twelve tribes. Literally, *Vezot Habrachah* means "and this is the blessing." The word "and" implies that this portion is a continuation of previous events. Ibn Ezra (Deut. 33:1) says that these blessings parallel those given by Jacob to his sons (Gen. 49:1-28). Although both are poetic in form, Moses predicts a bright and happy future for each tribe in its appropriate setting, and is forgiving of past sins, unlike Jacob, who did not relate to past events in the most favorable manner. These blessings are also in strong contrast to the song of *Ha'azinu*, which ends on an optimistic note, but is mostly devoted to describing the calamities which Israel will suffer throughout most of its history as a result of its rebellious proclivities. In fact, Rashbam (Deut. 33:1) bases

Vezot Habrachah

his explanation of the introductory word "and" on the contrasting narratives, in the sense of "but."

Moses' blessings are sandwiched in between important messages for the nation as a whole. The introductory verses (Deut. 33:1-5) contain a short synopsis of the three principles of faith as formulated by R. Yosef Albo:[71]

1. God exists: "The Lord came from Sinai and shone forth from Seir to them; He appeared from Mount Paran and came with some of the holy myriads [Rashi: angels]" (Deut. 33:2), and it is the obligation and purpose of Israel in this world to obey His will: "And He was King in Jeshurun [literally, the nation which acts honestly; see Deut. 32:15, 33:26; Isa. 44:2], when the entire people were gathered and the tribes of Israel were together" (Deut. 33:5).

2. There is Divine Providence (reward and punishment):

    You certainly showed love for peoples [Rashi: the twelve tribes]; all His holy ones are in Your hand [Rashi: the souls of the righteous are hidden away with Him] for they let themselves be centered at Your feet [Rashi: they are worthy of this because they eagerly placed themselves at Your feet at the bottom of Mt. Sinai (when the Torah was given)], bearing Your utterances [Rashi: accepting upon themselves the yoke of Your Torah] (Deut. 33:3).

3. What God desires of Israel is that they live their lives by the laws of the Torah: "The Torah that Moses commanded us is a legacy for the congregation of Jacob" (Deut. 33:4).

    The epilogue (Deut. 33:26-29) attempts to provide the nation with the self-confidence and strength to accomplish the formidable task described in the prologue, namely to observe the

---

[71]. A more detailed account appears in Abba Engelberg, *The Ethics of Genesis* (2014), pp. 223-234.

Torah's commandments on a personal level and to adopt them in developing a national infrastructure capable of managing a sovereign nation. Ever since Harlow's monkey experiments,[72] the importance of cuddling, comforting, and providing self-assurance to infants is recognized, and the same is true of a nation. In the case of the nation's blessing, the comforting message has two parts. First, it is emphasized that God is omnipotent, and second, that God wishes to use his powers in support of Israel.

The first point is demonstrated by such phrases as: "there is none like God" (33:26) and "with His majesty [He rides] the skies, which are the abode for the eternal God" (33:26-27). The second is brought out by: "He Who rides the heavens is at your assistance" (33:26); "He expelled the enemy from before you, and said 'Destroy!'" (33:27); "And Israel will dwell safely and alone as Jacob [had blessed them], in a land of grain and wine; also their heavens will drip dew" (33:28) [Rashi: Isaac's blessing will be added to that of Jacob, which states, 'And God will give you from the dew of the heavens' (Gen. 27:28)]; "a people whose salvation is through the Lord, the Shield Who helps you, your majestic Sword" (33:29).

The Order of the Blessings

As noted, in addition to the tribes being blessed by Moses, their twelve progenitors were blessed by their father Jacob. The overall content of both sets of blessings is similar: military strength, agricultural bounty, spiritual excellence, and leadership in specific areas, with each tribe praised for its superior attributes. The order of the blessings bestowed by Jacob and Moses differs. One might expect that Jacob, as their father, would have learned from the tragic results of favoring Joseph that no partiality should be displayed, which would imply that the

---

72. H.F. Harlow; R.O. Dodsworth; M.K. Harlow, "Total Social Isolation in Monkeys," *Proceedings of the National Academy of Science, USA* (1965).

Vezot Habrachah

blessings be bestowed upon the brothers in the order of their birth, namely: Reuben, Simon, Levi, Judah, Dan, Naphtali, Gad, Asher, Issachar, Zebulun, Joseph, and Benjamin (Gen. 29:32-30:34, 35:18).

However, Jacob ordered them as follows: Reuben, Simon, Levi, Judah, Zebulun, Issachar, Dan, Gad, Asher, Naphtali, Joseph, and Benjamin (Gen. 49:3-27).

R. Meir Gruzman[73] identifies fifteen listings of the tribes in the Pentateuch, noting that except for the three associated with the groupings for camping and marching (Num. 2, 7, 10), the orderings are different. In other words, perhaps one should not invest too much effort in justifying the specifc order used by Jacob, since the blessings may have been distributed in a random order. This would jibe with the Midrash which states:

> R. Yehoshua of Sachnin said in the name of R. Levi: The names of the tribes are not ordered identically everywhere. Rather, sometimes one name precedes another. Why is this so? So that people will not say that the sons of the wives take precedence and the sons of the maidservants follow, in order to teach you that one was no greater than the other (*Tanchuma Shemot* 3, *Exod. Rabbah* 1:6).

Matnot Kehunah contends that the handmaidens, as well as Leah and Rachel, were daughters of Laban; before marrying them, Jacob freed them, converted them, and performed a proper marriage. Thus, the twelve sons all had the same pedigree.

However, although the varying orders may have been meant to convey an important lesson, the order of the blessings administered by Jacob and Moses was most definitely premeditated. The thirteen other listings were dictated by God as the narrator of the Torah, but those of Jacob and Moses were bestowed with great forethought, and

---

73. Meir Gruzman, "*Sidram shel Shivtei Yisrael ba-Torah*," *Da'at Limudei Yahadut va-Ruach, Kitvei Eit, Niv ha-Midrashiyah*, 1978.

they must certainly have chosen their order with great deliberation.

The order of Jacob's blessings does not differ greatly from the birth order, which would indicate that he made every effort to avoid potential strife. Nevertheless, the following minor differences are noted:

1. Both Jacob and Moses mention Issachar after Zebulun, even though their birth order is the reverse. Moses blesses them jointly as follows: "Rejoice, Zebulun, in your departure, and Issachar, in your tents" (Deut. 33:18), which the Midrash (*Gen. Rabbah* 49:9) explains to refer to the tribe of Zebulun departing from the Land of Israel to engage in trade, while the tribe of Issachar stays behind in their tents to study Torah. The Midrash sees this same distinction in Jacob's blessing, in which Zebulun was said to "dwell on [actually near] the coast of the seas" and to be "at the harbor of the ships" (Gen. 49:13), while Issachar was compared to "a boney donkey [bearing the yoke of the Torah], lying between the boundaries [like students who sit on the ground before their teachers (*Gen. Rabbah* 49:10) and hardly rest from their studies (Rashi, Gen. 49:14)]." The Midrash, as cited by Rashi, proceeds to explain the reversal as follows:

   Zebulun and Issachar entered into a partnership [with the following agreement]: Zebulun would dwell at the seashore and go out in ships, to trade and make profit and provide food for Issachar, while they would sit and occupy themselves with the study of Torah. Therefore, Moses mentioned Zebulun before Issachar [even though the latter was the elder of the two], because Issachar's Torah was enabled by Zebulun.

   It should be noted, however, that Rashi did not envision the tribe of Zebulun as being totally void of Torah study, nor Issachar as living in isolation and exclusively engaged in learning. On the phrase stating that "they will be nourished by the abundance of the seas" (Deut. 33:19), Rashi understands the plural pronoun "they" to imply that both "Issachar and Zebulun [will be nourished] and thereby, they will have free time to study the Torah." Likewise, on the phrase with regard to Issachar, "he saw a good resting place" (Gen. 49:15), Rashi adopts the exegesis of Onkelos that "he saw that his territory was blessed and good for producing fruits," i.e., although the tribe of Issachar did not travel great distances to obtain merchandise, since doing so would detract from their immersion in their Torah studies, they were involved in agriculture, since it could be engaged in locally. Furthermore, Issachar's Torah knowledge was not to be confined to that tribe alone, but rather to be put at the service of the entire nation. On the continuation of the verse, which states that "he became an indentured servant," the Midrash explains that the tribe of Issachar was to serve its brother tribes by instructing them in Torah, correcting their mistakes, and answering their questions (*Gen. Rabbah* 49:10), as well as by sharing its expertise with regard to the Jewish calendar, in consonance with the verse which enumerates those who accompanied David to Ziklag: "And of the sons of Issachar, who have an understanding of the times" (1 Chron. 12:32, *Tanchuma Vayechi* 11).

2. The order of mentioning the sons of the concubines—Dan, Gad, Asher, and Naphtali, diverges from the order of their appearance in Gen. 30:5-13, which is: Dan, Naphtali (children of Bilhah), Gad, and Asher (children of Zilpah). R. Menachem Leibtag ("*Vezot Habrachah—Seder Hashvatim*," VBM) claims, however, that the latter is not necessarily their birth order. It is clear that Dan was born as a result of Rachel's complaint to Jacob regarding her being childless and her suggestion that Jacob wed her hand-maiden. This would have preceded Leah making a similar proposal with respect to her hand-maiden, since Leah was not desperate, having already given birth to four sons, and

she might have made her request only in imitation of Rachel. However, Bilhah's second son, Naphtali, might have only been born after Leah's parallel request that Jacob marry Zilpah, and the birth of both of her sons, so that Dan (Bilhah), Gad (Zilpah), Asher (Zilpah), Naphtali (Bilhah) may have indeed been the true birth order.

On the other hand, R. Gruzman assumes that the order of their appearance in Genesis is their true birth order. However, he says that Jacob had already combined Bilhah and Zilpah into one maternal entity when he went to meet Esau, where it states: "And he placed the maidservants and their children first, and Leah and her children after, and Rachel and her Joseph last" (Gen. 33:2). Although Rachel and Leah are specified, the maidservants and their descendants are grouped together, and so the random order of the names of their sons may indeed show complete equality and the total absence of hierarchy and feelings of superiority, at least amongst themselves.

3. Issachar and Zebulun were actually born after the children of the concubines, since their birth is recorded in the Bible only as a consequence of the story of Reuben's mandrakes (Gen. 30:17-30), which itself follows the description of the birth of the children of the maidservants (Gen. 30:5-12). Jacob, however, blessed them prior to the sons of the maidservants. One would have expected Jacob to go out of his way not to engender feelings of inferiority among them, since that is exactly what Joseph had accused the brothers of doing (*Gen. Rabbah* 84:7; Rashi, Gen. 37:2).[74] One might say that Jacob was not as sensitive as he should have been to arousing feelings of jealousy, based on his behavior with respect to both Joseph and Ephraim and Manasseh (Gen. 48:14).

On the other hand, it is quite possible that Jacob mellowed following the story of Joseph, although it is not clear whether

---

74. According to R. Eliyahu Mizrachi (Gen. 37:2), the accusations were false, while according to *Kli Yakar, in situ,* they were true.

Vezot Habrachah

he ever realized that the brothers were responsible for his plight. The lesson which he learned is that each person must be steered in the direction of his strengths and praised for them. Jacob studied Torah with Ephraim, as noted in the Midrash (*Tanchuma Vayechi* 6), but Jacob must have also been aware of Manasseh's administrative abilities, which allowed him to become his father's assistant viceroy (*Gen. Rabbah* 91:8). In this case, Jacob was quite successful in his efforts to prevent jealousy, as stated by *Imrei Chen*:[75]

Between Ephraim and Manasseh there was no jealousy. Manasseh was not jealous of Ephraim in consequence of his grandfather placing his right hand on his [Ephraim's] head, and also Ephraim did not become vainglorious as a result of meriting that the right hand of his illustrious grandfather be placed on his head.

It will shortly be seen that Jacob also stressed his sons' positive qualities when he blessed them. Why, then, would he seemingly have discriminated against the sons of the maidservants by blessing them after their younger brothers, Issachar and Zebulun? One might say that he chose to bless the sons of the same mother (considering Bilhah and Zilpah as one mother) consecutively, and for that reason he completed Leah's children before moving on to those of the hand-maidens. In fact, the list composed after the birth of Benjamin (Gen. 35:23), the lists of those who left for Egypt (Gen. 46:8-14) and those who arrived there (Exod. 1:2-3), and even the list of princes who conducted the first census (Num.1:5-9) all started by enumerating the six sons of Leah.

The order of the blessings of Moses differs from that of Jacob. The

---

75. Chaim b. Natan b. Senyor, *Imrei Chen*, Vayechi, "Jacob's Blessing to His Grandchildren" (1996).

order here is: Reuben, Judah, Levi, Benjamin, Joseph, Zebulun, Issachar, Gad, Dan, Naphtali, Asher (Deut. 33:6-25).

Ibn Ezra (Deut. 33:6) believes that Moses ordered the blessings in terms of functionality. Reuben, as the biological first-born, was in first place to symbolize the traditional leadership role given to the eldest, even if he did not receive all of the concomitant perquisites. Ibn Ezra, unlike Rashi and Ramban, does not relate to Reuben's sin with Bilhah. Ibn Ezra (noted in brackets) interprets the blessings of Reuben and Judah non-Midrashically, as follows:

> **6** Let Reuben live and not die, and may his people not be limited in number. **7** May this [also] be for Judah. And he [Moses] said, "O Lord, hearken to Judah's voice and bring him [back] to his people [when he goes to war]; may his [own] hands suffice [alternatively: fight] for him, and may You be a help against his adversaries" (Deut. 33).

Reuben's blessing is joined to Judah's, and God is entreated to bless them each with military success on their respective fronts, Judah in the mainland and Reuben in Transjordan.

Ramban, of course, could not adjoin the two blessings, since the first refers to Reuben's guilt, which is not applicable to Judah. However, he does agree with the military leadership interpretation of Judah's blessing, and sees it as a continuation of Jacob's blessing bestowed upon Judah: "Your hand will be at the nape of your enemies" (Gen. 49:8), which the Midrash (*Gen. Rabbah* 98:9) sees as a prophetic reference to what David proclaimed in his song of praise: "And of my enemies, You have given me the back of their necks" (2 Sam. 22:41).

Ramban concludes by noting that the order of the blessings was divinely inspired, since they were clearly not given in birth order. Reuben was chosen first to stress that although he was deprived of the first-born's double portion and leadership role, he retained other perquisites, such as being first in this instance and in receiving his

Vezot Habrachah

inheritance (Josh. 13:15), and also to emphasize that he had not been disenfranchised from being one of the twelve tribes.

Next came Judah, who was the natural leader (for good or for bad) already from the time of the sale of Joseph (Gen. 37:26, 43:3-10, 44:14-30). He later served in numerous leadership positions, such as leading the eastern-facing, most important camp (Num. 2:3-9) and being the first to enter battle in the prophetic period (Judg. 1:2, 20:18), not to mention David eventually becoming the founder of the royal lineage, culminating, God willing, in the coming of Messiah b. David.

As far as the ordering of Levi after Judah, if one takes the functional approach, Levi represents spiritual leadership, which follows the political leadership of Judah, as the Sages have said: "Pray for the welfare of the government, for if not for the fear of it, a man would swallow alive his fellow-man" (*Avot* 3:2). Both Ramban and Ibn Ezra (Deut. 33:6), on the other hand, base the contiguity on geography, noting that many of the Levites resided in Jerusalem, which is adjacent to Judah (actually between the territory of Judah and Benjamin), paving the way for continuing the blessings with the tribe of Levi.

Rashi stresses the spiritual rather than the geographical connection, and uses the same rationale to justify the placement of Joseph's blessing immediately after that of Benjamin:

> Since Levi's blessing pertains to the sacrificial service and Benjamin's blessing pertains to building the Holy Temple within his territory, Moses juxtaposed one to the other. He then juxtaposes Joseph immediately after him [Benjamin] because Joseph too [had a sanctuary built within his territory, namely] the *Mishkan* of Shiloh was erected in his territory, as is said: "He rejected the tent of Joseph" (Ps. 78:67). And because the Holy Temple is dearer [to God] than [the *Mishkan* of] Shiloh, he mentioned [the blessing of]

Benjamin before [that of] Joseph [even though Joseph was older] (Rashi, Deut. 33:12).

As noted, Benjamin followed, not so much on its own merit, but rather on the coattails of the tribe of Levi, which dwelled in its territory.

Joseph was the first-born of his mother, Rachel, and received a double portion (Gen. 48:5) in terms of the tribes which emanated from him (Ephraim and Manasseh), with their concomitant land allocations. Additionally, Joseph was prominent because of his outstanding personal qualities and his leadership role both in Egypt and in the Kingdom of Israel, while it lasted (1 Kings 11:26, 12:20), and indeed his blessing was one of the longest given by both Jacob (Gen. 49:22-26) and Moses (Deut. 33:13-17).

The tribe of Zebulun, which displayed military prowess in the fight against Sisera (Judg. 5:18), and assumedly in other military confrontations, is next, followed by Issachar—the nexus between the two having been previously described. Why political leadership precedes spiritual leadership may be explained in a parallel manner to the precedence of Judah to Levi.

At this stage, Ibn Ezra points out that the sons of the wives have all been blessed. Apparently, Ibn Ezra felt that they had priority over the sons of the concubines, much as Rashi implies in his comment concerning the family arrangement when Jacob met Esau, where the Bible states: "And he placed the maidservants and their children first, and Leah and her children after, and Rachel and Joseph last" (Gen. 33:2), whereupon Rashi observes: "The further back, the more beloved" (based on *Gen. Rabbah* 78:8).

Continuing with the assumption that the remaining blessings were given in order of importance, Gad comes next because it is the only concubinal tribe which shared a flag with the sons of the wives (Num. 2:14); then Dan, who himself led a flag-group (Num. 2:25); followed by Naphtali and Asher, in birth order.

Vezot Habrachah

THE CONTENT OF THE BLESSINGS

THE BLESSINGS OF REUBEN AND JUDAH

The first three blessings given by Jacob were to Reuben, Simeon, and Levi. A cursory examination of their contents leads to the immediate realization that calling them "blessings" is a euphemism, since in fact, they were highly critical evaluations. On the other hand, only by being aware of one's faults, can one endeavor to overcome them.

The Torah states: "Reuben went and he lay with Bilhah, his father's concubine" (Gen. 35:22). The Talmud explains:

> R. Shimon b. Elazar said… how do I interpret "and he lay with Bilhah, his father's concubine"? He resented his mother's humiliation. He said: "If my mother's sister was a rival to my mother, will the handmaid of my mother's sister be a rival to my mother?" He [thereupon] arose and transposed her sleeping arrangement [by moving Jacob's bed to her tent] (BT *Shabbat* 55b).

Reuben was censured by Jacob (Gen. 49:3) for his impetuosity and sexual impropriety with respect to Rachel's maidservant Bilhah (Gen. 35:22, and Rashi thereon). Later in the Bible, his punishment is made very explicit:

> And the sons of Reuben, the first-born of Israel—for he was the first-born, but when he defiled his father's bed, his birthright was given to the sons of Joseph the son of Israel, but [Joseph was] not to be reckoned in the genealogy as first-born, because Judah prevailed over his brothers, and the one appointed as prince was to be from him, but the birthright belonged to Joseph (1 Chron. 5:1-2).

Rashi's exegesis of these verses is:

Now if you ask, since he [Reuben] was the first-born, why did the kingship not emanate from him? He was indeed the first-born, but when he desecrated his father's bed, his birthright was given to the sons of Joseph. Now if you ask, if so, why did the sons of Joseph not serve as kings? He therefore says, "but not to be reckoned in the genealogy as the first-born" [i.e., the sons of Joseph took one of] the perquisites of the birthright, but not the birthright [itself], because Judah, even if Reuben had not defiled the birthright and it had not been taken from him, was the most fit to reign.

Rashi is explaining that although the first-born generally gets a double portion, and is the first choice for leadership, he may be deprived by God of the former as a punishment, and of the latter if his own qualities do not meet the required standard.

Moses' blessings were more conciliatory toward those brothers who had been rebuked, for the following reasons: first, it was Jacob who experienced the strong sense of disappointment, not Moses; second, the brothers themselves had long passed away, and future generations are not to be punished for the sins of their fathers.

Reuben was told: "Let Reuben live [in this world (Rashi, based on BT *Sanhedrin* 92a)] and not die [in the next world], and may his people be counted in the number [of tribes]" (Deut. 33:6). Moses is praying that Reuben be absolved of his sins and continue to be considered one of the twelve tribes, in spite of the fact that his territory was not even contiguous to Israel's mainland (Sforno, *in situ*). *Bechor Shor* (*in situ*) notes that the tribe would also need special protection, because in addition to defending its own land, Reuben had volunteered to assist the other tribes in conquering theirs (Num. 32:25-27). Furthermore, Reuben's portion was located in an especially dangerous neighborhood, with the Moabites to their south and the Ammonites and Hagarites to the northeast (Josh. 13:15-23,

Vezot Habrachah

Da'at Mikra, p. 111), with whom there were frequent conflicts (1 Sam. 14:47, 1 Chron. 5:19).

Rashi notes that Moses' request reflects the Torah's approach, when it immediately follows the phrase "and he [Reuben] lay with Bilhah" with the inclusive words "and Jacob's sons were twelve" (Gen. 35:22). Reuben had been deprived of many aspects of primogeniture. Judah had been given royalty, Levi the Temple service, and Joseph a double portion of the land. Nevertheless, Ibn Ezra (Deut. 33:6) notes that even Jacob had hinted that in spite of his sins, Reuben would still be counted as one of the tribes, when he said: "[You have] the restlessness of water [and therefore,] you will not be superior" (Gen. 49:4)—indeed, you will not predominate in many of the ways associated with being first-born, but you will still be the founder of one of the tribes, and in fact, you will retain your privilege with respect to some priorities, such as being the first to officially take possession of land (Josh. 13:15).

Rashi in *Vezot Habrachah* (Deut. 33:7) explains why the blessings are not arranged in birth order, with Levi preceding Judah, as in Jacob's blessings (Gen. 49:5-8), by referring to a number of Biblical incidents and various Midrashic exegeses of them. Rashi explains: "He juxtaposed Judah to Reuben, because they both confessed to the wrong they had done."

Reuben had severely sinned in the case of Bilhah, and he had not been able to keep Joseph out of harm's way, but he had attempted to do so when he told the brothers: "Let us not deal him a deadly blow.... Do not shed blood! Cast him into this pit, which is in the desert, but do not lay a hand upon him" (Gen. 37:21-22). Furthermore, Reuben had every intention of delivering Joseph to safety, as is evident from the verse: "And Reuben returned to the pit, and behold, Joseph was not in the pit, so he rent his garments" (Gen. 37:29). But where had Reuben gone in the interim? The Midrash (*Gen. Rabbah* 84:19) explains:

The Ethics of Deuteronomy

> R. Eliezer said: He was busy with his sackcloth and his fasting [for moving his father's bed]. The Holy One blessed be He said to him: Nobody ever sinned before me and repented,[76] and you initiated [a process of] repentance. Your reward is that your descendant [Hosea] will initiate a process of repentance, as it says: "Return, O Israel, to the Lord your God, for you have stumbled in your iniquity" (Hos. 14:2).

In addition to Reuben's sin with Bilhah and his unsuccessful attempt to save Joseph, Rashi also refers to a third Biblical incident—the story of Judah and Tamar. Judah was to give his son Shelah to Tamar in a levirate marriage, after Shelah's two older brothers had passed away. Judah delayed the marriage an unreasonable amount of time, so Tamar chose to pose as a harlot, take collateral from Judah, and have relations with him, from which she became pregnant. The Bible describes the continuation of the story:

> Now it came about after nearly three months, that it was told to Judah, saying, "Your daughter-in-law Tamar has had illicit relations, and behold, she is pregnant from harlotry." So Judah said, "Bring her out, and let her be burned." She was taken out, and she sent to her father-in-law, saying: "From the man to whom these [objects of collateral] belong I am pregnant".... Then Judah recognized [them] and he said, "*She is right, [it is] from me,* because I did not give her to my son Shelah" (Gen. 38:24-26).

The Talmudic approach is that Judah's confession manifested a praiseworthy sense of contrition, stating: "Judah confessed and was not ashamed. What was his end? He inherited the life of the world to come" (BT *Sotah* 7b). His reward in this world was that his descendant

---

76. Actually, another Midrash (*Gen. Rabbah* 22:13) says that Cain ws the first to repent for sinning.

Vezot Habrachah

David established the royal dynasty (Rashi, *in situ*). The Talmudic text continues with a similar statement concerning Reuben:

> Reuben confessed and was not ashamed. What was his end? He inherited the world to come. His reward in this world was that he was given his portion of land in Transjordan before the other tribes received theirs (Rashi, based on Num. 32).... Who caused Reuben to confess? It was Judah [whose example he followed].

Tosafot (BT *Makkot* 11b, s.v. *mi*) wonder how the Talmud could say that Reuben was influenced to make his admission by Judah, when the previously cited Midrash says Reuben did so at the time of the sale of Joseph, which preceded the story of Judah and Tamar. Tosafot answer that Reuben confessed and repented for his sin twice. The first time was indeed at the occasion of the sale of Joseph, when he privately expressed his sincere regret and anguish over his indiscretion with Bilhah after the death of Rachel. The second time was in imitation of Judah's public confession, when Reuben was moved to do the same. In fact, the Talmud even queries why Reuben made his confession public:

> It is understandable that Judah [publicly] confessed so that Tamar should not be burnt, but why was it necessary for Reuben to confess [in public]? Surely, R. Sheshet has declared: Consider him arrogant who [publicly] specifies his sins [Rashi: because it appears that he is not embarrassed by his behavior]. [Reuben confessed] so that his brothers should not be suspected [by their father Jacob of committing the offence of moving his bed] (BT *Sotah* 7b).

Of course, the Torah does not mention Reuben's confession, neither privately nor publicly. It was noted before that Reuben's private confession was mentioned in *Gen. Rabbah*. As far as the public confession, Rashi (BT *Sotah* 7b, s.v. *Yehudah*) states:

> *Midrash Aggadah* of R. Tanchuma says that when Judah said, "She is more righteous than I" (Gen. 38:24-26), Reuben arose and said: "I moved my father's bed."

Although not found in the extant versions of *Midrash Tanchuma*, this content is found in *Midrash Aggadah* (Buber, Num. 1:5). *Tosafot* (BT *Makkot* 11b, s.v. *mi... she-hodah*) found a second source in Onkelos, who translates the phrase "Judah, your brothers will thank you" (Gen. 49:8) as "Judah, you confessed and were not ashamed to do so; similarly, your brothers will confess," i.e., since you initiated confession, Reuben came and did the same. This explanation is based on the fact that the Hebrew words for thanking and confessing (*hoda'ah*) are homonyms.

The continuation of Rashi's explanation is based on a number of additional Midrashic sources. On the verse: "Moses took Joseph's bones with him, for he had made the Children of Israel swear, saying: 'God will surely remember you, and you should bring up my bones from here with you'" (Exod. 13:19), the Midrash wonders how Joseph could tell the brothers to bring his bones with them. They themselves would certainly not still be alive at that point. The Midrash answers that "with them" means with their bones—not only Joseph's bones would be transported to Israel, but those of all of the brothers (*Mechilta Beshallach*, parsha A, cited by Rashi *in situ*).

A second source relates to when Judah told Jacob that he would guarantee the safe return of Benjamin, saying that if he did not bring him back, "I will have sinned against you forever" (Gen. 43:9). The Talmud considers Judah's words to be like an oath, and even though Benjamin did in fact return safely, the oath (implying that if he was not returned, it would be a sin) still needed to be absolved. The

Vezot Habrachah

Talmud interprets the verses "Let Reuben live and not die... May this [also be] for Judah. And he [Moses] said, 'O Lord, hearken to Judah's voice'" to mean that Moses was praying to God to listen to the voice of Judah and allow him to live, just as had been promised to Reuben, since the latter confessed his own sins only in imitation of Judah. This interpretation is based on the contiguity of the blessings of Reuben and Judah. The Talmud concludes:

> All through the forty years that Israel remained in the wilderness, Judah's bones were jolted about in their coffin [unlike the remaining brothers, whose bodies remained whole] until Moses stood up and supplicated for mercy on his behalf... Thereupon, joint slipped into socket. (BT *Makkot* 11b).

Rashi, in his second interpretation, explains that by placing Judah together with Reuben, Moses alluded to Judah's merit in influencing Reuben to confess and, in effect, "hearken to Judah's voice" is a prayer that Judah's bones would finally come to rest.

Levi's Blessing

Simeon and Levi were condemned by Jacob for the wholesale slaughter which they perpetrated against the entire city of Shechem, as well as for instigating the violence against Joseph when they said: "Behold, that dreamer is coming, so now, let us kill him" (Gen. 37:19-20; Rashi, Gen. 49:5).

Reuben had sincerely repented for his actions regarding Bilhah, and had actively shown his righteousness, if not his leadership, on the occasion of the selling of Joseph. Moses must have taken all of this into account in his maintenance of Reuben as a *bona fide* tribe and in his inclusion of it in his mostly positive blessings. With regard to Simeon, on the other hand, there is no record of him having repented for his desecration of God's name in Shechem, and as far as the selling of Joseph is concerned, the Midrash (*Gen. Rabbah*—Albeck 97:8; see also *Tanchuma Vayechi* 9) states:

> "So they said one to the other... And now, let us kill him" (Gen. 37:19-20). Who were "they?" If you say [that it was] Reuben, Reuben wanted to save him, for it says: "And Reuben heard, and he saved him from their hand" (Gen. 37:21). And if [you say it was] Judah, but it already says: "And Judah said to his brothers: 'What is the benefit of slaying our brother and covering up his blood'" (Gen. 37:26)? And if you say [that it was] the sons of the maidservants, [that cannot be, because] it already says: "and he was a lad [and was] with the sons of Bilhah (Gen. 37:2) [Rashi, Gen. 49:5: so their hatred toward him was not so intense that they would want to kill him. It could also not have been Issachar and Zebulun, because they would not have spoken before their older brothers.] So who were "they" [when it says] "they said one to the other?" [We must say that] they were Simeon and Levi, regarding whom it says: "Simeon and Levi are brothers; violent instruments are their weapons" (Gen. 49:5).

In fact, Moses did not bless the tribe of Simeon at all. Since his purpose was to support and encourage, and since he did not have Jacob's paternal relationship, he chose to simply skip any reference to the tribe of Simeon, rather than to speak negatively of it. Of course, Simeon's descendants should not suffer because of the sin of their forefather. *Midrash Shocher Tov* (90) and *Sifrei* (*Vezot Habrachah* 349) point out, however, that the tribe of Simeon had sinned much more recently at Shittim with Baal Peor, where most of the 24,000 slain worshippers (Num. 25:1-9) were from the tribe of Simeon, as indicated by the considerable population decrease reflected in Moses' second census (only 22,200 in Num. 26:14, vs. 59,300 in Num. 1:23).

Vezot Habrachah

Even the tribe's prince was among the slain (Num. 25:14).

Rashi (Deut. 33:7) and Ibn Ezra (Deut. 33:6) adopt the Midrash's approach, but Ramban (Deut. 33:6) sharply disputes it. He disagrees with the numerical proof, noting that Simeon's population had actually decreased by 37,100, which was greater than the total number who had died in the plague, so there must have been other factors at play. In addition, the tribe of Gad lost more than 5,000 and Ephraim lost 8,000. Although Zimri, a prince in the tribe of Simeon, is singled out by name (Num. 25:14), this did not necessarily mean that his entire tribe followed in his footsteps. After all, in Korah's rebellion, both the 250 congregational princes (Num. 16:2) and Korah himself were more acclaimed than Zimri, who was only a prince in his father's household. Nevertheless, the overwhelming majority of the nation did not join Korah, as the total number of victims was only about 15,000 (Num. 16:32, 35; 17:14). There are explicit phrases which indicate that all of the tribes were involved with Baal Peor, such as when God told Moses to rebuke "all the leaders of the people" (Num. 25:4); or when He praised Phinehas for preventing the destruction of "the Children of Israel" (Num. 25:11); or when King David mentioned this sin (Ps. 106:28), among others, upon addressing the entire nation. Ramban finalizes his proof by noting that the Midrash (*Num. Rabbah* 21:9) lists five families of the tribe of Benjamin as having perished as a result of sinning with Baal Peor, but only one from Simeon. Furthermore, whoever sinned did not survive, as the Bible says: "every man who went after Baal Peor, the Lord your God has exterminated from your midst" (Deut. 4:3), while to those who remained, God stated: "And you who cleave to the Lord your God are all alive today" (v. 4). So why were the righteous members of the tribe of Simeon deprived of their blessing?

Ramban accordingly suggests different reasons for the exclusion of the tribe of Simeon. He first points out that every time the tribes are recorded, only twelve are listed. When Jacob blessed his sons, Joseph was blessed rather than Ephraim and Manasseh (who were blessed separately in Gen. 48:20). Here, however, they were both included (Deut. 33:17), having already been listed separately with respect to the division into camps (Num. 2:18, 21), at the inauguration of the altar (Num. 7:48, 54), and in connection with the subdivision of the land (Num. 34:23-24). Furthermore, Joshua—from the tribe of Ephraim and the successor of Moses—is mentioned at the end of the portion (Deut. 34:9), so it is only proper to reference Ephraim's older brother as well.

If Ephraim and Manasseh are to both be included, the only remaining question is which tribe to eliminate. Although Levi was sometimes left out (Eze. 48:4-5), here it was important for it to be included, since it was Levi who brought the sacrifices which diffused grace upon the entire nation. Simeon, on the other hand, was an appropriate choice not to be included for the following reasons:

1. It was now a small tribe (Num. 26:14).
2. Jacob's blessing was minimal, when he said of Simeon and Levi, "I will distribute them throughout Jacob, and I will scatter them throughout Israel" (Gen. 49:7).
3. Specifically because the tribe of Simeon was scattered among the tribes, it would benefit from their blessings. With regard to its inheritance, the Bible states: "And the second lot came out to Simeon... and their inheritance was in the midst of the inheritance of the children of Judah (Josh. 19:1). The Midrash states:

Twenty-four thousand fell from the tribe of Simeon, leaving twenty-four thousand widows, and two thousand were given to each tribe, for it says: "I will distribute them throughout Jacob," and [in addition] anyone who circulates collecting charity is from the tribe of Simeon (*Gen. Rabbah* 99:6).

Rashi slightly expands the repertoire of their potential professions, when he says: "There are no [itinerant] paupers, scribes, or teachers of children except from [the tribe of] Simeon, so that they should be scattered" (Gen. 49:7).

Because of its assimilation into Judah and other tribes, Simeon may have actually lost its tribal identity. Already at the time of the judges, the tribe of Judah had said to Simeon: "Come up with me to my allotted land, and we will fight against the Canaanites, and I will also go with you into your allotted land" (Judg. 1:3). Indeed, the two tribes acted in tandem, as the Bible states later: "And Judah went with Simeon his brother, and they smote the Canaanites that inhabited Safed, and they destroyed it" (Judg. 1:17).

It should be noted that although Rashi states that Simeon was not blessed because of the sin at Baal Peor, he too agrees that because of their close association, Simeon was blessed indirectly in conjunction with Judah (Rashi, Deut. 33:7, s.v. *ve-el*).

Why Was Levi Blessed the Second Time?

As previously noted, Jacob utilized his last meeting with his twelve sons to bless most of them, but Reuben, Simeon, and Levi were actually censured. Moses, who chose not to explicitly criticize, followed Jacob's precedent by ignoring the tribe of Simeon altogether; however, he did bless Reuben and Levi. Reuben's blessing by Moses has already been discussed. The Midrash (*Sifrei, Vezot Habrachah* 349) suggests the reason for blessing Levi, but not Simeon:

> Simeon and Levi both drank from one glass, as it says: "Cursed is their wrath, for it is mighty, and their anger, because it is harsh. I will distribute them throughout Jacob, and I will scatter them throughout Israel" (Gen. 49:7). This is comparable to two who borrowed from the king. One repaid the king and later lent to the king, and one, not only did he not repay, but he also borrowed again. So it was with Simeon and

Levi. They both borrowed in Shechem, as it says: "Jacob's two sons, Simeon and Levi, Dinah's brothers, each took his sword, and they came upon the city with confidence, and they killed every male" (Gen. 34:25). Levi repaid what he borrowed in the desert, for it says: "And Moses stood in the gate of the camp and said: 'Whoever is for the Lord, [come] to me!' And all the sons of Levi gathered around him" (Exod. 32:26); and he later lent the Lord at Shittim, for it says: "Phinehas the son of Eleazar the son of Aaron the *kohen* has turned My anger away from the Children of Israel by zealously avenging Me among them, so that I did not destroy the Children of Israel because of My zeal" (Num. 25:11). Simeon, not only did he not repay, but he borrowed again, for it says: "The name of the Israelite man who was killed, who was slain with the Midianite woman, was Zimri the son of Salu, the prince of the Simeonite paternal house" (Num. 25:14).

As compensation for the staunch stand of the tribe of Levi with respect to the golden calf, that tribe took over the priestly duties originally allocated to the first-borns, as stated in the Bible: "And I have taken the Levites from among the Children of Israel in place of all first-borns" (Num. 3:12), which Moses takes into account in his blessing, when he says: "They will place incense before You, and burnt offerings upon Your altar" (Deut. 33:10). Additionally, they would serve as judges and teachers, as Moses indicates at the beginning of the verse, when he says: "They will teach Your laws to Jacob, and Your Torah to Israel." In short, although Levi may have been one of the vilest of the brothers, as manifested both with regard to his behavior in Shechem and at the selling of Joseph, the tribe which emanated from him became one of the most lauded, with the greatest leader and prophet, Moses himself, being one of its sons, and his brother Aaron the founding member of the priesthood. The tribe's spiritual destiny made it eminently appropriate for inclusion

Vezot Habrachah

in Moses' blessings. Although Korah was also from the tribe of Levi, many of his co-rebels were from the tribe of Reuben (Num. 16:1), so it may be assumed that he acted more as an individual than as a tribal representative.

The Blessing of Benjamin

Jacob had spoken of Benjamin's military prowess, saying: "Benjamin is a wolf which tears [its prey]; in the morning he will eat his plunder, and in the evening he will divide the spoil" (Gen. 49:27). *Est. Rabbah* (10:13) says that Jacob was alluding to Saul, who was of the tribe of Benjamin (1 Sam. 9:1-2) and very successful in defeating Ammon, Moab, and Amalek (1 Sam. 14:47-48) in the morning (i.e., at the dawn of Jewish history), and also to Mordechai and Esther, who were of the tribe of Benjamin (Est. 2:5, 15), and defeated the Persians when the Jews were in exile (which is compared to the evening). *Midrash Tanchuma* (*Vayechi* 14; see also Rashi *in situ*) notes that a synonym of "tearing" was used in conjunction with the near destruction of the Benjaminites in the story of the concubine of Gibeah (Judg. 21:21).

In contrast, Moses makes no unpleasant future prophetic references, and speaks only of God's love for the tribe of Benjamin and His choice of its territory as the location of the Temple. The Midrash *(Mechilta de-Rabbi Yishmael, Yitro, Mesechta de-ba-Chodesh* 4) explains that Benjamin's territory was chosen because he had not participated in the selling of Joseph, and also because he was the only one of Jacob's twelve sons born in the Land of Israel.

The Blessings of Ephraim and Manasseh

Maintaining Ramban's approach that the number of blessings had to be twelve, and since Simeon was not included, it became imperative to bless Joseph twice, once for Ephraim and once for Manasseh. Continuing with the functionality approach, which orders the

The Ethics of Deuteronomy

blessings in terms of centrality, importance, and leadership, Joseph's descendants (who replaced Reuben's primogeniture in terms of inheritance of the land) come next. The blessing is agricultural and military in nature. With respect to the former, it says: "His land will be blessed by the Lord… with the sweetness of the land and its fullness" (Deut. 33:13, 16). On v. 13, *Sifrei* says: "This teaches that Joseph's land was more fertile than all of the other lands [inherited by the tribes]".

The military blessing is:

> To his first-born ox [Rashi: refers to Joshua as royalty] is [given] glory. His horns are the horns of a buffalo. With them, he will gore peoples from the ends of the earth. These [Ramban: horns] represent the myriads [killed by Joshua of the tribe] of Ephraim, and the thousands [Rashi: of Midianites killed by Gideon (Judg. 8:10) of the tribe] of Manasseh (Deut. 33:17).

According to Ramban, the right horn represents Ephraim and the left Manasseh. *Sifrei, in situ* (cited by Rashi), explains:

1. "The ox is powerful, but its horns are not beautiful; a buffalo has beautiful horns, but it is not powerful. Joshua was given the power of an ox and the horns of a buffalo."
2. "Were all the thirty-one kings captured [by Joshua] from the Land of Israel? [The answer is that…] any king or ruler who did not acquire for himself a palace and a holding in the Land of Israel [although he was from another country] would say that he accomplished nothing [because the Land of Israel was considered distinguished by all of them]."

The blessings given by Moses to the tribes of Manasseh and Ephraim predict a parallel role to that played by their father. Their fertile land and powerful armies would serve as providers and protectors for the remaining tribes.

In consonance with the noted trend, Moses' blessings of Joseph are tribal and positive, while Jacob's (Gen. 49:22-26) are mostly personal and refer to Joseph's (and his mother's) beauty, his altercation with his brothers, and other unpleasant incidents which he experienced.

THE BLESSING OF GAD

The blessing of the tribes of Joseph's sons is followed by that of the tribes of Zebulun and Issachar. The symbiotic relationship between them, and the positive example which it represented, has been discussed previously. Next comes the blessing of Gad. Jacob had given this tribe a short militarily-oriented blessing: "[As for] Gad, a troop will issue forth from him, and it will return in its tracks" (Gen. 49:19). Rashi relates the blessing to the vow of the tribe of Gad to cross the Jordan and fight with the rest of the nation (Num. 32:17), which they fulfilled (Josh. 4:12), and only then to return to their inheritance in Transjordan, which is what happened (Josh. 22:9), with Jacob promising that miraculously there would be no casualties. Ramban relates the blessing to assurances of victory in their constant skirmishes with the Moabites and Ammonites, and in particular to the battle of the latter with the troops of Jephtah, which ended in a decisive Israelite victory (Judg. 11:32-33).

It will be recalled that when the tribes of Reuben and Gad asked to settle in Transjordan, Moses fiercely rejected the idea, responding with a ten-verse scolding (Num. 32:6-15). Even after accepting their pledge to accompany the nation in the conquest of Canaan, Sforno comments: "In order not to engage in an argument, Moses accepted their words" (Num. 32:33).

In the blessings of *Vezot Habrachah*, Moses is much more conciliatory. First, he thanks God for granting Gad a large portion: "Blessed is He Who grants expanse to Gad" (Deut. 33:20), which he is able to defend because "he dwells like a lion, tearing the arm [of his prey, together] with the head." He even praises Gad for choosing to settle in Transjordan, saying it did so "because there, the portion of the lawgiver is hidden" (Deut. 33:21), which the Talmud (BT *Sotah* 13b) interprets to mean that Gad knew through Divine transmission that the burial place of "the lawgiver," namely Moses, would be in his territory, and that is why Gad chose to dwell on that land, and not because of greed or selfishness, as might have been inferred from the tone of Moses' reprimand in the book of Numbers. Gad owes his placement in the blessings of Moses to his military leadership and prowess.

THE BLESSING OF DAN

The next blessing was given to Dan. Both Jacob's and Moses' blessings focus on military achievements. Before examining them, it is relevant to discuss Dan's allotted portion and the battles engaged in to attain it. The lands allocated to the tribe of Dan are detailed in the book of Joshua (19: 40-48). They stretched from the coastal plain (the area unsurprisingly referred to today as *Gush Dan*) eastward, through the Valley of Ayalon and Beit Shemesh, as far as Kiryat Ye'arim and Beit Choron. However, when it came to actually conquering these lands, the tribe encountered serious opposition, as the verse states: "And the Amorites forced the children of Dan to the mountain, for they would not let them come down to the valley" (Judg. 1:34). Apparently, the Amorites migrated westward after being defeated by Moses in their original Transjordanian habitat (Num. 21:24), although *Da'at Mikra* also records a conjecture that the term "Amorites" is generic and refers to any of the Canaanite nations. Whoever they were, they occupied all of the lowlands, squeezing the entire tribe of Dan into the southeastern corner of their allocation (bordering on the Judean Hills, near present-day Ma'aleh ha-Chamishah), which includes the sites of Tzor'ah, Eshta'ol, and Beit Shemesh.

The Philistines invaded the coastal plain from the south, leading

Vezot Habrachah

the Amorites to press the tribe of Dan even further to the east. Samson, of the tribe of Dan, buoyed the spirit of the Danites by battling the Philistines for about twenty years (Judg. 15:20). However, rather than leading a combined army of the entire nation, he fought as an individual engaged in guerilla warfare. It is not surprising that he eventually succumbed (Judg. 16:30) and the tribe of Dan remained homeless, as the Bible states: "In those days, the tribe of Dan was [still] seeking for themselves an inheritance in which to dwell, for until that day their inheritance among the tribes of Israel had not come into their possession" (Judg. 18:1). In desperation, they sent an army up north, conquered a town called Layish in the Golan (Judg. 18:27), and settled the entire area, which apparently satisfied their needs, although they continued to maintain a presence in the south as well (Judg. 5:17). The Talmud (BT *Bechorot* 55a) even notes that the name Jordan, *Yarden* in Hebrew, is a composite of the two Hebrew words *yored Dan* (it descends from the territory of Dan).

The conquest of the Golan is already mentioned in the book of Joshua, where it states:

> And the border of the children of Dan went out [Rashi: was extended; Radak: did not suffice] from them; and the children of Dan went up and fought against Leshem [a variant of Layish], and captured it, and smote it with the edge of the sword, and possessed it, and dwelt in it, and called Leshem Dan, after the name of Dan, their father (Josh. 19:47).

Both Rashi and Radak explain that the conquest of the north happened many years after the death of Joshua. In fact, Radak claims that the Golan was not originally allocated to any of the tribes, and only became part of Dan because of the previously described circumstances. Abravanel asks how it is possible for it to be recorded in the book of Joshua, which, other than the last five verses, was written by Joshua himself (BT *Bava Batra* 15a). He formulates what both Rashi and Radak had hinted at, namely, that the book was edited at a later stage, and the conquest of the north, which was not originally in the plan, was added next to the description of the original inheritance of Dan in the coastal plain region.

At this point, Jacob's blessing will be examined. He said:

> Dan [Rashi: Samson from the tribe of Dan] will avenge his people [Rashi: against the Philistines], representing the tribes of Israel. Dan will be a serpent on the road, a viper on the path, which bites the horse's heels, so its rider falls backwards [Rashi: just as a snake causes a rider to fall without making contact with him, so Samson caused the death of many Philistines by grasping the pillars of the temple of Dagon]. For Your salvation [Rashi: Samson asked for God's help in returning his strength (Judg. 16:28)] I hope, O Lord! (Gen. 49:16-18).

Yair Ganz[77] has asked why, according to Rashi, Jacob's entire blessing focuses on Samson, who was not especially successful in his mission. In the blessing, he is compared to a snake, which has negative connotations in Judaism ever since the Garden of Eden (Gen. 3:14). Finally, Samson himself is portrayed as being a shady character, with the Midrash (*Gen. Rabbah* 98:14) accusing him of being a womanizer.

Ganz answers that there is indeed a bit of negativity associated with Dan, as well as with Gad, since they are the first-born children of the maidservants of Rachel and Leah, respectively. Dan's name itself, derived from the word for "judgment" (Radak, Gen. 30:6: Rachel said that she was judged to be worthy of children, just like Leah), implies a degree of contentiousness, while Gad's name is associated with Jacob's disloyalty to Leah (Rashi, Gen. 30:11). Furthermore, Dan and Gad, as well as Asher and Naphtali, as sons of the concubines, were

---

77. Yair Ganz, "Megamat ha-Piyus be-Birchotav shel Moshe be-Parshat Vezot Habrachah," *Shma'atin* (1994), pp. 115-116.

belittled and rejected by the sons of the wives (Rashi, Gen. 37:2, based on *Gen. Rabbah* 84:7).

Now compare the blessing of Jacob to that of Moses: "Dan is a young lion, leaping forth from Bashan" (Deut. 33:22). Once again, Moses attempts to reconcile. There is no reference here to Samson, and in fact no reference to the losing battles against the Philistines, which Dan fought in its southern region. Rather, only Bashan in the Golan is mentioned, where Dan scored an easy victory. Finally, Moses compares Dan to a majestic lion, the same animal to which Judah has been compared (Gen. 49:9: "A cub and a grown lion is Judah"), as if to say that the sons of the concubines are equal in status to their brothers.

THE BLESSINGS OF NAPHTALI AND ASHER

The tribes descended from Jacob's wives were blessed first by Moses, perhaps in deference to Rachel and Leah, who were the principal wives, while Jacob took the concubines only as a result of Rachel's barrenness. The blessings of the sons of the concubines apparently proceeded in a certain geographical order, from Gad who dwelt in Transjordan, westward to Dan in the Ayalon Valley, stretching all the way to the coast. Moses continued with the blessing of Naphtali, whose territory was in the north, and finished with Asher, whose land paralleled that of Naphtali's to the west, reaching until the coast.

Both Jacob's and Moses' blessings of Naphtali relate mainly to the fruitfulness of his inheritance. Jacob says that "Naphtali is a swift gazelle; [he is one] who utters beautiful words" (Gen. 49:21), with the swiftness referring to the speed of fruits ripening in the fertile Jordan valley of Ginosar, and the words uttered are blessings of God for creating such beautiful fruits (Onkelos).

The Midrash (*Gen. Rabbah* 99:12) sees Jacob's blessing as paralleling that of Moses, who said: "Naphtali is favorably satisfied and full of [fruits upon which people pronounce] the Lord's blessing"

(Deut. 33:23). The fruits were fit for kings, and when presented to them as gifts, were capable of transforming the evil intentions of monarchs into "the Lord's blessing." Moses' blessing concludes by saying: "He will possess the sea and the south" (Deut. 33:23). The sea referred to is the Sea of Galilee, along whose southern shore were spread fishing nets (Rashi, *in situ*).

A second interpretation of Jacob's blessing cited by the Midrash (*Gen. Rabbah* 98:17) is military in nature, with the "swift gazelle" referring to the ten thousand soldiers from the tribe of Naphtali who "rushed into the valley with their feet" (Judg. 5:15) to defeat the army of Sisera (Judg. 4:6), and the "beautiful words" uttered referring to those of Deborah in her famous poem (Judg. 5:1).

Both Jacob's and Moses' blessings of Asher were centered on the outstanding produce of its fertile land. Jacob had said: "From Asher will come rich bread, and he will yield regal delicacies" (Gen. 49:20), while Moses said: "More blessed than the other sons will be Asher. He will be pleasing to his brothers [*Chizkuni*: because olives are plentiful], and [one may] immerse his foot in oil" (Deut. 33:24). The Midrash (*Num. Rabbah* 14:11) explains that the fruitfulness and fertility of the plots of Naphtali and Asher, which lay side by side in the Galilee, were equivalent. Jacob blessed Asher first, while Moses reversed the order. Perhaps Moses, in his quest for reconciliation, harmony, and brotherly love, placed Naphtali first this time in order to neutralize any potential feelings of jealousy.

The Midrash (*Tanchuma Vayechi* 13) cites an alternate explanation of the blessing of Asher, saying it refers to the beauty of the women of that tribe. In the verse from Genesis, Asher is referred to as "rich bread," a euphemism for women fit to wed kings. This is also the gist of the phrase in Deuteronomy: "He will be pleasing to his brothers, and immerse his foot in oil," namely, that he will be much appreciated by his brothers, who will take beautiful wives from among his daughters, who will frequently marry high priests and kings anointed with oil. A second Midrash (*Gen. Rabbah* 71:10) cites a verse stating that Malchiel, a grandson of Asher, was "the father of Birzaith [literally, the son of the olive]" (1 Chron. 7:31), interpreting the verse to mean that he was so called because his daughters married anointed priests and kings.

Summary

Unlike Jacob, the blessings bestowed by Moses were not given in near birth order. Jacob related to his children as a father to his sons; he therefore clung to their birth order, and allowed himself the prerogative of a parent to constructively criticize his offspring when called for. Moses, on the other hand, related to the tribes as independent units, each with its own function. Furthermore, he went out of his way to salve any hard feelings that might have remained from earlier times, making sure to relate positively to both Reuben and Levi, in spite of their having been reproved by Jacob. With regard to Simeon, whom he did not bless, it is not clear whether it was because he had nothing positive to say, or because Simeon was eventually absorbed into the other tribes, so that it shared the blessings of the other tribes. Moses was thus able to leave this world with the satisfaction that he had generated good feelings and positive inertia among the various factions composing the Children of Israel, and had minimized the likelihood of jealousy and rivalry among the tribes. Of course, as Robert Burns wrote: "the best laid schemes of mice and men often go awry," and even Moses our teacher was not able to prevent the frequent friction and civil wars which prevailed throughout the books of Judges, Samuel, and Kings.

Appendix I:
Jewish Dietary History
From Adam to Noah

The book of Genesis (ch. 1) opens with a description of Adam's prescribed diet:

> **28** And God blessed them, and God said to them, "Be fruitful and multiply and fill the earth and subdue it, and rule over the fish of the sea and over the fowl of the sky and over all the beasts that tread upon the earth." **29** And God said, "Behold, I have given you every seed-bearing herb which is upon the surface of the entire earth, and every tree that has seed-bearing fruit; it will be yours for food. **30** And to all the beasts of the earth and to all the fowl of the heavens, and to everything that moves upon the earth, in which there is a living spirit, every green herb to eat," and it was so.

V. 28 states that man will rule over the animal kingdom, but as far as his diet is concerned, v. 29 specifies it as consisting of herbs and fruits, as noted in the Talmud:

> R. Yehudah said in Rav's name: Adam was not permitted to eat flesh, for it is written, "[Behold, I have given you every seed-bearing herb....] it will be yours for food, and to all the beasts of the earth" [vv. 29-30], implying, but the beasts of the

earth are not for you [the herbs and fruits have been given to you and to the beasts of the earth, but the beasts of the earth have not been given to you for food]. And when the sons of Noah arrived, He permitted them [animals—to be eaten], as it says, "[Every moving thing that lives will be yours to eat] like the green vegetation, I have given you everything" (Gen. 9:3) [just as the green vegetation may be eaten, so may the beasts be eaten] ... One may ask: "And rule over the fish of the sea" (v. 28), certainly this must mean that they are for eating? No. [It means they may be used] for work [the Talmud proceeds to describe how even fish and fowl may be utilized for work] (BT *Sanhedrin* 59b).

Rashi (BT *Sanhedrin* 59b, s.v. *lo hutar*; Gen. 1:29) understands that the diet of both mankind and the animal kingdom was meant to be the same at the time of creation, consisting of fruits and seed-bearing vegetables (e.g., kernels of wheat, barley, and rice—v. 29) and other herbs (v. 30), while Ramban (Gen. 1:29) holds that the former verse delineates a higher grade of sustenance for humans, and the latter indicates an inferior level of feed for all other creatures. Only after Adam sinned was his diet extended to include the green herbs originally designated for animals (Gen. 3:18), which were considered to be lower-grade, and which would now constitute a major portion of his diet.

Ba'al ha-Turim (*Tur ha-Aroch*, Gen. 1:30) comments that initially, meat was repulsive to man, for no distinction was made between killing humans and other creatures. Ramban explains that meat was prohibited because all creatures have a soul, even if animal souls are inferior to those of humans. In his own words (Gen. 1:29):

> The reason for this [prohibition of eating meat] was that moving creatures have some qualities of soul regarding which they are similar to intelligent beings—they can choose their

preferences and vittles, and they flee from potential pain and death. The verse says: "Who knows that the spirit of men is that which ascends on high and the spirit of the beast is that which descends below to the earth?" (Ecc. 3:21).

Ramban interprets the latter verse as a question, in accordance with *Targum Yonatan*. Kohelet (the author of Ecclisiastes) certainly does not doubt the eternity of the human soul, he just questions whether animals too have souls (*Da'at Mikra*).

The Sages of the Talmud initially thought that ruling "over the fish of the sea" implies that Adam was permitted to eat the inferior creatures, but conclude that this was not so; rather, he could at most benefit from their labor. The simple meaning would then seem to be that although their power could be harnessed, man dare not harm the bodies of his fellow creations. *Aruch le-Ner* (BT *Sanhedrin* 59b) points out that this was not the case, but rather it was permissible to kill animals, as long as there was no intention of eating their meat. He bases his view on the following Midrash:

> On the day that Adam was created, when he saw the sun setting, he said: "Alas, because I have sinned, the world is becoming dark and the world will once again become void and unformed—this then is the death which I have been punished with from Heaven!" He sat up all night fasting and weeping, and Eve wept opposite him. When dawn broke, he said: "This is the usual course of the world!" He then arose and offered a bull [as a sacrifice to the Lord] (BT *Avodah Zarah* 8a).

Furthermore, *Aruch le-Ner* notes that Abel sacrificed the first-born of his flocks, leading to God's acquiescence (Gen. 4:4), while Noah selected sacrifices from among all of the clean animals (Gen. 8:20), which were considered by the Lord to produce a pleasant aroma

(Gen. 8:21). He thus concludes that killing animals was permitted for any objective other than eating, whether as service to the Lord or to make use of their hide or fat.

Not only was it permitted to kill animals for non-eating purposes; it was also permitted to eat meat as long as the creature was not slaughtered by human beings, as is evident from the following Midrash:

> R. Yehudah b. Tema said: Adam reclined in the Garden of Eden, while the ministering angels roasted flesh and strained wine for him… There it refers to flesh that descends from heaven. Is there flesh which descends from heaven? Yes; as in the story of R. Shimon b. Chalafta, who was walking on the road, when lions met him and roared. He said: "The young lions roar for prey" (Ps. 104:21) and two thighs descended [from heaven]. They ate one and left the other. He took it and went to the *beit midrash*, and asked regarding it: Is this an unclean item or a clean item [fit for food]? They said to him: Nothing unclean descends from heaven. R. Zera asked R. Abbahu: What if something in the shape of a donkey were to descend? He said to him: "You stupid jackal. Did they not tell him: 'No unclean thing descends from heaven'" (BT *Sanhedrin* 59b).

From Noah to the Exodus

Ramban

As has been noted, after the flood, meat became permissible, based on the verse: "Every moving thing that lives will be yours to eat like the green vegetation, I have given you everything [just as the green vegetation may be eaten, so may the beasts be eaten]" (Gen. 9:3). Having previously explained the prohibition to kill living creatures as stemming from their possession of a soul, even if of inferior quality to that of human beings, Ramban (Gen.1:29) attempts to justify the transition which now occurred:

> And when they sinned and it was decreed that they die in the flood [since "all flesh had corrupted its behavior on the earth" (Gen. 6:12)], and for the sake of Noah, He saved [some] of them in order to preserve the species, He gave them permission to slaughter and eat them, since their existence was for his [Noah's] sake [as they were deserving of death, and were only spared because of his righteousness].

It is not clear from Ramban whether permission was granted as a reward for Noah's efforts in nurturing the multiplicity of creatures, or as punishment for their corrupt ways.

At any rate, so that the allowance to eat once-living creatures should not have a deleterious effect on mankind, God circumscribed the means of slaughtering and eating meat, as Ramban states *in situ*:

> Yet with all this, He did not give them permission regarding their souls, and He prohibited them from eating a limb cut off from a living animal, and in addition He gave us the mitzvah prohibiting the eating of all blood, because it is the basis of the soul, as it is written: "for the soul of any flesh is its blood" (Lev. 17:14), for He permitted the eating of the body of once-living creatures which could not speak, after they have died, but not the soul itself. And this is the reason for the commandments regarding slaughtering, and for what they said: "Preventing the suffering of beasts is a Biblical command" (BT *Bava Metzia* 32b), and this is the [basis for] the blessing [before slaughtering]: "Who has sanctified us by His commandments and commanded us to perform [the mitzvah of] *shechitah* [ritual slaughter]."

R. Isaac Aboab of Castile, in his commentary on Ramban (Gen. 1:29, s.v. *hinei natati lachem*), provides the following exegesis of the two reasons for *shechitah* suggested by Ramban:

> For blood is prohibited to us, and there is no location in the animal to let all of its blood other than the neck, and also since preventing the suffering of beasts is a Biblical command, it is therefore required to attempt, to the greatest possible extent, not to pain the animal, and that is by slaughtering on the neck [which is less painful than any other method].

Chatam Sofer (Responsa, 1:54 [*Orach Chaim*]) notes that Ramban includes the blessing said upon slaughtering to emphasize that he interprets the phrase "commanded us to perform *shechitah*" to mean "commanded us to be merciful toward all creatures."

Malbim

Malbim (Gen. 9:3) explains the change as resulting from a natural evolution in the wake of the flood, when the nutritional content of fruits decreased and, in addition, men relocated to colder climates. Both of these factors created increased nutritional requirements, which necessitated incorporating more protein into the human diet.

Malbim also claims that after the flood, the level of mankind actually rose. Until the flood, man was on the level (shared by animals) of the living (*chai*), and partook of roughly the same diet. After the flood, man became a *medabber*—an intelligent being capable of intelligent conversation and introspection. Malbim continues: "Just as there is no impropriety when the *chai* eats that which grows, since in doing so vegetation is elevated by becoming part of the body of the *chai*, so is there no impropriety if the *medabber* eats the *chai*, since in doing so, the *chai* is elevated by turning into part of the *medabber*."

Why did the transition from *chai* to *medabber* take place only after Noah alighted from the ark? Since the eating of meat has been related to man's use of his mental faculties (specifically for the study of Torah) and since the first step in this direction is represented by the presentation of the seven Noahide laws, which concluded with God transmitting to Noah the prohibition for man to eat the flesh of a *living* animal only (*Hilchot Melachim* 9:1), it is reasonable to assume that at this point man officially became a *medabber,* especially since the more barbaric people had been eliminated in the Great Flood.

This approach fits in well with the interpretation of *Akeidat Yitzchak* (*Beshallach* 41) of the following Talmudic excerpt:

> An ignoramus (*am ha-aretz*) may not eat the flesh of cattle, for it says: "This is the law [Torah] of the beast and of the fowl" (Lev. 11:46). Whoever engages in [the study of] the Torah is permitted to eat the flesh of beast and fowl, but he who does not engage in [the study of] the Torah may not eat the flesh of beast and fowl (BT *Pesachim* 49b).

Akeidat Yitzchak explains that uneducated people who do not exploit their intellectual potential, by remaining on the level of *chai,* forfeit the option to eat meat available to those who achieve the level of *medabber.* Of course, the more straightforward explanation of the Talmudic segment is that ignorant people have not mastered the intricate laws of *kashrut* (Ritva).

MIDRASH

An alternate rationalization for the transition that occurred after the flood is based on a comparison of two verses:

1. And God said, "Let us make man in our image, after our likeness, and they shall rule over the fish of the sea and over the fowl of the heaven and over the animals and over all the earth and over all the creeping things that creep upon the earth" (Gen. 1:26, at creation).

2. And your fear and your dread will be upon all the beasts of the earth and upon all the fowl of the heaven; upon everything that creeps on the ground and upon all the fish of the sea, [for] they have been given into your hands (Gen. 9:2, after the flood).

The Midrash (Maharzo, *Gen. Rabbah* 34:12) explains that when God created man, He gave him dominion over all other creatures; i.e., they were to both fulfill his requests and fear him, as indicated by the first verse. In punishment for the sins of the generation of the flood, man lost his ascendance over the animal kingdom, and was vulnerable to attack by wild beasts. Only after Noah brought his sacrifices was man's sovereignty returned, though only to the extent that he was feared by the animal kingdom, but not obeyed by it, as indicated by the second verse. According to Maharzo, their initial ability to comply with man's commands placed animals on a level close enough to man to make it odious for them to be consumed by him. Once that facility was lost, the gap between the functionality of man and beast was so great, that it became reasonable for man to eat such creatures, much as he eats fruits and vegetables.

In contrast to Maharzo, who felt that the reduced mental capacity of animals made them into a potential food supply for man, R. Yehonatan Grossman ("*Bein ha-Olam ha-Rishon ve-ha-Sheni*," VBM) believes that eating meat became acceptable for mankind not because of the shrinking ability of animals, but rather because man's own stature decreased (which also differs from the view of Malbim, who suggests that man's level actually rose). Initially, man ruled over the animal kingdom as a benevolent despot, enjoined by the necessity to nurture his subjects. He failed in this function, allowing all flesh to become corrupt and violent (Gen. 6:11-12). Once his dominion disappeared, he was actually a typical creature, a bit more intelligent, but not intrinsically different than the others and with no special responsibilities toward them. In short, he became one more carnivorous beast.

Man's initially elevated status is displayed in v. 1:26 above, which appears after all of the lesser creatures have been created, because man is meant to be God's partner in running the world, having been created in His image (Gen. 1:27). Alas, the task proved to be beyond man's ability, and so he was demoted to being just one of the many living creatures which populate the earth, as indicated by the fact that Noah and his family leave the ark before all of the animals contained in it (Gen. 8:18-19), no more God's helpmate and the pinnacle of creation, but just one more creature.

The Midrash concludes by noting that man's dominion over the animal kingdom returned (apparently briefly) during the reign of Solomon, as attested to by the use of that very word in the verse: "For he had dominion on this entire side of the river, from Tiphsah even to Gaza" (1 Kings 5:4). The implication is that at some point during Solomon's tenure, man's kingship over all creatures resumed, leading to the renewal of the antediluvian prohibition of meat consumption, based on the interpretation of the Midrash according to either Maharzo or R. Grossman. At any rate, in view of the fact that Jews have been carnivores for thousands of years, the interdiction could not have been very long-lived.

From the Exodus to the Giving of the Torah

After leaving Egypt, the Israelites were free to eat whatever their hearts desired—fruits and grains from the time of creation, vegetables from the time Adam sinned (according to Ramban), and meat from when Noah's ark landed. The only problem was that in the desert no food was available, leading to the nation's complaint: "If only we had died by the hand of the Lord [Rashbam: of old age (in a natural manner) and not of starvation] in the land of Egypt, when we sat by pots of meat, when we ate bread to our fill" (Exod. 16:3). God immediately responds by addressing Moses in the next verse and telling him:

"Behold! I am going to rain down for you bread from heaven." Ibn Ezra explains that the Hebrew word for bread is *lechem*, which can denote any staple—be it bread, meat, or even fruit, as is confirmed when Moses elaborates God's message by telling the Israelites that they will become cognizant of the Lord's glory "when He gives you in the evening meat to eat and bread in the morning [with which] to satisfy yourselves" (Exod. 16:8).[78] Noting that eating to satisfaction is mentioned only with regard to bread, the Talmud states: "Here the Torah teaches good behavior—that one should not eat meat to satiety" (BT *Chullin* 84a).

In conjunction with their request for meat and bread, the Talmud states:

> The flesh for which they asked improperly [Rashi: on a full stomach, for they had plenty of cattle. Rashi on Exod. 16:8: and furthermore, it was possible for them to get along without meat] was given to them improperly [Rashi: it descended at night, when it could no longer be prepared in time for the meal (and was thus usable only the next day)]. Bread, for which they asked properly [Rashi: for it is impossible to live without bread], was given to them properly [Rashi: in the morning, when there is time to prepare it; Rashi on Exod. 16:7: with dew over it and dew under it, as if it were lying in a box]. Here, the Torah teaches good behavior—that one should eat meat only at night (BT *Yoma* 75a-b).

Maharsha explains that the last statement is based on the verse itself (which stipulates that meat would be supplied in the evening),

---

78. In Exod. 16:12, God confirms that this is indeed what He meant. Ibn Ezra explains that God's promise is repeated at the time of implementation, since part of the implementation was the realization by the nation that God was indeed transmitting his intentions to Moses, while Ramban justifies the repetition as necessary to stress that their complaint displayed a lack of gratitude and was thus sinful.

not on the unbecoming conduct of the Israelites. *Torah Temimah* (Exod. 16:15) explains that meat should be eaten at night because it is generally part of a large meal, after which it is preferable for one to rest (*Hilchot De'ot* 3:4), just as the large carnivorous animals do in nature, and during the day one is too busy to do so. God's supplying meat at night was improper not because it was not to be eaten then, but rather because there was not sufficient time to prepare it.

In the book of Numbers, the Israelites once more revealed their lust for meat and their nostalgia for their (imagined) experience in Egypt, when they cried out: "Who will feed us meat? We remember the fish that we ate in Egypt free of charge, the cucumbers, the watermelons, the leeks, the onions, and the garlic" (Num. 11:4-5). God was repulsed by their falsification and lack of gratitude, yet He acquiesced to their request, but punished those who were most guilty:

> **19** You will eat it not one day, not two days, not five days, not ten days, and not twenty days. **20** But even for a full month until it comes out of your nose and is loathsome to you. Because you have despised the Lord, Who is among you, and you cried before Him, saying, "Why did we ever leave Egypt?".... **32** The people rose up all that day and all night and the next day and gathered the quails. [Even] the one who gathered the least collected ten heaps. They spread them around the camp in piles. **33** The meat was still between their teeth; it was not yet finished, and the anger of the Lord flared against the people, and the Lord struck the people with a very mighty blow. **34** He called that place Kivrot ha-Ta'avah [Graves of Lust], for there they buried the people who lusted (Num. 11).

Regarding the narrative in Numbers, there exists an internal contradiction. On the one hand, v. 20 states that the quail would last for a month, while v. 33 says that those who partook died when the meat was still between their teeth. The Talmud (BT *Yoma* 75b) explains that the mediocre sinners died immediately, and that was a blessing, while the incorrigible sinners lingered on for a month, and only then died.

On the same page of the Talmud it is stated that the quail which fell miraculously had to be slaughtered in the kosher manner. This is difficult to understand since, according to R. Akiva (BT *Chullin* 17a), whose view is accepted, kosher slaughtering was not required until the nation entered the Land of Israel. *Tosefet Yom ha-Kippurim* (BT *Yoma* 75b) answers that the requirement to slaughter the quail (which was not yet in force with regard to other forms of meat) was a punishment for the lack of gratitude which many had displayed. When the righteous heard that God had said that they would be eating quail until it came out of their noses (v. 20), they realized that the necessity to perform *shechitah* was a penalty. They concluded that by performing ritual slaughter, they would be doing penance for the nation's sins. In order to atone for the entire community, they slaughtered a large number of quail, as the verse says: "The one who gathered the least collected ten heaps" (Num. 11:32*). Tosefet Yom ha-Kippurim* notes that no one person would need such a large quantity. However, the righteous people, who had no intention of eating them, slaughtered them to expiate the offenses of their brethren.

A major question with regard to their present complaint at Kivrot ha-Ta'avah, where they whined, "Who will feed us meat?" (Num. 11:4), is that a month after their departure from Egypt (Exod. 16:1) they had recalled the bread and meat which they consumed in Egypt, which had led God already at that early stage to respond: "In the afternoon you will eat meat, and in the morning you will be sated with bread" (Exod. 16:12), upon which Ramban comments:

> Our Rabbis were of the opinion that the quail were with them from that day [15th of Iyar] on, like the manna, and so it would appear, for they complained about two things,

and regarding both of them He heard their complaint and He satisfied their craving, for what would it bring them and what would it add to them having meat for [only] one or two days.

Ramban actually relates to the apparent contradiction in the continuation of his commentary:

> The subject of the second incident of quail at Kivrot ha-Ta'avah is that they did not receive enough of them to be satiated, as it says [in the first incident]: "meat to eat and bread [in the morning with which] to become sated" (Exod. 16:8,12). It is possible that only the adults gathered it—or it may be that they were found by chance only by the pious ones among them—while the young hungered and craved for them, since Scripture does not relate concerning the quail, "both the one who gathered much and the one who gathered little" [Exod. 16:17, implying everyone gathered], as it does concerning the manna. It is for this reason that Scripture says there [in the narrative of Kivrot ha-Ta'avah]: "And the multitude among them began to have strong cravings" (Num. 11:4), and it says [in the continuation of the verse], "then also the Children of Israel began to cry once again," meaning that some of the Children of Israel were also weeping for it, but not all of them. He then gave of it [quail] to them in great quantity, as it says: "The one who gathered the least collected ten heaps. They spread them around the camp in piles" (Num. 11:32), and they ate for a month's time out of that abundance, and then the quail reverted to their normal incidence. In accordance with the plain meaning, the whole affair with the quail happened only at intervals, but the manna, which was their staple, was always available.

To summarize, Ramban holds that they did in fact have meat

previously, but they complained at Kivrot ha-Ta'avah for one of three reasons:

1. They did not receive enough to be satiated.
2. The older and stronger people received a portion, but the youngsters were deprived.
3. The quail as described in the book of Exodus were available once every couple of months, while the murmurers demanded it on a more frequent basis.

Ramban's understanding of the straightforward meaning is strengthened by the research of Zechariah Dori,[79] who found that quail are among the migratory birds who spend their summers in Europe and Asia, and their winters in Africa, migrating to the south in the fall and returning to the north in the spring. On their northerly migration in the spring, the quail pass through southern Israel and the Sinai Peninsula after completing a 750-kilometer (470-mile) flight in about ten hours. By the time they arrive in Israel, they are in a state of weakness and exhaustion, flying at a very low altitude of no more than a meter and a half (5 feet), which allows them to be caught very easily in trappers' nets.

According to the Biblical account, both stories of God raining down quail occurred in the spring month of Iyar (Exod. 16:1, in the first year after the exodus; Num. 10:11, in the second year after the exodus), when the quail fly over the Sinai Peninsula and southern Israel. According to the simple explanation, the quail did not appear daily but rather periodically; therefore, it is reasonable to propose that they were accessible twice a year, on their way to and from Africa. The complaint at Kivrot ha-Ta'avah was that in contrast to the manna, which was available on a daily basis, the availability of the quail was much more infrequent. It would seem that in the second year after

---

79. Zechariah Dori, *Daf Shavui* 846 (2010), *Parshat Beshallach*, Bar Ilan University.

the exodus, the size of the migratory flock was exceedingly large, as emphasized in the descriptive phrase: "[Even] the one who gathered the least collected ten heaps" (Num. 11:32).

Zechariah Dori also points out that quail meat from the spring flocks is mildly poisonous, apparently as a result of the comestibles which they consumed in Africa. This toxicity has been mentioned by Aristotle, Pliny the Elder, and even modern scientists.

The miraculous aspects of the normally natural phenomenon which occurred at Kivrot ha-Ta'avah were three-fold. One was the abnormally large size of the flock, in accordance with God's prediction that they would be eating quail "until it comes out of your nose and is loathsome to you" (Num. 11:20). The second was the higher than normal degree of toxicity manifested when "the Lord struck the people with a very mighty blow" (Num. 11:33). Finally, apparently, only the most ardent of the murmurers were negatively affected.

From the Giving of the Torah until Entering the Land of Israel

The eating of meat, which had been permitted from the time of Noah, was limited for Jews by the laws of the Torah, which allowed only certain creatures; in addition, many of those creatures had to be ritually slaughtered in order to be considered kosher. Ritual slaughter, with its myriad of detailed laws, is a complicated process, and it will be shown that it was only partially implemented in the desert. The following verses describe a transition in terms of the consumption of meat upon arrival in the Land of Israel:

> **20** When the Lord your God expands your boundary, as He has spoken to you, and you say, "I will eat meat," because your soul desires to eat meat, you may eat meat to your heart's content. **21** If the place where the Lord your God chooses to put His Name is distant from you, then you may slaughter

the cattle and the sheep which the Lord has given you as I have commanded you, and you may eat it in your cities to your heart's content. **22** But as the deer and the gazelle are eaten, so may you eat them; the unclean and the clean alike may eat of them (Deut. 12).

Based on a simple reading, v. 20 seems to be extending the available options for eating meat. On the other hand, v. 21, which speaks of slaughtering as commanded, implies a degree of restriction. In fact, in the Talmud, one Tanna focuses on the first verse and extends the range of permissible meats, while another derives new limitations from the second verse. Regarding v. 20, the Talmud states:

> R. Yishmael says this verse is stated specially in order to permit the Israelites to eat flesh which the soul desires [free of religious obligation], for in the beginning they were forbidden to eat flesh which the soul desires. Upon entering the Land of Israel they were permitted to eat flesh which the soul desires (BT *Chullin* 16b).

Rashi explains:

> [In the desert] they could only eat the meat of peace offerings. If they slaughtered without bringing the animal as a sacrifice, they would be punished by excision, as it says: "Any man of the House of Israel, who slaughters an ox, a lamb, or a goat inside the camp, or who slaughters outside the camp, but does not bring it to the entrance of the Tent of Meeting to offer up as a sacrifice to the Lord before the *Mishkan* of the Lord, [this (act) shall be counted for that man as blood; he has shed blood, and that man shall be cut off from among his people]" (Lev. 17:3-4).

The Ethics of Deuteronomy

According to Rashi's interpretation of R. Yishmael (and Ramban's commentary on Lev. 17:2), the verse in Leviticus specifying a punishment of excision refers to slaughtering an animal outside of the Tabernacle, whether for sacrificial purposes or otherwise, thus implying that non-sacrificial meat consumption was prohibited. *Tosafot* (BT *Chullin* 16b, s.v. *she-be-hatchalah*) argue with Rashi and hold that although slaughtering non-sacrificial meat was prohibited, it was not punishable by excision.

R. Akiva argues with R. Yishmael and believes that non-sacrificial meat was always allowed, even during their travels through the desert. Regarding v. 21, the Talmud states:

> R. Akiva says this verse is stated specially in order to prohibit the flesh of a stabbed [not halachically slaughtered] animal. For in the beginning, the Israelites were permitted to eat the flesh of a stabbed animal [Rashi: this is derived from this verse, for it says: "If the place... is distant from you *then you may slaughter*," implying that until now they were not commanded to slaughter]. From the time they entered the land, stabbed meat was prohibited (BT *Chullin* 17a).

One may ask, according to R. Akiva, why v. 21 relates the newly imposed requirement of ritual slaughter to living far away, since it is relevant to those living nearby as well. It may be answered that because of their great distance from the Temple, people might refrain from bringing sacrifices, and the entire slaughtering procedure could lapse into desuetude. It was accordingly reinforced by making ritual slaughter a prerequisite for all meat consumption.

The Talmud proceeds to pinpoint the different views of R. Yishmael and R. Akiva:

> In what do they differ? R. Akiva maintains that at no time was it ever forbidden to eat flesh which the soul desires. R.

Yishmael maintains that at no time was it ever permitted to eat the flesh of a stabbed animal.

Rashi explains R. Akiva's opinion:

> The verse "but does not bring it to the entrance of the Tent of Meeting" (Lev. 17:4) is referring only to holy sacrifices, and that which it says, "[and you say 'I will eat meat,' because your soul lusts to eat meat,] you may eat meat to your heart's content," is not meant to permit flesh which the soul desires [which was already permitted], but to teach the dictum of R. Eliezer b. Azariah...: "The Torah here teaches a rule of conduct, that a person should not eat meat unless he specially desires it [when he is nearly full, so he eats a small amount, but not when he is hungry and eats a lot; Rashi (BT *Chullin* 84a, s.v. *ella be-hazmanah*) explains, so that he not become impoverished], and "if the place... is distant from you *then you may slaughter*" comes to require slaughtering [of kosher animals] upon entry into the land.

According to R. Akiva, in contrast to R. Yishmael, the verse in Leviticus specifying a punishment of excision for slaughtering animals outside the sanctuary refers only to consecrated animals.

What is the conceptual difference between R. Yishmael and R. Akiva? R. Yishmael may have looked at the sojourn in the desert as an incubatory period, when most food was supernaturally supplied (such as the manna and quail), with the reins transferring to the Israelites only upon their arrival in Israel. Alternatively, being that the laws of ritual slaughter had been transmitted to Moses at Sinai, perhaps the Israelites were not yet sufficiently sophisticated to properly observe the legal intricacies inherent therein. In fact, as noted earlier, even after their arrival in the Land of Israel, the Talmud (BT *Pesachim* 49b) prohibits the uneducated from eating meat for fear of improperly implementing the laws of slaughtering (Ritva), although Maharsha notes that fish, which do not require ritual slaughter, are permitted. R. Akiva says they may have been permitted, because he takes into account that the Israelites would not yet have been able to master the complex laws of ritual slaughter. God's approach was one of gradual training, starting with the seven Noahide laws, with additions to Amram and at Marah. The initial emphasis was on the morally-oriented laws, and only gradually did God institute more ceremonial and ritually-oriented laws.

The Talmud asks and answers the following question on R. Yishmael's view:

> According to R. Akiva, who maintains that at no time was it ever forbidden to eat flesh which the soul desires, the implication [that meat was eaten in the desert] of the verse "but as the deer and the gazelle are eaten, so may you eat them" (Deut. 12:22) is acceptable; but according to R. Yishmael, was the gazelle or the hart ever permitted [to be eaten, since they could not be brought as sacrifices]? When the Divine Law prohibited [the eating of flesh which the soul desires], it was only the flesh of an animal that was fit for a sacrifice, but [the flesh of] a wild animal that was not fit for a sacrifice it did not prohibit (BT *Chullin* 17a).

In other words, even according to R. Yishmael, the meat of kosher undomesticated animals was permitted in the desert, but animals which could be brought as sacrifices could be eaten only in that context. *Or Sameach* (*Hilchot Shechitah* 4:17) points out that by the same token, fowl could also have been eaten, as it too may not be brought as a peace offering.

Jewish Dietary History

Upon Entering the Land of Israel

Although certain dietary limitations were already mentioned in the book of Genesis, the Torah added many more restrictions, leading to a final code which was fully operational upon the arrival of the Israelites in the Land of Israel, and may be summarized as follows:

1. Flesh of animals which do not have either of the following two signs: chewing of their cud and split hoofs is prohibited (Lev. 11:3, Deut. 14:6); accordingly, camels (no split hoofs—Lev. 11:4, Deut. 14:7) and pigs (do not chew their cud—Lev. 11:7, Deut. 14:8) are prohibited.
2. The part of the hind quarter containing the sciatic nerve of kosher animals is prohibited (Gen. 32:33).
3. Fish that do not have either of the following two signs: at least one fin, at least one easily removable scale are prohibited (Lev. 11:9-12, Deut. 14:10).
4. Birds of prey are prohibited (Lev. 11:13-19, Deut. 14:12-18).
5. Reptiles and insects, other than certain types of locusts, are prohibited (Lev. 11:10, 20; Deut. 14:19).
6. Animals and birds which have not been properly slaughtered (*shechitah*) by a ritual slaughterer (*shochet*) are prohibited.[80] An animal which dies a natural death or is killed by any method other than *shechitah* (including a faulty *shechitah*) is called a *nevelah*, and is forbidden (Lev. 11:40; Deut. 14:21).
7. Cooked foods containing meat mixed with milk are prohibited (Exod. 23:19, 34:26; Deut. 14:21), repeated thrice to prohibit

---

80. The details of how to slaughter are considered to be *halachah le-Moshe mi-Sinai* (laws transmitted orally to Moses at Sinai). The Torah hints at the existence of such laws in the verse: "If the place which the Lord your God chooses to put His name there is too far from you, then you should slaughter from the herd and of the flock, which the Lord gave you, as I have commanded you, and you can eat within your gates, as much as your soul desires" (Deut. 12:21).

cooking, eating, and deriving benefit.

8. Blood is prohibited (Lev. 7:26, 17:10; Deut. 12:23); to remove all blood, meat must be salted and soaked before cooking.

9. An animal or bird suffering from an injury (after being attacked by a wild beast) or a disease, either of which will lead to its death within a year,[81] is called a *trefah*, and is forbidden (Exod. 22:30), even though it has been properly slaughtered.

10. Eating a limb cut from a living creature is prohibited. The prohibition is one of the seven Noahide laws (BT *Sanhedrin* 56b) and is explicated after the flood (Gen. 9:4). Previously, meat had been forbidden, so Rambam explains that it was not yet relevant (*Hilchot Melachim* 9:1), while *Tosafot* (BT *Sanhedrin* 56b, s.v. *achol*) say it was already given to Adam in order to prohibit such meat even if not torn off by man. After the Torah was given, the law forbidding one to "eat flesh while there is still life" was repeated (Deut. 12:23).

11. Slaughtering a female animal with its young on the same day is prohibited (Lev. 22:28). The Mishnah (*Chullin* 5:1) states that although the act is prohibited, the meat of both is kosher (*Hilchot Shechitah* 12:1), although *Behag* says that the meat of the second to be slaughtered is prohibited for one day.[82]

12. Sending away the mother bird before taking her young or her eggs is mandatory (Deut. 22:6-7). If one did not do so, and slaughtered the mother or her young, he is permitted to eat them (*Hilchot Shechitah* 13:1).

13. Food which one vowed not to eat is prohibited (Num. 30:3).

---

81. BT *Chullin* 42a, 57b; *Yad ha-Chazakah, Hilchot Shechitah* 11:1.
82. *Tur, Yoreh Deah* 16. *Bach* (16:3) quotes Ran, who says it is a rabbinically enacted penalty, but he himself says it is a Torah law. *Perisha* (16:3) says it is rabbinical and only applies to the person who slaughtered it, and *Aruch ha-Shulchan* (16:14) extends it to his entire family.

Appendix II: Vegetarianism

Mishnaic Source

A potential source for vegetarianism could be the Mishnaic phrase: "the most respected among the butchers is a partner of Amalek" (*Kiddushin* 4:14). The Mishnah seems to be hinting that moral degeneration may not necessarily result from eating meat, but rather from slaughtering animals. However, since the former is impossible without the latter, the implication is that meat should not be eaten. Nevertheless, this idiom may be interpreted in various ways.

Rashi feels that butchers are being accused of financial greed. Since it is forbidden to eat improperly slaughtered animals, there is a strong temptation to pass off such animals as being kosher, especially if their actual status is in doubt.

More surprising is the view of R. Rafael Immanuel Chai (*Hon Ashir*), who actually interprets the phrase as being complimentary to butchers. Extracting the sciatic nerve thoroughly (*traibering*) involves declaring large segments of the meat unacceptable—to be designated for allocation to non-Jews, here termed Amalekites, who thus get as large a section of every cow as if they were partners. Alternately, proper *traibering* requires dissecting the hind quarter into minute pieces, reminiscent of the Amalekites' cruelty.

Other Mishnaic commentators, however, do emphasize a moralistic motivation. *Tiferet Yisrael* holds that the Mishnah indicates that a butcher is likely to develop a cruel disposition.

> Since he spends all day engaged in bloodshed, he becomes

naturally cruel just like Amalek, which fought Israel not in order to inherit their land or take their valuables, for they [Israel] left prison as a poor and wretched nation. Did this wicked one know of the Egyptian booty and the bounty at the sea? Only due to his excessive pride did he allow his cruelty to rage wildly with the intention of destroying a poor and impoverished nation (*Tiferet Yisrael, Kiddushin* 4:14).

Tosafot Yom Tov (based on *Tanchuma Ki Teitzei* 9 and cited by Rashi, Deut. 25:18) compares the butcher's cruelty to that of Amalek, which was the only nation that dared attack Israel after seeing all of the miracles which accompanied the exodus and the discomfiture suffered by the Egyptians both in Egypt and at the Reed Sea, thereby encouraging other nations to indulge in warfare.

Sefer ha-Ikkarim

The heretofore recorded commentators have directed their critique at the ritual slaughterer. It was noted that R. Eliezer b. Azariah said that meat should be eaten sparingly, but Rashi explained that this was due to the relatively high cost of meat (BT *Chullin* 84a, s.v. *ella behazmanah*). *Kli Yakar*, on the other hand, sees the verses in Deut. 12:20-22 as indicating that one should seriously limit, if not totally cease, one's intake of flesh. He interprets the words: "If the place where the Lord your God chooses to put His Name is distant from you" (Deut. 12:21) to mean that one has distanced himself from God and as a result is not ashamed to say, "I will eat meat" (Deut. 12:21). God will grudgingly permit it, "but as the deer and the gazelle are eaten, so may you eat them" (Deut. 12:22), i.e., meat may be eaten, but only intermittently, when one is unable to control his appetite, and this is the meaning of "because your soul desires to eat meat" (Deut. 12:20). The deer and gazelle are wild animals, available only infrequently, after undertaking a hunting trip. Domesticated animals as well should be eaten with the same degree of infrequency, so as not to get into the habit, which would only stimulate one's carnivorous tendencies.

Kli Yakar may have based his opinion on *Sefer ha-Ikkarim* (3:15), where R. Albo provides two reasons for abstaining from meat. The first is that it habituates one to bad traits, such as shedding the blood of innocent creatures (similar to what *Tiferet Yisrael* said concerning ritual slaughterers). Second, in a somewhat mystical sense, eating meat products leads to cold-heartedness or, in Biblical terminology, an uncircumcised heart (Jer. 9:25), which can characterize a Jew in spite of being physically circumcised (Malbim, *in situ*). When Jews take it upon themselves to return to God, the verse states that "the Lord your God will circumcise your heart" (Deut. 30:6), which Ramban explains to mean the suppression of tendencies to be greedy, lustful, and violent.

R. Albo supports his view from the wording "your soul *desires* to eat meat," which he interprets as "your soul *lusts* to eat meat," with its negative connotation. In fact, he places this issue in the same category as marriage to a captive of war (Deut. 21:11), concerning which the Talmud states: "The Torah takes into account the evil inclination; it is better for Israel to eat flesh of [animals] about to die, yet [ritually] slaughtered, than flesh of animals which have died [and were not slaughtered]" (BT *Kiddushin* 21b)—not an especially enthusiastic recommendation. R. Albo believes that Scripture emphasizes its great fear of such behavior causing a weakening of a Jew's appreciation of the sanctity of life by the three repetitions (Deut. 12:23, 24, 25) in the section of the prohibition to eat blood, which symbolizes life.

Although R. Albo opposes eating meat for the reasons enumerated, those reasons do not include negation of the opportunity for the animal to continue living. On the contrary, R. Albo believes that Cain's sin was that he equalized human and animal life. It will be recalled that Adam's diet was vegetarian. Cain brought a vegetable sacrifice to praise God for endowing him with dominion over vegetation. He did not bring an animal sacrifice, since he assumed that the prohibition to eat their meat implied that he was not inherently superior to them. However, if the two are equal, since animals spend their lives in search of food, totally unaware of spirituality, the implication would be that man too should lead a hedonistic life with no interest in values. Cain's deduction was quite contrary to God's purpose in creating man.

When Abel's sacrifice was accepted, since Cain equalized man and animal, he drew the conclusion that it must be permissible to kill humans as well, and that is how he came to murder Abel. Interestingly, R. Albo criticizes Abel as well, based on the phrase: "And Abel, he too brought of the first-born of his flocks and of their fattest" (Gen. 4:4). Why is the word "too" added here? R. Albo answers that Abel too made the same mistake as Cain by believing that man is not superior to animals, just that he felt that as God is superior to both man and animal, the latter could be sacrificed to Him, but certainly not slaughtered for the benefit of their equal—human beings. As punishment for his misunderstanding, Abel was killed. However, Abel did at least believe that man has limited dominion over animals to the extent that he can sacrifice them to the Lord, and he did bring his sacrifice of the choicest ("of the first-born of his flocks and of their fattest"). Cain's *Weltanschauung* was even farther from God's. He brought his sacrifice from the inferior "fruit of the soil" (Gen. 4:3) which, according to R. Albo, means vegetables as opposed to fruits. For those reasons, God accepted Abel's sacrifice and not Cain's. In summary, according to R. Albo, it is important that people be aware that humans are permitted to eat animals, but it is preferable that they not do so.

Abravanel

Abravanel, in a number of places, speaks out against consuming meat. In the paragraph which permits Noah and his descendants to eat meat, the following verse is found: "However, flesh with its soul, its blood, you shall not eat" (Gen. 9:4). According to the Talmud (BT *Sanhedrin* 57a), this is the source of the prohibition to eat a limb cut

Vegetarianism

from a living animal. Rashi explains that "flesh with its soul" means that the flesh should not be eaten as long as it is still associated with its soul, which indicates that the animal is alive. Abravanel (Gen. 9:1) comments: "Since by killing living creatures as food they will learn to be cruel, He prohibited eating the limb of a live animal, which is even crueler."

This citation is not an absolute proof that Abravenel opposed the eating of meat, because he might simply be saying that since killing animals can be done in a brutal manner, especially by non-Jews who are not bound by the laws of ritual slaughter, the existence of the prohibition of tearing off limbs from live animals will remind one of the importance of being merciful when obtaining meat for consumption.

In the portion dealing with the manna, where the Hebrews complained that they were undernourished and longed for the meat and bread which was their wont in Egypt (Exod. 16:3), Abravanel is more explicit. He notes the difference between God's immediate reply to their grievances and His later reaction in response to Moses' prayer.

In the first case, the verse states: "Behold! I will rain down for you bread from heaven" (Exod. 16:4). According to Abravanel, God was telling Moses that He had always intended to supply the nation with bread, "rain" implying a natural process, and so there was no reproof for this aspect of their complaint. Abravanel continues:

> Meat is not an essential form of nourishment, but rather a question of gluttony, eating to satiation, and intense craving, even though meat generates bad blood and cruelty in humans, and for that reason you will find that the carnivorous beasts and fowl are vicious and wicked, but sheep and cattle, chickens, doves, and turtle-doves, which are herbivorous—are not vicious and wicked, and thus the prophet specifies that at the time of redemption, "a lion, like cattle, will eat

straw" (Isa. 11:7, 65:25). For that reason, God did not tell Moses that He would provide Israel with meat, but only with bread, which is foodstuff that is suitable and necessary for a person's temperament (Abravanel, Exod. 16:4).

In the second case, the verse states: "I have heard the complaints of the Children of Israel. Speak to them, saying: 'In the afternoon you can eat meat, and in the morning you will be sated with bread'" (Exod. 16:12). Abravanel comments that only here does God rebuke them for complaining, and the reprimand is only with reference to the meat.

In summary, Abravanel certainly accepts the first reason of R. Albo for vegetarianism (*shechitah* habituates violence), and possibly the second as well (eating meat mystically flaws the personality).

Rav Kook

The views of R. Avraham Yitzchak Kook on the subject of vegetarianism were gathered in a pamphlet, *A Vision of Vegetarianism and Peace*,[83] which is a compilation of excerpts from two of his early essays, titled *Streams in the Desert* and *Dewdrops of Light*. R. Kook's disciple, R. David Cohen, collected the material and gave it its title.

Some of the points which R. Kook makes are:

1. Mankind instinctively considers it immoral to take the life of any creature, even if philosophers have attempted to justify doing so (ch. 1).
2. It is inconceivable that God would have created man such that he could not survive without eating meat, and thereby be forced to negate his moral sensibilities through the shedding of blood, albeit the blood of animals (ch. 1).

---

83. The pamphlet is available on the Internet, having been translated by Jonathan Rubenstein, and has been helpful in presenting this review.

3. Our Sages did not take the approach of the philosophers, but rather understood that it is a principle of the Jewish faith that one must have mercy on every creature, based on the following Talmudic extract:

> The suffering of Rebbi occured as a result of a certain incident and departed as a result of a certain incident... A calf was being taken to the slaughter, when it broke away, hid its head under Rebbi's clothing, and cried [in terror]. "Go," he said, "for this were you created." Thereupon they said [in heaven], "Since he has no pity, let us bring suffering upon him." [The suffering departed as follows:] One day Rebbi's maidservant was sweeping the house, and there were some young weasels lying there. She started sweeping them away. "Let them be," he said to her, "It is written: 'He has mercy on all of his creations'" (Ps. 145:9). They said [in heaven], "Since he is compassionate, let us be compassionate to him [and his suffering ceased]" (BT *Bava Metzia* 85a).

Here, R. Kook diverges from the view of R. Albo. The latter did not relate to the suffering of creatures or even the value of their lives. He discouraged slaughtering and eating them only because of the bad effect that doing so could have on mankind.

4. R. Kook refers to the Talmudic view that meat was prohibited to Adam (BT *Sanhedrin* 59b), which indicates that, in his opinion, "at one time all of humanity was encouraged to raise itself to this exalted moral state [of not shedding blood in order to obtain food]." Of course, in the end God permitted the descendants of Noah to eat meat; however, R. Kook (in ch. 1) says: "Is it possible to imagine that a very valuable moral virtue, which had already existed as a part of the human legacy, should be lost forever?"

5. In this world, only the *tzaddikim* (saints) are on a high enough ethical level to be punctilious with regard to vegetarianism, but

that will change in the next world. In the words of R. Kook:

> The same intellectual insight which, at the time of the spirit's degeneration, is the possession of only a small part of humanity from among its loftiest saints and Sages, will become the way of the many, when that which is written will be fulfilled: "And all your children will be taught of the Lord" (Isa. 54:13); "I will place my teaching into their innermost being and inscribe it upon their hearts" (Jer. 31:32). It is understood that we can in no way set a time for this [spiritual and moral] elevation, and it is put in the same broad category which includes other lofty qualities that are distinct from one another: that is to say, the category of the future to come, which includes among its aspects the coming of the Messiah and the revival of the dead.

6. The Torah is not satisfied with the present situation which condones carnivory, as is evident from the use of the word "lust" (Deut. 12:20) with regard to the eating of meat, implying that it is not initially desirable, and is only permitted *ex post facto*. The Torah yearns for the day that eating animal meat will be as repulsive to people as eating human meat (ch. 3).

7. Why did the Lord allow the prevalent moral corruption, according to which eating meat is acceptable? R. Kook says that sometimes it is necessary to forego perfect morality in order to allow important processes to take place in this world, and it is dangerous for mankind to attempt to accelerate them, lest he impede the required progression toward the ideal world. In the words of R. Kook:

> At times it is necessary to concede an important part of moral practices, in order that this laxity prepare humanity to achieve its own higher moral standard, and then this very concession becomes holy and exalted, and it is impossible for

these matters to be determined except through the mind of the God of [superior] knowledge… for if we had started out with that which should have been delayed, then we would have lost everything (ch. 4).

8. R. Kook suggests justifications for God permitting carnivory in the meantime. The first is that the world is so corrupt, with people being murdered and tortured, that it would be hypocritical and disingenuous to suddenly display mercy toward other creatures when men are suffering so much.

How ludicrous it would be if it [humanity]… would remove its hooves [mislead]… as if everything had already been set aright, the rule of evil and falsehood had been banished; hatred between peoples, national rivalries, racial animosity, and family strife, which cause so many mortalities and spill streams of blood—as if all these had already disappeared from the earth, and the only way left in which to elevate human piety was to attend to the establishment of a moral foundation in regard to animals (ch. 4).

9. R. Kook expands the view of R. Albo that if it were forbidden to eat meat, simple people would relate to humans and animals as if both had the same spiritual charge, and would not distinguish between deviant behavior toward animals (which at any rate exists) and human beings. As R. Kook says:

There is no doubt that if the prohibition of the killing of animals were publicized as a religious and moral pronouncement, this circumstance would result in many mishaps. When the animal-like craving to eat meat would become overpowering, it would make no distinction between the flesh of human beings and the flesh of animals, since in any case the life of an animal is proscribed as a prohibition and a violation of law, and the killing and sacrificing of human beings in order to eat their flesh would become a widespread phenomenon, to the point that the natural abhorrence which civilized humanity possesses at the present time would not exist (ch. 4).

10. In the fifth chapter, R. Kook expands the idea proposed in the fourth:

> Since human morality is still weak, humanity's animal-like self-love might overcome it to the point that all laws of justice and uprightness are destroyed, until the glory of morality becomes a mere game. It is clear that it is necessary for humanity to perceive itself as existing in a sphere far removed from the society of animals—a vast and profound distance, so people will not feel that they are simply one of them, for then the bestial habits, which drag humanity's spirit down to the muddy depths of the animals, whose world consists of nothing more than natural sensory instincts, with all their crude restrictions and limitations, would influence humanity.
>
> All of these concerns were taken into account by the exemption which the Torah grants [to humanity] from many moral obligations that pertain to animals, allowing humanity to obtain what it desires even to the extent of taking their lives, so that on this account humanity will come to the profound recognition of its superiority in relation to them [animals], so that its spirit will be elevated to the highest moral aspirations, which by their nature come with the elevation of the human spirit, by means of the sanctity of actions and superior character traits, until finally absolute moral truth will triumph, when knowledge of God will truly be present throughout the earth, until humanity will no

Vegetarianism

longer have any need for any moral concessions and it will be possible for the world to be judged by the letter of the law, as was originally intended.

11. If God were to formally prohibit the murder of any creature, it could possibly lower the overall level of morality. Even wicked people may have pangs of conscience when they behave immorally. Were there laws necessitating ethical behavior with respect to animals, the wicked would possibly observe them, and in doing so exempt themselves from exhibiting even a modicum of morality in dealing with their fellow human beings. Only if there is no such demand regarding animals is the wicked person forced to display some ethical values in his behavior toward humans, since otherwise he would not even minimally satisfy his conscience. As R. Kook says:

> And occasionally you find a thoroughly wicked person who is happy to act justly with respect to a certain moral issue in order to assuage by this action the pangs of conscience and the natural remorse which exist within him. And if kindly behavior toward animals were publicized as a fixed means of righteousness for humans, then we would find a great multitude of evil people who would be filled with relief by virtue of their kindness toward animals; for the causes which bring about abuses in the rule of human beings over each other to their detriment, and which for the most part come about because of hatred, jealousy, and the like, do not exist with respect to animals, who do not compete against them for food, honor, or other cravings of these evil people.
>
> Therefore, the Divine approbation sees that only it is capable of paving the way within the conscience and the heart [to achieve morality] by severing the cord which connects the human being to the animals, in order to focus the human moral core on its own unique goodness. Then, and only

then, will it [the moral core] succeed in bringing about its happiness in the end of days (ch. 6).

Between R. Albo and R. Kook

Both R. Albo and R. Kook believe animals to be on a lower spiritual level than humans. According to R. Albo, that fact, in principle, exempts one from dealing ethically toward animals; nevertheless, if one engages in animal slaughter, it will likely negatively affect his relationship to humans. Accordingly, it is best to desist from eating meat. R. Kook, on the other hand, feels that although they are on a lower spiritual level, animals have souls and are living creatures whose lives are valuable and forbidden to be destroyed by mankind. However, he fears that if morality were enforced with respect to all creatures, man would never reach the proper level of ethical interaction with his fellow humans. He feels that the Torah thus prefers to concentrate on engendering ethical behavior among human beings, and to save application and enforcement of the full range of ethical behavior for some future world.

Personal Behavior of R. Kook

R. Shlomo Aviner, a devoted student of R. Zvi Yehudah Kook (son of R. Avraham Yitzchak Kook), reports that he saw R. Zvi Yehudah eat meat on Sabbaths and holidays, as well as at festive religious meals (*se'udot mitzvah*) during the week, and he assumes that his father acted in the same way (*Serugim*, 11.5.2014).

When asked whether their sparse eating of meat indicated a tendency toward vegetarianism, R. Aviner answered that it indicated a tendency toward asceticism in general, rather than specifically vegetarianism. However, R. Kook in *Orot ha-Kodesh*, pt. 3, suggests that for most people, the middle path is to be preferred, as Rambam says: "The proper path is to find the midpoint temperament of each and every trait that man possesses" (*Hilchot De'ot* 1:4).

Vegetarianism

In Favor of Vegetarianism

Some people believe that R. Kook would have insisted on vegetarianism had today's conditions been prevalent during his lifetime. Specifically, they relate to the following reasons:

Ethical: The unimaginable cruelty practiced by the meat industry was non-existent at the time of R. Kook. Some of the immoral practices recorded by Asa Keisar (*Ve-Lifnei Iveir ha-Shalem*, Internet) are grinding male chicks to death, de-beaking chicks without anesthesia, genetic breeding (which raises birds as fast as possible, causing severe physiological deformations), holding calves in small crates so that they can't move (in order to have softer meat), and separating calves from their mothers on the day of birth and feeding them milk substitutes (so that the calf does not drink any of the milk which can be sold). These acts fall in the rubric of *tza'ar ba'alei chaim* (causing pain to creatures) which, according to most decisors, is Biblically prohibited (*Peirush ha-Mishnayot, Beitzah* 3:4).

Furthermore, in many cases, today's *shechitah* is halachically problematic if a bird or animal is slaughtered in front of another one, causing its lungs to shrink due to fear, making it non-kosher (*treifah*), according to *Ben Ish Chai* (*Tazria* 2:15) and *Aruch ha-Shulchan* (*Yoreh De'ah* 36:70), not to mention that this is also another instance of *tza'ar ba'alei chaim*.

Healthwise, at the time of R. Kook, meat was thought to be among the healthiest foods. Today it is well-known that red meat is a source of cholesterol and other unhealthy substances. Also, mass production of chickens and animals frequently leads to sick specimens, which are then consumed by humans. On the other hand, animal products are sources of iron, protein, and B12, so anyone who refrains from meat must find adequate substitutes for these necessary substances. Both Rambam (*Hilchot Rotze'ach* 11:4) and *Levush* (*Yoreh De'ah* 116) consider taking care of one's health to be a Torah-level requirement.

Environmental: Being considerate of others is included in the command to "love your neighbor as yourself" (Lev. 19:18). To produce meat, one must feed plants to animals, which causes the production of more greenhouse gases (such as methane and carbon-dioxide) than if the plants are eaten by people. These gases in turn cause global warming, which has negative impacts on the climate, agriculture, and human health. However, taking food-value into account, chicken, eggs, and milk are actually less destructive of the environment than tomatoes, broccoli, and potatoes.[84]

In summary, although uncontrolled meat production and consumption can be deleterious to moral values, health, and the environment, if monitored properly, these negative effects can be minimized so that a well-balanced diet can include moderate portions of certain meats.

---

84. Tamar Haspel, "Vegetarian or Omnivore: The Environmental Implications of Diet," *Washington Post* (March 10, 2014).

Appendix III:
The Sanctity of Marriage

In Jewish tradition, sexual relations are permitted in the context of marriage. Premarital, extra-marital, incestuous, and homosexual relationships, as well as caressing and other forms of endearment between non-married partners, are prohibited.[85]

Adulterous, incestuous, and homosexual relationships were already precluded in the Noahide laws (BT *Sanhedrin* 56a, 58a), and are punishable by the death penalty (BT *Sanhedrin* 57a). God even appeared to Abimelech in a dream to personally inform him that any potential sexual relationship which might develop between him and Abraham's wife, Sarah, would lead to his death (Gen. 20:3). As far as Jews are concerned, the Torah specifies in numerous locations that adultery is punishable by death, although the specific form of capital punishment varies with the details of the case.[86]

A Jewish woman who has a consensual adulterous relationship is prohibited to continue living with her husband, as well as with the adulterer (*Sotah* 5:1); however, if a married woman is raped, she may continue living with her husband unless he is a *kohen* (BT *Ketubot* 51b).

As far as sexual harassment is concerned, if it involves improper seclusion (*yichud*) or touching (*negiah*), those acts are known to be

---

85. See Abba Engelberg, *The Ethics of Leviticus* (2018), pp. 159-193.
86. Exod. 20:14; Lev. 18:29, 20:10, 21:9; Deut. 5:17, 22:21; Rambam, *Sefer ha-Mitzvot*, negative command 347.

forbidden.[87] Furthermore, any comments which make the victim uncomfortable are forbidden based on the Biblical commandment not to verbally pain one's colleague (Lev. 25:17; BT *Bava Metzia* 58b) and the requirement to love one's neighbor as oneself (Lev. 19:18).

SEXUAL RELATIONS BETWEEN UNMARRIED INDIVIDUALS
Rambam states:

> Before the Torah was given, if a man met a woman in the marketplace and he and she desired, he could give her payment, engage in relations with her on the highway, and then depart, and such a woman is referred to as a harlot. When the Torah was given, [relations with] a harlot became forbidden, as it states: "There may not be a harlot among the Children of Israel" (Deut. 23:18). Therefore, any person who has relations with a woman for the sake of lust, without formal marriage (*kiddushin*), receives lashes as prescribed by the Torah, because he had relations with a harlot (*Hilchot Ishut* 1:4).

Rambam incorporates this law in his *Sefer ha-Mitzvot* (negative command 355). Ra'avad, *in situ*, disagrees with Rambam and believes that the verse cited refers only to a promiscuous woman who has multiple, indiscriminate trysts; but engaging in a single, long-lasting relationship is what the Torah refers to as a concubinal relationship, and is permitted.

Rambam is consistent in his requirement of formal marriage, when he says that concubines were only permitted to kings. *Kesef Mishneh* (*Hilchot Ishut* 1:4) cites a responsum of Ramban in which he agrees with Ra'avad, and points out that many commoners had concubines—not only the patriarchs, who lived before the giving of the Torah, but also judges and prophets such as Caleb (1 Chron.

---
87. See Abba Engelberg, *The Ethics of Leviticus* (2018), pp. 160-168.

The Sanctity of Marriage

2:48) and Gideon (Judg. 8:31), who lived afterwards.[88] *Kesef Mishneh* points out, however, that those concubines may have started out as maidservants, who are permitted by Rambam, so that finding does not conflict with his viewpoint. In addition, *Kesef Mishneh* notes that even Ramban was not in favor of allowing concubines from a practical point of view, suggesting in his responsum that the fact that the Torah permits concubinal relationships be concealed, lest it lead to having relations with menstrual women.

Tur (*Even ha-Ezer* 26 and, in his footsteps, R. Yosef Karo in *Even ha-Ezer* 26:1) prohibits transient relationships based on the verse in Deuteronomy prohibiting harlotry, and proceeds to prohibit permanent relations which are not formalized by marriage. It is not clear if the latter prohibition is rabbinical, or if he associates it with the same verse as does Rambam. If it is rabbinical, Radbaz (cited in *Birkei Yosef, Even ha-Ezer* 26:1) holds that it follows from King David's decree prohibiting seclusion with unmarried women (BT *Avodah Zarah* 36b). However, Rema cites the opinion of Ra'avad, which he understands to permit concubinage even on a rabbinical level. Ritva (also cited in *Birkei Yosef*) agrees with Ra'avad, as does Ran (Responsa, ch. 68). On the other hand, R. Yonah comes out quite clearly in agreement with Rambam, writing that intercourse is only permitted in the framework of marriage, and concubines were available exclusively to kings (*Sha'arei Teshuvah* 3:94-95).

The previously quoted views were expressed by *Rishonim*, Sages who lived before the time of R. Yosef Karo's *Shulchan Aruch* (*Code of Law*). There is a well-known lenient view of a famous *Acharon*, a Sage who lived after R. Karo, namely R. Ya'akov Emden (1697-1776). He felt that concubines should be permitted for those who were unsuccessful in finding wives or could not have children (in order to fulfill the mitzvah of *peru u-revu*—procreation), as well as for successfully married men, including Torah scholars, to satisfy their sexual needs during periods when relations with their wives

---

88. Responsa of Rashba, 284 (ascribed to Ramban).

are forbidden, such as during their menstrual period or after giving birth (*She'eilat Yavetz* 2:15). Although some have claimed that this responsum provides a halachic basis for taking a concubine, they probably missed the following sentence near the end: "At any rate, I do not want anyone to rely on me regarding this unless he has the approval of the *gedolei ha-dor* (greatest Sages of the generation)." Since that has never happened, apparently R. Emden himself does not wish the Jewish world to utilize his permissive decision.

To summarize, sexual relations not sanctified by formal marriage have never been accepted. Rambam says they are forbidden by Torah law, others say they are rabbinically forbidden, and yet others say they are actually permitted. However, in the absence of a plurality of decisors permitting such behavior, the discussion remains in the realm of the theoretical. In certain very extreme and sometimes *ex post facto* circumstances, some decisors have adopted elements of R. Emden's approach, e.g., R. Eliyahu Abergil in *Dibrot Eliyahu* 8:93.

Appendix IV:
The Value Attached to Life

The following conundrum, called "the trolley dilemma," examined in an article by Laura D'Olimpio, pits one life against a multitude of lives:

> Imagine you are standing beside some tram tracks. In the distance, you spot a runaway trolley hurtling down the tracks towards five workers who cannot hear it coming. Even if they do spot it, they won't be able to move out of the way in time. As this disaster looms, you glance down and see a lever connected to the tracks. You realize that if you pull the lever, the tram will be diverted down a second set of tracks away from the five unsuspecting workers. However, down this side track is one lone worker, just as oblivious as his colleagues. So, would you pull the lever, leading to one death, but saving five?[89]

The same article presents the following variation:

> Imagine you are standing on a footbridge above the tram tracks. You can see the runaway trolley hurtling towards the five unsuspecting workers, but there's no lever to divert it.

---
89. Laura D'Olimpio, "The Trolley Dilemma: Would You Kill One Person to Save Five?" *The Conversation*, June 3, 2016.

However, there is a large man standing next to you on the footbridge. You're confident that his bulk would stop the tram in its tracks. So, would you push the man on to the tracks, sacrificing him in order to stop the tram and thereby saving five others?

If someone believes it is permissible to push the large man, would he also be willing to sacrifice a perfectly healthy person, as described in the following example from the same article:

Imagine you are a doctor and you have five patients who all need transplants in order to live. Two each require one lung, another two each require a kidney and the fifth needs a heart. In the next ward is another individual recovering from a broken leg, but other than his broken bones, he is perfectly healthy. So, would you kill the healthy patient and harvest his organs to save five others?

The article cited implies that more people would be willing to pull the lever in the first case than to physically push the large man in the second. And even fewer would be willing to transfer the organs of the healthy patient to the five dying patients. In trying to explain these different results, it is pointed out that in the first case, the bystander does not interact with the single worker directly, but rather concentrates on saving the five workers. If the single worker is killed, it is done indirectly as a byproduct of a positive action, as opposed to the second case, where the bystander directly engages the large man. In the medical example, not only would an innocent person be carved into pieces, but the victim is perfectly healthy, while in the second case, some would relate to the overweight person as being defective.

As far-fetched as these examples might seem, every country that has an army is in some sense making such a decision. Young healthy men and women, frequently against their will, are being placed in harm's way in order to protect the larger civilian population. Some might consider this to be more immoral than the trolley car examples, in which the victims work for the transit system, and by accepting employment are tacitly acknowledging that they may be placing themselves in danger on occasion and at the mercy of the higher-level decision-makers in the transit company's administration. Of course, the comparison is not absolute, since the soldiers will not necessarily be killed, nor are the lives of the civilian population necessarily threatened.

Sheba b. Bichri, Background Material

A few Talmudic sources, drawing upon Biblical narratives, deal with this type of question. In 2 Sam. 18, the ignominious fate of Absalom, who rebelled against his father David, is described. Upon his defeat, the tribes suggested that King David, who had escaped to Transjordan, be returned (2 Sam. 19:11). King David, apparently surprised that such a request did not come exclusively from the tribe of Judah, where the rebellion had started (in Hebron, 2 Sam. 15:9), invited that tribe to accompany him on his return to Jerusalem (2 Sam. 19:12-13), which it did after gathering in Gilgal (2 Sam. 19:15-16).

Upon crossing back over the Jordan, David was accosted by the lame Mephibosheth (son of Jonathan and grandson of Saul, 2 Sam. 19:25), whose servant Ziba had maligned him to David, resulting in the latter ceding all of Mephibosheth's estate to Ziba (2 Sam. 16:4). The servant had accused his master of wishing to re-establish the kingdom of Saul as a result of the weakening of David's kingship by Absalom, and Mephibosheth had come to inform David that on the contrary, he had loaded a number of donkeys with a generous amount of supplies for David in his place of refuge, but Ziba had abducted the donkeys, leaving Mephibosheth behind, and presented David with a contrived scenario. David did not know who was telling the truth and apparently did not wish to invest the time to find out, so he flippantly decided that Mephibosheth and Ziba should split the estate (2 Sam. 19:30). David's frivolous decision was looked askance upon in the Talmud (BT *Shabbat* 56b), which states:

> R. Yehudah said in the name of Rav: When David said to Mephibosheth, "You and Ziba divide the land," a Heavenly Echo came forth and said to him: "Rehoboam and Jeroboam will divide the kingdom." R. Yehudah said in the name of Rav: Had David not paid heed to slander [of Ziba], the kingdom of the House of David would not have been divided, Israel would not have engaged in idolatry [by worshipping the idols set up by Rehoboam, 1 Kings 12:28], and we would not have been exiled from our country [in punishment for idolatry, BT *Yoma* 9b].

When David arrived in Gilgal, near the western bank of the Jordan, there arose a confrontation between the tribe of Judah and the remaining tribes, who were not invited to accompany the king in his crossing back over the Jordan. When Judah answered that they were invited because they were kinfolk, David being a member of the tribe of Judah, the remaining tribes replied:

> "We have ten parts in the king [Rashi: we are ten tribes], and also in David we have more right than you [Rashi: although he is related to you, we are more drawn to him since we represent ten parts]. Why then did you slight us [Rashi: by preceding us (in the king's escort)]? Now was not our word the very first to return our king?" [Rashi: for our words to reinstate him came first, as it is written: "And the word of all of Israel came to the king" (2 Sam. 19:12).] And the words of the men of Judah were harsher than the words of the men of Israel (2 Sam. 19:44).

The Value Attached to Life

The Murder of Sheba b. Bichri

Logic seems to have been on the side of the ten tribes (Simeon was considered to be part of Judah), since they were the majority of the nation and had initiated the move to reinstate David, so they should certainly not have been sidelined. David himself, however, empowered and prioritized his own tribe of Judah by sending a letter to them alone, in which he termed them his own "bone and flesh" and asked for accompaniment upon his transversal of the Jordan (2 Sam. 19:12-13). Judah's harsh response was meant to cover up the weakness of their argument and the blatant favoritism displayed by David's behavior.

At this point, Sheba b. Bichri appeared on the scene, in revolt against King David, touting the slogan: "We have no portion of David, neither have we an inheritance in the son of Jesse; every man to his tents, O Israel" (2 Sam. 20:1). As is true in many social scenarios, the acts of the unstable reflect the turmoil of the society in which they find themselves. Sheba himself was from the tribe of Benjamin, whose royal family member (Mephibosheth) had been treated unfairly by David, and of course, Benjamin was one of the ten tribes who were at odds with the tribe of Judah. At any rate, such traitorous words were not to be taken lightly by the king, who readily dispatched his generals to deal with the situation (2 Sam. 20:4-16). Sheba was located in Abel of Beth-maacah, whose wall was about to be demolished and whose inhabitants were about to be massacred by the troops of Joab.

Thereupon, a wise woman from inside the walls asked why Joab wished to destroy their entire city. When Joab answered that he had nothing against the inhabitants and merely sought Sheba, the wise woman replied: "His head will be thrown to you from the wall" (2 Sam. 20:21). That is exactly what transpired, the siege was removed, and Joab and his army returned to Jerusalem.[90]

---

90. A more detailed account appears in Abba Engelberg, *The Ethics of Genesis* (2014), pp. 200-202.

The Ethics of Deuteronomy

Talmudic Discussion of the Murder of Sheba b. Bichri

The moral question that arises is whether it was ethical to sacrifice a single person in order to save the entire community. Although Sheba had rebelled against the king, and might have been convicted in court, here an instantaneous decision was called for. This problem is dealt with in the following source:

> A group of people were told by Gentiles: "Give us one of you and we will kill him, and if not, we will kill all of you." (A) [In such a situation,] rather they should all be killed than one Jewish soul be given to them. (B) However, if they specified [one particular person], as they specified Sheba b. Bichri, he may be given to them rather than they all be killed. (C) R. Yehudah said: "That is true if he [the Gentile] is inside and they are outside, but if he is inside and they are inside, since in any case one will be killed and the others will be killed, they should give up the one rather than allow all to be killed, and so it says: 'And the woman came to all the people in her wisdom, and they cut off the head of Sheba the son of Bichri and threw it to Joab' (2 Sam. 20:22)." R. Shimon says: "Whoever rebels against the kingship of the House of David is deserving of the death penalty" (Tosefta *Terumot* 7:23, Gen. *Rabbah* 94:9).

The question arises whether the words of R. Yehudah refer to (A) or (B). The commentary *Minchat Bikkurim*, on the Tosefta, says he refers to (A) and means to say that they should not submit in that case, because in that situation some members of the group may manage to escape even if they do not deliver one to the Gentile. However, if both the Gentile and the Jews are inside, then even if he does not specify, apparently the group may choose one by lottery and accept the Gentile's condition. R. Shimon argues and says the group may submit only if the Gentile names a specific person and that man is

The Value Attached to Life

indeed guilty. According to R. Yehudah, there are cases where the group itself chooses the victim, although this must be done in a fair manner. *Minchat Bikkurim* also accepts an emendation of the Vilna Gaon that the case where the Jew is not delivered is when the Gentile is outside and the group inside (and certainly the reverse situation).

Matnot Kehunah on *Gen. Rabbah*, however, believes R. Yehudah refers to (B), and holds that even when it is permitted to deliver the person specified, that is only when both the Gentile and the group are inside, but if the Gentile is inside and the group outside, where some of them might escape (including the specified person) even if they do not submit, they are not to accept the condition. According to this view, if the Gentile does not specify a particular individual, the group may never accept the Gentile's condition. If he does specify a particular person, they may accept the condition even if that person is innocent; however, R. Shimon says that the condition may be accepted only if the person is known to be guilty. The view of R. Yehudah is adopted by R. Yochanan, and that of R. Shimon by Reish Lakish, in the Jerusalem Talmud (*Terumot* 8:4), which also cites the following story:

> Ula bar Kushav was sentenced to death by the [Gentile] king. He fled and went to R. Yehoshua b. Levi in Lod. The army surrounded the city and said to them: "If you do not deliver him [Ula], we will destroy the entire city." R. Yehoshua went up to him [Ula], persuaded him [to surrender], and delivered him. Elijah the prophet, who used to reveal himself to him regularly, did not do so [for a while]. He fasted a number of times and he [Elijah] revealed himself [to him]. He [Elijah] said to him: "Do I reveal myself to informers?" He [R. Yehoshua b. Levi] said to him: "Did I not act according to the Mishnah [the Tosefta]?" He [Elijah] said to him: "Is this Mishnah directed at the most pious [*chasidim*]?"

Me'iri (BT *Sanhedrin* 72b) and *Taz* (*Yoreh De'ah* 157:7) both wonder what type of pietism allows innocent people to be slaughtered when the law does not actually require it; i.e., the criticism leveled against R. Yehoshua b. Levi seems unjustified. *Taz*[91] answers that in principle it was permitted to deliver Ula to the non-Jewish authorities; however, this should have been done by the populace rather than by a leading Sage.

R. Yissachar Temer (1896-1982), in *Alei Tamar* (*Terumot* 8:4), points out that if such deeds are done by great Rabbis, the masses will allow individuals to be taken even when no one specific is demanded. As an example, he relates to the drafting of young Jews in Russia for twenty-five years of service during the reign of Czar Nicholas. This was comparable to a death sentence, yet the wealthier Jews allowed the poorer element to suffer. R. Temer apparently felt that the entire community should have presented a united front, rather than allowing impoverished individuals to be drafted under those circumstances.

Me'iri suggests two more explanations for Elijah's criticism. One is that R. Yehoshua acted too hastily. Had he dragged out the negotiations, perhaps it would have become clear that the Gentiles were only threatening, with no real intention of destroying the entire city. The second is that the pietistic approach is to deliver the individual only if he is guilty (R. Shimon and Reish Lakish); in the present situation, Ula was indeed liable to the death penalty, but only according to civil law, and not Jewish law.

As far as the final law, Me'iri (BT *Sanhedrin* 72b) posits in accordance with R. Yehudah and R. Yochanan, while Rema (*Yoreh De'ah* 157:1) cites both views. Rambam (*Hilchot Yesodei ha-Torah* 5:5) posits quite clearly in accordance with R. Shimon and Reish Lakish, but then goes even further by stating that even when the Gentiles demand a man who is guilty by Jewish standards and who should therefore be delivered, "initially this instruction should not be conveyed to them [the populace]." *Taz* explains that Rambam is relying on the story of Ula bar Kushav, from which it emanates

---

91. This answer also appears in *Gen. Rabbah* 94:9.

The Value Attached to Life

that the *beit din* should not issue such an edict, but rather allow the congregation to act on its own behalf.

Appendix V: The Later Years of the Second Temple[92]

In 333 BCE, Alexander the Great (of Macedonia) conquered the Near East and defeated Persia. Upon his death, the generals Ptolemy and Seleucus fought, after which the former remained in control of Egypt, while the latter became ruler of Syria. Palestine, right in between the two kingdoms, was eventually taken over by Ptolemy. In Palestine, the prominent family of Tobias the Ammonite (from a Jewish faction in Ammon) favored Hellenism, while the populace remained faithful to classical Jewish practice.

In 198 BCE, Antiochus III pressured Egypt to give up Palestine. His successor, Seleucus IV, pursued the same policy. The Jews were divided in their loyalties: Joseph b. Tobias collected taxes for Egypt, and so preferred that Egypt control Palestine, but his brothers favored Syria. Seleucus IV was succeeded by his brother Antiochus IV (who called himself Epiphanes—meaning the visible god, but the people called him Epimanes—the madman), who planned to conquer Egypt. In order to stabilize his control of Palestine, he wished to increase its degree of Hellenization.

Pro-Syrian Jews bribed Antiochus IV to remove the high priest Onias III, who was faithful to traditional Jewish practice, and replace him with his Hellenized brother, Jason. When he too proved to be too conservative, they bribed Antiochus once again to replace Jason with

---

92. Unless noted otherwise, the historical review in this section is taken from Solomon Grayzel, *A History of the Jews* (1968).

The Later Years of the Second Temple

Menelaus, who was not even a member of a priestly family. The latter sold Temple vessels in order to raise the bribe money which had been promised to the king.

In order to further the Hellenization of the Jewish population, in 168 BCE Antiochus prohibited the observance of the Sabbath and holidays, as well as the performance of circumcision. He placed a statue of Jupiter which resembled himself over the altar, pigs were offered as sacrifices, and the traditional Temple service was abandoned. The practice of Judaism became illegal. The Jews violently resisted, but Antiochus soon discovered that by attacking them on the Sabbath, he could easily liquidate them without even waging a battle.

Hasmonean Dynasty

Mattathias of Modi'in, a descendant of the Hasmonean dynasty (founded by his great-grandfather, Asmoneus[93]), had five sons: Simon, Eliezer, Judah, Johanan, and Jonathan. When the Syrian soldiers set up an altar in their town, Mattathias refused to obey the order to sacrifice a pig, but a Hellenizer volunteered to do so (following which, all those present would have to eat of it). Mattathias grabbed a soldier's sword, killed the Hellenizer and the Syrian soldiers, and called out to the citizens: "Whoever is on the Lord's side, let him join me" (from Exod. 32:26). Mattathias died soon afterwards, and was replaced by his son Judah.

In 165 BCE, after Hasmonean victories in a number of battles, the Temple was rededicated, but the war continued. In 150 BCE, Jonathan took over the leadership after Eliezer and Judah were killed in battle, becoming both the governor and the high priest. In establishing self-government, Jonathan displayed political as well as religious goals, as opposed to his brother Judah, for whom attaining religious freedom had sufficed. Jonathan initiated an alliance with Rome, under the assumption that both were enemies of the Syrian regime, but this eventually (about one hundred years later) led to serious problems.

---

93. See Wikipedia, Hasmonean dynasty.

The Ethics of Deuteronomy

When Jonathan was treacherously murdered by a Syrian general, the only remaining son of Mattathias was Simon. He gathered together the Great Assembly, who voted him in as both high priest and ruler, but as he was already quite old, he let his son Johanan Hyrcanus do the fighting. Simon was killed by his own son-in-law, Ptolemy, but Johanan Hyrcanus managed to overcome him.[94] Later, he forced the Idumeans to accept Judaism (as opposed to his grandfather Mattathias, who was in favor of religious freedom) and conquered the coastal cities, which became part of the Jewish entity.

During this period, the Pharisees and Sadducees emerged. The former were mainly interested in observing the religion, although not forcing it upon others, while the latter saw religion as an instrument for uniting the state and assimilating its conquered peoples. The Pharisees developed the Oral Law, which enabled Judaism to be extended to all facets of life; they were internally-oriented, devoting their efforts to self-perfection and observance of the law. The Sadducees upheld a strict interpretation of the written Torah, but rejected the Oral Law; they were open to adopting guidelines for administration and culture from other civilizations. Both sects were acceptable to Johanan Hyrcanus, but his children, who were Greek-trained, preferred the Sadducees, whose view of religion and general outlook were much like that of the Greeks.

Johanan Hyrcanus was succeeded by his eldest son, Judah (Hebrew name) Aristobulus (Greek name), who immediately sent three of his brothers to prison, where two of them starved to death. He continued the policy of conquering pagan cities. This typically non-Jewish behavior disgusted the Pharisees, who were not upset when he died of drink and disease after a reign of only one year. He was followed by Alexander Jannai, the only brother to survive his stay in prison. His outlook did not differ from that of his brother, and he continued the conquest of pagan territory.

---

94. Max Margolis; Alexander Marx, *A History of the Jewish People* (1927), p. 151.

The Later Years of the Second Temple

In 89 BCE, Alexander Jannai suffered a severe loss in battling the Arabs in the south. When the Pharisees took advantage of his temporary weakness by pelting him with *etrogim* (citrons, which played a role in the prayer service in the Temple on Sukkot), he ordered his soldiers to kill hundreds on the spot. A rebellion broke out, and when the Pharisees secured Syria's help, Alexander Jannai was forced to flee to the mountains. At this point, many of the Pharisees realized that they did not really wish to lose their independence, so they flocked back to Alexander Jannai and helped him to expel the Syrians. Displaying a disgraceful lack of gratitude, he made a victory banquet for the Sadducee leaders, where he crucified 800 Pharisees, making eventual compromise between the sects impossible for all practical purposes.

In 76 BCE, on his deathbed, Alexander Jannai appointed his wife, Salome Alexandra (originally the wife of his older brother Aristobulus), to be his successor. She reigned until 67 BCE. There is a tradition that in his testament, Alexander Jannai had told his wife to favor the Pharisees, which she did by appointing them to the Sanhedrin, and they instituted religious schooling for all children.

Antipater

Alexander Jannai and Salome Alexandra had two sons: Hyrcanus, the elder, was the high priest in the lifetime of his mother and was favored by the Pharisees to succeed her; Aristobulus was the head of the army in his mother's lifetime and was favored by the Sadducees, who sought military victories (as opposed to the Pharisees). Initially, the elder brother reigned as Hyrcanus II, but soon Aristobulus's military prowess enabled him to take over as King Aristobulus II, whereupon Hyrcanus claimed that he had never wanted the kingship in the first place, and he vowed peace with his brother. To cement the relationship, Aristobulus's eldest son, Alexander, married Hyrcanus's only daughter, Alexandra. The harmonious idyll came to an end when Antipater, an Idumean Jew by religion if not necessarily parentage, convinced Hyrcanus to rebel against Aristobulus with the help of the Nabatean Arabs.

At this time, Pompey was capturing territories in the east, while Caesar was doing so in the west. Both wished to become the Roman emperor. Pompey received three delegations: one from Aristobulus, who gave him a gold vine, which he sent off to the Temple of Jupiter in Rome; one from Antipater representing Hyrcanus, who offered him control of Judea; and a third composed of Pharisees organized by the Sanhedrin, who asked Pompey to depose both Hyrcanus and Aristobulus, and to let the high priest rule under the guidance of the Sanhedrin. Pompey received the delegations and his troops then invaded Judea and killed twelve thousand Jews in the Temple area, after which he entered the Holy of Holies. In 61 BCE, Antipater was able to engineer that Hyrcanus would become the (puppet) ruler under his and Rome's control, thus ending Jewish self-government after eighty years of independence. To publicize his great victory, Pompey took Aristobulus and his two sons, Alexander and Antigonus, back with him to Rome to participate in a victory march.

Antipater ruled under the auspices of Rome and appointed his sons as governors—Phasael over Jerusalem and Herod over Galilee. In the struggle between Caesar and Pompey, the former sent Aristobulus II back to Palestine to help against Pompey, but Antipater had him and his son Alexander poisoned in Greece. When Caesar defeated Pompey, Antipater together with Hyrcanus knew how to change sides and give their allegiance to Caesar, who even rewarded them by returning Jaffa to them.

Cassius and Brutus became controllers of the east, where they imposed heavy taxes, which were collected by Antipater and his family. Antipater was soon murdered, possibly in revenge for his killing of Aristobulus or his ruthless methods of tax collection. When Mark Antony and Octavius beat Cassius and Brutus, a delegation of Jews went to Rome to ask to be rid of the Idumeans (who had sided with Cassius), but Herod also went to Rome and managed to

The Later Years of the Second Temple

convince Antony to appoint him governor (possibly because both the Romans and the family of Antipater were equally despised). Antony then had the Jewish delegation executed.

Antigonus, the remaining son of Aristobulus, found refuge with the Parthians, east of the Euphrates. Antony's eastern empire had become weakened by the neglect resulting from his affair with Cleopatra, enabling Antigonus and the Parthians to successfully invade Judea in 40 BCE. Phasael and Hyrcanus were lured into the Parthian camp, where the former committed suicide. Antigonus cut off one of the earlobes of Hyrcanus to disqualify him from remaining as the high priest; he then assumed the kingship and high priesthood under the name Mattathias, and Hyrcanus was exiled to Parthia.

HEROD

Antigonus proved to be a weak king. Herod, who had not been entrapped by Antigonus, took Alexandra, the daughter of Hyrcanus, with her daughter, the beautiful Mariamne (or Miriam, to whom he was engaged), and Mariamne's younger brother Aristobulus to a fortress in southern Palestine. He then left to join Antony in Egypt, but upon his arrival he discovered that Antony had left Cleopatra for Rome to make peace with Octavius. In Rome, Herod suggested that Aristobulus (grandson of Hyrcanus II and his prospective brother-in-law) be king under the tutelage of Herod, but Antony preferred to appoint Herod. With the help of the Romans, Herod retook Jerusalem and killed Antigonus, thus spelling the end of the Hasmonean dynasty.

Herod married Mariamne, who was the granddaughter of both Hyrcanus and Aristobulus. Her Hasmonean lineage could contribute legitimacy to his rule and, in addition, he apparently was deeply in love with her. She bore him three sons and two daughters. To strengthen his kingship, he soon killed forty prominent Sadducees, thus ridding himself of potential enemies and giving him a lot of money, which he used to pay mercenaries (since he did not trust

The Ethics of Deuteronomy

Jews). His fear of being replaced by the Hasmoneans led him to kill Mariamne's younger brother Aristobulus (who was found drowned). After inviting back the older Hyrcanus from Parthia, he accused him of plotting against him and had him killed. He even killed his beloved wife Mariamne, based on false accusations advanced by Herod's sister Salome (who claimed she had committed adultery and was plotting to poison her husband), driving him into a state of depression. He also killed two of his sons with Mariamne (in 7 BCE) on suspicion of plotting against him, as well as Mariamne's mother, Alexandra.[95]

Herod removed all political power from the Sanhedrin. He supported Antony, but when the latter was killed by Augustus, he went to Rome and made peace with Augustus, who allowed him to retain his kingship of Judea, Samaria, and the Galilee, and even add lands across the Jordan and some pagan coastal cities. He built Sebastes (meaning royal city) and Caesarea, which he named in honor of Augustus, and contributed to temples and amphitheaters in Greek cities. He encouraged Hellenization by building a theater and hippodrome in Jerusalem. To appease the Jews, he proposed the enlargement of the Temple, but the Jews were so suspicious of him that they would not let him tear down the existing Temple or suspend the sacrificial services, so he was forced to build around and over it while it remained standing. Since he favored the pagans economically, and identified with them culturally, he was hated by the Jews.

Archelaus (a name meaning "leading the people") was the son of Herod and Malthace the Samaritan, and was the brother of Herod Antipas and half-brother of Herod Philip. He came to power either after the death of his father (in 4 BCE) or while his father was still alive, but could no longer effectively rule due to his deteriorating health.[96]

According to Herod's will, which was more or less approved by

---

95. Max Margolis; Alexander Marx, *A History of the Jewish People* (1927), p. 171.
96. Ibid., p. 177; Archelaus in Wikipedia.

The Later Years of the Second Temple

Rome, Archelaus was to be king, Antipas was to be prince of Galilee, and Philip prince of the northeastern districts. Augustus had initially realized that Archelaus was problematic, so it was no surprise that he was exiled to Gaul after ten years and replaced by Roman officials called procurators. One of them, Pontius Pilate (26-36 CE), killed many Jews who were protesting against taking Temple money to finance an aqueduct which he constructed. Antipas, the ablest of the successors, built Tiberias and married the wife of his living younger half-brother, in contradiction to both morality and the Jewish religion. When he was rebuked by John the Baptist, Antipas had the latter killed. He was deposed by Rome in 37 CE. Only Philip had a peaceful reign.[97]

In 38 CE, the insane emperor Caligula appointed his fellow gambler Agrippa, a grandson of Herod and Mariamne, to be the king of the Upper Galilee. When Agrippa passed through Alexandria, the Jews celebrated (since this indicated the return of some degree of Jewish sovereignty, his father being Jewish), while the pagans under Apion mocked the Jewish king. To protect themselves from the wrath of Caligula, the pagans attacked the rich Jews of Alexandria for not erecting statues of Caligula in their synagogues, and managed to get some of the Jewish privileges cancelled, until they were reaffirmed by the emperor Claudius, the replacement for Caligula after the latter was assassinated.

Agrippa had been a rake, profligate, and spendthrift in Rome, but surprisingly turned into a responsible, religiously observant king, who mingled with the common people and was cherished by the Jews. Claudius enlarged his governorship to include Judea and Samaria, so that he controlled all of the territory once ruled by Herod. Unfortunately, he died suddenly in 44 CE, after ruling only six years. Although loved by the Jews, the pagans disliked his pro-Jewish policy, so Rome returned the procurators to Jerusalem, giving his son Agrippa II only a little kingdom north of Palestine, in addition to

---

97. Ibid., pp. 178, 181.

oversight of the Temple and appointment of high priests.[98]

In 66 CE, the rapacious procurator Florus robbed the Temple. The Jewish populace was so enraged that they belittled him by passing around a basket as if to gather donations for him. He retaliated by killing thousands of Jews and demanding an apology. The high priest convinced the people to acquiesce by extending a greeting to a new contingent of Roman soldiers upon their arrival. Florus had ordered the soldiers not to respond, which the Jews took as an insult and started grumbling, whereupon the soldiers charged the crowd, killing many more. Florus then tried to gain control over the Temple in order to plunder it, but the Jews arrived first, and Florus departed from the city.

Agrippa II hurried in from his kingdom and told the people to submit to Florus rather than protest to Rome about the behavior of Florus. This advice was vigorously opposed by the people, who proceeded to drive him out of the city while he, on his part, continued to side with Rome. Eleazar, the son of a former high priest, openly rebelled against Rome by refusing to bring sacrifices for Gentiles (including the emperor). At this stage, the aristocrats and the peace party asked Agrippa II to send forces, which he did, and, together with the Roman army, they fought the radical *Sicarii* (wielders of the small dagger), who were joined by the masses. The revolutionaries managed to burn the debt records and Agrippa II's palace, and surrounded the enemy in a fortress. Agrippa's soldiers were set free, but the Roman soldiers were killed after they laid down their weapons, in spite of having been promised that they would be freed.

The friction in Jerusalem encouraged Gentiles to attack the Jews in Caesarea and Alexandria as well. The Jews repulsed Gallus, the Roman governor of Syria, when he attacked Jerusalem. A government of Judea was formed from the more moderate element, including Hanan, a former high priest; the aristocrat Joseph b. Gurion; and the first-generation *Tanna*, Shimon b. Gamliel (fourth in Hillel's dynasty

---

98. Ibid., p. 191.

The Later Years of the Second Temple

after Hillel, Shimon, and Gamliel). The first two took over the defense of the capital.[99] The government's first mistake was to appoint Josephus (Joseph b. Mattathias, who claimed to be of Hasmonean lineage) commander of Galilee. Their logic was that he had been to Rome, was cool-headed, and had a Jewish education. The problem was that he did not want to use power in the struggle against Rome, since he thought that the Jews could never be victorious. Accordingly, he did not prepare the young men for war, nor did he build forts, gather resources, or inspire the wavering people. Instead, the Galilee was left exposed to the enemy.

To quell the Jewish rebellion, the Roman emperor Nero sent General Vespasian with three legions. In Antioch, his forces were reinforced with additional soldiers from Syria and from Agrippa II. Sepphoris and all of the nearby cities surrendered. In Yodfat, a hard battle ensued, while Josephus hid in a cave and surrendered a few days after it fell. From then on, he served Rome by providing them with vital information and weakening the morale of the Jews. The only remaining Galilean city was Tiberias, where the Jews fought hard, but were once more overpowered. When the survivors fled to Judea, the Galilee was in the hands of the Romans in its entirety.

The relative ease with which the Galilee fell discouraged the Jews of the Diaspora from sending help. Only the royal house of Adiabene, a kingdom whose entire populace had converted to Judaism, sent food and men.

In Jerusalem, zealots executed all of the members of the level-headed ruling body, since they had appointed Josephus the traitor, and the assumption was that they too must be traitors.[100] Although the majority of the population was moderate, the zealots mobilized the martial Idumeans, who were ardent patriots, by telling them that the moderates were willing to surrender Jerusalem to the Romans.

---

99. Max Margolis; Alexander Marx, *A History of the Jewish People* (1927), p. 195; Solomon Grayzel, *A History of the Jews* (1968), p. 159.
100. Solomon Grayzel, *A History of the Jews* (1968), pp. 164, 187.

The Ethics of Deuteronomy

Together, they were able to neutralize the moderates.

The only defenders left at this stage were members of three rival groups who battled each other, thus depleting their provisions and diminishing their manpower. Vespasian and his son Titus waited patiently while the Jews weakened each other.

When Nero committed suicide, Vespasian became a candidate for imperial power, which necessitated his return to Rome. Since he had no real opposition in Rome, he was able to leave his army in Palestine, with Titus in charge, thus enabling the Romans to continue the battle and achieve a complete victory.

Titus began his siege of Jerusalem in early spring of 70 CE. He sent Josephus to convince the Jews to surrender, but he was greeted with a hail of stones and curses. The Romans would not let the civilians escape, in order to increase the hunger within the city, while the zealots on their part prevented anyone from escaping, since they did not want the Romans to know how little food they had.

On the seventeenth of the Jewish month of Tammuz, the daily Temple sacrifices ceased and the third and innermost city wall was breached (*Ta'anit* 4:6). On the ninth of the next month, Av, the gates of the Temple area were set on fire and the Temple was burned. As soon as the Temple was in flames, Titus rushed into the Holy of Holies, apparently to see if it was true that the Jews did not worship any images.

Below appear lists of the Hasmonean and Herodian dynasties, with the numbers in parentheses indicating years of reign.

The Hasmonean Dynasty

- Simon (142-135 BCE), Eliezer, Judah, Johanan, Jonathan (152-142 BCE)—sons of Mattathias.
- Johanan Hyrcanus I (134-104 BCE)—son of Simon.
- Aristobulus I (104-103 BCE), Alexander Jannai (103-76 BCE)—sons of Johanan Hyrcanus.
- Salome Alexandra (76-67 BCE)—wife of Aristobulus I, then

The Later Years of the Second Temple

of his brother, Alexander Jannai.
- Hyrcanus II (67 BCE), Aristobulus II (66-63 BCE)—sons of Alexander Jannai and Salome Alexandra.
- Alexandra—daughter of Hyrcanus II.
- Alexander, Antigonus (40-37 BCE)—sons of Aristobulus II.
- Mariamne, Aristobulus III—children of Alexander and Alexandra.

The Herodian Dynasty
- Phasael I, Herod (37-4 BCE), Salome—children of Antipater the Idumean.
- Archelaus (4 BCE-6 CE), Herod Antipas (4 BCE-39 CE, Galilee)—sons of Herod and Malthase.
- Philip—son of Herod and Cleopatra of Jerusalem.
- Aristobulus IV, Shlomzion (Salampsis)—children of Herod and Mariamne.
- Phasael II—son of Phasael I
- Berenice—daughter of Salome and Costabarus (from noble priestly Idumean family; see Josephus, *Antiquities* 7:9).
- Agrippa I (41-44)—son of Aristobulus IV and Berenice.
- Cypros—daughter of Shlomzion and Phasael II (cousin of Shlomzion).
- Agrippa II (50-100)—son of Agrippa I and Cypros; ruled under procurators.

Herod in the Talmud

The Talmudic portrayal of Herod supports the historical description in general, although it differs in some of the important details. It is in agreement as far as his Gentile (Idumean) origins, his brutality, and his wish to be involved with the Hasmonean family in order to legitimize his rule. According to the Talmud, he did not realize his ambition to actually marry into the family, in contrast to the historical account,

The Ethics of Deuteronomy

according to which he actually married Mariamne the Hasmonean and had four children (two boys and two girls). According to both versions, he was deeply in love with her. The Talmud states:

> Herod was the slave of the Hasmonean house, and had set his eyes on a certain maiden [of that house, Mariamne]. One day he heard a voice from heaven say: "Every slave that rebels now will succeed." So he rose and killed all the members of his master's household, but spared that maiden. When she saw that he wanted to marry her, she went up on to a roof and cried out: "Whoever comes and says, I am from the Hasmonean house, is a slave, since there remained of them only this maiden [me], and I am throwing myself down from this roof." He preserved her body in honey for seven years. Some say that he had intercourse with her, others that he did not. According to those who say that he had intercourse with her, his reason for preserving her was to gratify his desires. According to those who say that he did not have intercourse with her, his reason was so that people would say that he had married a king's daughter (BT *Bava Batra* 3b).

In addition to his great passion for her, Maharsha (*in situ*) explains that Herod desired to marry Mariamne based on Rebbi's view: "If a slave marries a free woman in the presence of his master, he automatically becomes a free man" (BT *Gittin* 39b-40a).

Maharsha explains that since Herod had wiped out the entire dynasty other than Mariamne, she became his sole master, so that the slave would be freed simultaneously with her marriage to him and he would become a free full-fledged Jew, who would thus be suitable for royalty, based on the verse:

> You should surely place a king over you, whom the Lord your God will choose; from among your brothers you should

The Later Years of the Second Temple

place a king over you; you may not put a foreigner over you, who is not your brother (Deut. 17:15).

However, this explanation is problematic. According to Rashi (BT *Gittin* 40a, s.v. *yotzei le-cherut*), a deed of emancipation is a prerequisite for a former slave to marry a Jew. The only reason that the marriage is valid in this case is that it is assumed that the master must have issued such a deed either to the slave himself, or to another person who accepted it on his behalf, perhaps even without the slave's knowledge. But if Herod married Mariamne by force, she would certainly not have given him a deed of emancipation. The simplest answer is that even if Herod was aware of the ruling in the Talmud (which had not yet been written), he may not have appreciated the reasoning behind it (as suggested by Rashi). He may have taken it in the literal sense to mean that the act of marriage itself frees the slave. Another possibility is that if either of them did understand the rationale, and had Mariamne chosen to live, then she would have wished to comply with this requirement.

The Talmud assumes that Herod did not succeed in extricating himself from his slave status. He had already eliminated all of the pretenders to the throne, but he still faced the opposition of the Rabbis, upon whom he now focused his wrath. Herod noted that the previously cited Biblical verse says: "From among your brothers you should place a king over you," which would imply that any Jew is permitted to be a king, even a Canaanite slave, since upon becoming a Jew's slave, he is immediately converted and obliged to observe the same laws as a Jewish woman. It was only the Rabbis (BT *Bava Kamma* 88a) who interpreted "from among your brothers" to mean "from the choicest of your brothers," thereby excluding slaves (Tosafot *Bava Batra* 3b). Manifesting his brutality once more, Herod then murdered all but one of the Rabbis.

The Talmud proceeds (BT *Bava Batra* 4a) to state that Herod eventually chose to express some degree of regret and repentance by embellishing the Second Temple. Concerning the final product, the Talmud states:

> He who has not seen the building of Herod has never seen a beautiful building. Of what did he build it? Rabbah said: Of green and white marble. Some say, of blue, green, and white marble. Alternate rows [of the stones] projected, so that the mortar would stick. He originally intended to cover it with gold, but the Rabbis advised him not to, since it was more beautiful as it was, looking like the waves of the sea.

Interestingly, archeologist Dr. Gabriel Barkay has recently reconstructed some of the Temple's marble tiles from disinterred ancient fragments.[101] The tiles are geometrically shaped and are of various colors, resembling their description in the Talmud.

---

101. Nir Hasson; Ruth Schuster, "Archaeologists Restore Second Temple Flooring from Waqf's Trash," *Ha-aretz*, Sept. 6, 2016.

Appendix VI:
The War of Gog and Magog

At the end of the book of Ezekiel (chs. 38-39), the prophet speaks of Messianic days, when Israel will be restored to the land of its fathers. The return of Israel to its homeland will not pass unchallenged. Formidable armies from the extreme north (Ezek. 39:2), under the leadership of Gog from the land of Magog, will attack the fledgling country, stimulated to do so by God Himself (Ezek. 38:4). Radak (Ezek. 38:8) explains that Gog had been shut off from the rest of the world by a wall built by Alexander the Great, but would now be released.[102] This would all occur after Israel had been populated by Jews who had resettled there after having been exiled to all corners of the earth (Ezek. 38:8). Gog's intention will be to capture and despoil the peaceful Israelite immigrants, living in unprotected villages (Ezek. 38:11-12). However, all this will be to no avail, because God will utterly destroy Gog and his armies by generating a great earthquake, spreading pestilence, and raining down upon them a shower of large hailstones, fire, and brimstone, thus causing his armies in their confusion to inadvertently turn their swords against each other (Ezek. 38:21-22). Ravenous birds and beasts will devour the flesh of the fallen soldiers (Ezek. 39:4), whose great number would take the Israelites seven months to bury (Ezek. 39:14). God would scourge not only the invaders on the battlefield, but also the countries from

---

102. Based on a story in the Qur'an (Sura 18). See S. Frisch, *Soncino Books of the Bible*, Ezekiel, p. 254.

which they emanated (Ezek. 39:6). The Children of Israel will issue forth from their abodes, having heretofore been totally uninvolved in the warfare, to gather the wooden parts of the enemy's multitude of weapons for fuel, a process that will take seven years (Ezek. 39:9).

As a result of the Divine intervention, God will be magnified and sanctified in the eyes of the nations, leading to their recognition of Him as the creator, controller, and supervisor of the entire universe (Ezek. 38:23; 39:7, 27-28). The awe of the nations will certainly also be inspired by Israel's benevolent behavior in burying the bodies of their erstwhile enemies, by their delivery on the part of God without the necessity to even participate in the fighting, and by their total trust in God, which will enable them to permit themselves to be weapons-free. The manifestation of God's omnipotence will prove to the nations that Israel's suffering in exile was not because of God's inability to save His people, but because they had sinned (Ezek. 39:23).

The defeat of their enemies and the security and abundance that the Children of Israel will experience after their ingathering and resettlement in the Land of Israel will attune them to the fact that their punishment was no more than retribution for their misconceived past behavior, which they will deeply regret (Ezek. 39:26-28). Finally, God will promise to never again conceal His face from them, meaning that His holy message will be transmitted through prophecy, a phenomenon that did not exist in the Second Temple (Malbim, Ezek. 39:29); and, as a result, the nation will be prevented from sinning (*Metzudat David*, Ezek. 39:29). Having served their term of punishment after breaking their covenant with the Lord, during which time God hid His face, as predicted by Moses (Deut. 31:16-18), they would now be ready to experience the bliss of Messianic times. The war of Gog and Magog initiates what the Talmud (BT *Megillah* 17b) terms *atchalta de-ge'ulah* (the beginning of redemption), and it serves as the gateway of the Messianic era. Today, many look upon the establishment of the State of Israel, especially having occurred after the tragedies of World War II, as the *atchalta de-ge'ulah*.

The War of Gog and Magog

The Talmud states that the prophetic reading (*haftarah*) for the Sabbath which falls during the intermediate days of Sukkot starts with the verse: "When Gog comes against the Land of Israel" (Ezek. 38:18, continuing until 39:16). Rashi (BT *Megillah* 31a, s.v. *be-yom*) states that the battle referred to is that which is described in Zech. 14, in which the prophet speaks of an apocalyptic vision of the salvation of Jerusalem and God's judgment against the heathen nations which attacked it. In both texts, surrounding nations will fight against Israel unprovoked (Ezek. 38:11, Zech. 14:2); threatening natural and supernatural phenomena will occur (Ezek. 38:22, Zech. 14:6); a powerful earthquake will take place (Ezek. 38:19-20, Zech. 14:4-5); many of the enemy will die by the hand of fellow soldiers because of the total confusion (Ezek. 38:21, Zech. 14:13); and many humans and other creatures will perish as the result of pestilence (Ezek. 38:22, Zech. 14:12,15).[103]

One difference is in regard to the future status of the Gentile world. While in Ezekiel it states that as a result of God's treatment of Israel, the nations will realize that there is a Divine plan in human affairs (Ezek. 38:16, 23; 39:7, 24, 28), it does not explicitly mention how this will affect their behavior. In Zechariah, on the other hand, the prophet makes it quite clear that the survivors of the nations of the world will accept God as the Ruler of the universe, and praise Him together with the Jewish population by congregating at the Temple on the holiday of Sukkot (Zech. 14:16), while those who do not would be punished (Zech. 14:17-19).

The mention of Sukkot in Zechariah but not in Ezekiel leads to a question. It is understandable why the prophetic portion from the former is selected for the first day of Sukkot, but why is the latter narrative read on the Shabbat which falls during the intermediate days of Sukkot? Rashi, cited previously, attempts to answer this question

---

103. Although Ezekiel does not mention animals dying as a result of a plague, he does speak of birds and animals preying on the carcasses of those who died in the plague (Ezek. 39:4), so it may be assumed that the wildlife was affected as well.

when he says that both texts refer to the same battle. However, the battle *per se* seems to have no direct connection to Sukkot. Rashi might mean to say that since the pilgrimage of the nations on Sukkot resulted from the battle, as mentioned in Zechariah, the holiday is related to the narrative of Ezekiel as well, which after all relates to the same battle. Radak and Abravanel (Zech. 14:16) solidify this answer by stating that the fight against Magog will take place on Sukkot, and the reason for the surviving Gentiles' ascent to Jerusalem on that holiday will be to commemorate the miraculous victory and to express their gratitude for being spared and for being enlightened as to the belief in one Supreme Being. The verse states that in Jerusalem they will "prostrate themselves to the King, the Lord of Hosts" (ibid.), which Ibn Ezra interprets to mean that they will prostrate themselves to the king whom the Lord of Hosts will anoint, namely the Messiah, similar to that which was stated with regard to Solomon: "And all kings will prostrate themselves to him; may all nations serve him" (Ps. 72:11).

It is now clear why the non-Jews will celebrate Sukkot together with the Jews, but no intrinsic reason has been given for why the miracle took place specifically on that holiday and at no other time. An answer may be proposed based on a Talmudic text:

> R. Elazar stated: To what do the seventy bulls [that were offered during the seven days of Sukkot] correspond? To the [traditional number of] seventy [Gentile] nations [Rashi: to atone for them, in order for rain to fall throughout the world, because the world is judged regarding water on Tabernacles (*Rosh Hashanah* 1:2)].... R. Yochanan said: Woe to the idolaters, for they have lost but do not know what they have lost [by the destruction of the Temple]. When the Temple was in existence, the altar atoned for them, but now, who will atone for them (BT *Sukkah* 55b)?

The War of Gog and Magog

In other words, Sukkot is a holiday which is intrinsically dedicated to non-Jews, for whose welfare Jews pray on that festival. R. S.R. Hirsch (*Chorev—Ra'ayonot al Chovot Yisrael ba-Golah*) notes that Sukkot embodies an important lesson, both for Jews who keep the laws of the Torah and for Gentiles who are expected to obey the seven Noahide laws, namely to minimize the importance of material wealth by leaving one's comfortable dwelling place and living in temporary, less esthetic surroundings, where one can more readily concentrate on eternal values such as belief in a Supreme Being, peaceful co-existence, and inclusiveness in "the big tent." That the *sukkah* inculcates ethical qualities is indicated by the Jew's daily request of God in his evening prayers to "spread over us the tabernacle of Your peace."

THE TWO PORTIONS COMPLEMENT EACH OTHER
The lesson of Sukkot may be extended, based on the initial command as formulated in the Torah: "You should dwell in booths for seven days. Every resident of Israel should dwell in booths, in order that your [future] generations know that I had the Children of Israel dwell in booths when I took them out of the land of Egypt" (Lev. 23:42-43). The following difference of opinion appears in the Talmud:

> For I made the Children of Israel to dwell in booths: These [booths] were clouds of glory, [these are] the words of R. Eliezer. R. Akiva says: They made for themselves real booths (BT *Sukkot* 11b).

Clouds of glory may be considered to symbolize the Divine Presence and to represent what is expected of a Jew, namely belief in God and observance of His *mitzvot*, i.e., a person's output in his relationship with the Lord. On the other hand, the booths which God provided may be considered to represent what is expected of God, i.e., God's output with respect to human beings. These two categories may be seen in R. Yosef Albo's previously mentioned three basic principles of

The Ethics of Deuteronomy

Judaism (which may be used to characterize all of the monotheistic religions), which are:

1. The existence of God,
2. God's concern with the fate of each individual human being (also called *hashgachah pratit* or *sachar ve-onesh*),
3. The requirement to live by God's law.[104]

The first and third principles fit into the first category by describing what is expected of man, while the second describes what man can expect of God. These principles summarize a Jew's worldview, but also that of a Gentile who observes the Noahide laws.

Examining the two portions dealing with the war of Gog and Magog, although both categories are hinted at in each portion, each seems to emphasize a specific category. Ezekiel's prophecy contains the verse: "And I will magnify Myself and sanctify Myself, and I will make Myself known to many nations, and they will know that I am the Lord" (Ezek. 38:23), a clear prerequisite to the acceptance of the first category principles. The recognition of God's omnipotence and His redemption of Israel will catalyze universal acceptance of His sovereignty and His law. On the other hand, as part of Zechariah's prophecy, he states: "And on that day spring water will come forth from Jerusalem, half of it to the eastern sea and half of it to the western sea, in summer and in winter will that occur" (Zech. 14:8). In other words, Jerusalem will be the source of many streams which will irrigate the entire region. Here, God's concern for humanity is manifested, a declaration belonging to the second category.

In review, the holiday of Sukkot symbolizes basic principles applicable to Gentiles as well as Jews, and hence is an appropriate time for God's pre-Messianic intervention in the natural order.

---

104. A more detailed account appears in Abba Engelberg, *The Ethics of Genesis* (2014), pp. 223-234.

Appendix VII: Mashiach b. Yosef

The earliest mention of Mashiach b. Yosef is in *Targum Yonatan* (Exod. 40:11), who speaks of Moses' disciple Joshua, of the tribe of Ephraim, and "his descendant Mashiach b. Ephraim, through whom Israel will defeat Gog and his allies in the future, at the end of days." In *Shir ha-Shirim* (Song 7:4), the Targum compares Mashiach b. David and Mashiach b. Yosef to Moses and Aaron, respectively. The next reference is in tractate *Sukkah*, in a discussion concerning a description by the prophet Zechariah of a great day of mourning in Jerusalem (Zech. 12:10-12), which the Talmud (BT *Sukkah* 52a) describes as being for the demise of Mashiach b. Yosef, who would be slain in the battle of Gog and Magog according to Rashi (s.v. *ve-safda*, which he assumes is the battle of Judah against all of the nations that is portrayed in Zech. 12), implying that he will be the precursor of Mashiach b. David, the herald of the Messianic age. Yisrael Knohl (*Be-Ikvot ha-Mashiach*, pp. 68-69) has written that Mashiach b. Yosef was actually mentioned much earlier, in the *Book of Zerubabel* (who governed during the early years of the Second Temple), although the authenticity of the presently available version (from the seventh century) is questionable. By the time of the appearance of most Midrashic works (late Talmudic and post-Talmudic), the role of Mashiach b. Yosef was well established, and there are numerous references to it.[105]

---

105. *Num. Rabbah* 14:1, *Tanchuma Bereishit* A, *Eliyahu Rabbah* 18, *Mishnat Rabbi Eliezer* 12, *Lekach Tov – Balak, Bereishit Rabati Vayigash* 46:28, *Bereishit Rabati Vayechi* 48:19, *Sechel Tov Bereishit, Vayishlach* 33:17.

The Ethics of Deuteronomy

Drawing on various Biblical verses, Saadiah Gaon (882-942), in his *magnum opus* (*Emunot ve-De'ot* 8:5), used the Midrashic tradition to compose the following narrative:

1. If the Jews do not prove themselves worthy of Messianic salvation by repenting, God will force them to do so by exposing them to a tyrannical Edomite king, whose decrees are as harsh as those of Haman, causing them to repent and allowing them to be redeemed (view of R. Yehoshua, BT *Sanhedrin* 97b). Saadiah Gaon found a scriptural basis for the prediction that this king will conquer Jerusalem in the verse: "And saviors will ascend Mt. Zion to judge the great city [literally, the mountain] of Esau [assumedly Jerusalem, conquered by Edom]" (Obad. 1:21).

2. In consequence of these persecutions, a scion of the tribe of Joseph will arise and attempt to wrest Jerusalem from the hands of the Edomites, that is, from the Christians. That this precursor of the Messiah would emanate from the north is implicit in a Talmudic segment which lists the various stations of the Sanhedrin during the Roman period after leaving Yavneh, all of which were in the north, with the last being in Tiberias. Thereupon, R. Yochanan said (BT *Rosh Hashanah* 31b): "And from there [Tiberias] they are destined to be redeemed, as it says: 'Shake yourself from the dust [Maharsha: of Tiberias], arise [from the ground] and be seated'" (Isa. 52:2). More specifically, R. Saadiah found a verse which, according to the Midrash, implies that their leader would be from either the tribe of Ephraim or Manasseh: "Therefore, hearken to the counsel of the Lord, which He advised concerning Edom… indeed the young of the flock will drive them out and He will make their dwellings desolate" (Jer. 49:20). According to the Midrash (*Gen. Rabbah* 73:7), "the young of the flock" refers to the youngest of the tribes, namely those stemming from Rachel, whose patriarchs are Joseph's two sons. Maharsha (BT *Sukkah* 52a) found a different verse indicating the same: "[And the house

of Jacob will be fire] and the house of Joseph a flame, and the house of Esau stubble, [and they will ignite them and consume them, and the house of Esau will have no survivors]" (Obad. 1:18). Thus, Mashiach b. Yosef will create a fighting force from the survivors of the Edomite persecutions, who will then march toward and conquer Jerusalem (at least temporarily).

3. The army to be gathered by the Ephraimite Messiah will consist of only 30,000 soldiers. R. Saadiah bases the small size on the Biblical prediction: "Return, backsliding children, says the Lord, for I possessed you and I will take you, one from a city and two from a family, and I will bring you to Zion" (Jer. 3:14), which he takes to mean that although only a small number will volunteer to fight, all would be redeemed (based on R. Yochanan's exegesis of the verse in BT *Sanhedrin* 111a). This miniature force will face an immense heathen army, to be led by their king, Armilus, who will conquer and plunder the Holy City, killing one million[106] of its inhabitants, including Mashiach b. Yosef (R. Saadiah cites the previously noted sources: Zech. 12:10-12, BT *Sukkah* 52a). This will lead to a general campaign against the Jews, creating friction with all of the surrounding nations, from which they will be expelled, forcing them to flee into the desert, where they will suffer hunger and hardship. This prediction, as well, R. Saadiah bases on a Biblical narrative:

Behold! A day of the Lord is coming, and [the enemy will feel so secure that] the spoils which he takes from you will be divided in your midst. And I will gather all the nations to Jerusalem to wage war; and the city will be captured, and the houses will be plundered, and the women will be ravished, and half the city will go forth into exile; but [in God's mercy]

---

106. The numbers 30,000 and one million are based on the depiction found in Jellinek's *Beit ha-Midrash* collection, as is the forty-five-day period to be mentioned later (see: Armilus, *Jewish Encyclopedia*).

the rest of the people will not be cut off from the city (Zech. 14:1-2).

The undue suffering, according to R. Saadiah, is prophesied by Daniel: "It will be a time of distress that has never occurred from the time nations existed" (Dan. 12:1), while the desert exile resulting from being hated by the various nations is based on the Biblical phrase: "And I will bring you to the wilderness [as a result of the enmity] of the peoples" (Ezek. 20:35). Finally, the starvation they will endure appears in the next verse in Ezekiel: "As I contended with your forefathers in the wilderness of the land of Egypt [by depriving them of food (Deut. 8:3)], so will I contend with you."

Interestingly, although in one place the Zohar (*Ki Teitzei* 189a) accepts the Talmudic opinion that Mashiach b. Yosef would be killed, in a number of other places (*Mishpatim* 119b, *Pinchas* 223a, *Tikkunei Zohar* 7:146b) the Zohar states that he will not die.

4. After an interval of forty-five days, during which Jews unworthy of the Messianic glory will die out (similar to what occurred at the time of the exodus, according to Rashi on Exod. 13:18, based on *Mechilta* 18), the remnant will display their true worth in sore trials in the desert. R. Saadiah derives this period of bitter suffering and purification from the continuation of Ezekiel: "And I will cause you to pass under the rod [of punishment], and I will bring you [back] into the tradition of the covenant" (Ezek. 20:37). The harsh tribulations will bring the less staunch believers to defect from the religion, as described in the next verse: "And I will separate from you those who rebel and those who transgress against Me." When they have been purified by sorrow and pain, Elijah and then the Messiah will appear, gather the dispersed of Israel, and proceed to Jerusalem. R. Saadiah bases this on the verse: "Behold, I will send you Elijah the prophet before

the coming of the great and awesome day of the Lord [arrival of Mashiach], so that he may turn the heart of the fathers back through the children, and the heart of the children back through their fathers" (Mal. 3:23-24).

5. Armilus, inflamed against the Jews, will march against the Messiah. But now God Himself, or the Messiah, according to R. Saadiah, will fight against the army of Armilus, who will be slain by the Messiah.

6. The name Armilus is first mentioned by *Targum Yonatan*, who translates the phrase (associated with Mashiach) "with the breath of his mouth he will put the wicked to death" (Isa. 11:4) as "with the breath of his mouth he will put the wicked Armilus to death." For R. Saadiah, Armilus is merely an alias for Gog. In *Midrash va-Yosha*, Armilus is taken to be Gog's successor and is represented as a monstrosity—bald-headed, with one large and one small eye, deaf in the right ear, and maimed in the right arm, while the left arm is two and one-half ells long. Others relate the name to Romulus, the founder of Rome (see: Armilus, *Jewish Encyclopedia*).

An Important Function of Mashiach b. Yosef

Maharsha (BT *Sukkah* 52b) points out that "there will not be a complete redemption until the arrival of Mashiach b. David." However, Malbim, on the narrative of the valley of dry bones, outlines a very important goal to be achieved by Mashiach b. Yosef, based on the following text:

> **16** And you, son of man, take for yourself one stick and write upon it: For Judah and for the Children of Israel his companions; and take one stick and write upon it: For Joseph, the stick of Ephraim and all the house of Israel, his companions. **17** And join them one to another into one stick, that they may become one in your hand. **18** And when the

children of your people speak to you, saying: "Will you not tell us what you mean by these?" **19** Say to them: "So says the Lord God: 'Behold I will take the stick of Joseph, which is in the hand of Ephraim and the tribes of Israel his companions, and I will place it together with the stick of Judah, and I will make them into one stick, and they will become one in My hand.'" **20** And the sticks upon which you will write will be in your hand before their eyes. **21** And say to them: "So says the Lord God: 'Behold I will take the Children of Israel from among the nations where they have gone, and I will gather them from every side, and I will bring them to their land. **22** And I will make them into one nation in the land upon the mountains of Israel, and one king will be to them all as a king; and they will no longer be two nations, nor will they be divided into two kingdoms any more. **23** And they will no longer defile themselves with their idols, with their detestable things, or with all their transgressions, and I will deliver them from all of the dwelling places where they sinned, and I will purify them, and they will be to Me as a people, and I will be to them as a God. **24** And My servant David will be king over them, and one shepherd will be for them all, and they will walk in My ordinances and observe My statutes and perform them. **25** And they will dwell in the land that I have given to My servant, to Jacob, where your forefathers lived; and they will dwell upon it, they and their children and their children's children, forever; and My servant David will be their prince forever. **26** And I will make a covenant of peace with them. It will be an everlasting covenant with them; and I will establish them and multiply them, and I will place My Sanctuary in their midst forever. **27** And My dwelling place will be among them, and I will be their God, and they will be My people. **28** And the nations will know that I am the Lord Who sanctifies Israel, when My Sanctuary is in their midst forever'" (Ezek. 37).

Mashiach b. Yosef

Malbim (Ezek. 37:19) provides the following explanation of the parable of the sticks:

> The rabbinic tradition is that initially, Mashiach b. Yosef will reign as king from the ten tribes, and he will fight in battles, and all of Israel will gather under his flag, until afterwards [Mashiach] b. David will arrive and he will rule over them. The first parable will relate to the uniting of Israel under the flag of Mashiach b. Yosef, and He commanded that he should take one stick and write "For Judah and for the Children of Israel his companions," since initially Judah and Benjamin who were exiled at the [time of the destruction of the] First Temple and were gathered under Zerubabel in the days of Cyrus and became one nation in the days of the Second Temple, and even after the destruction of the [Second] Temple when they were dispersed, still they were united and hoping for the [final] redemption. In the end of days the ten lost and remote tribes will gather under the flag of Joseph, who is [under the leadership of] Mashiach b. Yosef, who will gather the far-flung tribes, for that was the second parable of the stick to Joseph's branch through Ephraim and to the entire house of Israel, who will join him at the time of the end, and afterwards also the children of Judah, who were already gathered, will be united under his rule and government, and will become one nation by God's miracles and wonders.
>
> And that is what is written in the parable, that afterwards he will take a stick and write on it "For Joseph, the stick of Ephraim," which is the united ten tribes in the end of days, and afterwards he will bring them close to each other and the first coming near will be of the children of Judah to the children of Joseph under Mashiach b. Yosef, and that is what it states: "Behold I will take the stick of Joseph, which is in the hand of Ephraim and the tribes of Israel his companions,

and I will place it together [with the stick of Judah]" (v. 19). In other words, first He will place him over them, that is He will place the tribes of Israel on the branch of Joseph, i.e., they will gather under the flag of Mashiach b. Yosef, and also the branch of Judah He will place under him, so that Judah will also stand under his flag, and in this [is fulfilled the end of the verse]: "and I will make them into one stick, and they will become one in My hand," miraculously.

Malbim's point is that one of the most important tasks of Mashiach b. Yosef will be to reunite those tribes which composed the Kingdom of Israel with those of the Kingdom of Judah, so that in the end of days the twelve tribes of Israel will be united once more into one nation.

Why Are Two Messiahs Needed?

The above question was posed by R. Kook (*Ma'amarei ha-Ra'ayah*, p. 94). Maharal mi-Prague (*Netzach Yisrael*, ch. 37) explains that the Nation of Israel is like a person composed of twelve organs (corresponding to the twelve tribes), two of which control the others, namely the head and the heart. The head, where the soul is to be found, is the Godlier of the two and it represents the tribe of Judah, as in the Biblical phrase: "Judah will be at the head" (Judg. 1:2; the literal meaning is that Judah will lead in battle). Joseph, like the heart, is always in the middle, as with the gifts of the princes at the inauguration of the Tabernacle, where the tribe of Ephraim (Joseph's son) made its donation as the seventh of the twelve tribes (Num. 7:48). When the kingdom is righteous, it is the recipient of the glory of God and there is one united kingdom of the House of David. However, when they do not merit it, they are not entitled to God's complete grace, and then the kingdom is divided, with the majority of the organs gravitating toward the heart, representing positive emotions, but also subservience to materialistic drives, and only a minority to the head, which is deficient. At that stage, the Judean kingdom consists of Judah and Benjamin alone, which are the tribes most worthy of receiving God's glory, and the Temple is located in their portion. The remaining organs do not follow in their path, so they are not at a high enough level to contain God's glory.

Generally, only kings of the Davidic dynasty are anointed (BT *Horayot* 11b), since it is the head, which is represented by them, which is anointed. However, the ten tribes are also entitled to a Messiah, and since the tribe of Ephraim is considered to be royalty, as it is compared to the heart, they too will in the end have their own leader, Mashiach b. Yosef. However, foreign nations led by Gog will overpower them. Since the heart is inferior to the head and eventually the nation will overcome its evil inclination, which is associated with the heart, he will be killed and this attribute will be aborted, at which point the nation will be ready for the arrival of Mashiach b. David.

R. Kook (ibid.), elaborating on the suggestion of Maharal, speaks of the body (parallel to Maharal's heart) and the soul. The virtues of the former are represented by Mashiach b. Yosef, who will initiate the practical and logistical stages, such as national, military, and industrial frameworks, which will enable the absorption of the diaspora from the four corners of the earth. The qualities of the latter are represented by Mashiach b. David, the spiritual and ideological Messiah, who will elevate the nation to its spiritual pinnacle.

Joseph was the governor and economist (Gen. 42:6) whom the Lord sent as a savior to revive a starving country (Gen. 50:20), and he also supplied Jacob and his family with material goods and enabled them to secure a livelihood (Gen. 47:11-12). He was a man of the world, who knew seventy languages (BT *Sotah* 36b), yet he was imbued with a belief in God and was aware of the holiness associated with living a moral life (Gen. 39:12). It was because of this unique combination that it was decreed that Esau would fall as a result of the efforts of the progeny of Rachel (*Gen. Rabbah* 73:7), and for 369 years God dwelt in the Tabernacle in Shiloh, in the tribal land of Ephraim, which King David speaks of as "the tent that He had stationed among men" (Ps. 78:60). Judah, on the other hand, embodied the unique holiness of the Nation of Israel, capsulized in the phrase: "Judah became His holy nation" (Ps. 114:2). The original intention was that the two strengths represented by the Kingdoms of David and Ephraim would supplement each other—the material strength becoming refined and sanctified as a result of its contiguity to Israel's unique holiness, and the spiritual strength being reinforced and revitalized on a strong physical platform, thus enabling God's splendor and glory to shine upon Israel and consequently be promulgated among the nations, as predicted in a previously cited verse: "The root of Jesse will stand as a banner for peoples; nations will inquire of him, and his resting place will be magnificent" (Isa. 11:10). The ideal is that rather than seeing the material and spiritual as two opposing powers, there exists between them a symbiotic enhancing relationship which would represent the most supreme and sublime source of pride and joy.

Unfortunately, as a result of their sinful behavior, the ten tribes separated from Judah; instead of the material coalescing with the spiritual, they each developed independently, as if they had nothing in common with each other, leading to the loss of both kingdoms. Jeroboam, monarch of the kingdom of Ephraim, was initially appointed by Solomon as a tax marshal, due to his competency in practical matters, as it says: "And Solomon saw that this young man was a diligent worker, and he appointed him to be in charge of all of the [tax] burdens of the house of Joseph" (1 Kings 11:28). Regrettably, he shed his allegiance to the unique holiness which characterized the Jewish people, as seen from his chastisement by the prophet Ahijah: "You have gone and made for yourself foreign gods and molten images to anger Me, and you have cast Me behind your back" (1 Kings 14:9), leading to a situation in which "Ephraim mingles with the peoples [losing its identity]; Ephraim was as a cake which was not turned over [half burnt, half unbaked—neglected by his leaders]" (Hos. 7:8). As for Judah, to overcome the lack of material support from Ephraim, it

Mashiach b. Yosef

was in need of significant spiritual excellence in order to maintain its spirituality while satisfying its material needs. Unable to achieve that level, it degenerated spiritually, as Hosea and Isaiah predicted: "Judah too will stumble with them" (Hos. 5:5); "For Jerusalem has stumbled, and Judah has fallen, for their tongue and their deeds are against the Lord, to provoke the eyes of His glory" (Isa. 3:8).

Even as separate entities, had either kingdom been susceptible to the influence of the other, they might have been able to maintain their special attributes, but this was also not to be, as indicated in the Talmud:

> "After this thing, Jeroboam turned not from his evil way" (1 Kings 13:33). What is meant by "after this thing [the simple meaning is the miracle of the drying up and later regeneration of Jeroboam's hand (vv. 4-6)]?" R. Abba said: After the Holy One, blessed be He, had seized Jeroboam by his garment and urged him: "Repent, then I, you, and the son of Jesse [David] will walk in the Garden of Eden." "And who will be at the head?" inquired he. "The son of Jesse will be at the head." "If so [he replied], I do not desire it" (BT *Sanhedrin* 102a).

This story indicates that even if the material and spiritual characteristics were to be developed as separate entities, it would still be possible for Israel to perfect itself and become "a light unto the nations" (Isa. 42:6, 49:6, 60:3), as long as they allow themselves to be cross-pollinated, with Judah adopting from Ephraim the means of material and social perfection, and Ephraim accepting from Judah the Divine influence which stimulates Israel's holiness, its devotion to the laws of the Torah leading to sublime personal attributes, and its cultivation of prophecy for those having such capabilities. It was necessary, however, that Ephraim accept the spiritual guidance and superiority of Judah. By refusing God's offer, Jeroboam exposed the Jewish nation to the constant threat of decimation, being the smallest of the nations, and to continual suffering and exile.

R. Kook's view of the ideal relationship between Mashiach b. David and Mashiach b. Yosef is comparable to that between Issachar and Zebulun. The Midrash (*Gen. Rabbah* 99:9) explains that Zebulun was involved in commerce and Issachar devoted extra time to Torah study. Nevertheless, Zebulun appreciated the spiritual aspect of Judaism and was therefore willing to support Issachar's efforts. Issachar appreciated the help it received form Zebulun, but also engaged in agriculture, leaving only the marketing aspect to Zebulun. As the enabler, Zebulun was given precedence in both the blessings bestowed by Jacob (Gen. 49:13-14) and those given by Moses (Deut. 33:18).

R. Kook says that at times, the nation will excel in its material achievements, represented by Ephraim, and at others, in its spiritual attainments, and this period is termed "the birth-pangs of Messiah" (*chevlei Mashiach*), actually of two Messiahs. However, since it is the spiritual aspect which provides the guidance and determines the direction, it must be the more dominant of the two, and this will be symbolized by Mashiach b. Yosef's death.

R. Kook goes on to reveal that the two kings Ahab and Josiah possessed the attributes of Mashiach b. Yosef and Mashiach b. David, respectively. Concerning Ahab, the Mishnah (*Sanhedrin* 10:2) speaks of three kings who will have no portion in the world-to-come: Jeroboam, Ahab, and Manasseh. The Bible mentions the dire sins of King Jeroboam numerous times.[107] However, regarding Ahab, the Talmud has the following to say:

> R. Yochanan said: The lightest [sins] committed by Ahab were equal to the gravest [ones] committed by Jeroboam… [Regarding the verse:] "Their altars are like heaps in the furrows of the fields" (Hos. 12:12), R. Yochanan said: [This

---

107. Such as 1 Kings 16:3, 26, 31; 21:22; 22:53; 2 Kings 3:3; 10:29; 13:2, 11; 14:24; 15:9, 18, 24, 28; 17:21; 23:15; 2 Chron. 13:6.

teaches that] there is no furrow in the Land of Israel upon which Ahab did not set up an idol and bow to it. From where [do we know] that he will not enter the future world? For it says: "[I will bring disaster upon you and I will destroy you] and I will cut off from Ahab every male child and those that are restrained [slaves] and those that are free [princes] in Israel" (1 Kings 21:21). Restrained [implies] in this world; free, in the next (BT *Sanhedrin* 102b).

As horrific as were the sins of Ahab, and as extreme as the punishment allotted him was according to the Mishnah (no portion in the world to come), interestingly, the Gemara (BT *Sanhedrin* 104b) cites the following alternative viewpoint:

The interpreters of verses maintained: "All of them [Rashi, *in situ*: the kings mentioned in the Mishnah] will enter the world to come, as it is written: '[King David says] Gilead will be mine [Rashi: I must bear the burden of their sins so that they may be exonerated]' (Ps. 60:9).... this refers to Ahab, who fell at Ramoth-gilead" (1 Kings 22:35).

What is the basis for absolving Ahab from his multitudinous transgressions? R. Kook bases it on a number of positive attributes, namely his love for the Land of Israel, his respect for the Torah and its scholars, and his bravery in defending the nation unto his own death. The first two traits derive from the following excerpt:

Why did Omri [father of Ahab] merit sovereignty? Because he added a region to Palestine, as it is written: "And he bought the hill Samaria of Shemer for two talents of silver, and built on the hill, and called the name of the city which he built after the name of Shemer, owner of the hill, Samaria" (1 Kings 16:24). R. Yochanan said: Why did Ahab merit royalty for twenty-two years? Because he honored the Torah [by being willing to surrender his silver and gold, but not his Torah scrolls, to Ben-hadad].... R. Nachman said: Ahab was equally balanced [Rashi: half sins and half merits].... Ahab was generous with his money, and because he used to benefit scholars with his wealth, half [his sins] were forgiven (BT *Sanhedrin* 102b).

His bravery and unmitigated stubbornness in defending the nation is highlighted in BT *Mo'ed Katan* 28b, which speaks of Ahab as having done one good thing, based on the verse: "The battle became more intense that day and the king was standing in the chariot against the Arameans. He died at evening and the blood of his wounds ran out into the inside of the chariot" (1 Kings 22:35). Rashi explains: "He exerted himself to remain standing so that the Israelites would not become aware of his wound and flee, for flight is the beginning of defeat." The well-being of the nation of Israel was important to him, even when he personally had nothing to benefit from it, and this love of the Jewish nation is forever held to his credit.

According to R. Kook, Mashiach b. David—signifying pure spirituality—was represented by King Josiah, concerning whom the Bible states: "And before him there was no king like him, who returned to the Lord with all his heart and with all his soul and with all his possessions, [behaving] according to the entire Torah of Moses, and after him no one [like him] arose" (2 Kings 23:25). The only sin attributed to Josiah is based on the Midrashic interpretation of his death as described in Chronicles:

> **20** After all this, when Josiah had reinstated the Temple [service], Neco, the king of Egypt, went up to wage war in Carchemish on the Euphrates [Rashi: against the king of Assyria (2 Kings 23:29)], and Josiah went forth toward him [in battle; Rashi: Scripture complains (of the injustice) and

Mashiach b. Yosef

laments Josiah, for a miracle was not performed for him as it had been for Hezekiah (2 Chron. 32:21)]. **21** And he [Neco] sent messengers to him, saying, "What do I have to do with you, king of Judah? Not against you [do I go] today, but to my place of war, and God has commanded to hasten me. Desist from [meddling with] the god who is with me, and he will not destroy you." **22** But Josiah did not turn his face away from him, but he disguised himself [as did Ahab (2 Chron. 18:29), so as not to be recognized by the enemy] to wage war with him, and he did not hearken to the words of Neco from the mouth of God, and he came to wage war in the valley of Megiddo [on Neco's route to the Euphrates]. **23** And the archers shot at King Josiah, and the king said to his servants: "Take me away, for I am sorely stricken!" **24** And his servants took him away from the chariot, and they put him into his second chariot and brought him to Jerusalem, and he died and was buried in the graves of his forefathers, and all of Judah and Jerusalem mourned for Josiah (2 Chron. 35).

The Talmud (BT *Ta'anit* 22b) and Midrash (*Lam. Rabbah* 1:53) deal with the question of why Josiah insisted on attacking Neco:

On what did Josiah rely? [On the verse:] "And the sword will not pass through your land" (Lev. 26:6). What sword? Is it a sword of war? But it is already stated [at the beginning of the verse]: "And I will give peace in the land." Rather, it must even refer to the sword of [an army passing through], and he did not know that his generation was not worthy [of this blessing]. When he [Josiah] was dying, Jeremiah saw that his lips were trembling and he feared that perhaps, Heaven forbid, he was saying something improper as a result of his great pain; he bent down and overheard him justifying [God's] decree against himself saying: "The Lord is righteous, for I have rebelled against His word" (Lam. 1:18). He [Jeremiah] then said of him: "The breath of our nostrils, the anointed of the Lord" (Lam. 4:20).

Josiah is seen to be an outstandingly righteous person, who simply made a mistake in Biblical interpretation. However, if that were the case, why did he suffer such an ignominious death? The Talmud *in situ* suggests that it was "because he should have consulted Jeremiah and he did not." This explanation could be interpreted in two ways. One might say that in Judaism, any momentous decision by a political ruler should be made in consultation with religious leaders, taking into account what is today called *da'at Torah*. *Chizkuni* (Lev. 10:2), on the other hand, compares it to the sin of Nadab and Abihu, which was that they made decisions in the presence or in proximity of their teacher, which is considered to be a grievous transgression.[108] Here too, Jeremiah was Josiah's mentor, and it was forbidden for him to interpret Scripture on his own regarding a matter that might have halachic repercussions. Rashi, in his commentary on *Ta'anit* 22b as printed in *Ein Ya'akov*, says that when the Talmud states that Josiah did not know that his generation was unworthy, he was partially to blame for his ignorance, since he was certainly aware of Jeremiah's prophecies of doom, and he should have realized that the prophet would not have threatened such dire tribulations, were there no reason to do so.

R. Kook relates Josiah's mistake to his thesis regarding the characterization of the two Messiahs. Josiah was so spiritual that he could not imagine any kind of tolerance for idol worshippers. *Sans* the practicality of Mashiach b. Yosef (who would have stressed the future potential of Israel as a light unto all of the world's nations, as well as the uncalled-for risk involved in battling Neco), Josiah's isolated view of the message of Mashiach b. David caused him to commit a serious error.

---

108. For a more thorough discussion of this topic, see Abba Engelberg, *The Ethics of Leviticus* (2018), pp. 90, 320-323.

Appendix VIII:
Birth Pangs of the Messiah

According to tradition, the final redemption will be preceded by a period of great suffering, as clearly expressed in the Midrash (*Shocher Tov* 45:3): "Israel said before the Holy One, blessed be He: 'Master of the world, when will You redeem us?' He said to them: 'When you will descend to the lowest depths.'" The Midrash then cites two consecutive verses from Psalms:

> **26** For our soul is bent down to the dust, our belly clings to the earth. **27** Arise to assist us and redeem us as a manifestation of Your kindness (Ps. 44).

The first verse says the nation will be completely humiliated, and only afterwards does the second verse speak of redemption. In another location, the Midrash points out that the darkest time of night is when the moon and stars are no longer visible, and the sun has not yet risen (*Shocher Tov* 22:4). This period is called *chevlei Mashiach* (birth pangs of the Messiah), based on the verse:

> As a pregnant woman comes near to give birth, she shudders, she screams in her pangs, so were we because of You, O Lord [Rashi: because of Your decrees, which we see as signs of (upcoming) salvation and redemption (in the metaphor, the birth of the baby)] (Isa. 26:17).

The Ethics of Deuteronomy

The Talmud (BT *Sanhedrin* 98b) derives the existence of this period from a Biblical verse:

> Rav said: The son of David will not come until the wicked power rules over Israel [Rashi: throughout the world, wherever they are scattered] for nine months, as it is written [in reference to Messianic times]: "Therefore, He will deliver them [Rashi: into the hands of their enemies] until the time a woman in confinement gives birth [for nine months], and [then they will be redeemed and] the rest of his brothers [Rashi: the rest of the tribe of Judah] will return with the Children of Israel [Rashi: Judah and Benjamin will join the other tribes and become one kingdom, and they will no longer be divided into two kingdoms]" (Mic. 5:2).

Alternatively, the Talmud cites a series of verses from Jeremiah which describe a terrible period preceding the arrival of the Messiah:

> **6** Ask now and see whether a male gives birth. Why have I [God] seen every man with his hands on his loins like a woman in confinement, and every face has turned to pallor? **7** Ho! For that day is great, with none like it, and it is a time of distress for Jacob [i.e., birth pangs of Messiah], from which he will be saved. **8** And it will be on that day, says the Lord of Hosts, [that] I will break his yoke off your neck, and I will break your straps, and strangers will no longer enslave them (Jer. 30).

V. 7 clearly speaks of a period of suffering. Rashi (BT *Sanhedrin* 98b, s.v. *mi*) explains v. 6 to be comparing God to a woman giving birth; He empathizes with the Children of Israel, who are undergoing a period of great distress, as well as with their enemies, who are also God's creations.

Birth Pangs of the Messiah

A second name found in the Mishnah (*Sotah* 9:15) for *chevlei Mashiach* is *ikvot Meshicha* (the footsteps of the Messiah; Rashi: "at the end of the exile, before the arrival of the Messiah"). It is described as a time of considerable social unrest. According to the Mishnah, at that time:

> Insolence will increase and inflation will soar; the vine will yield its fruit, but wine will be expensive [Rashi: because everyone will be partying]; the government will turn to heresy and there will be no rebuke [Rashi: since everyone will be sinners]; the house of meeting [of the Sages] will become a house of prostitution [Rashi: nobody will study Torah, it will be deserted, and lechers will gather there, because study halls will be located outside of the city]; and Galilee will be destroyed and Gavlan [possibly Golan] will be desolate; and the frontier people [possibly Galilee people] will wander from city to city without anyone pitying them; and the wisdom of scholars will be dishonored; and fearers of sin will be despised; and truth will be absent. Young men will put old men to shame. The old will stand in the presence of the young. [The following verse will be fulfilled:] "A son disgraces his father, a daughter rises up against her mother, a daughter-in-law against her mother-in-law, a man's enemies are the members of his household" (Mic. 7:6). The face of the [leaders of the] generation is like the face of a dog. A son will not be ashamed [to act corruptly] before his father (*Sotah* 9:15).

When the Mishnah mentions a dog, it does not specify the nature of the dog. If it refers to a vicious dog, it might refer to its ferocity and impudence. On the other hand, if it refers to a domesticated dog, it might be referring to its being satisfied with a tasty morsel with no moral qualms about its origin, just as unscrupulous leaders gladly accept bribes and plunder the weak.

A parallel text in BT *Sanhedrin* 97a stresses the widespread poverty, scarcity of students and scholars, and prevalence of apostates, denunciators, and slanderers. It notes that Messiah will not come until the nation has completely despaired of his potential arrival, and the general feeling among the Jews is that they have neither a Supporter nor a Helper.

In summary, the idea of the birth pangs of Messiah is that the nation will suffer great travail to the extent of almost giving up, and only when the nation is at its nadir will the Messiah arrive.

Appendix IX: Entitlement to the World to Come

The world to come (*olam ha-ba*) is the world of life after death, where righteous people are compensated for their good deeds, and wicked people are punished for their bad deeds.

The Talmud amplifies the question which Moses asked of God: "Let me know Your ways" (Exod. 33:13) as follows: "Moses said before Him: Lord of the Universe, why is it that some righteous men prosper and others are in adversity, some wicked men prosper and others are in adversity" (BT *Berachot* 7a). The Talmud suggests two alternative responses which God may have given to Moses:

> R. Yochanan [said God answered that]… A righteous man who prospers is a fully righteous man; a righteous man who suffers adversity is not a fully righteous man. A wicked man who prospers is not a fully wicked man; a wicked man who suffers adversity is a fully wicked man. Now this is in opposition to the saying of R. Meir. For R. Meir said [the answer to this question]… was not granted to him. For it is said: "And I will be gracious to whom I will be gracious" (Exod. 33:19), although he may not deserve it (BT *Berachot* 7a).

Maharsha explains that according to R. Yochanan, a righteous man who has some sins is treated poorly in order to execute the minor punishment associated with those sins in this world and allow him to be fully rewarded in the next world, while a wicked person who has performed some good deeds is treated kindly in this world in order to implement the minor reward associated with those deeds in this world and allow him to be fully punished in the next.

R. Meir, on the other hand, holds that God does not want His hands to be tied. He reserves the right to reward even partially righteous people in this world, and punish even partially wicked people. The account will be balanced in the world to come. Both R. Yochanan and R. Meir, then, believe in the afterworld, with their only difference being the amount of flexibility God maintains in carrying out His judgments.

In review, the necessity of there being an afterworld is based on two central beliefs of Judaism:

1. God has commanded His nation, and all nations, to obey certain laws.
2. God is just.

Since perfect justice demands that obedience be rewarded and transgressions be punished, and since, by observation, it is clear that the righteous do not always have a joyous life and the wicked do not always have a miserable life, it must be that each person's fate will be re-evaluated in some form of existence which is not part of this world, hence the next world.

Appendix X: The Halachic Decision Regarding *Tza'ar Ba'alei Chaim*

The View that *Tza'ar Ba'alei Chaim* Is Prohibited by the Torah

Although Rava (BT *Bava Metzia* 32a), a highly respected Amora, states that *tza'ar ba'alei chaim* is *mi-de-oraita*, the majority of the sources cited in the portion of *Ki Teitzei* point in the direction of assuming it is *mi-de-rabanan*. In certain instances, the text so clearly indicates that it is rabbinical, that the only way out is to say that that particular source follows the view of R. Yosi ha-Glili, who is known to hold that view. Nevertheless, Rosh (BT *Bava Metzia* 2:29) states that the *halachah* is that it is indeed *mi-de-oraita*. He was apparently swayed by a Talmudic segment (BT *Shabbat* 128b) which discusses an animal that falls into a ditch on Shabbat. If it can be fed while in the ditch, that is the best option; however, if it cannot, by leaving it there unfed, it could suffer an agonizing death due to starvation and perhaps cold. Rav permits one to place cushions under its feet so that the animal could possibly climb out, even though doing so is forbidden rabbinically, since formerly usable cushions are being made unusable—either because they become water-logged (Rambam, *Hilchot Shabbat* 26:25, as interpreted by *Maggid Mishneh*) or because, in the likely event that the animal does not succeed in extracting itself, they are serving as a basis for the animal, which is considered to be *muktzeh* (prohibited to move on Shabbat), thus making the basis *muktzeh* as well (Rashi, BT *Shabbat* 128b, s.v. ve-

ha). The Talmud justifies the decision of Rav by stating that: "[The avoidance of] *tza'ar ba'alei chaim* is Biblical, and a Biblical law can override a rabbinical [decree]." Rosh may have based his decision on the code of his predecessor, Rabbeinu Alfasi (Rif 51a, *Shabbat*), who also quotes this justification and associates the Biblical law of unloading with *tza'ar ba'alei chaim* (Rif 17b, *Bava Metzia*).

On the other hand, Me'iri (BT *Bava Metzia* 32b) cites a view (which he himself rejects) that holds that *tza'ar ba'alei chaim* is *mi-de-rabanan*, based on a segment toward the end of the tractate of *Shabbat* (154b) which speaks of an animal laden with glass surgeons' horns used for bloodletting, which are *muktzeh* on Shabbat. If one unties the straps holding the glass vessels, they will fall to the floor and break, so the Talmud permits one to place mattresses and pillows on the ground to ease their fall and thus prevent breakage. However, this is permitted only if the bags of glassware are small enough for the pillows to be pulled away from under them. If the bags are large, so that the pillows cannot be removed, it is forbidden to use them to catch the glassware, since the cushions then become unusable as a basis for an object which is *muktzeh*. Note that this is identical to the previously cited example of the animal that fell into the ditch, yet there it was permitted because of *tza'ar ba'alei chaim*, and here it is not, even though the animal suffers if not unloaded. This law was cited in the name of R. Huna (the greatest student of Rav and Shmuel), who inherited the position of Rav as *Rosh Yeshiva* of Sura, the largest and most dominant yeshiva in Babylonia, and was the teacher of the next great generation of Amora'im, including Rabbah, R. Chisda, and R. Sheshet.

The Talmud proceeds to describe the case of R. Gamliel, whose donkey was laden with *muktzeh* merchandise which would have ruined the cushions had it fallen on them, and as a result he allowed it to remain on the donkey until after Shabbat, when the donkey died. The Talmud explains that because R. Gamliel held that *tza'ar ba'alei chaim* is *mi-de-rabanan*, he could not allow the pain of the donkey to override the rabbinical law of *muktzeh*. Apparently, an opinion attributed to one of the greatest Tanna'im and one of the greatest Amora'im was accepted by those holding the alternative view quoted by Me'iri as sufficient to determine that *tza'ar ba'alei chaim* is indeed only rabbinical in nature.

The View that *Tza'ar Ba'alei Chaim* Is only Prohibited by the Rabbis

The Mishnah in *Bava Metzia* (32a) states that one is required to help unload his friend's donkey, but not to load it according to the Rabbis, while according to R. Shimon both loading and unloading are required. The Talmud interprets this to actually mean that he must help his friend in both cases (since there is a Torah verse for each case), but in the latter he may ask to be paid, and according to R. Shimon he must do both without remuneration. Rava derives from the fact that he gets paid for loading according to the Rabbis, that *tza'ar ba'alei chaim* is *mi-de-oraita*, and therefore, if he did not get paid for loading, one would have known that he must unload *a fortiori* by virtue of the fact that there is a verse which requires loading. The only justification for two verses is to clarify that for loading one gets paid, but not for unloading. Even R. Shimon, who requires both to be done without pay, holds that *tza'ar ba'alei chaim* is *mi-de-oraita*. He says that each verse could be interpreted as either referring to loading or unloading. Only by having two verses is it clear that both are required. According to Rava's interpretation of R. Shimon, had the verses been clearer, he would have agreed with the Rabbis that it would have been sufficient for the Torah to merely include the verse in Deuteronomy that requires loading, and we would have derived that unloading is also required without pay because *tza'ar ba'alei chaim* is *mi-de-oraita*.

Additionally, although the verse states that the requirement to unload is only when the owner loaded the animal in a responsible manner, as the verse says "under its [normal] burden," the mainstream view of the Mishnah is that one must unload the animal even if it was overburdened, clearly because the animal is suffering even more then, and *tza'ar ba'alei chaim* is *mi-de-oraita*.

Pnei Yehoshua (BT *Bava Metzia* 32b) notes that these two proofs of Rava that *tza'ar ba'alei chaim* is *mi-de-oraita* can be refuted. The view of the Rabbis that one is to be paid for loading can be derived without resorting to *a fortiori* logic. In contradistinction to Rava—but as stated in the Talmud (BT *Bava Metzia* 33a)—the phrase "under its burden" (Exod. 23:5) may be used to imply that the burden is still on the animal and has not fallen off, thus excluding a situation where the burden has already fallen off. But this would mean that loading is not required at all, and would be contradictory to the second verse, which states: "You must pick up [the load] with him" (Deut. 22:4). The contradiction would then be reconciled by the Rabbis explaining that loading is in fact required, but the helper is entitled to ask for money. R. Shimon, on the other hand, holds that since there are two verses, one for laoding and one for unloading, each must be performed gratis.

As far as the proof from the fact that the animal must be unloaded even when overburdened, if the phrase "under its burden" is used to stress that the verse in Exodus refers only to unloading, it cannot be used again to indicate that one is exempt if the animal is overburdened, and one remains with the default that the verse in Deuteronomy is referring both to normal and oversize loads. Hence the views of both R. Shimon and the Rabbis in the Mishnah in *Bava Metzia* may also be derived under the assumption that *tza'ar ba'alei chaim* is rabbinical in origin.

Rambam

Because of the great esteem in which Rambam is held, his views are always taken very seriously, even, and perhaps especially, when they seem to be contradictory. In the latter situation, much energy is expended on trying to reconcile the contradiction. A number of citations will be examined:

Tza'ar Ba'alei Chaim

1. The requirement to help unload "applies whether the animal was carrying a burden appropriate for it or a burden greater than it could bear" (*Hilchot Rotze'ach* 13:1). This seems to imply a Biblical approach, although the previously cited *Pnei Yehoshua* shows that it does not necessarily negate a rabbinical approach.
2. "If the owner of the animal was there and sits down, telling the passer-by, 'Since the mitzvah obligates you, if you would like to unload it yourself, unload it'—in this case, he [the passer-by] is not obligated" (*Hilchot Rotzeach* 13:8). This seems to indicate a rabbinic approach, since if Biblical, then *tza'ar ba'alei chaim* should still apply.
3. The following decision does not even mention *tza'ar ba'alei chaim*, implying acceptance of the Talmudic interpretation according to the view that it is rabbinic:

If the animal is owned by a Gentile, but the burden is owned by a Jew, if the Gentile is the one driving his donkey, one is not obligated toward him. If not, one is obligated to unload and reload it with him because of the distress suffered by the Jew. Similarly, if the animal is owned by a Jew, but the burden is owned by a Gentile, one is obligated to unload and reload it because of the distress suffered by the Jew. However, if both the animal and the burden are owned by a Gentile, a passer-by is only obligated to concern himself with the animal because of the possibility that animosity will be aroused (*Hilchot Rotze'ach* 13:9).

Those who say that Rambam holds that *tza'ar ba'alei chaim* is *mi-de-oraita* point out that Rambam does mention it as the rationale for the requirement to help unload in *Hilchot Rotze'ach* 13:13. They assume that paragraphs 8 and 9 refer only to the requirements of the laws of loading and unloading, but not to unloading from the facet of *tza'ar ba'alei chaim*. *Kesef Mishneh* (*Hilchot Rotze'ach*

13:9) explains that the first sentence of paragraph 9 speaks of loading exclusively. Unloading is mentioned only in the second sentence. R. Nachum Rabinovitch (*Yad ha-Peshutah* 13:9) claims that although Rambam does consider *tza'ar ba'alei chaim* to be *mi-de-oraita*, it only applies to one's own animals and not to those of others.

4. In the following citation, Rambam accepts the explicit view of Rav (BT *Shabbat* 128b), who permits neutralizing a vessel on Shabbat, which is only prohibited rabbinically, in order to prevent an animal's suffering, since the latter is considered to be Biblically prohibited:

Regarding an animal that fell into a pit or a water conduit, if one can attend to its needs while it is there, one should do so until after Shabbat. If not, one may bring cushions and blankets and place them beneath it. If this [enables the animal] to ascend, it ascends. Although one is neutralizing a vessel—for one is throwing it into a pit with water—when an animal suffers, they [the Sages] did not decree [that it is forbidden to neutralize a vessel] (*Hilchot Shabbat* 25:26).

Or Same'ach comments *in situ* that even if *tza'ar ba'alei chaim* is considered to be rabbinical, there is a special Biblical law that on Shabbat "your ox and donkey must rest" (Exod. 23:12), and this command overrides any rabbinic prohibition.

5. A previously cited Talmudic extract (BT *Shabbat* 154b) notes that R. Gamliel did not permit usage of a cushion to be nullified on Shabbat, even though that led to the death of his donkey. Similarly, cushions were not permitted to be used to break the fall of large bags of glassware with which a donkey was laden, in spite of the obvious pain that the animal suffered if they remained on his back. These are clear indications that *tza'ar ba'alei chaim* is rabbinic. Rambam, however, says in clear contradiction to R.

Tza'ar Ba'alei Chaim

Gamliel, that the animal may never be pained, apparently even if it would require the neutralization of a cushion (as explicated in *Shulchan Aruch ha-Rav* 266:25):

> If the sacks were large, containing glass utensils and the like, one should unload the sacks gently, and in any case he may not leave them on the animal because of the pain of the animal (*Hilchot Shabbat* 21:10).

FINAL HALACHIC DECISION

It was noted that Rif and Rosh say explicitly that *tza'ar ba'alei chaim* is prohibited on a Torah level, as do *Tur* (Rosh's son, *Choshen Mishpat* 272:11) and Rema (*Choshen Mishpat* 272:9). Mordechai (a student of R. Meir mi-Rottenberg, *Avodah Zarah*, comment 799) says, regarding the Talmud's statement that an animal that is sanctified when there is no Temple must be locked up until it dies (BT *Avodah Zarah* 13a-b) in spite of the pain, that this is permitted because *tza'ar ba'alei chaim* is only rabbinical, and any other solution involves transgressing other rabbinical prohibitions. However, after the Talmudic discussion in *Bava Metzia* (comment 263), Mordechai says it is *mi-de-oraita*. *Chiddushei Anshei ha-Shem* (*Bava Metzia*, comment 40) resolves the contradiction by explaining that severe pain is prohibited on the Torah level and lesser pain only rabbinically.

As to the view of Rambam, it has been noted that the previously enumerated point 3 tends toward a rabbinical approach, while 4 and 5 lean towards a Torah-level law. Both the Vilna Gaon (*Choshen Mishpat* 272:11) and *Or Same'ach* (*Hilchot Shabbat* 25:26) give precedence to point 3 (especially the exemption from helping unload the animal of a Gentile, which the Talmud associates with the view that *tza'ar ba'alei chaim* is rabbinical), and the previously cited *Or Same'ach* explains that points 4 and 5 are not contradictory to this view. R. Yosef Karo in *Kesef Mishneh*, also cited previously, gives preference to points 4 and 5, and reinterprets point 3. In summary, the Vilna Gaon and *Or*

Sameach believe that Rambam holds *tza'ar ba'alei chaim* is rabbinical, and R. Karo believes that he holds it is *mi-de-oraita*. A very potent proof of R. Karo's view is the fact that Rambam himself in his *Peirush ha-Mishnayot* (*Beitzah* 3:4) says that *tza'ar ba'alei chaim* is *mi-de-oraita*. According to R. Chaim Ben Attar's exegesis of Rambam's understanding of the Mishnah (*Rishon le-Tzion*, BT *Beitzah* 26a), if a first-born animal which had a passing defect (and is thus still holy) fell into a pit on a holiday (causing the defect to become permanent, thus allowing the animal to be slaughtered), although the animal is *muktzeh*, since it was forbidden to be eaten when the holiday started, *tza'ar ba'alei chaim*, being *mi-de-oraita*, overrides *muktzeh*, so it may be raised from the pit and slaughtered on the holiday.

Source Material

Akeidat Yitzchak: Classical work of ritual matters and moralizing legends by R. Yitzchak Arama.

Aruch ha-Shulchan: Yechiel Michel Epstein's code of law, based on Karo's *Shulchan Aruch*, but also containing the sources and development of halachic decisions. Influenced by Rambam, R. Epstein generally took a lenient approach, frequently arguing with the earlier *Mishnah Berurah*. He also wrote *Aruch ha-Shulchan ha-Atid* on agricultural and sacrificial laws not included in the *Shulchan Aruch*.

Aruch la-Ner: Glosses on various Talmudic tractates by R. Ya'akov Ettlinger.

Avot de-Rabbi Natan: Tannaitic work by R. Natan, parallels *Ethics of the Fathers*.

Avodat ha-Melech: Commentary by R. Menachem Krikovski on *Sefer ha-Madda* of the Rambam.

Ba'al ha-Turim: Commentary on the Torah by the halachist Ya'akov b. Asher, called *Tur*.

Bechor Shor: Commentary on the Torah by Yosef Bechor Shor.

Be'er Sheva: Supercommentary on Rashi by R. Meir Binyamin Menachem Danon.

Beit ha-Levi: Book on weekly portion by R. Yosef Soloveitchik I, which shows the connection between the Midrash and the Torah.

Bereishit Rabbati: Collection of Midrashim, assembled by R. Moshe ha-Darshan (early 11th-century head of Narbonne Yeshiva), according to Zunz; or containing excerpts from the works of R. Moshe ha-Darshan, according to A. Epstein. Published by Chanoch Albeck, 1940.

Covenant and Conversation: Series of essays on the weekly portion by R.

Jonathan Sacks, on the Internet and published as books.

Da'at Zekenim mi-Ba'alei Tosafot: Commentary on Torah written by the Tosafists in the 12th and 13th centuries, mostly from the school of Rashi in Germany and France, but some from England and Italy.

Divrei Chaim: Responsa and Torah commentaries of R. Chaim Halberstam.

Ein Ya'akov: Compilation of all the aggadic material in the Talmud, with commentaries by R. Ya'akov ibn Habib and (after his death) by his son, R. Levi ibn Habib.

Emunot ve-De'ot: First systematic attempt to integrate Jewish theology with components of Greek philosophy. Written by Saadiah Gaon.

Eshel Avraham: Commentary on *Orach Chaim* by R. Avraham David Wahrman. Gives greater background to halachic discussions than comparable works. Frequently termed *Eshel Avraham Buchach* to distinguish it from the commentary of the same name by R. Yosef Te'omim (*Pri Megadim*).

Etz Yosef: Commentary on Midrash, *Ein Ya'akov, Seder Olam Rabbah*, and the Siddur, by R. Chanoch Zundel b. Yosef.

God, Man, and History: Basic Jewish philosophy by Dr. Eliezer Berkovits.

Guide for the Perplexed: Rambam's principles of Jewish philosophy.

Haggadah: Manual with prayers and customs for conducting the Passover Seder.

Ha'amek Davar: Commentary on the Torah by the Netziv, Naftali Zvi Yehuda Berlin.

Harchev Davar: Commentary on the author's *Ha'amek Davar*, both written by Naftali Zvi Yehuda Berlin.

Hon Ashir: Commentary on the Mishnah by R. Rafael Immanuel Chai Ricchi.

Kesef Mishneh: Commentary by R. Yosef Karo on Rambam's *Yad ha-Chazakah*.

Kli Yakar: Commentary on the Torah by R. Shlomo Ephraim Luntschitz.

Kur Zahav: Commentary on Ramban by R. Aryeh Leib Steinhardt (1936).

Lechem Mishneh: Commentary on Rambam by R. Avraham de Bouton, started before he saw *Kesef Mishneh*, which included Rambam's sources. Afterwards, he only included items not handled in *Kesef Mishneh*, but analyzed words of previous commentators – *Kesef Mishneh* and *Maggid Mishneh*.

Legends of the Jews: Compilation which weaves together Midrashim in the order of the events presented in the Bible, by Prof. Louis Ginzberg. Extensively footnoted and annotated.

Levush: Series of books by R. Mordechai Yafeh. He wished to enlarge upon the *Shulchan Aruch,* but be more concise than *Beit Yosef. Levush ha-Orah* explains Rashi and Mizrachi. *Eliyahu Rabbah, Zuta,* and *Malbushei Yom Tov* are commentaries on *Levush.*

Likutei Batar Likutei: Anthology on the Torah, Megillot, and *Avot*, by R. Shmuel Alter, rabbi in Vienna, Cuba, and Brooklyn.

Likutei Moharan: Chasidic interpretations of Biblical and Midrashic stories by R. Nachman of Breslav, published and disseminated after his death by his disciple, Reb Nosson. Moharan stands for Moreinu ha-Rav Nachman.

Magen Avraham: Commentary on *Shulchan Aruch* by R. Avraham Abele ha-Levi Gombiner, published after his death. Incorporates 17th-century Polish-Jewish customs and Kabbalistic customs of Safed. The author wished to call it *Ner Yisrael*, not mentioning his name out of modesty, but his son, either to honor his father or because it was to be printed with *Magen David* of *Taz* as part of *Meginei Aretz*, called it *Magen Avraham*.

Maggid Mishneh: Commentary on entire *Mishneh Torah* by Vidal of Tolosa. By 1906 only those parts were extant which cover about half of *Mishneh Torah*, specifically: *Zemanim, Nashim, Kedushah* (chs. 1-9 only), *Nezikin, Kinyan* (chs. 1-3 only), and *Mishpatim*.

Matnot Kehunah: Simple, well-documented commentary on *Midrash Rabbah* by R. Yissachar Ber ha-Kohen Katz.

Mechilta de-Rabbi Yishmael: Halachic Midrash on Exodus. Based on the teachings of R. Yishmael b. Elisha, R. Akiva's contemporary, and redacted by Rav.

Mechilta de-Rashbi (R. Shimon b. Yochai): Halachic Midrash on Exodus. Based on the teachings of R. Akiva. Compiled in the 5th century.

Meshech Chochmah - Torah commentary by R. Meir Simcha ha-Kohen of Dvinsk. Inter alia, warns of the danger of living in Europe.

The Ethics of Deuteronomy

Metzudat David: Commentary on the entire Bible (except for Esther, Ruth, and Lamentations) by R. David Altschuler, which culls in a clear, simple, and concise manner from earlier exegeses. R. David's son, R. Yechiel Hillel, divided the commentary into *Metzudat David*, which explains content, and *Metzudat Tziyon*, which translates difficult words.

Midrash Aggadah: Midrash on the Torah publicized in Vienna in 1894 by Shlomo Buber from a single manuscript found in Haleb, Syria. The author, who lived in the 12th or 13th century, drew from the Talmud, R. Moshe ha-Darshan, *Midrash Lekach Tov*, etc.

Midrash Lekach Tov: see *Pesikta Zutrata*.

Midrash Rabbah: Name given to ten sets of Midrashim on Torah and the five Megillot. Compiled and edited between the 6th-10th centuries.

Midrash Sechel Tov: Compiled by the European Jew Tuviah b. Eliezer, during the time of Rashi and Rif. Collection of Midrashim gathered from the Talmud and earlier Midrashic sources.

Midrash Shocher Tov: Ancient Midrash on Psalms, first published in Turkey (1512); later, based on mauscripts, by Shlomo Buber (1891).

Midrash Vayosha: Short Midrash on the Song of the Sea (Exod. 15:1-18) and the preceding verses (Exod. 14:30-31). It appeared in two versions, the first in Ashkenazi countries around the 11th century and the second expanded version in the 12th century in Islamic-ruled countries. Cited by Rabbeinu Bachya and in the *Yalkut Shimoni*.

Migdal Oz: One of the earliest commentaries on Rambam, which provides Rambam's sources and attempts to answer objections raised by Ra'avad. Author owned an original manuscript of Rambam, which he referenced when responding to Ra'avad. He believes Rambam was familiar with Kabbalah, although Ra'avad doubts it. Some attribute this work to Ritva, but Chida insisted it was written by Shem-Tov Even-Gaon. Some (Maharshal, Shach, Radbaz, *Chatam Sofer*) felt its support of Rambam was excessive.

Minchat Chinuch: Commentary on *Sefer ha-Chinuch*, published in 1869 by R. Yosef b. Moshe Babad, which cites the sources and provides an erudite analysis of the subjects related to in *Sefer ha-Chinuch*. It derives its name from the sacrifice brought by neophyte priests in the Temple, and includes appendices on the thirty-nine forbidden forms of work on the Sabbath and on the fifty *mitzvot* which Ramban substitites for those of Rambam and *Sefer ha-Chinuch*.

Mishneh Torah: see *Yad ha-Chazakah*.

Mizrachi: Super-commentary on Rashi, written by R. Eliyahu Mizrachi.

Mul Etgarei ha-Tekufah: Essays on the Jewish approach to modern issues by Prof. Yehudah Levi.

Netivot Shalom: Series of books by the Slonimer Rebbe, R. Shalom Noach Berezovsky, on the Torah, holidays, chasidism, and Talmud.

Netzach Yisrael: Book by Maharal on Tisha b'Av and the final deliverance.

Or ha-Chaim: Commentary on the Torah written by R. Chaim Ben Attar.

Or Same'ach: Commentary of R. Meir Simcha ha-Kohen on Rambam.

Orot ha-Kodesh: Philosophical (*Chochmat ha-Kodesh*) and ethical (*Mussar ha-Kodesh*) writings of R. Kook.

Oznayim la-Torah: Commentary on the Torah by R. Zalman Sorotzkin.

Perisha: Commentary of R. Yehoshua Falk Katz, in the *Tur Shulchan Aruch*.

Pesikta de-Rav Kahana: Aggadic Midrash with homilies for special *Shabbatot*, including the four *parshiyot*, from Pesach to Shavuot, from 17 Tammuz until Rosh Hashanah (three weeks of mourning and seven weeks of comfort), and holidays. *Pesikta* comes from the word *pasuk*, "verse." Some are quoted in the name of R. Kahana. Compiled at the time of *Bereishit Rabbah*, 5th -7th centuries.

Pesikta Zutrata: Also called *Lekach Tov* - each homily starts with *tov*. Written by R. Tuvia b. Eliezer, Rashi's contemporary. Explains weekly portions and Megillot.

Pirkei de-Rabbi Eliezer: 54-chapter *Midrash aggadah*. Retells Biblical stories. Traditionally ascribed to R. Eliezer b. Hyrcanus, but Zunz claims it was written in the 8th century in an Islamic country.

Piskei Tosafot: Composition which summarizes the halachic decisions of Tosafot, appearing at the end of Talmudic tractates. According to Chida, it was wrongly attributed to Rosh or his son, *Tur*. Some attribute it to R. Meir of Nordhausen, who died a martyr's death, together with the Jews of his town, in riots following the advent of the Black Plague. Both Chida and *Chatam Sofer* note that there was frequently a dissonance

The Ethics of Deuteronomy

between a tractate's Tosafot and its *Piskei Tosafot*.

Rif: Hebrew acronym for R. Yitzchak Alfasi, and also for R. Yoshiyahu Pinto, author of the eponymous commentary on *Ein Ya'akov*.

Sefer Chareidim: Written by R. Elazar Azikari in Safed in the 16th century. Divides the 613 commandments according to body parts (eyes, ears, etc.), deals with their essence and ramifications, especially Israel-oriented laws. Chareidim means "fearful ones," stressing fear of God, needed for proper fulfillment of *mitzvot*. Quotes from *Orchot Tzaddikim*. Printed posthumously in 1600. Contains his *piyut* (liturgical poem), *Yedid Nefesh*.

Sefer Chasidim: Book of R. Yehuda ha-Chasid, containing laws, customs, prayer interpretation, and moralistic lessons reflecting the worldview of the Ashkenazi pietists of the 12th century.

Sefer ha-Chinuch: Systematic discussion of the 613 *mitzvot*, published anonymously in 13th-century Spain, variously attributed to Aharon ha-Levi or his brother, Pinchas. Based on Rambam's count, ordered according to the weekly portion. Gives Biblical sources, philosophical underpinnings, basic laws.

Sefer ha-Ikkarim: Written by R. Yosef Albo. Proposes three principles of faith: existence of God, revelation, and Divine justice (i.e., reward and punishment).

Sefer Yerei'im: Written by R. Eliezer mi-Metz. Based on the 613 commandments according to R. Yehudai Gaon. Mainly halachic, with ethical digressions. Commandments are grouped into seven categories of prohibitions, such as sexual, dietetic, financial, etc. Quoted by Rabbeinu Tam in *Sefer ha-Yashar*, and by many prominent decisors, such as *Sefer ha-Ittur, Shibbolei ha-Leket, Sefer ha-Terumah, Or Zaru'a*, Rosh, and Mordechai.

Seridei Eish: Responsa of R. Yechiel Ya'akov Weinberg, written in Montreux. Deals with halachic questions sent from all over the world, concerning problems of modern life (technological, social, and personal). Based on his *Mechkarim be-Talmud* (1938), which combines traditional Lithuanian and modern scientific approaches to Talmud study.

Sha'arei Teshuvah: Moral and ascetic work, allegedly written by Rabbeinu

Yonah to atone for earlier attacks on Rambam. It preaches simple piety, modesty, and sincerity in the worship of God as a means of reaching a higher religious level.

She'elot u-Teshuvot Noda be-Yehudah: Responsa by R. Yechezkel Landau. Esteemed for its logic and independence from other Achronim, while adhering to writings of Rishonim. Inter alia, limits autopsies to preventing clear and present dangers in others.

Sifra (Torat Kohanim): *Midrash halachah* (legal Biblical exegesis) on Leviticus. Rambam attributes it to Rav, and Malbim to R. Chiya. From school of R. Akiva. Quoted frequently in Talmud.

Sifrei: *Midrash halachah* (legal Biblical exegesis) on the books of Numbers and Deuteronomy, preceded and followed by aggadic sections. Final redaction in the time of the Amora'im.

Tanna de-Vei Eliyahu: Midrash taught to 3rd-century Amora, Anan, by Elijah (BT *Ketubot* 106a). Consists of *Seder Eliyahu Rabbah* (larger) and *Seder Eliyahu Zuta* (smaller). Final redaction - end of 10th century. Describes development of the world and Jewish history.

Tanchuma: Aggadic interpretations of the weekly portions, attributed to R. Tanchuma. Edited in 5th century, before *Midrash Rabbah* and Talmud, which quotes it.

Targum Onkelos: Official Aramaic translation when reading the Torah in Talmudic times (and today for Yemenites). Tradition: conveyed to Moses at Sinai, mostly forgotten until it was recorded by Onkelos the convert. "Reading the weekly portion twice and *targum* once" refers to *Targum Onkelos*.

Targum Yonatan: Official Aramaic translation of Prophets, ascribed to Yonatan b. Uziel. *Targum Yonatan* on the Torah (pseudo-Yonatan) composed in 7th or 8th century.

Tiferet Ya'akov: Commentary on tractate *Gittin* by R. Ya'akov Gesundtheit, 19th-century rabbi and rabbinical judge in Warsaw.

Tiferet Yisrael: Commentary on Mishnah, composed by R. Yisrael Lifshitz, in two parts (after the two Temple pillars): Yachin - basic explanation; Boaz - new ideas, more analytical.

Torah Shleimah: Encyclopedia of oral teachings on the Torah, edited by R.

M.M. Kasher.

Torah Temimah: Collection of Talmudic and Midrashic teachings related to the verses of the Torah, with commentary. Prepared by R. Baruch ha-Levi Epstein.

Tosafot Yom Tov: Mishnah commentary by R. Yom Tov Lipmann Heller. Comparable to Tosafot on the Talmud, just as Bartenura's Mishnah commentary is comparable to Rashi.

Tzeror ha-Mor: Kabbalistic and Midrashic commentary on the Torah by R. Avraham Saba. First printed in Venice in 1523.

Yad ha-Chazakah: Code of law containing 14 books (the Hebrew numerical value of *yad* is 14), written by Rambam. Also called *Mishneh Torah* – the repetition of the Torah. Compiled ca. 1170-80, while Rambam was living in Egypt. Lithuanian yeshiva rabbis used it as a guide to Talmudic interpretation and methodology.

Yad Ramah: Commentary on *Bava Batra* and *Sanhedrin* by R. Meir b. Todros ha-Levi.

Yalkut Shimoni: Anthology of Midrashim, arranged according to the books of the Bible, with 963 sections on the Pentateuch and 1,085 sections on *Nevi'im* and *Ketuvim*. Halachic sources include the Talmud, *Seder Olam Rabbah*, *Mechilta*, *Sifra*, and *Sifrei*. Aggadic sources include *Tanchuma*, *Midrash Rabbah*, *Pesikta de-Rav Kahana*, *Pirkei de-Rabbi Eliezer*, *Lekach Tov*, and *Midrash Shocher Tov*. Compiler uncertain. Best conjecture is R. Shimon Ashkenazi of Frankfurt (early 13th century), whose name appears on title page of the Vienna edition (1566). Earliest citation is by R. Yitzchak Abravanel.

Yefei To'ar: Commentary by R. Shmuel Yafeh on *Midrash Rabbah* on the Torah. A summarized version appears in the Vilna edition of *Midrash Rabbah*.

Zohar: Literally, splendor. Foundational work of Jewish mystical thought known as Kabbalah. Discusses the nature of God, structure of the universe, nature of the soul.

Commentators

Abergil, Eliyahu (b. 1948): Born in Morocco, immigrated to Israel at age 10, studied at Yeshivat Porat Yosef. Chairman of heads of religious courts in Jerusalem and rabbi of the Baka, Jerusalem neighborhood. Published his halachic decisions in *Dibrot Eliyah*.

Abravanel, Yitzchak (1437-1508): Born to a wealthy family in Lisbon, Portugal; employed by King Alfonso of Portugal as treasurer. Facilitated the ransom of 250 Jews when Alfonso captured the town of Arzilla in Morocco. Abravanel tried to use his relationship with the king to prevent future edicts against the Jews, but Torquemada, the Grand Inquisitor, overruled the king. Wrote three types of works: exegesis of Bible and Haggadah, philosophy, and apologetics. His works include: *Ma'ayanei ha-Yeshu'ah*, a commentary on the Book of Daniel; *Yeshu'ot Meshiho*, an interpretation of rabbinic literature about the Messiah; and *Mashmi'a Yeshu'ah*, a commentary on the Messianic prophecies in the prophetical books, all part of a larger work entitled *Migdal Yeshu'ot*.

Abulafia, Meir b. Todros ha-Levi (1170-1244): Born in Spain. Kabbalist, poet, Talmudist and halachic decisor. Was *rosh yeshiva* and *dayan* in Toledo, together with grandson of Ri Migash and Avraham b. Natan ha-Yarchi (author of *Sefer ha-Manhig*). Author of *Yad Ramah* on *Bava Batra* and *Sanhedrin*, and responsa, as well as commentaries on other tractates, which have been lost.

Albo, Yosef (1380-1444): Born in Monreal, Aragon. Student of Hasdai Crescas. Had medical knowledge, was versed in Aristotle. Wrote *Sefer ha-Ikkarim*.

Alfasi, Yitzchak (Rif, 1013-1103): Born in Algeria. Studied in Kairouan,

Tunisia, under Rabbeinu Nissim b. Ya'akov and Rabbeinu Chananel b. Chushiel. Compiled summary of halachic conclusions in each tractate, *Sefer ha-Halachot*, on which Ran wrote a commentary. Headed yeshiva in Fez. Students include Yosef ibn Migash (Ri Migash) and Yehuda Halevi. Left responsa in Arabic, translated as *She'elot u-Teshuvot ha-Rif*.

Altschuler, David (1687-1769): Born in Jaworow, Galicia, to a family of refugees from Portugal, who brought stones from Portuguese shuls with them and built them into a new synagogue in Prague (apparently the Altneuschul - altschul means old synagogue). He served as a rabbi in Jaworow and later in Prague. His magnum opus is his commentary on *Tanach, Metzudat David*, which he wrote when he noticed that *Tanach* was not studied enough, and felt it was because there was no simple commentary. His son, Yechiel Hillel, continued as rabbi in Jaworow and also completed the commentary.

Arama, Yitzchak (1420-1494): Born in Spain. Talmudist, philosopher. Wrote *Akeidat Yitzchak* (Binding of Isaac), a philosophical, homiletic commentary on Torah.

Asevilli, Yom Tov b. Avraham (**Ritva**, 1260-1320): Born in Seville, Spain (Asevilli means from Seville). Student of Ra'ah and Rashbah. Became rabbi of Saragossa. Famous for his commentary on the Talmud.

Asher b. Yechiel (**Rosh, Rabbeinu Asher**, 1250-1327): Born in Germany. Great-grandson of Ra'avan (Tosafist). Student of Meir of Rothenburg. Worked in money-lending, wealthy. Fled to Toledo, became rabbi after being recommended by Rashbah. Magnum opus – abstracts of Talmudic law printed at the end of each tractate. Father of *Tur*.

Ashkenazi, Yissachar Baerman: see Katz, Yissachar Ber ha-Kohen.

Avraham ben David (**Third Ra'avad**, 1120-1198): Became rabbi and *rosh yeshiva* in Posquières. Wrote critiques on Rif and Rambam, as well as *Ba'alei ha-Nefesh*, and studied Kabbalah.

Azikari, Elazar (1533-1600): Born in Safed. Wrote *Sefer Chareidim*, a basic text of Jewish ethics in the Middle Ages. A poet, Kabbalist, orator, and Talmudic commentator (*Nedarim, Gittin, Yerushalmi Berachot, Beitzah*). Ordained by R. Yaakov Beirav. Studied under R. Moshe Cordovero, influenced by the Ari and is buried next to him. Compatriots were Yosef

Karo, Shlomo Alkabetz, Chaim Vital, Yisrael Najara.

Azulai, Chaim Yosef David (Chida, 1724-1806): Born in Jerusalem. Studied under R. Chaim Ben Attar (*Or ha-Chaim*). On the basis of his scholarship, was elected to become an emissary for the Jewish community in Israel in 1755. In Europe, met the Vilna Gaon and the *Pnei Yehoshua*. Wrote 70 works on Bible, Talmud, *halachah* (*Birkei Yosef* on *Shulchan Aruch*), Kabbalah, and bibliography (*Shem ha-Gedolim*). His travel diaries place him in the ranks of Benjamin of Tudela by providing a comprehensive account of Jewish life and historical events throughout Europe and the Near East. Died in Leghorn, Italy; re-interred in Israel in 1960.

Babad, Yosef (1800-1874): Born in Galicia. Served as rabbi in various Galician towns until appointed rabbi of Tarnopol (1857). Close friend of *Shoel u-Meishiv* (R. Shaul Natanson), R. Naftali of Ropshitz, and R. Chaim of Sanz (his brother-in-law). Known mainly for his commentary on *Sefer ha-Chinuch*, known as *Minchat Chinuch*.

Bach: see Sirkis, Yoel.

Bachya b. Asher ibn Halawa (1255-1340): Born in Saragossa, student of Rashba. Like Ramban, used Kabbalah to interpret the Bible. Principal work - commentary on Torah, called Rabbeinu Bachya, which refers, inter alia, to *Sefer ha-Bahir* and *Zohar*.

Bazak, Amnon (b. 1966): Born in Jerusalem, grandson of R. Zvi Pesach Frank. Serves as a *rosh yeshiva* at Yeshivat Har Etzion, where he was ordained. He has published books and articles on Biblical topics.

Bechor Shor, Yosef (1140?-1210?): Most scholars consider him to be R. Yosef b.Yitzchak mi-Orleans, a Tosafist who was a close student of Rabbeinu Tam. Known for his eponymous text-oriented commentary on the Torah, in which he defends the behavior of the patriarchs, moderates the supernatural aspect of miracles, and rationalizes many *mitzvot*. Wrote *piyutim* regarding Christian persecution that he witnessed, and disputations in which he participated.

Ben Attar, Chaim (1696-1743): Born in Meknes, Morocco. Talmudist, Kabbalist. Wrote *Or ha-Chaim*, commentary on Torah. One of four called holy (*kadosh*), in addition to Ari, Alshech, and *Shlah*. Teacher of Chida. Buried on Mount of Olives.

Berezovsky, Shalom Noach (1911-2000): Born in Baranovitch, Belarus. Moved to Israel in 1936. Re-established Slonimer *chasidut* after WWII, became rebbe in 1981. Magnum opus is *Netivot Shalom*.

Berkovits, Eliezer (1908-1992): Born in Nagyvarad, Hungary. Ordination from R. Akiva Glasner (*Dor Revi'i*) and R. Yechiel Weinberg at Hildesheimer Rabbinical Seminary. Ph.D. in philosophy, U. of Berlin. Wrote *Tnai be-Nisu'im u-ve-Get*; *God, Man, and History*.

Berlin, Naftali Zvi (Netziv, 1816-1893): Born and learned in Mir, Belarus. First wife was daughter of R. Yitzchak of Volozhin; second wife was his niece, daughter of R. Y.M. Epstein (*Aruch ha-Shulchan*). Rosh yeshiva of Volozhin, 1854-92. Wrote *Ha'amek She'eilah* (on *She'iltot*), *Ha'amek Davar* (on Torah).

Breish, Mordechai Ya'akov (1896-1976): Belzer chasid, born in Galicia. After serving as rabbi in communities in Poland and Germany, escaped from the Nazis to Zurich, where he served as rabbi and strengthened the *chareidi* community. Wrote 3 volumes of responsa, called *Tiferet Ya'akov*.

Chanoch Zundel b. Yosef (1790?-1867): Lived in Bialystok, where he taught Midrash, and composed commentaries on Midrash (*Tanchuma, Midrash Rabbah, Pesikta de-Rav Kahana*), *Ein Ya'akov, Seder Olam Rabbah*, the Siddur, and the Haggadah (*Meishiv Nefesh*). Commentaries are in two parts and named after his father: *Etz Yosef* (short explanations), *Anaf Yosef* (longer explanations).

Chatam Sofer: see Sofer (Schreiber), Moshe.

Chaviva, Yosef (Nimukei Yosef, 1340-1420): Born in Saragossa, Spain. Studied under Ran and, upon his demise, the latter's student, Chasdai Crescas. Famous for his commentary on Rif, called *Nimukei Yosef*, in which he cites his predecessors, especially Ran and Ritva, and to which he added his own explanations.

Chayut, Zvi Hirsch (Maharatz Chayes 1805-1855): Born in Brody, Galicia; studied under Ephraim Zalman Margaliot (*Mateh Ephraim*), who ordained him, and under Shalom Yehudah Rappoport (Shir). Also learned French, German, Italian, Latin, natural sciences, and history, and was the only rabbi who obeyed a new law requiring rabbis to obtain an academic degree (from University of Lvov, where he excelled in philosophy, logic, and metaphysics). Served as rabbi in Galicia and Russia. One of few rabbis who were close to the *Haskalah* movement. Wrote Talmudic commentary.

Chizkiya b. Mano'ach (**Chizkuni**, 1250-1310): Born in France. Wrote *Chizkuni*, based on Rashi, but used twenty other commentaries. Wandered the world to find proper explanations. Quotes by name only Rashi, Dunash ben Labrat, *Yosippon*, and *Physica*.

Danon, Meir Binyamin Menachem (1780?-1854): Born in Bosnia, studied under R. David Pardo, became rabbi and *rosh yeshiva* in Sarajevo. Settled in Jerusalem in 1839, where he wrote his commentary on Rashi, *Be'er Sheva*.

De Bouton, Avraham (1545-1588): Born in Salonika to refugees from the Inquisition. Studied under Maharashdam (Shmuel de Medina). Known for commentary on Rambam, *Lechem Mishneh*. Also wrote responsa, *Lechem Rav*.

Dichovsky, Shlomo (b. 1938): Born in Tel Aviv, studied at Yeshivat Chevron. Ordained by Rabbis Unterman, Sarna, Shmuelevitch, and Zholty. Served as rabbi in Tel Aviv and Talmud teacher at Kerem be-Yavneh and Sha'alvim. Appointed to *Beit ha-Din ha-Rabbani ha-Gadol* (1988); was offered a position on the Supreme Court (1994) by Aharon Barak, but was advised by R. Elyashiv to decline. Sought solutions for *agunot* and attempted to harmonize secular and religious law.

Eidels, Shmuel Eliezer ha-Levi (**Maharsha**, 1555-1631): Born in Krakow, Poland to Maharal and Klonymus families. Mother-in-law, Eidel, supported him. Wrote commentary on Tosafot and aggadic parts of Talmud. Knew Kabbalah, believed in reincarnation.

Einhorn, Ze'ev Wolf (**Maharzo**, 1790?-1862): Born in Grodno, Lithuania. Wrote commentary on *Midrash Rabbah*, which he extended in *Netiv Chadash*. Showed that Midrashic interpretation follows from a detailed analysis of the Hebrew text of Biblical verses.

Eliezer mi-Metz: see Mi-Metz, Eliezer.

Emden, Ya'akov (**Yavetz**, 1697-1776): Born in Germany. Involved in business, except when rabbi of Emden. Accused Yonatan Eybeshitz of being Sabbatean. Friendly with Moses Mendelssohn. Believed Christianity and Islam have important roles to play in God's plan. Wrote commentary on Jewish prayer book (*Siddur Beit Ya'akov*) and the Mishnah (*Lechem Shamayim*), and responsa (*She'eilat Yavetz*).

Epstein, Baruch ha-Levi (Torah Temimah, 1860-1941): Lithuanian rabbi, son of author of *Aruch ha-Shulchan*. Learned in Volozhin under his uncle the Netziv. Wrote *Torah Temimah* - commentary on Torah and Megillot, citing Talmud and Midrash on each verse, with explanations.

Epstein, Yechiel Michel ha-Levi (Aruch ha-Shulchan, 1829-1908): Born in Belorussia to Sephardi family (Benvenisti, descendants of Aharon ha-Levi, author of *Sefer ha-Chinuch*), which found refuge in Epstein, near Frankfurt, after the expulsion. Studied in Volozhin, married sister of Netziv. After short unsuccessful business career, became a *dayan* and then rabbi of Navardok. His son was the *Torah Temimah*, and his daughter married her uncle, the Netziv. Wrote *Aruch ha-Shulchan*.

Ettlinger, Ya'akov (1798-1871): Born in Karlsruhe. Studied under Abraham Bing in Würzburg, where he attended university. Was chief rabbi of Altona from 1936. R. S.R. Hirsch and R. Azriel Hildesheimer were his students. He wrote *Bikurei Ya'akov* on the laws of Sukkot, *Aruch la-Ner*, and responsa titled *Binyan Tziyon*. He requested in his will that nobody should call him tz*addik* (righteous), and that the inscription on his tombstone merely contain the titles of his works and the number of years he was rabbi of Altona.

Falk, Ya'akov Yehoshua (Pnei Yehoshua, 1680-1756): Born in Krakow to prominent family, named after great-grandfather (who wrote *Meginei Shlomo* to answer questions of Tosafot on Rashi and was descended from Rashi and Rabbeinu Tam). In Lvov, hometown of his wife, he conducted a yeshiva in his house until an explosion occurred, killing his wife and daughter. He vowed that if he escapes alive, he would complete the work of his great-grandfather to answer questions on Rashi, which became his magnum opus - *Pnei Yehoshua*, which Kotsker Rebbe said he wrote only after completing *Shas* 36 times.

Feinstein, Moshe (1895-1986): Born in Uzda, Belarus, on 7 Adar; was great-great-grandson of brother of Vilna Gaon. Studied under R.

Isser Zalman Meltzer. Moved to N.Y. in 1936, headed Mesivta Tifferet Yerushalayim and *Mo'etzet Gedolei ha-Torah*. Considered foremost posek in U.S. Wrote *Igrot Moshe* (responsa), *Dibrot Moshe* (Talmudic novellae), *Darash Moshe* (weekly portions). Died in 5746, and 5746th verse in the Torah states: "Moshe had finished writing down the words of this Torah" (Deut. 31:24).

Frand, Yissocher: Born in Seattle. Educated at Ner Yisroel in Baltimore, where he became a senior lecturer. Skilled orator. Author of numerous books on Jewish topics, especially the weekly portions.

Gerondi, Yonah b. Avraham (Rabbeinu Yonah, 1180-1263): Born in Gerona, Spain (birthplace of R. Zerachiah ha-Levi, Ran, and Ramban). Student of R. Shlomo Min Hahar, and teacher of Rashbah. Talmudic works: commentary on Rif (only *Berachot* preserved) and *Aliyot de-Rabbeinu Yonah* (novellae on *Bava Batra*). Ethical works: *Sha'arei Teshuvah* and commentary on *Ethics of the Fathers*.

Ginzberg, Louis (1873-1953): Born in Vilna, a descendant of the Vilna Gaon, educated at Telz. Arrived in the U.S. in 1899. Wrote commentary on Yerushalmi, six volumes of *Legends of the Jews*, and *Ge'onica* on Babylonian Ge'onim. Professor at Jewish Theological Seminary.

Gombiner, Avraham Abele ha-Levi (Magen Avraham, 1635-1682): Born in Gombin, Poland; parents and many relatives killed in Chmielnicki massacres of 1648. Wrote commentary on *Shulchan Aruch* called *Magen Avraham*, and *Zayit Ra'anan* (commentary on *Yalkut Shimoni*). He calculated the day from dawn until nightfall (as opposed to the Vilna Gaon, who reckoned from sunrise to sunset), making morning rituals earlier. Taught in Kalisch, where *Shach*, upon visiting, realized his great potential and asked for him to become rabbi, but he was too modest to dislodge the incumbent.

Grossman, Yonatan (b.1970): Professor of Biblical studies at Bar-Ilan University.

Grunfeld, Isidor (Yishai ha-Kohen, 1900-1975): Born and educated Jewishly and academically (as a lawyer) in Germany. Escaped to England with rise of Nazis, where he became a rabbinical judge and author associated with the London *Beit Din*. Best known for his popular works on Jewish law and his translations of the works of R. Shimshon Rafael Hirsch.

Gruzman, Meir (b.1935): Born in Israel, ordained at Chevron Yeshiva. Lectured at Bar-Ilan University (Talmud Department) and other educational institutions. Wrote numerous books and academic articles in the areas of Talmud, Bible, and Jewish prayer and holidays.

Ha-Kohen, Meir Simcha (1843-1926): Born in Lithuania. Rabbi in Dvinsk, together with R. Yosef Rozin (Ragotshover) of chasidic community. Wrote *Or Same'ach* on Rambam. *Meshech Chochmah* on Pentateuch published posthumously.

Ha-Kohen,, Yisrael Meir (Chafetz Chaim, 1839-1933): Born in Belarus, studied in Vilna, lived in Radin, where he was supported by his wife's store, enabling him to open a yeshiva in 1869. Was active in Agudat Yisrael, favored the establishment of Beit Ya'akov, and mediated in the argument between students of R. Kook and R. Sonnenfeld. Among his students were R. Elchanan Wasserman and R. Yosef Kahaneman. Wrote *Chafetz Chaim* and *Shemirat ha-Lashon* on ethical behavior, and the universally accepted *Mishnah Berurah* commentary on *Orach Chaim*.

Halberstam, Chaim (Sanzer Rebbe, 1793-1876): Born in Tornograd, Poland. Studied under R. Naftali Zvi of Ropshitz. Became rabbi in Sanz, Poland, where he founded a chasidic dynasty (today Sanz-Klausenberg and Bobov), attracting many followers due to his piety. Outstanding Talmudist, *posek*, and Kabbalist, and champion of the poor, establishing many charitable organizations. He studied with his brother-in-law, R. Yosef Babad, author of the *Minchat Chinuch*.

Hame'iri, Menachem (1249-1306): Born in Provence, France. Magnum opus is *Beit ha-Bechira* on the Talmud, which provides background and conclusions on each topic based on Rashi, Rambam, Ra'avad, Rif, and Ri Migash. Not universally available until 1920, and accordingly not utilized in halachic development. Wrote *Kiryat Sefer* for scribes. Held that discriminatory laws against Gentiles only related to idol worshippers.

Hartom, Elia Shmuel (1887-1965): Born in Torino, Italy. Served as rabbi in Florence, director of rabbinical seminary in Rome, and high-school teacher in Italy and Israel. Known for his scientific and popular Hebrew translation of the Bible, associated for publicity reasons with his famous brother-in-law, the Italian Biblical scholar Prof. Moshe David Cassuto (1883-1951). His book *Chayei Yisrael ha-Chadashim* stresses that the Jewish nation and the State of Israel will prosper to the extent that they are imbued with Torah knowledge.

Heller, Yom Tov Lipmann ha-Levi (1579-1654): Born in Bavaria; studied under Maharal. Wrote *Tosafot Yom Tov* on Mishnah, *Ma'adanei Yom Tov* on the Rosh. Rabbi in Krakow. Ancestor of Aryeh Leib Heller *(Ketzot ha-Choshen)* and his brother, Yehuda Heller Kahana (*Kuntras ha-Sfeikot*).

Hertz, Joseph (1872-1946): Born in Hungary, left for New York in 1884. Ordained at Jewish Theological Seminary in 1894, was a rabbi in the U.S. and South Africa before becoming chief rabbi of Great Britain in 1914. Wrote commentary on Torah and the Siddur.

Hirsch, Shimshon Rafael (1808-1888): Born in Hamburg; student of R. Ya'akov Ettlinger. Rabbi in Frankfurt. Father of Torah with *derech eretz* movement. Wrote *Nineteen Letters of Ben Uziel* in defense of tradition; *Chorev*, an explanation of *mitzvot*; commentary on the Torah.

Hoffman, Dovid Zvi (1843-1921): Born in Hungary. Studied philosophy, history, and Oriental languages; doctorate from University of Tübingen, 1871. Rabbinical training by Moshe (Maharam) Schick and Azriel Hildesheimer. Became rector of Rabbinical Seminary of Berlin in 1899 after the death of Hildesheimer. Adapted German-Jewish approach of openness toward general culture and society. In Pentateuchal commentary, defended against Biblical criticism. Wrote responsa, *Melamed le-Ho'il,* which deals also with modern questions.

Horovitz, Yeshayahu (1565-1630): Born in Prague. Magnum opus is *Shnei Luchot ha-Brit* (basis of the acronym, *Shlah ha-Kadosh*), an encyclopedic compilation of ritual, ethics, and mysticism. Moved to Eretz Israel in 1621.

Ibn Ezra, Avraham (1089-1167): Born in Tudela. Excelled in philosophy, astronomy/astrology, mathematics, poetry, linguistics, and Biblical exegesis. In Granada, met his friend (and perhaps father-in-law) Yehuda

Halevi. Wrote Biblical commentary.

Ibn Habib, Ya'akov (1460-1516): Born in Spain; after expulsion, settled in Salonika. Collected all *aggadot* from Babylonian Talmud and many from Jerusalem Talmud in *Ein Ya'akov*. Died after two of six orders printed. Son, Levi, completed it, without *aggadot* of Jerusalem Talmud.

Isserles, Moshe (**Rema**, 1520-1572): Received questions from Yosef Karo. Wrote *Ha-Mappah* on Karo's Code, *Darkei Moshe* on the *Tur*, and *Torat ha-Olah* on the philosophy of the laws concerning the Temple. Inscribed on his tombstone is: "From Moshe [ben Maimon] until Moshe [Isserles] there was none like Moshe."

Karo, Yosef (**Mechaber**, 1488-1575): Born in Toledo. After the Spanish expulsion, the family went to Portugal, then Morocco and Turkey. He arrived in Safed in 1535, where he was ordained by R. Ya'akov Beirav, and taught R. Moshe Alshech and R. Moshe Cordovero. For 32 years, he wrote and proofread his *Beit Yosef* commentary on the *Tur*, which he then summarized in his classic Code of Law (the *Shulchan Aruch*), based on majority decisions of Rambam, Rosh, and Rif.

Kasher, Menachem (1895-1983): Born in Warsaw; moved to Israel in 1924 at the behest of the Gerrer Rebbe, whom he brought to Israel at the beginning of WWII. He received the Israel Prize in 1963 in rabbinical literature and was a prolific writer. Magnum opus is *Torah Shleimah*, an encyclopedia of oral teachings on the Torah. He also published works of the Rogotchover.

Katz, Yehoshua Falk (**Perisha**, 1555-1614): Born in Krakow. Talmudic scholar who studied under Rema and Maharshal, also knowledgable in Kabbalah, philosophy, and astronomy. Wealthy father-in-law built his yeshiva in Lvov and financed the printing of his famous works: *Perisha* (short explanations) and *Derisha* on the *Tur Shulchan Aruch*, and *Sefer Me'irat Einayim* (*Sma*) on *Choshen Mishpat*. Famous Students: Shlah and his son, R. Yissachar Eilenberg (*Be'er Sheva*), R. Yehoshua Heschel (*Maginei Shlomo*).

Katz, Yissachar Ber ha-Kohen (1500s): Born in Poland. Wrote *Matnot Kehunah* on *Midrash Rabbah*, *Mar'eh Kohen* on *Zohar* and Jewish theology. Student of Rema. Knew medicine, astronomy. False rumor:

emigrated to Israel, became student of R. Moshe Cordovero.

Keisar, Asa (b. 1973): Israeli Talmudic scholar, known for his view that the Jewish religion demands vegetarianism of its adherents.

Kimchi, David (Radak, 1160-1235): Born in Provence. Wrote commentaries on Prophets, Genesis (seeks historical, ethical underpinnings), Psalms, Chronicles. Influenced by Ibn Ezra and Rambam; favored the latter in the controversy regarding his works. Delved into philosophy and science.

Knohl, Israel (b. 1952): Professor of Biblical studies at Hebrew University. His books deal with the integration of scientific and archaeological discoveries with Biblical accounts, early Israelite beliefs, and how and where the Israelites originated.

Kook, Avraham Yitzchak (1865-1935): Born in Latvia, student of Netziv, son-in-law of Aderet. Became rabbi of Yafo (1904), then first Israeli chief rabbi (1921), and founded Merkaz Harav (1924). Close with secular, religious, Zionist, and *chareidi* communities. Wrote on Talmud and Jewish thought.

Kramer, Eliyahu (Vilna Gaon, 1720-1797): Born in Grodno. Teacher: Moshe Margalit, author of *Pnei Moshe*. Talmudist, halachist, Kabbalist. He stressed critical examination of texts and made textual emendations when necessary. Considered greatest Torah scholar in recent generations. He never held a communal position. Strongly opposed chasidism. Encouraged study of secular sciences. Most of his writings on *Tanach* (e.g., *Aderet Eliyahu*), Mishnah, Talmud, Kabbalah, and Hebrew grammar were dictated to his students and publicized by them, but *Bi'ur ha-Grah* on *Shulchan Aruch* he wrote himself. Main students: Chaim of Volozhin, Yisroel of Shklov, and Hillel Rivlin (descendants founded neighborhoods in Jerusalem).

Krikovski, Menachem (1869-1929): Born in Lithuania. Uncle of R. Moshe Feinstein, great uncle of Rabbi J.B. Soloveitchik. Educated at Volozhin Yeshiva. Succeeded R. Yechiel Michel Epstein in Navardok and later became rabbi in Vilna. Founded a *chareidi* newspaper called *Ha-Shavua*. His magnum opus was *Avodat ha-Melech* on all of *Mishneh Torah*, but only his commentary on *Sefer ha-Madda* survived.

The Ethics of Deuteronomy

Landau, Yechezkel (Noda be-Yehudah, 1713-1793): Born in Poland, a descendant of Rashi. Studied in Brody and became a *dayan* there in 1734, then rabbi in Yampol, where he mediated tactfully between R. Yaakov Emden and R. Yonatan Eybeshitz in the controversy about Shabtai Zvi. Jews in Prague hired him as rabbi in 1755. Established a yeshiva, where R. Avraham Danzig (author of *Chayei Adam*) studied. Wrote *Noda be-Yehudah* responsa (Yehudah was his father), *Dagul me-Revavah* on *Shulchan Aruch*, and *Tziyun le-Nefesh Chayah* on Talmud (Chayah was his mother).

Leibtag, Menachem: Faculty member at Yeshivat Har Etzion, founder of the Tanach Study Center, www.tanach.org.

Lifshitz, Yisrael (1782-1861): Grandson of rabbi who aranged Cleves *get*. Born in Danzig, became head of local *Beit Din*. Wrote *Tiferet Yisrael* on Mishnah, *Shvilei de-Rakiya* on rabbinical astronomy, and *Derush Or ha-Chaim* on age of the universe.

Loew, Yehuda b. Betzalel (Maharal mi-Prague, 1520-1609): Born in Poznan, Poland. According to tradition, of Davidic descent. Served as rabbi in Nikolsburg, Poznan, and Prague. Important Talmudic scholar, mystic, philosopher. Wrote *Gur Aryeh,* supercommentary on Rashi; *Gevurot Hashem* on Passover; *Netivot Olam* on ethics; and numerous philosophical works. Teacher of Yom Tov Lipman Heller (*Tosfot Yom Tov*) and David Ganz (*Tzemach David*). Influenced R. Dessler, R. Kook, and R. Hutner. Ancestor of Alter Rebbe and R. Nachman of Breslav.

Luntschitz, Shlomo Ephraim (1550-1619): Born in Luntschitz, Poland. Student of Maharshal. *Rosh yeshiva* in Lvov. Rabbi of Prague after Maharal. Student - Sheftel Horowitz, son of *Shlah*. Wrote *Kli Yakar* (magnum opus) and *Olelot Ephraim* (sermons).

Maharal mi-Prague: see Loew, Yehuda b. Betzalel.

Maharsha: see Eidels, Shmuel Eliezer.

Maimonides: see Rambam.

Meir Leibush b. Yechiel Michel (Malbim, 1809-1879): Born in Ukraine. In 1859 became chief rabbi of Bucharest. Argued with upper class, who wanted changes. Imprisoned, then liberated with the help of Moses Montefiore, on condition that he leave Romania. Magnum opus is his commentary on the Bible.

Me'iri: see Hame'iri, Menachem.

Meir of Rothenburg (Maharam of Rothenburg, 1215-1293): Born in Worms. Studied under R. Yitzchak b. Moshe (*Or Zaru'a*) of Vienna, and R. Yechiel of Paris, where he witnessed burning of the Talmud in 1242. Upon return to Germany, recognized as outstanding Ashkenazi decisor and established yeshiva in Rothenburg. Famous students were Rosh, Shimshon b. Tzaddok (*Tashbetz*), Mordechai, Meir ha-Kohen of Rothenburg (*Hagahot Maimoniyot*). Captured and imprisoned in Ensisheim, refused to be ransomed. Wrote 1,500 responsa (codified by Rosh), Tosafot on *Yoma*, liturgical poems (*piyutim*), and halachic codes on kosher slaughtering (*shechitah*), blessings (*brachot*), and mourning (*aveilut*).

Merzbach, Eli (b. 1950): Born in Paris. Professor Emeritus of Mathematics at Bar-Ilan University, head of the Israeli Organization of Orthodox Jewish Scientists. Wrote *Alei Higayon* on weekly portions and holidays.

Mi-Metz, Eliezer (1120-1198): Outstanding and respected student of Rabbeinu Tam (together with R. Chaim ha-Kohen) in Ramerupt. Subsisted by lending money to Gentiles. Teacher of the Tosafists Ravya and R. Elazar of Worms (*Ba'al ha-Rokeach*). Wrote *Sefer Yerei'im*.

Mizrachi, Eliyahu (Re'em, 1435-1526): Born in Turkey. Knew Arabic and Greek. Discovered how to extract square roots. In 1495 became chief rabbi of Turkey. Sensitive to *agunot* and Karaites. Wrote commentary on Rashi, math book, and responsa used by R. Yosef Karo.

Moelin, Ya'akov ben Moshe Levi (Maharil or **Mahari Segal,** 1360-1427): Born in Mainz, Germany. Succeeded his father as rabbi in 1387, and established a yeshiva where R. Ya'akov Weil (Mahari Weil) studied. He lived through a mass slaughter of Jews in Austria in 1420. He composed *piyutim* for the synagogue as a *chazan*, and ruled that traditional melodies should not be changed. Wrote *Minhagei Maharil*, which contains details of religious observances cited frequently by Rema.

Mordechai b. Hillel (1250-1298): Born in Austria. Devoted student of Meir of Rothenburg, and later of Rabbeinu Peretz of Corbeil, among the last

Tosafists. Appointed rabbi and *rosh yeshiva* in Nuremburg, Germany in 1291. His book of halachic decisions, *Mordechai,* adapted decisions of Rif to Ashkenazi practice. Descended from Ra'avyah and Ra'avan. Son-in-law of R. Yechiel of Paris, brother-in-law of R. Yitzchak of Corbeil (*Smak*) and R. Meir ha-Kohen of Rothenburg (*Hagahot Maimoniot*). Died as a martyr with his wife and five children at Reindfleish.

Nachman of Breslav (1772-1810): Born in Medzhybizh, Ukraine, great-grandson of Ba'al Shem Tov. Founder of Breslav chasidism. Believed in closeness to God, speaking to God as with a best friend, and *hitbodedut* - unstructured, spontaneous prayer.

Nachmanides: see Ramban.

Navon, Chaim (b. 1973): Born in Ramat Gan, studied under R. Aharon Lichtenstein at Yeshivat Har Etzion, where he was ordained, and received an MA in Jewish philosophy from Hebrew University. He has written extensively on *halachah* and the philosophy of R. Soloveitchik, and serves on the rabbinical council of Tzohar.

Netziv: see Berlin, Naftali Zvi.

Nissim b. Reuven of Gerona (Ran, 1320-1376): Born in Barcelona, student of R. Peretz ha-Kohen. Physician, astronomer, and scribe. Received queries from entire diaspora. Wrote sermons and commentary on Rif, Talmud, Bible. Students: Rivash, Chasdai Crescas, Yosef Chaviva (*Nimukei Yosef*).

Noda be-Yehudah: see Landau, Yechezkel.

Onkelos (first century): Nephew of Hadrian, who converted and translated Torah into Aramaic. Contemporary of R. Akiva and R. Yishmael.

Ra'avad: see Avraham ben David.

Rabbeinu Bachya: see Bachya b. Asher ibn Halawa.

Rabbeinu Peretz (1225?-1295): Born in Corbeil, France, where he became *rosh yeshiva.* Studied under R. Yechiel of Paris. In Germany, met R. Meir of Rothenburg, later wrote commentary on book of his customs. He wrote glosses on *Sefer Mitzvot Katan (Smak)* of R. Yitzchak of Corbeil and on Tosafot. He also wrote his own Tosafot on many tractates, and is considered to be one of the last Tosafists.

Rabinovitch, Nachum (1928-2020): Born in Montreal. Ordained at Yeshivat

Ner Yisrael, and obtained a doctorate in mathematics. Served as a rabbi in the U.S., as the dean of Jews' College in London, and as *rosh yeshiva* of Yeshivat Birkat Moshe in Ma'aleh Adumim. His magnum opus is an exhaustive commentary on the Rambam, *Yad Peshutah*. Studied under R. Yitzchak Ruderman and R. Eliyahu Henkin, and taught R. Jonathan Sacks.

Radak: see Kimchi, David.

Ralbag (Levi b. Gershon or Gersonides, 1288-1344): Born in Provence, France; philosopher, Talmudist, mathematician, and astronomer/astrologer. Never had a rabbinical post, maybe because of the uniqueness of his opinions. Wrote commentary on *Tanach*. Served as a doctor for the courts of the nobility in Southern France. Invented an instrument to observe the stars and planets. Produced a camera that anticipated features of the modern camera. Wrote *Milchamot Hashem* to reconcile religion and Aristotle, but that work was opposed by many. Wrote *Ma'aseh Choshev* on square and cube roots, and combinatorics (using mathematical induction), as well as other mathematical works.

Rambam (Moshe b. Maimon or Maimonides, 1138-1205): Born in Cordoba. Wrote commentary on Mishnah, *Sefer ha-Mitzvot*, *Yad ha-Chazakah*, *The Guide for the Perplexed*. Court physician. Buried in Tiberias. Epitaph: From Moshe (Rabbeinu) to Moshe (Maimonides) there was none like Moshe.

Ramban (Moshe b. Nachman or Nachmanides, 1194-1270): Born and became rabbi in Gerona. Medical doctor. Wrote Torah commentary, *Chiddushei ha-Ramban* on Talmud, *Iggeret ha-Kodesh* on marriage. Students: Rashbah, Ra'ah (*Chinuch*). In 1263, won debate with Pablo Christiani, but had to relocate to Israel.

Ran: see Nissim b. Reuven of Gerona.

Rashbah: see Shlomo b. Avraham Ibn Aderet.

Rashbam: see Shmuel b. Meir.

Rashi: see Shlomo Yitzchaki.

Rema: see Isserles, Moshe.

Ricchi, Rafael Immanuel Chai (1687-1743): Born in Italy. As an orphan, he travelled between cities as a tutor, leaving one job because he held that

Ashkenazim living among Sephardim should be permitted not to wear *tefillin* on *chol ha-mo'ed*. After being ordained in 1717 and serving as a communal rabbi, he went to Israel, where he studied Kabbalah in Safed and completed his commentary on the Mishnah (*Hon Ashir*). When a plague struck, he returned to Italy, where he wrote his magnum opus, *Mishnat Chasidim*, on Kabbalah.

Rimon, Yosef Zvi (b. 1968): Born in Tel Aviv, studied at Yeshivat Har Etzion, where he continued as a *rosh metivta* (*ra"m*). He is a congregational rabbi in Alon Shvut, and became the head of the Beit Midrash at Merkaz ha-Academi Lev in 2015. He is the head of the Jewish educational project *Sulamot,* and founded the social welfare organization *La-ofek*. He has written many books on Jewish law, including the series *Halachah mi-Mekorah*, which traces the development of *halachah* regarding various topics.

Ritva: see Asevilli, Yom Tov b. Avraham.

Rosh: see Asher b. Yechiel.

Saadiah b. Yosef Gaon (882-942): Born in Egypt, studied in Tiberias, served as rabbi in Egypt. Jewish philosopher and exegete of the Gaonic period; appointed Gaon in Babylonia in 928. Active in opposition to Karaism and in defense of rabbinic Judaism. Founder of Judeo-Arabic literature. Magnum opus is *Emunot ve-De'ot* (Jewish philosophy).

Saba, Avraham (1440-1508): Born in Castillia. In Portugal, imprisoned and tortured, children kidnapped and baptized. Escaped to Morocco, then Turkey, where he rewrote his books on Torah (*Tzeror ha-Mor*), Megillot, holidays, and *Ethics of the Fathers*. Granddaughter married R. Yosef Karo.

Sacks, Jonathan (b. 1948): Born in London. Received degrees from Cambridge (MA), Kings' College (PhD). Ordination from Jews' College and Etz Chaim. Appointed chief rabbi after R. Jacobovits, in 1991. Wrote *Dignity of Difference* and *Covenant and Conversation* on the Torah, and commentaries on the Siddur, Machzor, and Haggadah.

Segal, David ha-Levi (1586-1667): Born in Ludmir, Ukraine. Student and son-in-law of *Bach* (Yoel Sirkis). Wrote a commentary on *Shulchan Aruch*, called *Turei Zahav*, known by the acronym *Taz*. Fled to Moravia from the pogroms of 1648; in 1654 became chief rabbi of Lvov.

Sforno, Ovadiah b. Ya'akov (1475-1550): Born in Cesena, Italy. Studied math, philosophy, medicine. Contacts: Reuchlin, Meir Katzenellenbogen, Maharik. Wrote commentary on Torah and Megillot, selecting from Rashi, Ibn Ezra, Rashbam, Ramban, and adding his own interpretations.

Shlah: see Horovitz, Yeshayahu.

Shlomo b. Avraham ibn Aderet (Rashbah, 1235-1310): Born in Barcelona. Medieval halachist, rabbi of main synagogue in Barcelona, leader of community, and successful banker. Student of Rabbeinu Yonah and Ramban, teacher of Ritva and Rabbeinu Bachya. Wrote Talmudic commentary, *Torat ha-Bayit* on *kashrut*, *Avodat ha-Kodesh* on the laws of Shabbat and holidays, and responsa.

Shlomo Yitzchaki (Rashi, 1040-1105): Born in Troyes. Student of Ya'akov b. Yakar (Worms), who was student of Rabbeinu Gershom. Wrote commentary on Talmud, *Tanach* (supercommentaries: *Gur Aryeh* by Maharal, *Ha-Mizrachi* by Re'em, *Yeri'ot Shlomo* by Maharshal).

Shmuel b. Meir (Rashbam, 1085-1158): Born in Ramerupt, Northern France. Son of Yocheved, Rashi's daughter. Shepherd, vintner. Rashi's student, elder brother of Rabbeinu Tam. Earliest Tosafist. Wrote basic commentary on Bible. Completed Rashi on *Bava Batra* and *Pesachim*.

Sirkis, Yoel (Bach, 1561-1640): Born in Lublin, cousin of *Levush*. Studied under student of the Rema. Became *Av Beit Din* and *Rosh Yeshiva* in Krakow. Most famous student and son-in-law was the *Taz* – Dovid b. Shmuel ha-Levi. Magnum opus is *Bayit Chadash* (lit. "new house," acronym *Bach*), commentary on *Tur* which traces Talmudic sources of the laws. Accepted Kabbalah, but rejected practices contrary to *halachah*; was critical of those who relied solely on *Shulchan Aruch*, rather than Talmud and Geonim. In his responsa, opposed religious stringencies, stating: "He who wishes to be stringent, let him be stringent for himself only."

Slifkin, Natan (b. 1925): Born in Manchester, ordained at *Or Same'ach*, and received a doctorate in Jewish history from Bar-Ilan University. His books deal with the intersectionality of Torah, science, and zoology. He founded and directs the Biblical Museum of Natural History in Beit Shemesh.

Sofer (Schreiber), Moshe (Chatam Sofer, 1762-1839): Born in Frankfurt, studied there under R. Nosson Adler and R. Pinchas Horowitz. He became rabbi and *rosh yeshiva* in Mattersdorf (1797) and Pressburg (1806). Produced rabbis for Hungarian Jewry: Avraham Shmuel Binyamin Sofer (*Ktav Sofer*, his son), Shmuel Ehrenfeld (*Chatan Sofer*, his grandson), Hillel Lichtenstein (Kolomea), Moshe Schick (Maharam Schick), Akiva Yosef Schlesinger. Strong opponent of Reform Judaism, saying: *chadash asur min ha-Tora*h (new is forbidden by the Torah). Wrote responsa, as well as novellae on the Torah, Talmud, and *Shulchan Aruch*, called *Chidushei Torat Moshe*.

Soloveitchik, Yosef B. (1820-1892): Born in Minsk, great-grandson of Chaim of Volozhin. Reputed to have one of the great minds of his time. He was the assistant head of Volozhin Yeshiva, but left when the Netziv was chosen as *rosh yeshiva*. He became rabbi in Slutsk (1865), where he taught Yosef Rosen, the Rogatchover Gaon. From 1877 until his death, he served as rabbi of Brisk, replacing R. Yehoshua Leib Diskin, who went to Eretz Yisrael, and he was succeeded by his son, Chaim Soloveitchik. He is buried in the Jewish cemetery in Warsaw. Both his commentary on the Torah and his responsa are called *Beit ha-Levi*.

Soloveitchik, Yosef Dov ha-Levi (1903-1993): Born in Pruzhany, Belarus. Descendant of R. Chaim of Volozhin and *Tosfot Yom Tov*. Mother was cousin of R. Moshe Feinstein. He learned the Brisker methodology devised by his grandfather, R. Chaim of Brisk, from his father, R. Moshe Soloveitchik. Graduated from the University of Berlin with a PhD in philosophy. In 1932, emigrated to Boston, where he established one of the first Jewish parochial schools, Maimonides, in 1937. Succeeded his father as *rosh yeshiva* of Yeshiva University's Rabbi Yitzchak Elchanan Theological Seminary (where he was known as the *Rav*) in 1941. Served as honorary president of the Agudat ha-Rabbanim of America, which he later left to lead the Rabbinical Council of America and the Mizrachi. Wrote *Lonely Man of Faith, Halachic Man*. Advocated compatibility of Torah and academic scholarship.

Sorotzkin, Zalman (1880-1966): Born in Lithuania; studied in Slobodka, Volozhin, and then Telz, where he married the daughter of the *rosh yeshiva*, R. Eliezer Gordon. Rabbi of Luzk, Ukraine. Escaped Holocaust to Israel in 1940. Wrote *Oznayim la-Torah, Ha-De'ah ve-ha-Dibur*. Headed Israeli Council of Sages.

Steinberg, Milton (1903-1950): Born in Rochester, N.Y; rabbi, philosopher, theologian, and author.

Strashun, Shmuel (Rashash, 1793-1872): Born in Lithuania. Studied under R. Avraham Danzig (*Chayei Adam*). When Napoleon invaded Russia, moved to Vilna, where he became a leader of the Jewish community. Wrote extensive annotations on Talmud and *Midrash Rabbah*. Like Vilna Gaon, eschewed *pilpul*, sought correct text and interpretation. Had wide knowledge of Hebrew grammar, history, geography, and foreign languages.

Taz: see Segal, David ha-Levi.

Temer, Yissachar (1896-1982): Born in Poland, educated in European yeshivot; immigrated to Israel in 1933 with the help of R. Kook, and became a congregational rabbi in Tel Aviv. Wrote a commentary on the Jerusalem Talmud called *Alei Tamar*. Upon his demise, his library was donated to Yeshivat Har Etzion.

Tur: see Ya'akov b. Asher.

Vidal of Tolosa (Maggid Mishneh, Rav ha-Maggid, 1283-1360): Born in Tolosa (either in Spain or France). Student of Rashbah or R. Aharon ha-Levi, both of whom were students of Ramban. One of the earliest and greatest commentators on *Mishneh Torah* of Rambam. Was older associate of Ran. In disputes concerning meaning of *Mishneh Torah* or Rashbah, *Maggid Mishneh's* view is accepted.

Vilna Gaon: see Kramer, Eliyahu.

Wahrman, Avraham David (1771-1840): Born in Ukraine. In addition to Talmud, studied Kabbalah, mathematics, astronomy, and natural sciences, maintaining that *Chazal* were also learned in science. Became rabbi of Buchach in 1814. Famous for his two commentaries on the *Shulchan Aruch*: *Eshel Avraham* on *Orach Chaim*, and *Ezer Mekudash* on *Even ha-Ezer*.

The Ethics of Deuteronomy

Weinberg, Yechiel Ya'akov (Seridei Eish, 1885-1966): Born in Poland, studied at Mir and Slobodka, where he was close with R. Nosson Zvi Finkel and R. Naftali Amsterdam. Received doctorate in 1923 from University of Giessen on *Targum Peshitata*, early Syrian Biblical translation. He was rector of the Hildesheimer Rabbinical Seminary in Berlin (1924-1939), where his students included R. Eliezer Berkovits and Dayan Yosef Hirsch Dunner. Refused offer to head London *Beit Din* by R. Yosef Hertz in 1934 because of students' pressure (position accepted by R. Yechezkel Abramsky). After WWII, R. Shaul Weingort brought him to Montreux, Switzerland, where he composed responsa, *Seridei Eish*.

Ya'akov b. Asher (Tur, Ba'al ha-Turim, 1269-1343): Son of Rosh, born in Cologne. Moved to Castile with his father. Wrote *Arba'ah Turim* (code of law); *Rimzei Ba'al ha-Turim* (concise Torah commentary); and *Peirush al ha-Torah*, which quotes Ramban, Saadiah Gaon, Rashi, and Ibn Ezra.

Yafeh, Mordechai (1530-1612): Born in Prague to a prominent family descended from Rashi. Studied under Rema in Krakow and Maharshal in Lublin. When Jews were expelled from Prague in 1561, went to Italy, where he learned mathematics, astronomy, philosophy, and natural science, as well as Kabbalah. Valued secular knowledge, in contrast to Maharshal. Later served as rabbi in Horodneh, Lublin, Prague, Kremnitz, and Posen. Wrote books called *Levush* on *halachah*, commentary of Rashi, and *Guide for the Perplexed*. Descendants: R. Akiva Eiger, R. Kook, Aryeh Leib Yafeh (head of Keren ha-Yesod), and R. Y.L. Kowalsky, European Mizrachi leader.

Yafeh, Shmuel b. Yitzchak Ashkenazi (1525-1595): Born in Turkey, studied in Constantinople (where he became rabbi of the Ashkenazi community in 1564) and in Adrianople, under R. Shlomo Alkabetz. May have been related to Mordechai Yafeh (author of *Levush*) and Shmuel Yafeh (father of *Bach*). Wrote commentary on *Midrash Rabbah* (*Yefei To'ar* on Torah, *Yefei Kol* and *Yefei Anaf* on Megillot), and on *aggadot* of Jerusalem Talmud (*Yefei Mar'eh*).

Yehuda ha-Chasid (1140-1217): Born in Germany, descendant of the Kalonymus family, which had moved from Italy. Became *rosh yeshiva* in

Regensburg. His students included Elazar of Worms (*Ba'al ha-Rokeach*), Yitzchak b. Moshe (*Or Zaru'a*), Baruch b. Yitzchak (*Ba'al ha-Terumah*) and Moshe mi-Kutzi (*Smag*). Wrote *Sefer Chasidim* and many other works, but because of his modesty did not sign his name. A critical commentary on *Tanach* and *Shir ha-Kavod* (*An'im Zemirot*) have also been attributed to him.

Yosef Chaim of Baghdad (Ben Ish Chai, 1835-1909): Born in Baghdad, where he served as unsalaried chief rabbi. Financially helped the Jewish community in the Land of Israel, where he bought a house and was involved in founding of Yeshivat Porat Yosef. He wrote more than 100 compositions, including responsa, *Ben Ish Chai* on *halachah*, *Ben Yehoyadah* on *aggadah*, as well as works on prayer, *Tanach*, and *Kabbalah* (which he also used in halachic decisions).

Yosef, Ovadia (1920-2013): Born in Baghdad, studied at Porat Yosef in Jerusalem. Served as rabbi in Egypt from 1947-50, sent by R. Uziel. In 1950s-60s, served as *dayan* in Petach Tikva and Jerusalem. Became chief rabbi of Tel Aviv in 1969; won Israel Prize for rabbinic literature in 1970. Served as chief rabbi of Israel from 1973-83; founded Shas Party in 1984. Wrote responsa: *Yabi'a Omer*, *Yechaveh Da'at*, as well as *Chazon Ovadia* on Shabbat and holidays. Generally, issued lenient rulings.

Zoldan, Yehuda (b. 1958): A prolific scholar, he taught at the Midrasha of Bar-Ilan and at Jerusalem College of Technology, and became Supervisor of Jewish Studies at the Israel Dept. of Education.

www.ingramcontent.com/pod-product-compliance
Lightning Source LLC
Chambersburg PA
CBHW020108240426
43661CB00002B/74